FOURTH EDITION

Motivation to Learn

Integrating Theory and Practice

Deborah Stipek
Stanford University

Allyn and Bacon

Boston ▪ London ▪ Toronto ▪ Sydney ▪ Tokyo ▪ Singapore

Series Editor: *Arnis E. Burvikovs*
Editorial Assistant: *Matthew Forster*
Marketing Manager: *Kathleen Morgan*
Editorial–Production Service: *Chestnut Hill Enterprises, Inc.*
Composition and Prepress Buyer: *Linda Cox*
Manufacturing Buyer: *Julie McNeill*
Cover Administrator: *Linda Knowles*
Electronic Composition: *Peggy Cabot, Cabot Computer Services*

Copyright © 2002, 1998, 1993, 1988 by Allyn & Bacon
A Pearson Education Company
75 Arlington Street
Boston, Massachusetts 02116

Internet: www.ablongman.com

Between the time Website information is gathered and then published, it is not unusual for some sites to have closed. Also, the transcription of URLs can result in unintended typographical errors. The publisher would appreciate notification where these occur so that they may be corrected in subsequent editions.

Library of Congress Cataloging-in-Publication Data

Stipek, Deborah J.
    Motivation to learn : integrating theory and practice / Deborah Stipek.—4th ed.
      p. cm.
    Includes bibliographical references and index.
    ISBN 0-205-34285-X
      1. Motivation in education.   2. Achievement motivation in children.
   3. Learning, Psychology of.   I. Title.

LB1065 .S82 2002
370.15'4—dc21   2001046136

Printed in the United States of America

10 9 8 7 6   06

CONTENTS

PREFACE

Why do some students approach school tasks eagerly and work diligently on school assignments, while others avoid schoolwork or work half-heartedly? Why do some children enjoy learning in and out of school and take pride in their accomplishments, while others rarely seek opportunities to learn on their own and are anxious and unhappy in school? These are motivation questions that have important implications for learning.

Motivation is relevant to learning because learning is an active process requiring conscious and deliberate activity. Even the most able students will not learn if they do not pay attention and exert some effort. For students to derive maximum benefits from school, educators must provide a learning context in which students are motivated to engage actively and productively in learning activities.

Purpose

This book gives readers a thorough understanding of motivation theories and research and an appreciation of the implications for educational practice. The focus is on classroom learning, but attention is also given to how strategies used to motivate students in school affect students' motivation to engage in intellectual activities outside of school. A primary goal is to demonstrate how achievement motivation theory and research can be used to help teachers develop autonomous, self-confident learners who value and enjoy learning both in and out of school and throughout their lives.

Terms are clearly defined so that a reader unfamiliar with the psychological theory and the academic research literature can understand the concepts used. All new terms introduced in the book are summarized in a table at the end of each chapter. Personal anecdotes and classroom observations are used to make the book more enjoyable to read.

This book also contains many specific and practical examples of how principles based on research and theory might be applied in the classroom. Charts, checklists, and questionnaires are included in the form of tables and appendices to assist teachers in assessing their own students' motivation and in monitoring their own practices.

The motivation literature is thoroughly updated. This new edition includes substantially more discussion of practical classroom applications. Teachers' own motivation and behavior is addressed in greater detail, and there is more discussion of the implications of motivation theory and research for students with special needs, and for minority and low-income children. Readers will also find an expanded discussion of the larger school context, including the role of principals.

Self-regulation in students, relationships between teachers and their students, and goal theory are treated in much greater detail in this new edition.

The book can be useful to individuals anticipating a teaching career as well as to practicing teachers; it also could serve as a supplementary textbook for courses on teaching methods or teacher preparation instructional methods and classroom management courses.

Because the book provides a broad overview of theory and research on achievement motivation, which is a central area of educational psychology, it could serve as a supplementary text in a survey course on educational psychology or as the primary text in a course on achievement motivation. The literature review is obsessively thorough and has been significantly updated in this edition.

Organization

The fourth edition is organized somewhat differently from the first three editions and contains one entirely new chapter (Chapter 10 on goals).

Chapter 1 describes hypothetical children with motivation problems that are commonly encountered in classrooms. A profile of each student's behavior in the classroom is used to make these common motivation problems appear more vivid. The hypothetical students are referred to in subsequent chapters, more in this edition than in previous editions, as concrete examples to illustrate theoretical constructs, research findings, and appropriate interventions.

Chapter 2 begins with an overview of the theoretical frameworks used by achievement motivation researchers and discussed in the book. This chapter also provides a brief history of these frameworks and discusses the links between them and their implications for how motivation problems are conceptualized, assessed, and remediated. The second half of the chapter discusses issues related to the identification of motivation problems in students.

Chapter 3 reviews traditional reinforcement theory and gives examples of the effective application of reinforcement principles to maximize student effort in the classroom. A detailed analysis of effective and ineffective praise illustrates some of these principles. The potential negative effects of over-reliance on extrinsic reinforcement are also considered.

Social cognitive theory, focusing on Bandura's theory and the concept of self-efficacy, is described in Chapter 4. This chapter also reviews several approaches to fostering self-regulation in students, including cognitive behavior modification, teaching metacognitive strategies for learning, and monitoring understanding and other study skills.

Cognitive theories of achievement motivation, including Atkinson's expectancy x value theory, Rotter's locus of control theory, and Weiner's attribution theory are described in Chapter 5. Chapter 6 focuses on cognitions directly related to ability. It begins with a discussion of different conceptions of ability, then describes Covington's self-worth theory, and summarizes research on gender and age differences in children's perceptions of their academic ability.

Chapter 7 provides a clear set of principles for classroom practice that can be derived from the theory and research reviewed in previous chapters on students' achievement-related beliefs. The principles are described in concrete and practical terms.

The concept of intrinsic motivation is introduced in Chapter 8, and research on the effects of extrinsic rewards on intrinsic motivation is reviewed.

Chapter 9 summarizes research on values and relationships in the classroom. The section on values reviews theory and research based in self-determiniation theory, with a focus on Eccles' expectancy x value theory. A discussion of research related to antiacademic values, especially among low-income and minority students, was added to this chapter. Chapter 10, on goals, makes a distinction between performance goals (e.g., develop understanding and mastery), and then broadens the discussion to include recent research on social and personal responsibility goals.

Chapter 11 summarizes, again in concrete and practical terms, the implications for classroom practice of theory and research on intrinsic motivation, goals, values, and relationships.

The causes and consequences of achievement anxiety for learning and performance in achievement contexts are discussed in Chapter 12. Here, specific recommendations are made for alleviating the negative effects of anxiety in the classroom. Research on ways that teacher expectations affect students' own beliefs about competence and learning is described in Chapter 13.

The practical implications of achievement motivation research and theory are integrated in Chapter 14, by discussing remedies to the problems of the hypothetical children described in the first chapter. One section discusses some of the complexities and obstacles teachers face in their efforts to increase student motivation. The second section steps back to examine teachers and classrooms in a larger school context, and discusses ways in which school-level practices and policies can support or undermine teachers' efforts to apply the principles of good classroom practice discussed in the book.

Acknowledgments

I am very grateful to Lisa Dingman, Andrea Christenson, and Kyung Park for their excellent editorial assistance and to Heather Littlejohn, Sarah Miles, Jeffery Port, and Breyana Rouzan for their help with indexing. I would also like to thank my colleagues who reviewed earlier editions as well as the current edition: Helene Anthony of Moorhead State University; Myron Dembo of University of Southern California, Los Angeles; John P. Gaa of the University of Houston; Okhee Lee of the University of Miami; Patricia A. Pokay of Eastern Michigan University; and Edmund L. Thile of San Diego State University.

1 Profiles of Motivation Problems

Like cold and flu symptoms, motivation problems come in many shapes and sizes. But they usually come in "packages," and some combinations of symptoms are more common than others. This chapter describes typical motivation "syndromes"—patterns of beliefs and behaviors that inhibit optimal learning. No child you meet will look exactly like any of the six hypothetical children described here. Indeed, these children are in some respects caricatures. But these vignettes should remind some readers of real children they have observed or taught. Later chapters will discuss the causes of the kinds of problems described here and ways to improve the motivation and learning of students who evidence problems like these six.

Defensive Dave

Dave is one of the worst students in his fourth-grade class. Poor performance, he assumes, is likely regardless of what he does. So he puts his energy into preventing his teacher and classmates from concluding that he lacks ability. Unfortunately, the strategies he uses to avoid *looking* dumb prevent him from *getting* smart.

Dave's strategies, often overlooked by the teacher, can be very clever. For example, one morning Dave works on an assignment to answer ten questions about a story the children in his reading group were supposed to have read. The teacher shifts her attention from one student to another to monitor their work. Dave asks the teacher several questions, but he is careful to give her the impression that he is working diligently to answer most of the questions on his own. Actually, he gets the rest of the answers by asking classmates or by copying his neighbor's paper. Thus, Dave manages to complete the assignment without reading or understanding the story.

That afternoon the teacher asks students to take out yesterday's assignment, which required them to use a dictionary. Dave makes a show of looking through his desk for an assignment that he knows, his teacher knows, and his classmates probably know, he has not completed.

During a social studies test Dave sharpens his pencil twice, picks up an eraser that has fallen to the floor, and ties his shoelaces. He makes no attempt to conceal his inattentiveness to the test. To the contrary, he seems to want everyone to notice that he is not trying. The teacher reminds him several times to get to work, publicizing the message that if he tried, he could do the test. This, of course, is exactly the interpretation Dave desires. He'd rather be known as a goof-off than as an incompetent student.

Dave's strategies serve their purpose, at least in the short term. He manages to complete some assignments with a respectable, if not excellent, level of performance. By fooling around while he is supposed to be taking tests (when other strategies, such as cheating, are not available), he at least avoids appearing dumb, the logical conclusion associated with performing poorly after trying hard. By not trying, he creates an alternative explanation for failure, leaving open the question of whether he would have done well on the test if he had tried.

The tragedy is that Dave's ingenious efforts to avoid looking dumb are self-defeating. He makes little progress in mastering the curriculum, and failure becomes increasingly inevitable. Eventually Dave will give up trying to preserve an image of himself as a capable student, and he will resign himself to the status of one of the "dumb" kids in the class. If he continues this self-destructive game, he will soon look like Helpless Hannah, who does not even try to look competent.

Helpless Hannah

Hannah has been sitting at her desk for nearly half an hour, doing nothing, as far as her fifth-grade teacher can tell. The teacher urges Hannah to try one of the arithmetic problems she is supposed to be working on. "I can't," claims Hannah without even looking at the problem the teacher is pointing to. She adds, "I don't understand what I'm supposed to do." The frustrated teacher replies, "But I just went over a problem exactly like this on the board; weren't you listening?" "I don't understand," Hannah repeats. The teacher goes through a long-division problem step by step, asking Hannah questions along the way. Hannah answers most of the questions correctly. She obviously has at least some understanding. "See, you know how to do these kinds of problems," the teacher observes. "Why don't you try one on your own now?" "I don't know how," Hannah stubbornly declares. "But you knew the right answers to my questions," the teacher responds. "You were helping me," is Hannah's ready reply. Not to be fooled, the teacher concludes firmly, "I think you know how to do these, and I want you to try some of the problems."

The teacher has the last word and turns her attention to another student, leaving Hannah alone with her arithmetic problems. Later, she passes by Hannah's desk and finds no progress. The scene just described is repeated, as it has been so many times that year. The end result is an exasperated teacher and a student who interprets the teacher's despair as confirmation of her own lack of competence.

Hannah is a classic example of what researchers refer to as "learned helpless." Her academic performance is uniformly poor, and she is regarded by her classmates as one of the "dummies." She has developed a firm view of herself as incompetent and unable to master any new academic material. Failure is inevitable, so she reasons, "why try?"

Hannah makes little academic progress and is nearly two grades behind in most academic subjects, but she is not disruptive. She isn't socially integrated into the classroom and therefore does not have the option of spending her time socializing. She is not an aggressive child, and rather than acting out, calling attention to herself, or interfering with her classmates, she sits quietly, spending much of her time gazing into space. She also makes few demands on the teacher. Hannah doesn't ask questions because she doesn't expect to understand or to be able to make use of the answers.

There are many variations of learned-helpless students. Some of the students who have given up trying to gain respect through their academic performance turn to other domains for recognition. They may become the class clowns or bullies, or turn to teasing others. Or, especially as they approach adolescence, they may engage in more serious antisocial behavior to gain respect in a peer group that publicly rejects academic achievement. It is unusual for the academically "helpless" child to turn to legitimate ways of demonstrating competence, such as excelling in athletics, music, or other arts. For some children the feeling of incompetence is so profound that they assume that there is simply no domain in which they can excel.

School offers little joy for students like Hannah. Their days are characterized by hopelessness, despair, and probably—because they spend little time working on academic tasks—boredom. They are often shunned by their classmates and sometimes ignored by their teacher.

Because they rarely try, helpless students rarely succeed. Their repeated failures confirm their perceptions of themselves as incompetent. When they do succeed, they are quick to deny responsibility. They attribute their success to some variable over which they have no control—an easy problem, the teacher's help, or even luck. The logic is elegantly consistent; the consequences of such reasoning are devastating.

Fortunately, pure cases of learned helplessness are rare; weak versions are more common, and some children become helpless in only one subject area (perhaps math, writing, or art). Learned helplessness is, however, the motivational problem most resistant to change by even the most clever and persistent teacher. Obviously, it is best to prevent it from developing. But teachers in later grades have no control over their students' experiences in earlier grades and children like Hannah occasionally appear in their classes.

Safe Sally

In her senior year of high school Sally's SAT scores are in the top 5 percent of her school. This does not surprise her teachers because she is a "straight-A" student. In many respects, Sally is a perfect student—well behaved, dependable, and highly motivated. A superficial look at her would reveal no motivational problems.

But despite Sally's high academic performance she is an underachiever. She is motivated, but only to achieve high grades and the accompanying respect of her teachers. She perceives a "B+" as a disastrous blemish on her record, something to be avoided at all costs.

A careful look at Sally's perfect record reveals a series of courses that offered little challenge. She took advanced placement English, but the teacher of this course is well known for giving every student in the class an "A," as long as the work is done reliably. She took only the required science courses, and she enrolled in a calculus course but dropped it after getting a "C+" on the first weekly quiz.

Sally religiously follows directions for every assignment. She is tuned in to her teachers and has an astonishing ability to predict what material will be stressed on tests. She over-studies, repeatedly reviewing the text and memorizing every possible fact that she might be asked to recall. She rarely reads anything that she is not required to read for a course or that she will not be tested on.

Sally is anxious, but her anxiety is not debilitating within the context of the intellectual demands she allows herself. She is constantly recognized by teachers for her achievements, and she appears to be academically self-confident. She enjoys the respect of her classmates and is socially active.

What is unfortunate for Sally is that she does not allow herself to be challenged. She systematically takes the safe route in all of her academic endeavors. In her classes she learns only what she is told to learn, exactly in the ways she expects to be evaluated on the material. It does not occur to her that learning has some intrinsic value aside from being a means to good grades and external recognition. Working methodically within the guidelines and structure given to her, she makes no effort to be creative.

Sally ignored the school counselor's suggestion that she take courses required for acceptance at a selective university. She knows that she is smart enough to excel in the carefully chosen, not-too-demanding courses she takes, but she is not at all sure she can handle a more challenging academic experience. She doesn't know the true boundaries of her competencies because she never tests them.

Sally will no doubt excel in college, and she will probably perform well in a responsible, albeit not intellectually challenging, job. But she will not, as an adult, stretch her knowledge and imagination. Learning, for Sally, is what you do in school. It has instrumental but no intrinsic value. It brings "A's," but no joy or excitement. Learning means memorizing somebody else's ideas, not developing her own. Sally's potential for creative thinking may never be tapped.

Satisfied Santos

Santos is the seventh-grade class clown. He is one of the first to arrive at school in the morning, and he often fools around with classmates on the school grounds long after school is over. He seems to enjoy school, is popular with peers, and only occasionally gets into trouble for his pranks.

Santos is a likable student, but he has frustrated many of his teachers. He is a "C+/B–" student who could easily be earning "A's." His scores on standardized aptitude tests consistently show him to be capable of achieving considerably beyond most of his classmates, and he occasionally demonstrates his unusual aptitude. On those rare days when he pays close attention, he is frequently the only student in the class who can answer a difficult question. His potential is also evident when he becomes seriously involved in a project, such as the prize-winning model of the solar system that he presented to his science teacher after several weeks of intense effort.

Typically, Santos shows little interest in schoolwork. Threats of bad grades have no effect because he is quite satisfied with a grade that requires little effort for him to achieve. He usually finishes his work, but he rarely does more than the minimum. He makes it a rule never to study for tests because he knows that he can pass by simply paying marginal attention in class. He knows he is smart, but he is not inclined to show off. He doesn't need to demonstrate academic excellence to gain respect from his peers, and he is not at all interested in gaining his teachers' respect. He is motivated to stay out of trouble—at least most of the time. Consequently, he does what is required to keep teachers "off his back."

At home Santos spends hour upon hour at his computer, playing intellectually demanding games. He is also interested in science. He reads every book on space that he can find, and often surprises his science teacher with comments that demonstrate sophisticated understanding—usually on topics that are not part of the science curriculum. Science fiction novels are another great love, and he has written several short stories himself. But his talent for writing is rarely evident on school assignments. His science classwork is average at best; he does exactly what he needs to do to avoid getting into trouble.

Santos' teachers know that he could do better in school. Each new teacher goes through essentially the same series of strategies. Noting his half-hearted effort on assignments, teachers first encourage him to spend more time on his schoolwork to achieve higher grades. But Santos is unresponsive to this admonition because high grades simply do not have the same value for him that they have for some other students, and he does not consider poor grades as punishment, unless they dip below his "C+" threshold of acceptability.

Santos sees no reason to push himself on school-related work. He enjoys intellectual challenges, but on his own terms. If his current interests happen to overlap with course requirements, he excels at school. More typically, his intellectual life is outside of the classroom and his life in the classroom is not intellectual.

Students like Santos are seen at all grade levels, although they are commonplace in junior high school. They frustrate parents and teachers alike. In contrast to Hannah, who convinces some teachers that she really cannot learn, Santos' teachers know that he could excel. But conventional strategies to motivate students like Santos are ineffective.

Anxious Alma

Alma is in the eighth grade. She is an average student in most subjects, but she is doing poorly in math. She often turns in tests with many problems unanswered. Sometimes correct answers have been written in and erased. Alma occasionally spends the math period in the nurse's room—claiming a headache, a stomachache, or some other ailment that miraculously disappears about the time her mathematics class ends.

For the first few weeks of the semester, Alma's mathematics teacher frequently asked her questions in an attempt to elicit her participation, and to assess her understanding of the concepts being studied. But Alma often just shook her head. The teacher, sensing that Alma was uncomfortable when questions were addressed to her publicly, stopped trying to engage her in class discussion.

In contrast to her class performance, assignments that she can take home are often returned completed and mostly correct. The teacher knows from conversations with Alma's parents that she does her homework on her own. Her mathematics teacher is puzzled by her reticence in class because she knows from Alma's homework assignments that she could figure out the answers if she tried.

Alma lacks self-confidence and apparently finds it less threatening to refuse to answer a question than risk giving a wrong answer. It is difficult for her to concentrate on math problems in class because she is distracted by her concerns about failure. However prepared she may be for a test, as soon as it is in front of her, she panics. She cannot remember the simplest procedures that she knew well the evening before. When the teacher asks her a question in front of the class, she is painfully conscious of the other students' evaluative gaze and she cannot concentrate on the question itself.

Alma will get through eighth-grade math with a passing grade, partly because she can compensate for her poor test scores and class performance with complete and correct homework, but she will take only the mathematics courses required to graduate. If she goes to college, she will major in an area that does not require any math. For the rest of her life she will claim, if the subject comes up, that she has no aptitude for numbers.

Alienated Al

Al is a tenth grader, although he is absent so frequently it is hard to say whether or not he attends school. He drops in to his large urban high school more to see friends than to be a student. Most of his friends have similarly weak ties to school.

When Al is at school he attends to the teacher and to his academic work intermittently and half-heartedly. Occasionally, almost in spite of himself, he gets engaged and shows a spark of enthusiasm and intelligence. But he appears to be embarrassed when he finds himself seriously involved in a classroom discussion, and reverts quickly to being disrespectful or cynical. He appears not to want to be seen as a serious student.

His mother, a single parent who works two jobs to make ends meet, pleads with him to take school more seriously. Again and again she tells him that he needs to graduate to make anything of himself. The high school counselor calls him in from time to time to threaten suspension for his poor attendance. Al is amused by the idea that they won't let him come to school as punishment for him often choosing not to attend. The counselor has never asked him why he doesn't come to school regularly. And aside from occasional lectures, there are no negative consequences.

Al's academic difficulties go back to early elementary school. He was slow to catch on to reading, and even now, as a tenth grader, his reading skills are at about the sixth-grade level. Trying to make sense of his classes requires a great deal of effort, more than he is willing to exert. He just doesn't see the purpose. The few friends he has who have completed high school don't have much better jobs than his friends who dropped out. Success is too remote and would require too much effort to achieve.

The high school is large and impersonal. Some of Al's teachers don't know his name, and most are unperturbed by his poor attendance and effort. They seem to expect it. In fact, his science teacher expressed only surprise when he turned in a completed project that showed some genuine effort and good understanding. The topic happened to grab him, and he got into it. The teacher's surprised reaction served only to confirm his view that no one expected him to do quality work.

Al will continue to hang out at his high school, although not very consistently. He'll pass most of his classes for showing up, and he might even graduate. But his skills will be so low that he will have difficulty finding work that pays a decent living.

Conclusion

The following chapters provide a theoretical framework for understanding the kinds of motivation problems presented by these six children. They also discuss research that can be used to guide classroom practices that will prevent and even reverse them. School learning is emphasized, but attention is also given to how strategies that are used to motivate students in school affect students' motivation to engage in intellectual activities outside the classroom. The underlying goal is for students to exert maximum effort on academic tasks in the classroom, but also to seek challenging learning activities outside of school and throughout their adult lives.

2 Defining and Assessing Achievement Motivation

Defining Achievement Motivation

This book is about behavior in achievement contexts. The problems described in Chapter 1 occur in classrooms—regular classrooms and classrooms for children with special needs or talents. But achievement contexts can be found anywhere—on the playing field, on stage, in an art studio, or even in a kitchen or a garden. To be sure, standards and even the definitions of success vary among contexts. In sports success usually means winning, although it could also be defined in terms of personal improvement. Success for a pianist might be measured in the length of applause or in newspaper reviews, for a hostess in the amount of food the guests consume, and for a surgeon in patient survival rates. This book focuses primarily on school contexts, but most of the issues discussed apply to any context that involves some standard against which performance can be measured—any situation that offers the opportunity to succeed or fail.

Theoretical Frameworks

Several psychological theories will be used to organize our analysis of achievement motivation. Theories of motivation are created to help us explain, predict, and influence behavior. If we can explain *why* individuals behave the way they do in achievement settings we might be able to change their behavior. Why does Defensive Dave pretend to be working when he is not, and how can we get him to exert genuine effort on school tasks? Why does Satisfied Santos put so much more effort into intellectual activities outside of school than those in school? What can be done to interest him in the school curriculum? Why doesn't Alienated Al attend school regularly, and how can we get him interested and engaged in academic work?

Motivation theories are important to discuss because everyone has them. And consciously or unconsciously, people rely on their theories of what causes behavior when deciding how to try to change their own or another's behavior.

The theory a researcher chooses for studying motivation influences how motivation is measured and defined in his or her studies, and what his or her notions are about appropriate interventions to address motivation problems. Some of the theories discussed in this book contradict each other; they cannot both be "right." More often different theories are compatible because they account for different aspects of achievement motivation or focus on different causes of behavior.

Over time, psychological theories are often modified in response to research evidence on their usefulness in predicting and changing behavior. New theories are also developed, and different theories become prominent at different times. In general, psychological theories that have been used to explain behavior in achievement contexts have shifted focus in the last few decades, from observable behavior to psychological variables—such as beliefs, values, and goals—that can be inferred but cannot be directly observed from behavior. Below is a brief overview of the theories discussed in this book.

Reinforcement theory, which dominated the educational literature until the early 1960s, conceptualizes motivation entirely in terms of observable behavior. According to traditional reinforcement theory, individuals exhibit a particular behavior in achievement or other settings because they have been reinforced (rewarded) for that behavior in the past. Accordingly, students who are rewarded (for example, with good grades) for working hard on school tasks and for persisting when they face difficulty will continue to work hard and persist in the future.

Reinforcement theory was originally derived from drive theories, which assumed that reinforcement necessarily involved the reduction of basic biological needs (e.g., hunger and thirst; Hull, 1943, 1951). Applications to achievement contexts, however, assume that other consequences (e.g., teacher praise) take on reinforcing properties by having previously been associated with the reduction of basic drives, and can therefore influence behavior. In contrast to drive reduction theories, the best-known reinforcement theory today, developed primarily by Skinner (1974), does not make any claims about particular qualities of reinforcements. Any consequence of a behavior that increases the likelihood of its future recurrence is, by definition, reinforcing.

Reinforcement theory is considered "mechanistic" because it is not concerned with beliefs, feelings, aspirations, or any other psychological variable that cannot be directly observed. It assumes that there is a direct link between the consequences to a behavior and the likelihood that it will be repeated.

The theory has clear implications for how motivation is conceptualized and measured. Motivation is not considered a quality of the person, but rather a set of behaviors and their contingencies (i.e., whether the behaviors are rewarded or punished). Any attempt to explain, predict, or influence motivation would involve measuring behavior and examining the consequences of the current and the desired behavior. A reinforcement theorist who wanted Defensive Dave to exert more effort, for example, would first closely examine the consequences of Dave's behavior. What happens to him when he spends 20 minutes sharpening his pencil and arranging his desk? What happens on those rare occasions that he completes tasks efficiently? The next step would be to adjust the environmental consequences so that the undesirable behaviors (wasting time) were punished, or at least not rewarded, and the desired behaviors (getting to work and completing tasks) were rewarded.

By the 1960s, most motivation researchers found such mechanistic assumptions about behavior unsatisfactory, and began to explore psychological variables that are not directly observable. *Cognitive motivation* theorists do not rule out external reinforcement as a cause of achievement behavior. They claim, however, that cognitions (beliefs), such as expectations, "mediate" the effect of rewards. Thus, for example, they claim that students work hard because their past experience leads them to expect hard work to be rewarded in the future, not simply because they have been rewarded for working hard in the past. In fact, a student might be convinced to expect a reward for doing something (e.g., by telling her that you will give her one), even though she has never actually been rewarded for that behavior in the past. According to cognitive motivation theorists, it is her belief, not her past history, that influences her behavior.

A motivated person, therefore, is conceptualized as someone with cognitions or beliefs that lead to constructive achievement behavior, such as exerting effort or persisting in the face of difficulty. Although expectations have been especially prominent in achievement motivation research, cognitive theorists are also interested in the effects of other beliefs—such as perceptions of ability ("I'm good at math"), control over achievement outcomes ("I determine whether I succeed or fail"), and the causes of achievement outcomes ("How well I do is determined by how hard I try").

Cognitive theorists are not satisfied with merely observing behavior and its consequences. They may want to assess students' beliefs about the consequences of behavior or the causes of performance outcomes. They may also want to measure how competent the students believe themselves to be in a particular domain, whether they expect to succeed, or whether they believe grading is fair.

The intervention cognitive theorist would design a program aimed at changing maladaptive beliefs. To get Helpless Hannah to exert effort on school tasks, therefore, the teacher might begin by interviewing her to ascertain her perceptions of her competencies (i.e., does she think she is incapable of completing school tasks? which ones?). Then she might try to increase her perceptions of her competencies on tasks she doesn't believe she can do. (This may also require changing tasks so that they are appropriate for her skill level.) A teacher might ask Dave what he thinks would happen if he tried hard to complete a task but wasn't able to do it. If he expected negative consequences (e.g., teacher disapproval, ridicule from his classmates), the teacher might try to change his expectations by reassuring him that his fears are not well founded, or by making sure that his fears are not, in fact, fulfilled in the classroom.

Cognitive theorists do not assume that beliefs are based entirely on previous experiences with contingencies (e.g., reward and punishment) to one's own behavior. People's expectations are based on many factors, such as observations of what happens to *others* when they behave a particular way, or even simply what they are told about what they can expect. When teachers call attention to the consequences of students' behavior ("Table 3 can go to recess because everyone is sitting quietly"), and when they promise rewards ("if you finish all your work before recess I'll let you play on the big kids' yard"), they are using cognitive motivation theory. They are attempting to influence behavior by influencing expectations about the consequences of desired behaviors.

Atkinson (1964) also emphasized expectations as an explanation of achievement behavior, but he added values as another explanatory variable. According to his *expectancy x value* theory, exerting effort and persisting on a task requires more than expecting to be able to complete it; the task must also have some value attached to it. Atkinson conceptualized value narrowly, in terms of pride in success and the avoidance of shame in failure. Other theorists have considered values more broadly, such as in terms of how important academic achievement is to self-concept and how useful particular kinds of achievement are in people's lives outside of school (Eccles, Adler, Futterman, Goff, Kaczala, Meece, & Midgley, 1983).

Researchers and teachers working from an "expectancy x value" theoretical framework, therefore, would need to measure students' perceptions of the value of rewards in any effort to predict or change behavior. Dave's teacher might try to find out whether Dave expects his effort on school tasks to lead to pride or shame, and then try to make sure that pride is more likely (e.g., by giving him tasks that he is sure to succeed in or by making sure that put-downs by classmates are not allowed). Satisfied Santos' teacher might try to increase the value Santos places on doing well in school by giving him examples of the long-term accomplishments or privileges of people who do well in school.

Intrinsic motivation theorists are also concerned with emotional as well as cognitive aspects of motivation, although they stress different emotions than the "expectancy x value" theorists. Intrinsic motivation theory is based on the assumption that humans are inherently motivated to develop their intellectual and other competencies, and that they take pleasure in their accomplishments (White, 1959). Part of the value of achievement striving is the intrinsic pleasure one feels from achieving higher levels of mastery or understanding. Intrinsic motivation researchers have examined factors that foster or inhibit human beings' intrinsic desire to engage in intellectual tasks.

They usually measure motivation by observing people's voluntary activities. Thus, to assess students' intrinsic motivation to read, researchers might find out how much they read on their own, when there is no external reward (e.g., a good grade) nor any punishment (e.g., a bad grade) involved. Or they might give them several activities to choose from and observe whether they do one involving reading.

For children who are not intrinsically motivated to engage in intellectual activities, intrinsic motivation theorists would determine first whether factors that research has shown to support intrinsic interest (e.g., feelings of control and competence) are present, and then manipulate those factors to increase interest (e.g., by providing students more autonomy or making sure they can succeed on tasks and feel competent).

While intrinsic motivation theorists emphasize feelings of enjoyment, *self-worth* theorists are concerned with feelings of being valued. Covington (1992, 1998) and others propose that students are naturally motivated to preserve a sense of personal worth. If a student believes his value in an educational context is based on academic competence, he will seek opportunities to demonstrate his competencies and, like Defensive Dave, avoid situations that may lead to a judgment of incompetence. Self-worth theorists, therefore, might assess students' beliefs about what others' regard is based on. Interventions might be aimed at making sure that students feel supported and admired for trying, regardless of the outcome of their efforts.

Related to self-worth theory, which emphasizes students' feelings of being valued, *self-system theory* claims that feeling socially connected is a basic human need and that people do not function well in environments where this need is not met. They study the quality of children's relationships with the teacher and classmates. They might suggest that a teacher make a greater effort to develop an emotionally close relationship with a child who is not exerting much effort. For example, a teacher or a counselor might reach out to Alienated Al to let him know that he or she cared about Al's academic success and is interested in understanding his feelings about school.

Recently *goal theorists* have pointed out that people engage in the same behavior for different reasons, and that the reason for engaging in a task is just as important as the level of effort, degree of persistence, or any other observable behavior. Most goal theorists promote the goals of learning, mastering, or understanding as the most conducive to learning. Unfortunately these goals are not usually the most prominent in school. Sally's goal is to get good grades. As a consequence, she does only what is likely to contribute directly to grades. Some students work to meet the school's minimum requirement for being on the football team (and stop working when this minimum requirement is achieved). Santos doesn't work hard at all on academic tasks because his goal is to enjoy himself. Dave engages in behaviors that achieve his goal of avoiding looking stupid. According to goal theorists, interventions designed to change maladaptive behaviors and increase student learning would require changing students' goals.

That children often have goals that are different from the teacher's is illustrated by Wentzel's (1989, 1991) research in which she asked high school students how often they tried to achieve each of 12 goals while they were in class. "Making or keeping friends" ranked the highest among students with average GPA's and second highest (after "having fun") among the lowest achieving students. Only the highest achieving students ranked "learning" above friends as an important goal in school.

Important Questions

Another way of thinking about motivation in achievement contexts is in terms of responses to three questions. Consider a child who has just been handed an assignment. Although she may not consciously ask these questions of herself, her subsequent behavior will depend on implicit answers to the following: First, *"Can I succeed at this task?"* This is the central question in the expectation component of "expectancy *x* value" theory. If, like Helpless Hannah, the student believes she has no hope of completing the task, she's not likely to try, or even to go on to the next question.

If our hypothetical student expects success, or at least believes success is a realistic possibility, the answer to the next question becomes important: "*Do I want to do this task?*" There are a number of different affirmative answers that are likely to lead her to get started on the task. She may "want" to do it because she fears she will be punished if she doesn't do it, or because she wants to achieve a good grade in that subject area. These would be extrinsic reasons. Or perhaps she wants to do the task for intrinsic reasons—because it looks like it will be fun or challenging, or she gets to work on it with her best friend. On the other hand, perhaps, like Satisfied Santos or Alienated Al, she finds no good reason for doing the task. It's boring, she doesn't care about the grade, and she sees no useful purpose in it. Thus even if the answer to the first, "can-I" question is affirmative, a student may not complete a task because she simply doesn't want to.

Assuming that our student decides to do the task, there still remains a third question—"*Why am I doing this task?*—that is relevant to the way she approaches the task and how much effort she puts into it. If, like Defensive Dave, her goal is to stay out of trouble for not trying, she might work half-heartedly, just to look busy. If she is more like Safe Sally, and her goal is to get a good grade, she will do whatever she believes is required for the grade she aspires, and no more. If her goal is to master a new skill, she may go beyond the minimal requirements, for example by making up additional problems for herself or by trying different strategies to see how they work.

These questions point out that there are many reasons for a student to exert low effort, or to work ineffectively, as well as many reasons for them to complete tasks. Motivation related to academic achievement, therefore, involves a rather complicated set of issues.

Is Motivation in the Person or in the Environment?

For reinforcement theorists, motivation is not in the person at all; it is in the environment. Changes in a person's behavior are produced by changing contingencies in the environment. Other motivation theorists conceptualize achievement motivation as a stable trait—something that an individual has either a lot or a little of, and that is only modestly changeable. For example, according to Atkinson's theory, achievement motivation is partly conceptualized as an unconscious trait (the motive to achieve success) which develops early in life primarily as a consequence of parenting practices. Thus, experiences in early childhood are assumed to play a continuing role in individuals' responses to achievement situations.

Still other theorists conceptualize achievement motivation as a set of conscious beliefs and values, influenced primarily by recent experiences in achievement situations (e.g., the amount of success or failure) and variables in the immediate environment, such as the nature and difficulty of the task at hand. A student's behavior when working on geography may differ from her behavior when working on algebra because of differences in her past performance in these two subjects, or because of differences in the two teachers' instructional approaches or the kinds of tasks in each subject.

Most theories allow for changes in achievement behavior—few assume that it is a fixed trait. And most theories assume that the context is important. Parents play a role, but teachers control most aspects of instruction as well as the social climate of the classroom. Although some students' motivational inclinations can create challenges for even the best teachers, I have seen teachers dramatically affect the motivation of even the most recalcitrant students.

The remainder of this book is about the theories of motivation mentioned briefly above, the research based on them, and their practical implications. Although most people do not know these psychological theories, everyone makes assumptions about why people behave the way they do; and their efforts to change others' and even their own behaviors are based implicitly on the theories this book describes. This book, therefore, acquaints readers with the formal language and details of psychological theories that should already be a part of their own explanations of behavior. A good understanding of these theoretical frameworks will make readers keener, more thoughtful observers and predictors of behavior, and help them become more effective in their efforts to change their own behavior as well as to influence students' achievement motivation.

Regardless of the theoretical orientation we take, our ultimate goal is to affect behavior. Before examining the theories in greater depth, we need a behavioral basis for judging when there is a need for intervention or changes in practices, and for evaluating whether changes made have had the desired effect. We turn, therefore, from a theoretical to a behavioral analysis of achievement motivation.

Identifying Motivation Problems

Observing Behavior

Whatever the cause of students' motivation problems, they usually manifest themselves in their behavior. The first step, therefore, is to do careful and systematic observations of student behavior. To provide a rough index of the degree and nature of students' motivation, Appendix 2-A lists behaviors that can be observed directly. Although motivation theorists and educators have varying interpretations of these behaviors, and varying beliefs as to which are most important, most would agree that all of them are desirable and their absence, particularly of the first 12, signals a problem.

Teachers should observe all students, including those who are achieving relatively well. And students should be observed working on different subject areas, in a variety of contexts, and on a variety of tasks. Some students work diligently in small groups but never finish tasks that are designed to be done individually. Some students work best in structured learning situations, others in unstructured situations, and so on. These differences will not be identified if students are observed in only one learning context. Analysis of these variations can provide hints about the causes of motivational problems and possible solutions.

It is important to observe students' emotional expressions as well as their behaviors. Do students approach tasks enthusiastically? Do they smile, get excited, even cry out occasionally when a major breakthrough is achieved? Or do they look depressed, bored, or anxious? Do they express pride in their achievements? Do they appear embarrassed or humiliated when they answer a question incorrectly? Emotions are important determinants of behavior and they can reveal a great deal about students' motivation.

From Identifying to Explaining

As essential as careful observations are, they are usually insufficient in diagnosing problems, and need to be supplemented with other strategies. The inadequacy of simply observing behavior is demonstrated in a study by Peterson and Swing (1982), in which some elementary school-age students who looked like they were attending faithfully to a mathematics lesson reported in subsequent interviews that they were actually thinking of other things. They claimed, for example, to be worrying about whether they would be able to solve the problems and whether they would be among the last to finish. Students' responses to questions about their thoughts during the time they were supposed to be working on the task predicted their achievement better than observers' judgments regarding their level of attention. As would be expected, children who claimed they were thinking about strategies to solve the problems performed better than those who claimed to be thinking about whether they could solve them.

This finding should not be surprising. What adult has not been guilty of feigning attention at a teachers' meeting or during a religious service while planning the evening's dinner menu or fantasizing about an upcoming vacation? What college student has not pretended to be taking notes in a lecture while writing a letter to a friend? Adults sometimes have elaborate strategies for looking attentive, and so do children. With a large group of students to observe, it is often difficult for the teacher to see through these ruses.

Teachers can supplement observations with other strategies for identifying and understanding motivational problems. Discussions with individuals or with small groups of students can be revealing if teachers encourage and do not penalize students for honesty and openness. Teachers are often surprised to hear some of their high-performing students claim that they do not like schoolwork and that they work hard only to get good grades. Some poor-achieving students, who teachers assume do not care about academic success, occasionally confess to being discouraged or fearful of failure. Conversations with students can provide other important information that can be used to get them on to a more productive pathway. If discussions don't work well or don't feel comfortable, teachers who are interested in assessing motivation problems can also give questionnaires for students to complete anonymously. Examples of questions that can be asked in discussions or on questionnaires are provided in various chapters throughout this book.

One of the purposes of this book is to help teachers identify and remedy motivational problems stemming from unobservable thoughts and feelings, such as levels of self-confidence, expectations for success, interest in academic work, feelings of autonomy, alienation, achievement anxiety, and fear of failure. Even if motivational problems are apparent from overt behavior, remedies require accurate diagnoses. Strategies for identifying the causes of maladaptive behavior will be described in later chapters to help teachers in this important process.

High Achievers Are Not Invulnerable

Teachers usually recognize the motivational problems of relatively low achievers. In contrast, motivation problems of high-achieving students like Sally, who are not realizing their potential for intellectual development, often go unrecognized. This is because teachers usually assume that students who do well in school do not have motivation problems. They rate students like Sally high in motivation and most of them enjoy having students like her in their class.

Studies of student motivation challenge this assumption. Phillips (1984), for example, studied 117 fifth graders who were above the 75th national percentile on the Stanford Research Associates (SRA) achievement tests. Twenty-three of these students seriously underestimated their actual levels of performance, set low achievement standards for themselves, and were less persistent than the high achievers in the sample who had high perceptions of competence. By setting low standards and by giving up easily, these high-ability students were not living up to their learning potential. (See also Kolb & Jussim, 1994; Phillips & Zimmerman, 1990.)

Research suggests that high-achieving girls and minority students are particularly vulnerable to motivational problems. In the Phillips study, for example, girls composed 66 percent of the students studied, but 100 percent of those who underestimated their competency. Steele's (1999) research on "stereotype threat" indicates that high achieving minority students often become so concerned about avoiding the stereotype of intellectual inferiority that they fall apart in situations in which they are asked to demonstrate their competency, such as on standardized tests.

It is easy to overlook relatively high-achieving students who are not performing at their capacity. Teachers who have as many as 25 or even 35 students in a class generally believe that their primary responsibility is to make sure that all students master the basic curriculum. As long as students consistently finish their work and are not disruptive they are usually not considered to pose problems. That some students finish assignments in half of the allotted time often goes unnoticed. This is especially true in classes in which there are many students who are having difficulty mastering the assigned material and who lay significant claims on the teachers' attention. Consequently, the "B+" student who could be getting "A's," and the student who gets "A's" without really trying are less likely to be noticed or to be perceived as problems than those students who are barely passing. Their talents are, as a consequence, not developed, and some become bored and disinterested. It is, therefore, important to scrutinize all students for motivational problems.

Looking Beyond the Student

What are seen as *students'* motivation problems are often problems with the academic context. If more than a few children seem unmotivated to complete school tasks, it is useful to examine aspects of the educational program and the social context of the classroom that might undermine motivation. Student motivation is strongly affected by the nature of instruction and the tasks given—for example, whether tasks are clear and at the appropriate level of difficulty, and whether they involve active participation and are personally meaningful. Students' motivation is also affected by the social context—for example, whether students feel valued as human beings, are supported in their learning efforts by the teacher and their peers, and whether they are allowed to make mistakes without being humiliated. Motivation problems that are observed in students' behaviors, therefore, often actually reside in the educational program.

Often an analysis of the fit between the student and the instructional program is required to understand motivation problems. This is because a program that is highly motivating for one student is not necessarily effective for another. For example, a student like Safe Sally, who is used to working for grades, may not work at all in a classroom in which grades are not given, at least not initially. A student like Satisfied Santos, who is motivated to do only the work he chooses, may work effectively in a classroom that allows a great deal of choice and autonomy, but not in a classroom that is very teacher-directed. Identifying motivation "problems," therefore, requires a complex analysis of students, the educational context, and the interaction between the qualities of students and contexts.

Grade Differences in Motivational Problems

Underachievement in the early elementary grades (i.e., kindergarten and first grade) usually has different causes than it does in later grades. Some young children do not work effectively on school tasks because they are having difficulty adapting to the demands of a new social context. Young children usually have not had experience in formal academic settings. Some have difficulty sitting still for more than a few minutes. They may also be easily distracted because they are not accustomed to the stimulation of many other children and activities. Sometimes young children, who are used to being able to choose their activities, are unenthusiastic about accepting constraints that the teacher imposes.

Although some children in kindergarten and first grade have difficulty following directions and completing tasks, most are eager and self-confident learners (although not necessarily on the tasks the teacher provides). Helpless Hannahs, Defensive Daves, Anxious Almas, and Alienated Als are rare in the early elementary grades. Indeed, most young children have unrealistically high expectations about their ability to complete tasks (see Stipek, 1984a, 1984b; Stipek & Greene, 2001; Stipek & Tannatt, 1984).

By second or third grade some students lose self-confidence, become anxious in learning contexts, and consequently engage in activities that inhibit rather than facilitate learning. Thus, although the kinds of adjustment problems experienced by very young children usually disappear with time and experience in a school setting, other problems emerge.

The older the child, the more serious the consequences of motivation problems. During their first 6 to 9 years of school, students have little choice in their educational curriculum. Because there are not many tasks they can avoid, children's motivational problems often appear in the form of low effort expenditure, poor attention, or disruptive behavior. High school students have more choice in the type and difficulty level of the courses they take, and even in how long they continue their education. Older students, like Sally, can avoid certain courses, or like Al, school itself. Thus, while the fifth grader who lacks self-confidence in mathematics may "forget" to do her homework, the older student may not take any courses in mathematics or more seriously, drop out of school.

Although the immediate consequences of motivational problems in the early grades of school may be less serious than those occuring in later grades, children's early experiences in school put them on a pathway that becomes increasingly difficult to change. Children's school performance as early as in kindergarten is highly predictive of their performance much later (Alvidrez & Weinstein, 1999; Luster & McAdoo, 1996; Stipek, 2001) and an accurate predictor of dropping out is failure in elementary school (Garnier, Stein, & Jacobs, 1997; Luster & McAdoo, 1996; Stipek, 2001). Motivational orientations that develop early in life no doubt play a role in this predictability. Indeed, some analysts consider low perceptions of competence resulting from early failure in school to be a major cause of dropping out of high school (Stipek, 2001). Achievement motivation, even in the first few years of school, therefore, has serious and life-long implications.

Summary

Careful observation of students' behavior is a critical first step in enhancing student motivation in achievement contexts. Thorough observations in variable contexts, supplemented with interviews and analyses of the educational program, are necessary to identify and understand motivation problems.

Psychological theories provide a coherent set of constructs and principles that can guide this analysis. Theories provide a framework for understanding, predicting, and changing behavior in achievement contexts. They also provide a framework for conducting research that will produce useful information about practices that promote student motivation. The remainder of this book is about how theory and research can be used to guide decisions in educational practice.

CHAPTER

3   **Reinforcement Theory**

Reinforcement theory was developed to explain all human behavior, not just achievement-related behavior. But a great deal has been written about the application of reinforcement theory to classrooms. Indeed, for many years a reinforcement model of motivation dominated the educational psychology literature. This chapter describes the theory and its applications in achievement settings. In the last section, praise is discussed in some detail to illustrate the principles of effective use of reinforcement.

The Theory

Reinforcement theorists assume that behavior is caused by events external to the person and that behavior can be understood in terms of simple laws that apply to both human beings and animals. According to the **law of effect,** behavior is determined by its consequences. Responses become more likely to occur as the result of some consequences and less likely as the result of others. Thorndike (1898) derived this principle from his observations of food-deprived cats placed inside a box with food outside. In their attempts to escape, the animals would, by accident, eventually operate a device that released the door, allowing them to consume the food. The animals subsequently operated the device more and more rapidly when placed in the box. Thus, an accidental behavior that originally had very low probability occurred with increasing frequency as a result of its consequence (being able to consume food).

Skinner (1974) expanded Thorndike's law of effect by systematically manipulating consequences and studying their effects on behavior. He coined the term **operant conditioning** to refer to the process of establishing a behavior or set of behaviors using the principles of reinforcement. Skinner defined consequences that increased the probability of behaviors that they were contingent upon as **positive reinforcers,** and consequences that reduced the probability of behavior as **punishments. Negative reinforcers** are consequences that increase the probability of a behavior by taking something away or reducing its intensity. Negative reinforcers are often confused with punishment. They actually have the opposite effect; because something unpleasant (for example, a noise or a teacher's angry stare) is terminated, negative reinforcers *increase* the likelihood of the behavior they follow. In contrast, when punishment follows a behavior, the behavior is *less* likely to be repeated.

Although originally reinforcement theory was derived primarily from research on animals, theorists assume that these principles apply to humans as well. Consider, for example, a teacher who wants to increase the amount of attention a child pays to his or her directions. This child likes **social reinforcement** (reinforcers that are linked to social approval, e.g., teacher smiles, verbal praise) and dislikes missing recess. If the teacher praises the child (positive reinforcement), or stops frowning (negative reinforcement) when he pays attention, he is more likely to pay attention in the future. If the teacher cancels the child's recess (punishment) when he is inattentive, his inattention will decrease.

Reinforcers and punishments are defined strictly in terms of their effects on behavior and cannot be identified independently of these effects. What is a positive reinforcer for some may, therefore, be punishment for others. An opportunity to perform in front of the class may be a real treat for an outgoing, self-assured student, and would serve as a positive reinforcer. The same "opportunity" may serve as punishment for a shy or insecure student. Consequences can become reinforcing by being linked to other consequences that are already reinforcing. These are called **secondary reinforcers.** Consider grades, for example. Grades have little effect on most kindergartners who have not yet learned their value. But kindergartners who bring home "A's" are likely to be praised by their parents and possibly given tangible rewards. As a result of being paired with consequences that are already reinforcing, "A's" take on reinforcing qualities that are independent of the rewards with which they were originally paired.

This pairing process also works for punishment. Most young students value teachers' positive attention, but after the first few grades of school, children who appear to be the teacher's pet are sometimes teased or rejected by classmates. What once served as positive reinforcement becomes punishment by being linked to an undesirable consequence. A child who previously sought and was reinforced by teacher approval may therefore cease engaging in behaviors that gain teacher attention.

If a previously reinforced behavior ceases to be reinforced, its rate of occurrence decreases; the desired behavior becomes **extinguished.** Thus, for example, if the attention of the boy described above does not continue to be reinforced, he will stop paying attention (i.e., attention will be extinguished). Although a reinforcer needs to be contingent upon a desired behavior from time to time, reinforcers do not have to follow every occurrence of the behavior. To the contrary, behaviors that are reinforced **intermittently** or partially (rather than every time the desired behavior occurs) actually take longer to extinguish; they will continue longer after reinforcement ceases altogether than behaviors that were always reinforced.

Another reinforcement principle explains the conditions under which behavior that has been reinforced will occur. Skinner found that unrelated external cues became signals for the availability of reinforcement or punishment. For example, if a rat is reinforced for pushing a lever only when a particular type of light is on, the rat will begin to push the lever when the light is turned on, and will not push it without the light. The light, according to Skinner, serves as a **discriminative stimulus**, and the lever-pushing response is under stimulus **control.** Thus, according to the principle of stimulus control, stimuli that become associated with consequences can cause behavior itself, and the behavior may occur only in the presence of those stimuli. The stimuli that are present when reinforcement occurs serve as a "signal" that particular behaviors will have particular consequences.

The principle of stimulus control applies to humans as well as to rats. For example, a teacher standing in front of the classroom may cause students to pay attention if, in the past, students were rewarded for paying attention or punished for not paying attention when the teacher stood in front of the class. A change in the stimulus, such as a substitute teacher or a student standing in front of the class, may not cue students to pay attention because these individuals were not previously associated with positive reinforcers or punishment. This principle may explain why discipline sometimes deteriorates when the teacher leaves the room for a few minutes or when a substitute takes over a class.

Fortunately, it is not necessary to positively reinforce every desired behavior. The effects of positive reinforcement and punishment for one response **generalize** to similar responses. This occurs because reinforcement for a particular behavior affects not only that behavior but a class of behaviors. For example, the likelihood of a student paying attention during a social studies lesson may be increased by rewarding her for paying attention during mathematics. A child who is punished for disrupting the class by throwing paper airplanes may, as a consequence, be less likely to disrupt the class by other means as well as by the specific behavior for which the punishment was received.

As mentioned in the previous chapter, reinforcement theory is considered "mechanistic" because no reference is made to such unobservable variables as choice, beliefs, expectations, or emotions (Graham & Weiner, 1996). The emphasis is exclusively on the environment and on observable behaviors. A strict reinforcement theorist, such as Skinner (1974), assumes that a person's behavior at any given time is fully determined by his or her reinforcement history and the contingencies in the present environment. Thoughts and feelings are considered irrelevant. According to the theory, we should look only at the environment to understand behavior, not to inner thoughts, such as self-perceptions of competence and expectations for success, or to emotions, such as fear and anxiety.

Strict reinforcement theorists, therefore, would not consider motivation as a characteristic of the individual. Individuals would be considered "motivated" only inasmuch as they exhibit behaviors that are believed or known to enhance learning, like paying attention or working on assignments. Faced with a student who is not working in school, a reinforcement theorist would ask, "What's wrong with the environment?" rather than "What's wrong with this student?" The only way to change a student's behavior is to change the reward contingencies (consequences to behavior) in the classroom.

Implications for Educational Practice

The educational implications of reinforcement theory for maximizing desired learning behaviors are straightforward. The teacher makes positive reinforcers contingent upon desired behavior and punishments contingent upon undesired behavior. The process of using reinforcement principles to change behavior is referred to as **behavior modification.** The simplicity of the theory is no doubt a major reason for its long-standing central role in educational psychology, and its widespread classroom application.

The first task is to determine what constitutes rewards and punishment for any given student. Teachers can try out making different consequences contingent on behavior, observe students' responses to each, and continue to use those that increase desired behavior and decrease undesired behavior. Rewards that are common in American classrooms include praise, good grades, public recognition, and privileges. Disapproval, bad grades, public humiliation, and staying after school are commonly-used punishments. I have also observed teachers make the opportunity to clean the chalkboard, do extra challenging math problems, and read a poem to the class contingent upon some desired behavior. In one kindergarten class that I visited, the teacher explained that the children were being especially good because homework was given only to the students who behaved well all day!

Teachers sometimes make positive reinforcers and punishment contingent on the whole class behaving or not behaving in a particular way. This can produce peer pressure for desirable behavior. For example, a teacher might hold a popcorn party on Friday afternoons, contingent upon the class completing all assignments; she may also shorten recess for the whole class as a consequence of too many students failing to pay attention during a lesson.

Reinforcement affects a particular behavior only if it is contingent on *that* behavior. The teacher must, therefore, reinforce only desirable behavior and ignore or punish undesirable behavior. Children often have no idea why there are happy faces and stars stamped on their papers. If they don't know what behavior the reinforcement is contingent upon, the desired behavior won't increase.

Clearly, if maximum learning is the goal, behaviors that enhance learning need to be reinforced and behaviors that inhibit learning need to be ignored or punished. Accordingly, students should be reinforced for paying attention to the teacher or the task at hand, selecting challenging tasks, persisting on tasks that are difficult, completing tasks, and engaging in other behaviors that enhance learning. Such behaviors as inattentiveness, giving up quickly, selecting very easy tasks, or turning in incomplete assignments, should be ignored or punished. Teachers also may reinforce helpfulness, generosity, responsibility, or other socially desirable behaviors.

Behavior or **contingency management** strategies are frequently applied to children who have serious behavioral problems, including conduct problems, antisocial behavior, or hyperactivity. Accordingly, teachers reward desired behaviors, such as sitting still, raising hands before speaking, making eye contact and saying hello, offering help, or waiting in turn. Speaking out of turn might be ignored; shoving another child may be punished with a time-out. Daily report cards have been promoted as a strategy for keeping track of behavioral change and communicating with parents (Jacob & Pelham, 2000).

Rewards and punishments might be used to change the behaviors of some of the children described in Chapter 1. According to reinforcement theory, a teacher who wants to increase Safe Sally's risk-taking should make positive reinforcers contingent upon her approaching challenging learning situations rather than on performing well. A different approach would be required to get Helpless Hannah to complete her assignments. For Hannah, rewards need to be contingent upon completing assignments.

This approach can only work, however, if Hannah actually completes an assignment. What can a teacher do if the desired behavior never initially occurs? The problem is particularly serious for students who almost never engage in desired behaviors. To address this problem, researchers developed a strategy called **shaping.** Skinner used this strategy to teach pigeons to play Ping-Pong. Needless to say, if Skinner had waited for his pigeons to begin a game of Ping-Pong so that he could reinforce the behavior, he would have had a long wait. Instead, he began by giving a pellet of food for the first behavior in a chain required for playing Ping-Pong. When that behavior began to occur with some frequency, he was able to reinforce the pigeon for the second behavior in the chain, and so on.

This same strategy can be used to shape behavior in a child. The teacher first makes clear to the child what the desired behavior is, and then begins reinforcing any behavior that approximates it. If a troublesome student looks in the teacher's direction, the teacher may praise him for paying attention, or maybe just smile approvingly. Presumably the student will, as a result of the reinforcement, look more often in the teacher's direction. The teacher may then praise the student for maintaining a gaze in the teacher's direction for more than a minute and gradually increase the length of time required for reinforcement. Thus, the teacher "shapes" the student's actions in the direction of the desired behavior—paying attention to the teacher for an extended period of time.

Because she has become completely disengaged from classroom activities, shaping would probably be necessary to get Helpless Hannah to finish assignments. The teacher might begin by praising her for opening her book and taking out her pencil after an assignment is given. This should, according to the theory, increase the probability of her preparing to work on future assignments. The teacher could then praise Hannah only for actually beginning the assignment (e.g., doing a few problems), and then "up the ante"—praise her for persisting on an assignment. If praise serves as a positive reinforcer for Hannah, she should eventually complete an assignment—which the teacher can then reward.

Token Economies

In some classrooms teachers have developed elaborate **token economies**—formalized systems of behavior modification. The essential components of a token economy are: (1) tokens (that can be exchanged for a reward), (2) target behaviors, (3) rules for earning and losing tokens, and (4) "back-up consequences" for which tokens can be exchanged. Tokens can be anything that is easily counted: points, play money, chips, stars, or checkmarks. They have no inherent value; rather, their worth is based on their ability to be exchanged for a valued "back-up consequence," such as candy, toys, trinkets, money, extra recess, or movies. Although token economies have been used primarily to improve social behavior— such as talking out of turn, being off task, and poor attendance—they have also been used to improve assignment completion and accuracy. A token economy can be implemented with one student, a small group of students, or the whole class.

In the case of programs designed to reduce undesirable behaviors (e.g., talking out of turn), students are initially given a set of tokens and are asked to give back a prespecified amount for engaging in the undesirable behavior. In programs designed to increase desirable behaviors (e.g., completing assignments), students are given tokens for exhibiting the target behavior.

All programs include specific rules for earning or losing tokens, which may be simple or complicated. Systems can be created to increase a single behavior or a combination of behaviors. For example, a teacher who desires to increase both task completion and task accuracy may allow students to earn one token for completing an assignment and two for completing it with at least 80 percent accuracy. A variable number of tokens may be earned for different degrees of accuracy.

A program developed by Cohen (1973) for a troublesome group of adolescent boys in a residential home illustrates how token economies are implemented. Most of the students in Cohen's study had dropped out of school and many had been found guilty of crimes. They were given points that could be exchanged for goods, services, and special privileges, such as recreational time in a lounge, books, magazines, extra clothing, mail-order supplies, a private shower, or a private room for sleeping and entertaining. (This list demonstrates the importance of tailoring reinforcers to the particular individuals whose behavior one desires to change.) Reinforcement was made contingent upon academic achievement and behaviors presumed to enhance achievement. Despite a long history of previous failed attempts to increase the motivation of these boys, their academic achievement improved dramatically under this token economy system.

Another form of a token economy is illustrated by Alschuler's (1968) performance contracting. In one program, students were advanced $2,000 in play money. Students determined their own performance goals, which they indicated on a written contract. The higher the goals, the greater the payoff; students lost money for not meeting their goals or for turning in assignments late. Consequently, unrealistically high goals generally resulted in losses and unnecessarily low goals resulted in very low payoffs. The system, therefore, encouraged moderate risks to produce the greatest amount of learning. In one study of fifth graders, Alschuler observed an average gain of three years of growth on standardized mathematics tests in one academic year.

Token economies can also be applied to one or two students in a class. McGinnis, Friman, and Carlyon (1999), for example, created a token economy to increase completion and accuracy of math problems for two middle-school boys. Both problem-solving accuracy and ratings of how much they liked math remained high even after the reward was withdrawn.

Different procedures for implementing token economies are required for students of different ages. High-school students may be able to comprehend complicated systems and to delay exchanging tokens for the back-up consequence for a relatively long period of time. Young children cannot understand or keep in mind complicated systems, and they are likely to lose interest in the tokens if the exchange is delayed more than a few days.[1]

Token economies were first developed primarily as a procedure of last resort with clinical, frequently institutionalized populations. They have since been applied to children with less serious problems and to children in regular classrooms. Studies have examined the effectiveness of token economy programs in changing behaviors, such as attention and persistence on tasks. Most studies find that tangible rewards, systematically applied, can produce substantial behaviorial change, even in the most recalcitrant subjects (see Abramowitz & O'Leary, 1991; De Martini-Scully, Bray, & Kehle, 2000; Williams, Williams & McLaughlin, 1991).

Research on the maintenance and generalization of desired behaviors in token programs shows less positive results. Reviews of data on how well behavioral changes are maintained after token programs are withdrawn, and on how well the desired behaviors generalize to other settings in which tokens are not administered are mixed (Kazdin & Bootzin, 1972; Kazdin, 1988; see also, Kohn, 1993). Although effects are sometimes evident even a few years after the program is concluded, removal of the tokens often leads to a rapid return to **baseline behaviors** (behaviors preceding the implementation of the token economy program). Behavior outside of the setting in which the tokens were given (sometimes referred to as "transfer") is generally not affected by the token economy. These and other limitations of external reinforcement are discussed in the next section.

Problems with Reward and Punishment

Teachers usually find that the promise of a reward or the threat of punishment can affect most children's behavior in the classroom. Behavioral methods have been particularly successful with children who behave extremely inappropriately in school settings. Indeed, it is hard to imagine a well-functioning classroom in which desirable behaviors are not reinforced in some way and undesirable behaviors are not ignored or at least occasionally punished.

---

[1] I discovered the importance of frequent exchanges when I tried to implement a token economy to motivate my 5-year-old to get dressed for school in the morning. She was allowed to put a star on a calendar each day that she was dressed by 7:30 a.m. I explained that when she earned 20 stars I would take her to a toy store and she could pick out a toy. The implementation of the star system had an immediate and dramatic effect on her behavior, but after about a week she lost interest in the stars and we returned to our daily morning conflict. Twenty days without linking the stars to a tangible reward was simply too long.

But research on the use of rewards to control student behavior suggests that rewards should be used thoughtfully and sparingly. Inappropriate application of reinforcement principles can adversely affect behavior, and over-dependence on rewards and punishments to influence achievement behavior can have long-term negative effects on student motivation (Kohn, 1993; Lepper & Henderlong, 2000; Ryan & Deci, 2000; Stipek & Seal, 2001). Next is a summary of some of the problems that teachers need to consider when using rewards and punishments.

Effectiveness of Rewards.   Consider first the problem of finding an effective reward. Rewards used in most American classrooms are not universally effective. Grades, for example, don't work for some children in early elementary school because they have no intrinsic value to that age group. Unless the value placed by teachers on grades is supported by parents and peers, even older students are unlikely to work for such a symbolic reward. Thus, for some students good grades are not sufficiently desirable to inspire high effort. Satisfied Santos, for example, is happy with a grade that requires a level of performance below what he could achieve with effort; higher grades are not reinforcing for him. A teacher who perseveres in promising good grades as a reward for positive achievement behaviors, and in threatening bad grades for negative ones, will not obtain desired behaviors in students like Santos.

The effectiveness of grades as reinforcers declines for some students in adolescence. In early adolescence peer approval becomes increasingly important and adult approval less critical. Unless peer acceptance is to some degree associated with high achievement, as has been found in studies of younger children (e.g., Leonard, Reyes, Danner, & de la Torre, 1994), grades may not hold any value for such students. In adolescence, it is common for some peer groups to sanction and reward poor grades (Graham, Taylor, & Hudley, 1998). Thus for rebellious or alienated adolescents, like Al, who explicitly devalue success in school, high grades may be perceived as embarrassing—a punishment rather than a reward. Recall that Cohen (1973) used private showers, magazines, and clothing, not good grades, to reinforce adaptive achievement behavior among delinquent boys. In a residential center such tangible rewards may be available and appropriate, but in most regular schools they are not. Alternatives to grades—such as candy and even money—have been used, but these have obvious problems in regular schools.

Teachers and students sometimes have different perspectives on the reward value of consequences to behavior other than grades. For example, for some students any form of teacher attention, including negative attention (e.g., threats, nagging, teasing), serves as positive reinforcement. For these students, a reprimand, which the teacher believes serves as punishment, actually increases the likelihood of the undesirable behavior. For adolescents who are eager to win approval from nonachievement-oriented peers, a teacher reprimand earns them points. This is why Al looks around the room when the teacher admonishes him for cracking a joke in class. Being sent to the principal's office is more desirable for some students than staying in class, and thus serves as a reinforcement rather than as a punishment.

Accessibility of Rewards.   If grades are based on competitive criteria (as they usually are), high grades will not be available to all students. By definition, all students cannot be above average. Moreover, students begin classes with varying levels of preparation, and some students learn new concepts more quickly than others. A few students, like Helpless Hannah, will find that they cannot get a high grade, regardless of how hard they work. Defensive Dave and Alienated Al doubt that good grades are really available to them, and thus do not exhibit the behaviors teachers desire.

The threat of a bad grade will not affect the behavior of students who believe that bad grades are unavoidable, whatever they do. The promise of a good grade will not increase the effort of students who believe that they will achieve a good grade whether or not they exert much effort. This principle holds for any reward that can be earned easily by some children and only with great difficulty (or not at all) by others.

The principle applies to other rewards that have become commonplace in American schools as incentives for academic achievement—including "student-of-the-year" awards, vouchers for toys or hamburgers, and scholarships (Webb, Covington, & Guthrie, 1993; Stipek & Seal, 2001). Such rewards will motivate only the students for whom the reward is genuinely accessible, sometimes a very small proportion of students and often those who are already working hard.

An analogous argument could be made for merit pay for teachers. If it is available only to a small percentage of them (e.g., 5 percent), most teachers would not perceive merit pay to be realistically available. Therefore, it would not serve to motivate most teachers, especially those who most need motivation. Reinforcement must be perceived by individuals to be genuinely available to them for it to affect their behavior.

There are also problems of timing. Many rewards, such as scholarships to college, are too far in the future to motivate the kinds of daily activities (e.g., finishing homework, studying for tests) that are required to achieve the reward. They may affect the behavior of high school students; they would probably have to be linked to more immediate rewards to motivate students in middle or elementary school.

Perceived unavailability of positive reinforcers explains why teachers often get a false impression that a student does not desire conventional rewards. Teachers often express dismay at a student's apparent unwillingness to engage in behaviors that will be positively reinforced. I often hear teachers complain: "I have told him over and over that if he would just put a little effort into his work he could get good grades; he just doesn't seem to care one way or the other."

Careful observations of these troublesome students often reveal that they never receive positive reinforcement, even when they do exert a little effort. Many actually care a great deal and would be delighted to receive teacher praise or good grades, but they don't believe that either of these positive reinforcers is genuinely available. It is not uncommon for such students to resort to alternative, often undesirable means of gaining recognition. Misbehaving to get negative teacher attention is not their preferred mode of operation; it is what they resort to when getting attention through more desirable behaviors doesn't seem to work.

Rewarding Desired Behavior.   Another problem with relying on reinforcement is that only observable behavior can be reinforced. Some "behaviors," such as attention, are not entirely observable. As mentioned in Chapter 2, students can look like they are intensely engaged in intellectual tasks while they are actually reliving the home run they made at recess or planning their strategy for getting a particular girl to go to the junior prom. Teachers can directly reinforce students for looking in their direction, but it is difficult to reinforce students for *listening* or *thinking* about the information.

Teachers can also reinforce observable outcomes, like good performance on tests, that are usually associated with paying attention. But if the student had cheated, or guessed, or didn't have to study at all to do well, the teacher inadvertently rewards cheating, guessing, or low effort. And, consistent with reinforcement theory, studies show that rewarding performance that required low levels of effort fosters relatively low levels of effort (Eisenberger, 1992).

If the teacher's goal is to increase effort, then effort must be rewarded. Studies have shown that rewarding serious effort and high (but achievable) levels of performance enhances effort and the quality of performance (Eisenberger, 1992). But effort, like attention, is not easy to assess in a classroom with many students. Teachers usually are not able to observe the level of effort directly, and even when they can, students like Defensive Dave become artful at giving a false impression of intense effort. To make accurate judgments teachers need very good observation skills (and eyes in the back of their heads).

Most of the time effort has to be inferred from performance, which, to be an accurate indicator, requires a very good knowledge on the teacher's part of her students' skill levels. It is often difficult to distinguish poor performance despite high effort from poor performance caused by low effort, or good performance despite low effort versus good performance that required high effort. As a consequence, for some children punishment (e.g., a low grade) follows high effort or reward follows low effort.

Negative Effects of Rewards on Behavior.   In several studies rewards have been shown to have a negative effect on children's willingness to attempt challenging tasks. In one study, for example, some children were offered an extrinsic reward for correct answers and others were not. Subjects who were offered extrinsic rewards chose significantly less difficult problems than subjects who were not offered rewards for correct answers (Harter, 1978b). Thus, under the reward condition children were less likely to select a challenging problem. Or, as Kohn (1993) points out, if children are offered a pizza for reading a certain number of books, how likely are they to select long, difficult books?

Rewards can also lead to very superficial learning behaviors, less flexible problem-solving strategies, and less creativity (Ryan & Deci, 2000; Hennessey, 2000). How carefully would you expect a child to read a book that she was reading solely for points toward a pepperoni pizza? I remember a "reading wheel" that my fourth grade teacher put on a bulletin board for each student in the class. For every book report we wrote in a particular set of categories, a part of the wheel was filed in. A prize was offered for the first student who completed the wheel. I can't remember whether I won the contest, but I do remember how competent I became at filling in the book report forms without really reading the books.

Extrinsic rewards affect teachers' as well as students' behavior. Garbarino (1975) describes a study in which sixth-grade children served as tutors for first-grade children. Tutors who were offered a reward for their success in tutoring exhibited a more "instrumental" orientation toward their pupils. They were more demanding and critical and created a more negative emotional atmosphere in the tutoring setting than tutors who were not offered a reward. The reward presumably focused these sixth-grade tutors' attention exclusively on their students' performance. Tutors consequently neglected behaviors like giving encouragement that may have seemed unnecessary, but actually would have helped them accomplish their goals.

This same instrumental orientation is likely to be seen when teachers' pay increases or bonuses are made contingent on the achievement test performance of their students. Teachers are more likely, under these reward conditions, to give students work that looks like the test items, and to provide students with fewer opportunities to engage in creative problem solving and other intellectual and social activities, which, although not tested, are extremely important. We return to these possible negative effects of using achievement test scores as the basis for rewards in Chapter 14.

Short-Lived Effectiveness.   A fifth problem with external reinforcement is that its effectiveness is often short-lived. Rewards may be effective in eliciting desired behaviors, but if the only reason for engaging in a behavior is to obtain a reward, the behavior will occur only under reward conditions. Indeed, evidence discussed in Chapter 11 suggests that under some circumstances when a reward is given and then later withdrawn, the desired behavior occurs even less frequently than it would have occurred if no reward had ever been offered (i.e., below baseline).

This limitation in the use of external reinforcement becomes increasingly important as children advance in school. The curriculum in the early elementary grades is generally broken down into small units with frequent opportunities for positive reinforcement. Most assignments are completed in less than half an hour and are reviewed by the teacher soon after. In the upper grades assignments are generally larger, less frequent, and span a longer time period.

Compare, for example, typical language arts assignments for elementary versus high-school students. The younger students may, in one day, be given as many as three short assignments for which they can receive reinforcement (e.g., a grade, a star, or teacher praise). High school students might be asked to write an essay based on assigned reading once every week or two. Consequently, although young children can be reinforced for every subcomponent of an academic task, older students must go through many steps without any reinforcement (i.e., they must read the assigned literature, think about it, make an outline, write, and perhaps rewrite the essay). The older student is not rewarded for the several intermediate tasks that are required to complete the assignment.

For students who enter college, many rewards (e.g., obtaining a degree, getting into graduate school, getting a good job) are far removed from the immediate situation requiring achievement behaviors. Even within a given course, a midterm and a final examination are often the only "products" of a semester of academic labor that the professor sees. Consequently, they are the only opportunities students have to be reinforced. The promise of such distant rewards will not be effective for students who are accustomed to being reinforced daily for every academic effort.

Reinforcing behavior also conveys the message that the behavior is not worth doing for its own sake. Compare the messages given by the teacher who tells students that they will be allowed to spend 15 minutes at the computer if they finish their math assignment to the message given by the teacher who announces that students who complete their 15 minutes on the computer can go out to recess. The former teacher is much more likely than the latter to foster the perception that working with computers is fun.

Providing positive reinforcements for all intellectual activities in school can, ultimately, undermine students' desire to be involved in *any* nonschool-related learning activity. I once gave a copy of *Tom Sawyer* to an eighth-grade boy. He graciously accepted the gift, but added that he had already written a book report for his English class that semester so he wouldn't be reading the book until the next semester. It apparently did not occur to him that a book could be read for reasons other than getting a grade in school. Safe Sally is another example of a student who has learned to participate in learning activities only for extrinsic rewards. She does not engage in learning activities outside of the classroom unless products are graded or are likely to bring some kind of social recognition. Even the novels she selects to read over the summer are on the high school reading list and may be included in the English curriculum the next year.

Effects of Punishment.   When the carrot approach is ineffective, it is natural to turn to the stick. I have seen teachers publicly humiliate children, and explain to me afterward that this is their strategy to get students to do their work and prepare for class discussions in the future. Perhaps for some children fear of humiliation or some other form of punishment motivates them to work. More often it has negative effects; it usually causes anxiety and alienation, which hinder learning.

Many children, like Defensive Dave, spend more energy trying to avoid such punishment than trying to understand the material in the curriculum or learning new skills. Some students avoid volunteering answers for fear of being criticized or embarrassed. They may turn in completed assignments with answers that they know are incorrect rather than try to figure out the right answers, because they have learned that punishment is more severe for not turning in an assignment on time than for poor performance. Other students, like Anxious Alma, become paralyzed by their fear of embarrassment or low grades.

Astute classroom observers have described these and other more elaborate measures that some children take to avoid punishment (e.g., Covington, 1992; 1998; Covington & Beery, 1976; see Chapter 6). Most of these behaviors accomplish the student's immediate goal, but they are self-defeating in the long run because they do not promote learning.

In the last decade there has been a proliferation of school-, district-, and even statewide sanctions for poor academic performance or attendance (Webb et al., 1993). Many states have "no pass/no play" rules requiring a certain level of school performance to participate in sports. States are also implementing "no pass/no drive" regulations that preclude poorly performing students from obtaining a driver's license. There is, as far as I know, no evidence on the effects of these policies on students' academic effort and school achievement. They have considerable face value, but their limitations and drawbacks need to be weighed against whatever positive effects are expected. The no pass/no drive law has the same limitation as rewards that come late in the educational game; they are probably too distant to motivate day-to-day behaviors necessary for school success in young children. Sports is often the only reason some relatively poor performing students stay in school, and the no pass/no play rule could effectively push out some students who otherwise might have persisted to graduation. While they may not have excelled in school, they would have kept the door open for further education.

Students need to be made accountable for their work, and there should be some consequences for low effort; yet punishment has to be used judiciously for the positive effects to outweigh the negative. And punishment should not be given for poor performance if there is evidence that the student has done his or her best. Research also suggests that some punishments work better than others. For example, reprimands given calmly, firmly, consistently, and immediately have been found to be more effective than those that are emotional or delayed (Abramowitz & O'Leary, 1991).

Using Rewards Effectively

Applying reinforcement theory effectively in the classroom requires considerable thoughtfulness. In addition to taking care to implement reinforcement and punishment in the most effective ways, teachers need to be vigilant about possible inconsistencies between the behavior they desire and the reinforcement contingencies in their classroom. A teacher once told me that he valued individual initiative and creativity and was disappointed that his students were passive and conforming. His students' behavior, however, was predictable based on his grading system, which conflicted with the values he espoused. Students lost points by failing to follow arbitrary rules, and their grades were determined almost entirely by accuracy. There were no rewards for personal initiative or creativity. To the contrary, students could be punished for straying slightly from the teacher's directions.

It is useful for teachers to reflect upon the kinds of rewards and punishments they use, the behavior upon which these consequences are contingent, and the degree to which rewards are available to all students. Appendix 3-A is provided to help teachers in this reflective process, which will occasionally reveal inconsistencies between values and actions.

Below are a few general principles that can also be used to guide the use of rewards:

1. Use rewards to get students to engage in an activity that they are otherwise not interested in doing, and then withdraw the reward when they show some interest. Often once children get going on something new, they find that it is not as difficult as they expected or more interesting than they thought it would be. Sometimes they even forget about the promised reward. They don't need to be reminded!

2. Make sure that it is clear to students what behavior the reward is contingent upon. Sometimes you can make a comment to clarify for a child what it is that you are rewarding. "I gave you an 'A' on this paper because I can see that you really put a lot of effort into it, and you've improved in your use of transition sentences."

3. Reward genuine achievements, such as high levels of effort and persistence, achieving a high standard, or personal improvement. Avoid rewarding relatively high levels of performance that required little or no effort.

4. Make sure that the behaviors you desire are rewarded. If you desire creativity or risk-taking, don't reinforce only accuracy and high levels of performance.

5. Use the most modest reward that will work. If an opportunity to play with the pet gerbil for a few minutes is effective, don't offer a popcorn party.

6. Use rewards that convey the intrinsic pleasure of educational activities—for example, spending time on the computer, doing brain teasers, reading topical magazines, or working on an art project.

7. Make sure the time between the desired behavior and the reward is not so great that the reward has no effect. The promise of getting into college is not very effective for first graders.

8. Make sure rewards are realistically available. The promise of a good grade won't affect the behavior of a student who is failing and knows that the most heroic effort will, at best, earn a "D." It is usually better to reward effort and improvement because this makes rewards available to all students.

Praise is featured in the next section because it is the most common reward used in educational settings, and because it illustrates the problems, limitations, and practical implications of using reinforcement effectively.

Praise

Brophy (1981) defines praise as ". . . reactions that go beyond simple feedback about appropriateness or correctness of behavior . . ." (p. 5). Simply indicating to a student that his or her answer is correct would not be considered praise. Congratulating the student for a right answer, or saying, "good job" or "you're really good at this" are examples of praise. Praise serves as a reinforcer for most students, especially very young children. According to the principles of reinforcement theory, behaviors followed by praise should increase in frequency. Studies of praise support the theory, demonstrating that well-administered praise can have positive effects on students' motivation (Sutherland, Wehby, & Copeland, 2000), even when administered by a computer (Fogg & Nass, 1997)!

Like other types of reinforcement, however, praise is not universally valued by psychologists. Kamii (1984) suggests that praise, as it is commonly used, may discourage children from developing personal criteria for judging their own work and may lead to dependency on adult authority figures. Schwartz (1996) claims that praise sends a message that adults "are always passing judgment on children's work and ideas and . . . are the ones to decide if things are good or bad" (p. 397). Other educational experts have claimed that because learning is intrinsically rewarding, praise is superfluous and can interfere with the natural disposition to learn (Kohn, 1993; see also Chapter 8), or that it can interfere with the goal of genuine achievement if given too freely (Damon, 1995). Another objection concerns the differential status it creates between the person giving the praise and the person receiving it, a situation that teachers who desire a more egalitarian relationship with their students may want to avoid (Brophy, 1981; Kohn, 1993). The remainder of this chapter discusses how to use praise in a way that effectively minimizes the kinds of negative effects mentioned above.

Consider first the principle that reinforcers, including praise, must be contingent on the behavior the teacher desires to maintain or increase. Brophy (1981) claims that praise is often not contingent on good performance or even on high effort, especially among teachers who have low expectations for student learning and for students who are typically poor performers. Anderson, Evertson, and Brophy (1979) found, for example, that the rate of praise following reading turns containing mistakes was slightly higher than the rate of praise following errorless reading turns. No doubt, teachers use praise to encourage poor performing students to try harder. But if praise is not contingent on high effort or good performance, it will not increase the likelihood of either one. If poor performance is just as likely to be praised as good performance, or if students are praised regardless of their effort, students learn that praise is not based on anything they do and they discount it.

Praise must also be credible to be effective. Praise that is either not contingent on effort or good performance, is not supported, or is contradicted by nonverbal behavior, is not believable praise. Brophy, Evertson, Anderson, Baum, and Crawford (1976) found that troublesome students sometimes received as much verbal praise as successful students. Aspects of teachers' nonverbal behavior, such as stern or distracted expressions on their faces, however, often indicated that they were expressing negative emotion or were not really paying attention while they were praising a student.

Some psychologists have raised the concern that praising the child can convey to children that their self-worth is contingent upon being able to perform in particular ways. Kamins and Dweck (1999) compared the effects of *person praise* (e.g., "I'm very proud of you"), *process praise* (e.g., "You must have tried really hard"), and *outcome praise* (e.g., "that's the right way to do it") on kindergarten-age children. The children who received person praise rated their products lower and assessed their ability lower than the children who received the other kinds of praise. These researchers concluded that praise directed at effort or some other aspect of the process (e.g., strategy) promotes the most positive motivational outcomes.

Praise given noncontingently and praise lacking in credibility can, under certain circumstances, also have negative effects on students' self-confidence. Praise for succeeding on a very easy task, for example, may be interpreted as an indication that the teacher has a low perception of the student's ability (Meyer, 1982, 1992; Miller & Hom, 1997). This interpretation is understandable in light of evidence that teachers tend to reward strong effort (Covington & Omelich, 1979b). Thus, if a teacher praises a student, presumably he or she believes the student exerted some effort, and strong effort to succeed on an easy task suggests low ability. (See Chapter 13 for further discussion of the paradoxical effects of praise.)

In contrast to older children and adults, who sometimes see negative implications in praise, research suggests that young children are more oriented toward pleasing adults, are more responsive to praise, and tend to accept it at face value (Meyer, 1992; Stipek, 1984a).

A compelling demonstration of this is seen in a study by Meid (1971) in which 6- and 10-year-old children were given either high-, medium-, or low-objective information (i.e., scores) for their past performance, and either praise, no comment, or a mildly negative comment. The younger children's expectations for performance on a subsequent task were based entirely on the social, verbal feedback, even when it conflicted with the objective feedback. The older elementary school-age children took both objective feedback and social feedback into account in their expectancy statements.

Although children in the elementary grades may accept praise at face value, young children who are praised when they have not exerted any effort will learn that effort is not necessary for reinforcement. There are, therefore, negative consequences to indiscriminate praise, even for very young children.

Praise can be used to inform students of the teacher's standards and to focus their attention on particular aspects of their performance. The elementary teacher who says "I like the way your letters are all in between the lines," or "What nice, neat handwriting" is providing information on what she values. This information function is best accomplished with praise that is specific and informative. A general "good job" is appreciated by most students. But more informative praise (e.g., "Your paper is well organized, clearly written, creative, persuasive, well researched, neat . . .") provides information on the teacher's standards and it provides guidance for improvement and future assignments.

Praise can also orient students toward particular kinds of standards. Praise that focuses students' attention on their own improvement or effort (e.g., "Your handwriting has improved"; "You obviously put a lot of time into this"; or "I think you are really beginning to understand this material") is better than praise that encourages social comparison (e.g., "This is one of the best papers in the class"). The former sets a high personal standard that all students can strive to achieve. All children can improve, and if they are praised for improvement, they must continue to progress to receive further praise. Children who are praised for relative performance need to continue to perform better than classmates, which for some children is impossible and for others requires neither effort nor improvement.

Praise for outcomes that are achieved with little effort gives students the message that effort is not valued. This is unproductive because optimal performance requires effort. Praise should be given, therefore, only for outcomes that require some effort to achieve, and it should sometimes be given for effort alone, regardless of the outcome.

Students should be encouraged to work for their own purposes, not to please the teacher or for external rewards. Comments such as, "You're really getting good at figuring out these problems," are better than "I'm really pleased at how well you are doing." The first focuses the student's attention on skill development, the latter on external approval.

Table 3.1 is Brophy's (1981) summary of effective versus ineffective ways to use praise. Most of these principles apply to any form of external reinforcement, not just praise.

It is difficult for teachers to monitor how they use praise because it is usually given spontaneously in the context of complex interactions in the classroom. It is useful, therefore, for teachers to have an aide, another teacher, or a parent observe them and give feedback. The form in Appendix 3-B is provided to help in this process.

Summary

Reinforcement techniques are used in virtually all classroom settings. When teachers praise students, give grades or gold stars, put students' papers on public display, or require students to stay after school for disruptive behavior, they are applying principles of reinforcement theory. The same is true for parents who praise children for cleaning their room and deny privileges for breaking rules. The basic notion that positive reinforcement increases the frequency of desired behavior and that punishment decreases the likelihood of undesirable behavior underlies all of these techniques.

Reinforcement strategies can be very effective in influencing students' behavior and are invaluable tools in educational settings. Promising a reward is particularly useful in getting children to try something they believe they won't like or won't be able to do, or to engage in an activity that simply cannot be made intrinsically interesting.[2]

---

[2]My daughter was finding mathematics frustrating (too slow) because she had not memorized the multiplication tables. This occurred despite my efforts to make practicing multiplication facts interesting. I finally resorted to the most tangible of rewards—money! I gave her a penny for every multiplication problem she did. I'm not recommending this strategy, but when all else fails. . . .

TABLE 3.1   Guidelines for Effective Praise*

Effective Praise

1. is delivered contingently
2. specifies the particulars of the accomplishment
3. shows spontaneity, variety, and other signs of credibility; suggests clear attention to the student's accomplishment
4. rewards attainment of specified performance criteria (which can include effort criteria)
5. provides information to students about their competence or the value of their accomplishments
6. orients students toward better appreciation of their own task-related behavior and thinking about problem solving
7. uses students' own prior accomplishments as the context for describing present accomplishments
8. is given in recognition of noteworthy effort or success at difficult (for this student) tasks
9. attributes success to effort and ability, implying that similar successes can be expected in the future
10. fosters endogenous attributions (students believe that they expend effort on the task because they enjoy the task and/or want to develop task-relevant skills)
11. focuses students' attention on their own task-relevant behavior
12. fosters appreciation of and desirable attributions about task-relevant behavior after the process is completed

Ineffective Praise

1. is delivered randomly or unsystematically
2. is restricted to global positive reactions
3. shows a bland uniformity which suggests a conditioned response made with minimal attention
4. rewards mere participation without consideration of performance processes or outcomes
5. provides no information at all or gives students information about their status
6. orients students toward comparing themselves with others and thinking about competing
7. uses the accomplishments of peers as the context for describing students' present accomplishments
8. is given without regard to the effort expended or the meaning of the accomplishment (for this student)
9. attributes success to ability alone or to external factors such as luck or easy tasks
10. fosters exogenous attributions (students believe that they expend effort on the task for external reasons—to please the teacher, win a competition or reward, and so on)
11. focuses students' attention on the teacher as an external authority figure who is manipulating them
12. intrudes into the ongoing process, distracting attention from task-relevant behavior

*From Brophy (1981). Copyright 1981 by the American Educational Research Association. Reprinted with permission of the publisher.

Although strict reinforcement theorists would not discuss the effects of rewards on students' thoughts, less traditional theorists might point out that rewards have the added value of conveying the teachers' values. By observing which behaviors are rewarded and which are not, students learn which behaviors the teacher believes are important. Thus, for example, students get different messages from teachers who reward effort and persistence regardless of the outcome and teachers who reward only high levels of performance. For those of us who believe that values are important and that children often emulate and internalize the values they see in significant adults, this is an important process. (See Chapter 9 for a more extended discussion of values.)

But, as we have seen, there are costs associated with over-reliance on reinforcement as a means of motivating behavior. The next chapter describes more recent theoretical developments as well as new classroom applications that are designed to maximize the benefits of reinforcement while minimizing these costs.

TABLE 3.2   Summary of Terms

Term	Definition	Example
Law of effect	Principle of reinforcement theory in which behavior is assumed to be determined by its consequences	Students complete assignments because this behavior is rewarded
Operant conditioning	Establishing a behavior (an operation) using the principles of reinforcement	Students learn to come into the classroom, sit at their desks, and begin work after recess
Positive reinforcer (rewards)	A consequence that increases the probability of the behavior that it is made contingent upon	Good grade; star; teacher praise; teacher attention
Punishment	A consequence that decreases the probability of the behavior that it is made contingent upon	Bad grade; loss of privilege; public criticism
Negative reinforcer	A consequence that increases the probability of a behavior if terminated or diminished	Teacher's angry stare; social isolation
Social reinforcement	Positive reinforcer linked to social approval	Praise; smile; pat on the back
Secondary reinforcers	Consequences that take on reinforcement properties by being paired with primary reinforcers	Grades (originally paired with praise)
Extinguish	Terminating a behavior as the result of terminating positive reinforcers	Students stop doing homework when teacher stops grading it

(continued)

TABLE 3.2   *(continued)*

Term	Definition	Example
Intermittent (partial) reinforcement	The reinforcement of some but not all occurrences of a response	Teacher praising some but not all correct answers
Discriminative stimulus	A stimulus that acquires the ability to to control behavior because of its association with reinforcement or punishment	Teacher standing in front of the classroom
Stimulus control	Behavior is influenced by the presence of a stimulus that has previously been associated with reward or punishment	Students become quiet when the teacher enters the room
Generalization	The principle that behavior will occur or not occur because a similar behavior has been positively reinforced or punished	A student who is praised for neatness on a math assignment subsequently write her spelling words more neatly
Behavior modification	The process of using reinforcement principles to change behavior	Calling on a student when she raises her hand to answer a question and ignoring her when she calls out an answer
Contingency management	Using principles of operant conditioning to change a person's behavior by modifying discriminant stimuli or consequences	Changing the contingencies for rewards in the classroom so that a specific set of positive social behaviors are rewarded and time-out is given for antisocial behavior
Shaping	Providing reinforcement for behaviors that increasingly approximate the desired behavior	Praising a child for opening a book, then for beginning, and then for completing assignments
Token economy	A system in which individuals receive or lose tokens that can be exchanged for a reward	A poker chip is earned for every assignment completed, and later exchanged for added recess time
Baseline behaviors	Frequency of behavior previous to intervention designed to increase or decrease it by reward or punishment	Proportion of homework assignments completed before a token economy intervention is implemented

4 Social Cognitive Theory

Introducing Cognitions

The powerful effect of reinforcement and punishment on behavior is well recognized today. But in the last few decades the theory has become more complicated.

Reinforcement theory was modified in part because it could not explain the results of new studies. Studies found, for example, that when people were not aware of the reinforcement they received for a particular behavior, their behavior was not affected by it (Dulany, 1968), and if people were led to believe that previously reinforced behavior would not be reinforced in the future, they would not engage in the behavior (Estes, 1972).

With these findings in mind, Bandura (1977, 1986, 1997) proposed that people are not entirely regulated by external forces; they are not passive respondents to environmental contingencies. As an alternative to strict reinforcement theory, he developed a social cognitive theory in which cognitions (thoughts, beliefs) are assumed to mediate the effects of the environment on human behavior.

Bandura's social cognitive theory focuses especially on people's *expectations* about the consequences of a behavior. He claims that reinforcement history does not necessarily have a direct effect on peoples' expectations. Rather, people's beliefs are filtered through personal memory, interpretation, and biases. Thus, for example, a student might not expect to get a reward for working on a task, even if one was received in the past, if the student thought this teacher didn't like her or is too hard a grader.

Social cognitive theorists, therefore, claim that people interpret events and develop expectations about reinforcement. These interpretations and expectations, in turn, affect their behavior. According to this theory, personal experience with reinforcement and punishment are not even required for behaviors to be manifested. What matters is what a person believes will happen in the future, not what has happened in the past.

This chapter summarizes the basic elements of social cognitive theory. Consistent with the theory's emphasis on personal agency, the chapter also discusses its implications for helping students learn to control and take more responsibility for their own learning.

Vicarious Learning

The emphasis on cognitions solves a problem traditional reinforcement theorists have in explaining new behavior. According to reinforcement theory, students' behavior is determined by their own reinforcement history. Children attend to the teacher and complete assignments because they have been reinforced for these behaviors in the past. Traditional reinforcement theorists rely on the principle of shaping to explain how children "learn" new behaviors, behaviors that have not previously been reinforced. But this explanation is not very satisfying because it would be too cumbersome for every behavior to be shaped by reinforcing successive approximations.

Bandura and Walters (1963) proposed that people exhibit behaviors as the result of observing another person being reinforced for the behavior. They refer to this process as **vicarious learning.** The process is illustrated in a classic study by Bandura (1965). Children were shown one of three versions of a 5-minute film that depicted aggressive responses to toys, including hitting and throwing objects at a Bobo doll. In the version shown to one group of children the child was rewarded by an adult for the aggressive behavior; in another version the child was punished; and in the third version there was no adult reaction. After they had viewed one of these three versions of the film, children were secretly observed in a room that contained the same toys shown in the movie. Children who viewed the rewarded model were most likely to repeat the model's aggressive behavior; children who viewed the punished model were least likely to repeat the behavior, with the third group falling in between. Thus, the likelihood of their demonstrating the behavior was a function of the reinforcement contingencies of the child they had *observed* in the film, not of their own reinforcement histories.

Note that all children were equally capable of reproducing the aggressive behavior. They nevertheless differed in the degree to which they actually engaged in the behavior, depending on which version of the film they had watched. This distinction between acquiring a behavior and manifesting a behavior in action—between learning and performance—is made by social cognitive theorists, but not by traditional reinforcement theorists.

Principles of vicarious learning are used frequently in elementary school classrooms. It is common for teachers of young children to reinforce one or a few children for a behavior that they desire in all children: "I like the way Jackson got to work on his assignment right away." "Table 5 is ready and can go to lunch." The effect can be dramatic. Before the children from Table 5 reach the door, children at the other tables are likely to have ceased talking and put on their most angelic expressions.

Personal Agency

People have much more agency in social cognitive theory. Bandura (1986) departs from strict reinforcement theory in stressing the importance of personal evaluation as positive reinforcement. He claims that most people value the self-respect and the self-satisfaction derived from a job well done more highly than they do material rewards. Thus, achieving a personal goal or meeting a personal achievement standard, and experiencing the accompanying self-satisfaction, can serve effectively as reinforcement.

Goals or intentions also play a central role in social cognitive theory. One way to influence students' behavior is to influence their goals. When students commit themselves to a goal, discrepancies between their goals and their accomplishments create self-dissatisfaction, which serves as an incentive for enhanced effort. The feeling of satisfaction for achieving a goal serves as a reward, which in turn increases future effort.

Social cognitive theory also portrays individuals as active agents in their behavior. According to Bandura (1977, 1986), the capacity to use symbols—especially language—provides humans with a powerful tool for dealing with their environment and a means of controlling their own behavior. Consequences of behavior have lasting effects on future behavior because they are processed and transformed into symbols that can be remembered. It is the cognitive representations of behavior and its consequences that guide future behavior. For example, a red light signals that you'll get hit by another car (or that you'll get a traffic ticket) if you pass through the intersection, so you stop. Children in a classroom in which the teacher dismisses the quietest table first may quiet down quickly before recess in the future, because they have a cognitive representation of the teacher's reaction to a quiet, orderly table.

The cognitive capacity for symbolic representation and forethought (e.g., of goals and expectations) also allows people to sustain effort over a long period of time. Thus, students who aspire to master a skill or to obtain high grades can, by keeping their goal and the expected reward in mind, continue to exert effort without regular reinforcement.

With age comes increased capacity for symbolic thought and a longer time-perspective, consequently gaining the ability to sustain effort for longer periods of time without reinforcement. Thus while a second grader should be able to keep working until recess without some consequence to his behavior, a college student is expected to be able to sustain effort until the end of the semester.

Another way human beings use their representational abilities to exercise self-control is by arranging the environment in a way that produces the behavior they desire. Setting an alarm clock to wake up at a particular time is a simple example. Making a reward (e.g., a chocolate chip cookie) contingent upon a particular behavior (e.g., finishing a homework assignment) is another way of regulating one's own behavior. According to social cognitive theory, students can shape their own experiences—including the frequency and nature of reinforcements—in academic contexts by choosing which courses to take, which assignments to work on, or which strategies to use to complete an assignment.

Self-Efficacy

Bandura claims that people's answers to the question, "Can I do this task?" is a critical determinant of their behavior. He refers to this belief as **self-efficacy** (Bandura, 1977, 1982, 1986, 1993, 1995, 1997; Schunk, 1989; Pajares, 1997;

Zimmerman, 1995). Self-efficacy pertains to a person's judgments of his or her performance capability on a particular type of task at a particular point in time. It is closely linked to perceptions of competence, discussed in Chapter 6, but unlike global perceptions that apply to many situations, the term "self-efficacy" usually refers to specific judgments in specific situations. (See Bandura, Barbaranelli, Caprara, & Pastorelli, 1996, and Bong, 1997, on the generality of self-efficacy beliefs.) There is evidence that self-efficacy is a more powerful predictor of academic performance than more general perceptions of academic competence (Pajares, 1996; Pajares & Miller, 1994; Pajares, Miller, & Johnson, 1999).

Sources of Self-Efficacy Judgments.   According to Bandura there are four principal sources of information for self-efficacy judgments in academic situations—actual experience, vicarious experience, verbal persuasion, and physiological arousal.

Actual experience, especially past successes and failures, is the most important source. Typically, successes raise self-efficacy and failures lower it. There is not, however, a simple relationship between objective experience and self-efficacy judgments. Self-efficacy judgments involve inferences, which are influenced by prior beliefs, expectations, difficulty of the task, amount of effort expended, amount of external help, and other factors.

For example, previous success will not contribute to perceptions of efficacy if the student believes that the task was easy or that she did not try very hard. Perceptions of the cause of outcomes also affect subsequent self-efficacy judgments. A student like Helpless Hannah, who is convinced of her academic incompetence, may attribute success to some external factor such as good luck or help from the teacher or a classmate. Her success, consequently, does not engender a feeling of efficacy.

Second, *vicarious experiences* affect self-perceptions of efficacy. For example, children can sometimes become persuaded that they are able to perform a task after watching another child the same age complete the task. I observed this when I taught swimming lessons. Individual lessons were often not as effective as group lessons for young children because seeing an age-mate execute a behavior (e.g., swim across the deep end, dive off the diving board, and so on) often convinced children that they could do the same. Observing a peer gave them a greater sense of efficacy than they would have gotten by observing an adult model the same behavior. Bandura (1986, 1992b) points out that vicarious experiences are most influential in situations in which people have little personal experience with the task.

Schunk and Hanson (1985) demonstrated the value of having children observe other children successfully complete an academic task. In their study, children who were having difficulty doing subtraction observed either a same-sex peer or a teacher demonstrate mastery. Observing a peer led to higher self-efficacy for learning the procedure, as well as to better mastery following a subsequent training intervention, than did observing a teacher.

Verbal persuasion is the third factor that influences self-efficacy judgments. Teachers and parents can sometimes persuade children that they are able to achieve some goal. Verbal persuasion is not likely to be effective unless it is realistic and reinforced by real experience. But in some circumstances, encouragement (e.g., "Try it, I know you can do it") can bolster a child's self-confidence for a new task, especially when given by a credible person.

The positive effects of encouragement are evident in a study involving interviews of females who had successful careers in mathematics, technology, and science (Zeldin & Pajares, 2000). All of the women interviewed referred to individuals who had expressed confidence in their competencies and encouraged them to persevere in math and science.

The final factor affecting self-efficacy judgments is *physiological arousal*. Consider, for example, Anxious Alma noticing that her palms are sweaty and her heart is beating rapidly while she is taking a math test. If a high state of anxiety has negatively affected her performance in the past, she may lose confidence in her ability to perform in this instance. The lowered perceptions of efficacy can, in turn, increase her anxiety, and consequently interfere with her ability to demonstrate what she understands.

Consequences of Self-Efficacy.   Perceived efficacy can affect people's behavior, thoughts, and emotional reactions in achievement settings. People don't seek out or enjoy doing things that they believe they can't do very well. This is why children who have high self-efficacy for reading read more than children who believe they lack reading skills (Wigfield & Guthrie, 1997).

People relatively high in self-efficacy also set higher goals (Zimmerman & Bandura, 1994), choose more difficult tasks (Sexton & Tuckman, 1991), and persist longer at tasks, even when perceptions of efficacy are experimentally induced (Bouffard-Bouchard, 1990; see also Berry & West, 1993; Zimmerman, 1995). Research has shown that self-efficacy judgments even predict career choices (Hackett, 1995; Hackett & Betz, 1992).

Self-efficacy beliefs also affect students' thoughts and behaviors while they work on tasks. Students who are not confident that they can complete a task often become anxious and preoccupied with concerns about failing, especially when they are being evaluated. In contrast, students who are convinced of their competence are task-oriented—they can concentrate on problem-solving strategies instead of worrying about whether they will be able to solve the problem (Bandura, 1986, 1992a, 1993; Bandalos, Yates, & Thorndike-Christ, 1995; Zimmerman, 1995).

A study by Pintrich and De Groot (1990) is illustrative of many. They found that the higher students' self-efficacy was, the more they used constructive strategies for learning (e.g., attempting to make connections between textbook and classroom instruction, rereading material, and creating outlines; see also, Bandura, 1992b; Berry & West, 1993; Bouffard-Bouchard, 1990; Meece, Wigfield, & Eccles, 1990; Pajares & Miller, 1994; Pintrich, Roeser, & De Groot, 1994; Randhawa, Beamer, & Lundberg, 1993).

Students with high self-efficacy also have more positive emotions while they work on tasks, which make them want to continue. Think of the novice skier who finally makes a successful run to the bottom of a hill. He is likely to want to go right back up the hill, or possibly even up a steeper hill, as a consequence of this success and the positive feelings it engendered. School tasks, like solving a difficult algebra problem, can also engender positive feelings of efficacy. The student who solves a difficult problem should feel efficacious and be eager to attempt more.

These consequences of high self-efficacy—willingness to approach and persist on tasks, reduced fear and anxiety, a focus on problem-solving strategies, and positive emotional experiences—affect achievement outcomes (see Zimmerman, 1995, for a review). The positive effects of self-efficacy on achievement were shown in a study by Collins (1982). Students who were low, average, and high in mathematical skills were first identified on the basis of scores on standardized tests. Within each skill group students with higher self-efficacy solved more problems correctly and chose to rework more problems that they had missed than did students low in self-efficacy. Self-efficacy thus predicted achievement behavior and performance over and above actual skill level in all three groups. These studies clearly point to the importance of fostering self-efficacy in learning situations.

Teacher Self-Efficacy.   The concept of self-efficacy applies to teachers as well as to students (Pajares, 1997). Teachers high in self-efficacy believe they can help the children in their class to succeed, regardless of their home circumstances or the children's skills when they enter their class; they are confident that they can "get through to even the most difficult students." Teachers low in self-efficacy think there isn't much they can do to overcome adverse conditions brought about by economic hardship or lack of parental support, or they think that some kids are just too far behind academically or not smart enough to handle their academic curriculum. Self-efficacy in teachers affects teachers' emotions and behavior, just as it does students'. These effects are discussed in detail in Chapter 13.

In summary, social cognitive theorists do not dismiss the effect of reinforcement and punishment on behavior, but they do not believe that the consequences to behavior are the only factors that affect behavior. Social cognitive theory assumes that people's thoughts—especially their expectations related to the likelihood of rewards—are the direct causes of behavior. Expectations themselves are influenced by observations, persuasion, and even physiological arousal, as well as by personal experiences with reinforcement and punishment.

People are considered active agents in their behavior in social cognitive theory. Cognitive representational abilities liberate humans by allowing them to manipulate their own stimulus conditions. Thus, people can arrange the environment to maximize the likelihood of desired responses. Social cognitive theory has, accordingly, inspired the development of a variety of techniques that can help people regulate their own behavior and thus influence the rewards they receive. The next section on self-regulation summarizes strategies that have been developed for students to play an active, constructive role in their own learning.

Self-Regulation

Some of the behavioral change strategies discussed below are referred to as **cognitive behavior modification (CBM).** The word "cognition" is included because the theory assumes that cognitions, not past reinforcement histories, affect behavior. The strategies are also sometimes referred to as "self-management" because students are invited to play an active role in managing their own behavioral change.

The final section of the chapter describes additional approaches for involving students in regulating their own learning. Some of these strategies focus more on active thought processes (e.g., planning and rehearsal) than on managing overt behavior, such as through CBM. Thus, they are referred to as **meta*cognitive* strategies.** Others concern structuring tasks and organizing the environment to facilitate learning.

Cognitive Behavior Modification

Hallahan and Sapona (1983) define CBM as "the modification of overt behavior through the manipulation of covert thought processes" (p. 616). (See also Robinson, Smith, Miller, & Brownell, 1999; Shapiro & Cole, 1994; Shapiro & Bradly, 1996; Wahlberg, 1998.) CBM is similar to approaches based on strict reinforcement theory in that it focuses on overt behavior and that reinforcement principles are assumed to be operating. It is different in the sense that the treatment involves modifying a person's cognitive operations in order to achieve a change in his or her behavior. It is also different in that it is not entirely regulated by some outside source. When CBM approaches are used, the teacher is not the only determiner of reinforcement contingencies or the sole dispenser of rewards, as is the case in behavior modification programs such as token economies. Cognitive behavior modification requires students to take responsibility, either by monitoring their own behavior, setting their own goals and standards, or administering their own rewards.

Personal involvement is believed to have a number of advantages over external monitoring and reinforcement. First, there are problems with external reinforcement that personal responsibility can resolve. It is difficult for teachers to monitor and reinforce many students' behavior at one time, while students are less likely than teachers to miss their own reinforcement opportunities (Fantuzzo & Polite, 1990). Furthermore, when rewards and punishment are always administered by an external agent, the agent may become a discriminative stimulus, and thus a necessary cue for the performance of the desired behaviors. The behavior, therefore, will not occur when the external agent is absent. As mentioned in Chapter 3, this is why classroom discipline can break down the moment the teacher steps out.

After contingent rewards are withdrawn, desirable behaviors should be maintained longer if students are involved in regulating their own behavior than if their behavior is manipulated by another. Personal involvement should also enhance understanding of the relationship between behavior and consequences, and therefore result in more generalization outside of the setting in which the rewards are given. In general, CBM is believed to result in less reliance on external agents to control behavior (Mace & Kratochwill, 1988; Shapiro & Cole, 1994), although even some CBM advocates claim that ultimately all behavior is controlled by the contingencies of external reward or punishment. Two of the most commonly used approaches, self-recording and self-reinforcement, are described below to illustrate CBM strategies.

Self-Recording.   One simple method that has been used to help children begin to take responsibility for their own behavior is to have them keep a record of it. Self-recording itself has been found to influence behavior, even without tangible reinforcements—an outcome referred to as **reactivity** (Kirby, Fowler, & Baer, 1991).

Children may be asked to record the duration of an activity, frequency of a particular behavior, task completion, or their level of performance (see Kirby, Fowler, & Baer, 1991; Mace & Kratochwill, 1988; Shapiro & Cole, 1994). For example, students may record how long they read at home each evening, each time they bring their homework home, each time they begin an assignment without asking the teacher to repeat the instructions, or each time they complete an assignment on time. They may record how many spelling words they practice or spell correctly on quizzes, how many math problems they complete independently, or how many pages they read.

Time-sampling methods also have been used. Kern, Dunlap, Childs, and Clarke (1994), for example, increased task engagement and decreased disruptive behavior by having children record, on sheets placed in the corner of their desks, whether they were or were not "on task" when a bell sounded at 5-minute intervals. Methods as simple as touching a child on the shoulder can be used to signal the time for self-assessments (Maag, Rutherford, & DiGangi, 1992).

What is recorded depends on the problem. A student who is not doing assignments at all might benefit from keeping track of assignments completed and not completed. A student who usually finishes assignments but does them carelessly should record error rates or some other index of quality. A predetermined performance standard has been shown to enhance the effectiveness of self-monitoring (Kazdin, 1974), presumably because it gives students a particular goal toward which to work. A few researchers have also found that self-monitoring is more effective in increasing desired behaviors than in decreasing undesirable behaviors (e.g., Litrownik & Freitas, 1980).

Self-recording can be done in a variety of ways. One of the simplest methods is to have students make a mark on a sheet of paper every time they engage in some behavior, and endeavor to increase the number of marks from week to week. Some CBM researchers have taped paper on to children's desks to record behavior. Shapiro (1984) describes "countoons"—simple stick figure drawings that represent the specific behavior to be self-monitored. Children place a tally mark next to each picture when the behavior occurs.

It is sometimes useful to have students graph their "scores" (see Shapiro, 1984, for examples). Some children are encouraged and excited when they see the line in the graph going up or down, depending on whether they are trying to increase or decrease the behavior.

Teachers can encourage personal responsibility by allowing students to set their own goals for improvement. Students may, for example, decide how many math problems they will do each day or how many spelling words they will get right on the next spelling test. Students may even choose the area in which they would like to improve their behavior. Personal choice and goal setting engages students' involvement and interest and makes them feel more responsible for their own behavior.

Personal goal setting also helps students learn how to set realistic goals, an important skill in achievement settings (see Schunk, 1990, 1995). Many students initially set goals that are either too easily achieved or too difficult for them. Teachers usually need to help students adjust their goals. Charting goals along with actual behavior demonstrates how close their progress is to their goal. If they are working hard but not meeting their goals, they may need to make them more realistic.

If goals are set too high, students will simply become discouraged when they cannot reach them. Teachers should encourage students like Helpless Hannah, who are doing very poorly in school, to set modest goals at first, such as simply remembering to take home their homework or getting started on seatwork without having to be coaxed. Once they have met a modest goal, the standard can be raised. Better performers, like Safe Sally, need encouragement to set ambitious goals. Research has shown that maximum learning occurs when goals or standards are gradually raised as a function of students' past performance.

O'Leary and Dubey (1979) point out that self-recording may be effective primarily for students who already want to engage in the desired behavior. Evidence for this comes from a number of studies on smoking behavior. Lipinski, Black, Nelson, and Ciminero (1974), for example, found that self-recording decreased smoking in subjects who volunteered for an experiment to reduce smoking, but not for subjects who volunteered for a general experiment involving smokers. Self-recording may, therefore, only be effective for students who genuinely desire to change their behavior. It may, for example, help an easily distracted student who is motivated to finish assignments, but not a student like Satisfied Santos, who doesn't care whether he completes his work.

Self-Reinforcement.   Another way to help students control their own behavior is to involve them in selecting and administering their own reinforcement. According to social cognitive theorists, self-reinforcement increases performance mainly through its motivational function. By making self-reward conditional upon attaining a certain level of performance, students create self-inducements to persist in their efforts until their performance matches the prescribed standard (Bandura, 1977). Self-reinforcement is an example of **reciprocal determinism** in social cognitive theory. People exercise control over their environment, which in turn influences their own behavior. Examples of self-reinforcement include promising oneself a piece of cake for finishing some predetermined amount of work (such as revising a section in a book chapter), or a vacation for not smoking for a specified length of time.

A practice common in elementary school classrooms is to give children opportunities to engage in desired activities (e.g., playing with a puzzle or game, using a listening center, or feeding the fish) when they finish their assigned work. This is a form of self-reinforcement when children choose the specific activity and administer their own reward. A common problem with this practice is that the reward may only be realistically available to a small subset of relatively fast workers. As a consequence, it will be motivating only for those students who are least likely to need an external incentive.

Another potential problem with making one set of activities contingent on completing another is that it gives an implicit message to students that the assignment that is reinforced is undesirable, and the activities that serve as the reinforcement are the desirable ones. As noted in Chapter 3, the teacher who tells students they can play games, pet the rabbit, or work on the computer when they finish their math assignment gives the message that the math assignment is not interesting or worth doing in its own right.

A few classroom studies in which students determined their own standards for reinforcement have found that children tend to select lenient performance standards (Rosenbaum & Drabman, 1979; Wall, 1983). If self-reinforcement is used, it might be necessary to have some incentive for selecting stricter standards. Research also suggests that publicly stated standards are more effective than private ones (Hayes, Rosenfarb, Wolfert, Munt, Korn, & Zettle, 1985). Studies documenting a fair amount of cheating (e.g., administering unearned rewards; Speidel & Tharp, 1980) suggest that some monitoring is required.

The CBM strategies described have been used primarily with children who have learning disabilities or attention or behavioral problems, and have focused on observable behavior. The metacognitive strategies described next have been used to assist children in regular classrooms as well as children with special needs to improve their learning, and often involve cognitive processes that cannot be directly observed.

Learning Strategies

Compare the following two children:

> Jennifer ate a snack, played with her new kitten, and watched a little TV when she got home from school. She intended to start her homework before dinner, but got sidetracked by a telephone call from a friend. By the time the dishes were done, and she had listened to her brother's new CD, it was 8:15. She opened her notebook and realized she had a history test the next day in addition to her regular home-

work. She stayed up late rereading the relevant chapters in her history textbook, with the TV on in the background.

When Samantha got home from school she had a snack, took her dog for a walk, and checked her notebook, where she had written down the homework that she had to do that afternoon. She made a schedule for completing her homework, fitting in some time for a favorite TV show. When she began studying for her history test she found it difficult to keep everything straight. So she made a chart to organize the information. When she finished reviewing the relevant chapters, she went over the questions from her weekly quizzes to ensure that she could answer them. When her brother turned up his stereo, she asked him to turn it down so she could concentrate. Later, she found that she was having trouble understanding her science homework, so she called a friend from class for help.

Samantha is not necessarily more motivated than Jennifer, but she regulates her environment and her behavior to support optimal learning. She writes down and reviews homework assignments to make sure she has time to complete them before she gets tired, and she uses active learning strategies for learning and self-assessment. She schedules in breaks and activities she enjoys to help her sustain her attention. She makes changes in the physical environment when it is not conducive to learning, and she makes use of social resources when she is having difficulty. All these self-regulation strategies contribute to her learning and to her academic performance.

What sometimes looks like a lack of motivation is really a lack of organization and planning skills, similar to those demonstrated by Jennifer. A number of researchers have observed that children with learning problems often lack two kinds of skills: **metacognitive skills** (awareness of what capabilities, strategies, and resources are needed to perform a task effectively), and **self-regulation skills** (e.g., planning, managing time, evaluating effectiveness of ongoing activities, or accessing help; Hallahan & Sapona, 1983). Both of these sets of skills are discussed below.

Metacognitive Strategies.   Walking out at the end of a lecture I realize I don't remember a word that was said. I ask a colleague about an article he just read and he has difficulty summarizing even the main points. My daughter stares at me blankly when I complain that she didn't clean her room as I had asked. We all have experienced this gap between hearing or reading the surface structure of words and actually *processing* the information contained in them. I "listened" to the lecture; my colleague "read" every word of the article; my daughter "heard" my request. But to process and remember the information we would have had to use more active cognitive strategies.

Researchers have investigated many kinds of metacognitive strategies—including planning and goal setting, asking questions and testing oneself for understanding, reflecting upon new material, searching for main ideas, making connections to what one already knows, making inferences and predictions and checking to see whether they are correct, taking and organizing notes, keeping records, practicing problems, rehearsing, paraphrasing, summarizing, mapping, making time lines, and creating mnemonics. Students who use these kinds of metacognitive strategies in educational contexts learn more, but not everyone uses them. Research indicates that individuals are most likely to use such active learning strategies when they believe that the task is interesting or important, and when they believe that they are capable of mastering the task at hand (i.e., when their "self-efficacy" is high; see Pintrich & De Groot, 1990; Printrich & Schrauben, 1992; Pintrich et al., 1994; Zimmerman & Martinez-Pons, 1992).

But even when there is a will, some children lack the way. They simply don't know how to use such strategies to foster learning. The good news is that metacognitive strategies can be taught (Hattie, Biggs, & Purdie, 1996; Hofer, Yu, & Pintrich, 1998; Pintrich, 1999). Children can learn to become more cognizant of the demands of a task and better able to plan and monitor their learning.

Wang and Palincsar (1989) recommend embedding instruction on meta-cognitive skills in regular instruction, rather than teaching it as a separate curriculum (see also Corno & Randi, 1999; Palincsar & Brown, 1984, 1987; Paris, Cross, & Lipson, 1984). Many studies have shown the value of teaching self-regulation skills in the context of reading (e.g., Guthrie, Van Meter, Hancock, Alao, Anderson, & McCann, 1998; Shawaker & Dembo, 1996) and writing (e.g., Butler, 1998).

The value of embedding the teaching of metacognitive strategies into subject matter instruction is supported by research indicating that training that was implemented in the context of the regular curriculum is more effective than training provided in a counseling or remedial center as a "general or all-purpose package of portable skills" (Hattie et al., 1996, p. 130). Studies also find that students need to be taught how to apply new strategies to material that is substantially different from the material on which they learned skills (Hattie et al., 1996), and that they need to understand the basis of how a strategy works and when it is appropriate to use it.

Wang and Palincsar (1989) recommend that teachers first assess the cognitive strategies their students currently use in learning situations. The simplest strategy is to ask them directly, e.g., what did you do to learn your spelling words, or to figure out how to complete this science experiment?

They suggest then introducing a cognitive strategy and explaining its usefulness. This is followed by modeling its use, and engaging students in guided practice. Teachers need to provide "expert scaffolding"—assisting students at first by giving them reminders, directions and hints—and then slowly withdrawing the assistance. The last step is to give students opportunities to apply and practice the strategy independently and in a variety of contexts.

Children with learning disabilities are less likely to use effective self-regulation strategies for learning, and interventions have been developed specifically for this population. Butler (1998a, 1998b), for example, has investigated the effectiveness of a program called "Strategic Content Learning," in which tutors work with students on tasks that are part of their regular coursework. The tutors help students analyze task demands and performance criteria. Learning activities are then planned, and the tutor helps the student analyze performance gaps and adjust strategies if the current ones are not achieving the student's learning goals. The tutor's role is to provide suggestions and help the student articulate goals and strategies, and to monitor and evaluate the effectiveness of those strategies.

An intervention developed by Shawaker and Dembo (1996) illustrates an approach using some of the same strategies used in cognitive behavior modification. Middle school students were taught a four-step process to enhance their comprehension of what they read. To help them implement the process, the students were taught to set proximal goals, make statements that promoted self confidence ("I can do this"), and use self-talk to guide their behavior, such as complementing themselves occasionally. Students also engaged in reciprocal teaching—taking turns with the teacher or with other students modeling the task process. The idea was to get students actively engaged in monitoring their own learning process.

These strategies concern the learning process itself: processing, making sense of, and remembering new concepts and material. But as the comparison between Jennifer and Samantha's approach to homework illustrates, there is more to being an effective learner. We turn next to some of the other behaviors included in Bandura's notion of self-regulation.

Planning and Organization.

Planning and Organization.   In addition to the metacognitive strategies mentioned above, effective learners like Samantha plan and organize tasks, create an environment conducive to learning, and use social and other resources effectively.

Teachers can help students develop these skills by structuring assignments to make planning and organization explicit or by embedding instructions on planning and organization in the curriculum. Having students turn in drafts several days before a paper is due is an example of embedding some planning into the task itself. It requires students to get started on a writing task in time for them to be able to revise before the assignment is due. Having a class discussion about how to divide a report into smaller pieces and create deadlines for each piece is an example of giving self-regulation instruction. Corno and Randi (1999) point out that it is also important to structure the classroom in a way that gives students opportunities to develop self-regulation skills. If students are always told exactly what to do and when and how to do it, they will not learn how to make wise choices and plan and organize tasks themselves. Examples of interventions designed to help children develop these skills are described below.

Time Management.   Dembo and Eaton (2000) describe a program for middle school students in which they teach children strategies for managing their time better. They ask students to record their activities 24 hours a day for one week and then organize them by category (e.g., eating, playing sports, studying, talking on the phone, sleeping). They report that students are often surprised at how inefficiently they had been using their time, and how much less time they spent studying than they had thought. Students then learn how to list the things they need to do, make priorities, and create a schedule. They are taught, for example, to keep logs in which they record study time and effort levels in small increments, in order to help them become more aware of how much time they are spending on tasks and how effectively they are working (see also Zimmerman, 1998).

Some schools provide students with homework calendars and give instructions on how to use them, as well as reminding them to write down assignments and tests dates. Teachers can also teach students strategies for planning and completing large, multidimensional tasks, such as a history or science report. For example, they can help students break down large tasks into parts and create a schedule for accomplishing each part.

Organizing the Physical Environment.   Students can be encouraged to assess the physical environment in which they do their work both at home and at school. Is the chair comfortable, the desk the right height? Is the lighting sufficient? Is there noise that interferes with concentration? If problems are found, what can be done to improve the environment or to improve support for learning? To promote attention to these issues, Dembo and Eaton (2000) asked students to rate different study environments (e.g., studying in the library or at the kitchen table, studying alone or with others) and to compare their behaviors in these different settings.

Using Social Resources.   Being able to decide when to persist alone and when to seek help, what kind of help to seek, and from whom to seek help are important self-regulation skills (Newman, 1998). Adaptive help-seeking behavior requires the ability to assess what you know vis-à-vis the demands of the task ("Do I have the skills to complete this task if I persist?"). Even after the decision to ask for help is made, students need to be able to analyze what they understand and what they don't understand, and articulate this to the helper. And they need to integrate the information or guidance they receive with what they already knew, which often requires rejecting previously held assumptions or understandings. Effective help-seeking thus can require considerable metacognitive awareness.

The type of help students request is also important. Nelson-Le Gall (1981, 1990, 1992, 1993) makes a useful distinction between "instrumental" or mastery-oriented help-seeking, which enables students to complete a task on their own, and "excessive" or dependency-oriented help-seeking, which involves getting someone else to solve problems that they have not earnestly attempted to solve independently. Nadler (1998) makes a similar distinction between autonomy and dependent help-seeking. Butler (1998) explains that "autonomous help-seeking"—help-seeking behavior that is initiated after spending time trying to solve a problem alone—involves requests for hints rather than for answers. It results in improved capacity to solve problems independently and allows students to take responsibility for their achievements.

Teachers can encourage students to seek productive help by modeling appropriate questions and providing independence-promoting assistance. If students who ask for answers are given clues instead, they will eventually stop asking for answers. Teachers can also reword or reframe students' questions in order to teach them the kind of reflective analysis they need to ask effective questions. Thus, the teacher might respond to the dependency-oriented question: "How do I do this problem?" with a series of questions designed to determine what the child does and does not understand. "Do you know how to represent the word problem in a calculation problem? Does the problem require multiplication? Where did you get stuck?"

The key in any effort to help students develop self-regulation strategies is to give them increasing responsibility. Teachers can teach the strategies directly at first, and remind students to use them. But with time, less and less intervention on the teacher's part should be required. After some direct teaching and practice with reminders and assistance, students should begin, on their own, to accommodate the different strategies to new situations as they arise.

Summary

Social cognitive theory represents a significant departure from strict reinforcement theory by including cognitions as mediators of behavior. It also reflects a trend away from depicting people as passive—controlled entirely by external reinforcement contingencies. Now people are viewed as active, thinking, and self-regulating. Thus, whereas previously motivation researchers focused entirely on the conditions of the environment, now they focus also on the causes of certain cognitions and on developing the skills students need to regulate their own learning.

As shown above, self-efficacy is a necessary ingredient in creating the will to engage actively in learning; people must believe that the strategies available to them will actually achieve their goal. The next chapter discusses other cognitive beliefs that affect students' motivation to learn.

Evolving out of social cognitive theory are specific strategies, such as cognitive behavior modification, that are designed to help students control their own behavior. Proponents of CBM claim that because cognitions mediate behavior, intervening in students' cognitions, i.e., helping them become self-conscious about their behavior, is an effective way to change behavior. The developers of the CBM procedures described in this chapter hoped that they would free teachers to spend more time teaching. They hoped also that children would continue to engage in desired behaviors even when they were not being monitored by adults and external reinforcement was not available.

Research implementing CBM procedures suggests that such procedures may be superior to behavior change programs that rely entirely on external reinforcement, and that they may actually increase independence and self-confidence.

It is still an open question whether they are effective in the long run, without being accompanied by contingent reinforcement. Teachers also sometimes view the intervention as too time consuming (Wood, Rosenberg, & Carran, 1993) and there remain many questions about its generalizability and applicability to regular classroom environments (Graham & Wong, 1993).

Research on metacognitive and other self-regulation strategies shows clearly that children can can be taught to be more effective learners. But even these approaches assume that children have the will to learn. Although reinforcement theory and social cognitive theory provide some answers as to the sources of children's will to learn, it is important to explore other motivational systems that may be tapped in learning contexts, such as those that will be described in Chapters 8 and 9.

TABLE 4.1 Summary of Terms

Terms	Definition
Vicarious learning	Engaging in a behavior as a result of observing the consequences to another individual engaging in it
Self-efficacy	Personal judgments of performance capabilities on a particular type of task at a particular point in time
Cognitive Behavior Modification (CBM)	Strategies for changing behavior that involve changing beliefs and expectations, and encouraging a more active role for the person whose behavior is being changed
Metacognitive strategies	Cognitive strategies used to enhance one's own learning—such as goal setting, planning, note taking, rehearsing, creating and using mnemonics, checking for understanding, and making and testing inferences and predictions
Reactivity	Behavior change that occurs as a result of self-recording of behavior
Metacognitive skills	Awareness of what capabilities, strategies, and resources are needed to perform a task effectively
Self-regulation skills	Regulating one's own behavior (e.g., planning and evaluating the effectiveness of ongoing activities)
Reciprocal determinism	Individuals exercise control over the environment, which in turn influences their own behavior

5 Cognitive Theories Applied to Achievement Contexts

Like social cognitive theory, the three theories discussed in this chapter emphasize beliefs as the direct causes of behavior. For all three, changes in behavior are assumed to require changes in cognitions. Reinforcement and punishment may affect those cognitions, but the cognitions, not the consequences of the behavior, are what actually influence behavior.

The theories differ, however, from social cognitive theory and from each other with regard to the particular beliefs they emphasize. Bandura's social learning theory, described in the previous chapter, focused on self-efficacy. Atkinson's expectancy x value theory, discussed in this chapter, also focuses on expectations for success, but is conceptualized somewhat differently from self-efficacy. Rotter's social learning theory emphasizes beliefs about the contingency of rewards, especially about whether rewards are within a person's control, and Weiner's attribution theory is concerned with beliefs about the causes of achievement outcomes.

Emotions, in addition to cognitions, play an important role in Atkinson's and Weiner's theories. Atkinson focuses primarily on pride and shame; Weiner on these two self-evaluative emotions as well as others that he believes affect behavior in achievement contexts.

The theories also differ in how much they emphasize stable dispositions. Atkinson and Rotter both consider stable individual differences as determinants of behavior, whereas Weiner emphasizes the effect of the immediate context.

Each of these three theories is described below. Some mention is made of practical classroom implications of the theories, but this topic is addressed in more detail in Chapter 7.

Atkinson's Expectancy x Value Theory

Atkinson's (1964) primary goal was to be able to predict whether a person would approach or avoid an achievement task. He conceptualized achievement behavior as a conflict between a tendency to approach tasks and a tendency to avoid tasks.

These two opposing tendencies are strengthened or weakened by stable individual differences in motives and by expectations about the likelihood of accomplishing a particular goal. Emotions are central to many of the constructs (psychological variables) in Atkinson's theory.

Consider first the stable factor affecting the tendency to approach tasks. Atkinson proposed that an unconscious **motive for success (MS),** or **need to achieve (Nach),** directs individuals toward achievement tasks. MS represents a relatively stable disposition to strive for success, conceptualized in the theory as a "capacity to experience pride in accomplishment" (Atkinson, 1964, p. 214).

The motive for success is usually measured by the Thematic Apperception Test (TAT), in which people are shown ambiguous pictures and asked to describe what is happening. It is assumed that people "project" their own achievement values and beliefs into their interpretations of the pictures. Their responses are scored according to the amount of achievement-striving content in their descriptions (i.e., references to accomplishments, achievement concerns, goals, expressions of achievement-related affect). The use of a projective test reflects a Freudian view that motivation is unconscious and expressed in fantasy (McClelland, 1961).

The **motive to avoid failure (MAF),** conceived of as a capacity to experience shame given failure, is the unconscious, stable factor that directs people away from achievement tasks. MAF is generally operationalized (measured) as anxiety aroused in testing situations.

Any achievement-related activity is assumed to elicit both positive (hope for success) and negative (fear of failure) emotional motives. What determines a person's behavior is the relative strength of these two motives—whether the person's hope for success (and the accompanying feeling of pride) is more or less than his or her fear of failure (and the accompanying feeling of shame).

According to Atkinson's theory, individual differences in both of the stable motives can be traced to parents' child-rearing behaviors. Children whose parents encourage their achievement efforts and provide opportunities for them to demonstrate competence should develop a relatively high motive to achieve success. In contrast, children whose parents punish their achievement efforts (e.g., become angry or frustrated when they are not successful or hold them to impossible standards) should develop a strong motive to avoid failure. People develop emotional associations to achievement contexts (pride in success or shame in failure) as a consequence of their experiences in early childhood, and these emotions are evoked in achievement situations when they are older, even though their parents are not present.

These assumptions related to the effects of early child rearing have not held up well in empirical tests. Some studies indicate that early independence training (Winterbottom, 1958) and high but realistic expectations (Rosen & D'Andrade, 1959) foster a strong achievement motive in children. But taken together, findings have been inconsistent. (See V. J. Crandall, 1963; V. C. Crandall, 1967; Trudewind, 1982, for reviews.)

Although Atkinson assumes the motives to strive for success and to avoid failure are unconscious, he also believes that people's behavior in achievement situations is influenced by their conscious beliefs about that particular situation. These situational variables, like the unconscious motives discussed above, direct people toward or away from achievement tasks.

Two conscious variables are believed to direct people toward achievement tasks—the **perceived probability of success (Ps)** and the expectation to feel proud, which Atkinson refers to as the **incentive value of success (Is).** According to the theory, people who expect to succeed (i.e., believe that the probability of success is high) on a particular task are more likely to approach it than people who are less certain about their chances for success.

Atkinson argues that greater pride is experienced following success at a difficult task (a task with a low probability of success) than following success at a task with a high probability of success. Thus an "A" in a difficult course has a higher incentive value than an "A" in an easy course. Because anticipated pride is determined entirely by the perceived probability of success, these two situation variables in the model are reducible to one. Emulating the physical sciences, Atkinson created formula to represent the psychological laws he proposed. Represented in a formula, $Is = 1 - Ps$.

Two situational variables also inhibit achievement efforts, perceptions of the **probability of failure (Pf),** and the anticipation of shame, which Atkinson refers to as the **incentive value of failure (If).** Shame is believed to be greatest following failure on very easy tasks, and least following failure on very difficult tasks. According to the theory, a "C" in physics might be experienced as less humiliating than a "C" in a course that is considered less difficult. Thus, again, because one of these situation variables (If) is determined by the other (Pf), they are reducible to one ($If = 1 - Pf$).

In summary, the tendency to approach tasks is determined by an unconscious stable factor (motive for success or need for achievement) and two conscious situational factors (expectations for success and anticipated pride). The tendency to avoid tasks is determined by an unconscious stable factor (fear of failure) and two conscious situational factors (expectations for failure and anticipated shame).

These two motivational tendencies—to approach tasks and to avoid tasks—are represented as opposing forces. **The resultant tendency to approach or avoid an achievement activity (TA)** is a function of the strength of the tendency to approach minus the strength of the tendency to avoid the task. If the tendency to approach is stronger, the person will approach the task; if the tendency to avoid is stronger, the person will avoid it. Atkinson combines these factors in a mathematical equation:

$$TA = TS - MAF$$

$$TA = (MS \times Ps \times Is) - (MAF \times Pf \times If)$$

To illustrate how the formula works, let us try to predict whether Anxious Alma or Satisfied Santos is more likely to approach a mathematics task. Alma's motive to avoid failure (MAF) is much higher (let's say, +5) than Santos' (let's say, +1); Alma's motive to succeed (Ms) is somewhat higher (+4) than Santos' (+2).

Their expectations for success (Ps) and expectations for failure (Pf) on the task are about the same (70% chance of success, 30% chance of failure); thus the incentive value of success (pride they expect to experience if they succeed on this particular task) is the same (Is = 1 − .70 = .30), as is the incentive value of failure (shame they expect to experience if they fail; If = 1 − .30 = .70). Note that the negative feelings expected for failure are stronger than the positive feelings expected for success. This is because the task is relatively easy (with an anticipated 70% chance of success). Which child, according to Atkinson's formula, is most likely to approach (TA) the math task?

$$\text{Alma: TA} = (4 \times .7 \times .3) - (5 \times .3 \times .7) = .84 - 1.05 = -.21$$

$$\text{Santos: TA} = (2 \times .7 \times .3) - (1 \times .3 \times .7) = .42 - .21 = +.21$$

Even though Alma's motive to achieve success is higher than Santos', she is less likely to approach the task because her motive to avoid failure is so much higher. Indeed, according to the formula, she is more likely to avoid than to approach the task (indicated by the negative TA), whereas Santos is more likely to approach the task than to avoid it.

The evidence on the effectiveness of the mathematical model in predicting behavior in achievement situations is mixed. There is, however, some evidence suggesting that, by measuring the components included in the model and combining them according to Atkinson's equations, modestly accurate predictions can sometimes be made regarding people's engagement in achievement tasks, the difficulty level of the tasks they choose, their level of aspiration or willingness to take risks, and their persistence in completing a difficult task. (See Weiner, 1980a, 1992 for reviews of this research.)

There are, however, many problems with Atkinson's model, which may explain why it has had only modest success in predicting behavior, even in highly controlled laboratory circumstances. The two major variables in the model, the motive for success and the motive to avoid failure, are difficult to measure. Since they are believed to be unconscious, they can be measured only indirectly. A second problem is that the incentive values of success and failure are fully determined by the probability of success, regardless of the importance of the task. Consequently, if the probability of success in a neighborhood bridge game and on the Graduate Record Exams is the same, success on these two tasks is assumed to generate the same amount of pride. Intuitively, it seems that a greater amount of pride would be aroused in the latter than in the former situation, but the model does not differentiate tasks according to their importance to the performer.

The model also assumes that task value is inversely associated with the probability of success—that people value success on tasks that they expect to fail more than on tasks on which they expect to succeed. This is a very narrow definition of value. Moreover, most research that assesses values using a broader definition suggests the opposite, that individuals place more value on tasks for which they believe they have high competence (e.g., Eccles & Wigfield, 1995; Wigfield & Eccles, 1992; see Chapter 9).

Despite these and many other problems, Atkinson made a major contribution to achievement motivation theory. His inclusion of expectations and addition of emotions as factors that influence achievement behavior paved the way for future cognitive motivation theorists, who have built on some of Atkinson's basic notions. Indeed, many contemporary motivation theorists base their research on Atkinsons' "expectancy x value" theoretical model. By elaborating on Atkinson's proposals, more recent cognitive theorists have developed models that have greater relevance to classroom practice.

Rotter's Social Learning Theory

Recall that the traditional reinforcement theorists discussed in Chapter 3 believe that the frequency of the occurrence of behaviors (e.g., paying attention to the teacher, approaching tasks and completing tasks) depends on whether the behaviors have been rewarded in the past. Rotter (1966, 1975, 1990), like Bandura, proposed that it is not the reward itself that increases the frequency of a behavior, but a person's *beliefs* about what brings about rewards. If people do not believe that the rewards they receive are caused by something about their personal characteristics or behavior, rewards will not influence their future behavior.

Consider, for example, good grades, which have reinforcement value for most students (Satisfied Santos being the exception). According to strict reinforcement theory, any behavior (whether it be studying or carrying a rabbit's foot) that preceded a good grade should be repeated. Rotter's more cognitive theory would predict increased studying or rabbit foot carrying only if a student believed that one of these behaviors caused the good grade. If everyone in the class received "A's" on their papers, students may believe that the teacher gives "A's" indiscriminately, regardless of the quality of the product or the amount of effort they exerted. They may not work hard on papers in the future despite the previous reward, because they don't believe that rewards ("A's") are contingent on effort.

Rotter, like Atkinson, assumes that expectancies (both generalized and specific) of reinforcements and the value of reinforcements determine behavior. He conceptualized value, however, more broadly than Atkinson; reinforcement value in Rotter's theory is linked not just to the probability of success, but also to a person's needs and to associations with other reinforcements. Thus, an "A" in chemistry may have particularly high value for a college student hoping to become a doctor because she believes good grades in chemistry will help gain admission to medical school. This student's effort in her chemistry class, therefore, is determined by her expectation that hard work results in *valued* reinforcement.

Expectancies are not always accurate; they are based on *subjective* perceptions of the probability that a behavior will be reinforced. Thus a rumor that a teacher is biased against girls, or never gives "A's", or is unpredictable in grading, can affect students' expectancies and thus their behavior, even if the rumor is pure invention.

Expectancies in a particular situation are determined not only by beliefs about reinforcement in that situation, but also by *generalized* expectancies based on experiences in other, similar situations. Rotter refers to people's generalized beliefs about the contingency of reinforcement as **locus of control (LOC).** He claims that people who generally believe that events or outcomes are contingent on their own behavior or on a personal characteristic, such as ability, have an *internal locus of control.* People who believe that events are caused by factors beyond their control (e.g., by luck, chance, fate, or biased others) have an *external locus of control.* Thus, while Atkinson focused on individuals' expectations for reward, Rotter is concerned with their beliefs about what causes them to receive or not receive rewards.

Although Rotter focuses on generalized beliefs that apply in a very broad set of contexts, more recent theorists have found evidence for more domain-specific beliefs, based on individual life experiences (Edelstein, Grundmann, & Mies, 2000). Thus, a person might have an external locus of control with regard to politics ("Politicians will do what they want regardless of what I or people like me want or think"), but an internal locus of control with regard to school achievement ("If I work hard I can get a good grade").

Students bring to each new class their own generalized belief system molded by past experiences in achievement situations. For example, students who have repeatedly experienced failure regardless of the amount of effort they have exerted often develop the belief that success is not contingent on effort. This generalized belief may override information to the contrary in any specific situation. Thus, students like Helpless Hannah, who come to believe that hard work will not be rewarded (e.g., by a good grade) are not likely to exert much effort, even in situations in which their effort would actually lead to success.

Once such beliefs are developed they are difficult to change (Schmitz & Skinner, 1993). A few success experiences may not convince a child like Hannah that rewards really are contingent on effort. Firm in her belief that there is nothing that she can do to achieve success, Hannah is likely to interpret any positive outcome as a result of good luck, an easy task, or even the teacher's mistake. She may tenaciously hold to her belief that effort does not lead to success, despite evidence to the contrary. This is why occasional success experiences frequently do not encourage greater effort in students like Hannah.

Rotter's theoretical work has spawned extensive empirical literature linking students' academic achievement with their locus of control (for reviews, see Lefcourt, 1976; Skinner, 1995). More recently, researchers have examined associations between perceptions of control and achievement behavior, such as effort and persistence (e.g., Patrick, Skinner, & Connell, 1993; Schmitz & Skinner, 1993). Rotter's distinction between the beliefs that rewards are contingent (internal) or not contingent (external) on individual characteristics or behavior has important educational implications, but practical classroom application requires certain refinements, some of which are described below.

Control = Strategy + Capacity

Skinner (1990, 1995) makes a distinction between **strategy (means–ends) beliefs** and **capacity (agency) beliefs** that is not in Rotter's theory. Strategy beliefs are about the extent to which certain strategies or means are sufficient to cause particular ends (e.g., "Will I get an 'A' if I understand everything in this book on motivation?"). Capacity beliefs refer to the extent to which a person has access to those means ("Am I *able* to understand the material in the book?"). Logically, a perception of control requires both beliefs, although Skinner points out that people do not always reason logically. (See Weisz & Stipek, 1982, for a similar distinction between *contingency* and *competence*.)

The distinction is useful in diagnosing and remedying motivation problems. One student, for example, may feel that she has the capacity to master motivation theory, but is unclear about how the professor grades (e.g., whether grades are based on class participation, memorizing names and studies, or understanding and being able to critically analyze the material). She therefore doesn't know what strategy is likely to be rewarded. Her sense of control could be increased by clarifying the grading criteria. Another student may be clear about the criteria for a good grade, but he believes he lacks the capacity to achieve those criteria. The remedy here is to persuade him that he can meet the criteria, perhaps by providing additional assistance.

Measuring LOC

According to Rotter, locus of control is a relatively stable trait and can be measured by a questionnaire. He developed the internal–external (I–E) control scale, which pits an internal belief against an external belief using a forced-choice format. The items are classified into six subcategories: academic recognition, social recognition, love and affection, dominance, social-political beliefs, and life philosophy (Rotter, 1966). Note that locus of control is operationalized very broadly in this scale, as general beliefs about control over rewards in many domains of life.

Several scales have been developed to be used with children, and some focus on control over outcomes in achievement contexts (see Weisz & Stipek, 1982, for a review). One measure frequently used to assess children's perceptions of control in achievement situations is the Intellectual Achievement Responsibility (IAR) Scale, developed by Crandall and associates (Crandall, Katkovsky, & Crandall, 1965). The IAR scale has the advantage of systematically dividing questions into positive and negative outcomes. An example of a positive item is: "When you do well on a test at school is it more likely to be (a) because you studied for it (internal response), or (b) because the test was especially easy (external response)?" Children who believe that positive outcomes are contingent on their own characteristics or behaviors have relatively high internal scores on the success subscale. Children who believe that negative outcomes are contingent on their own characteristics or behavior have relatively high internal scores on the failure subscale.

This distinction made in the IAR between perceptions of control for success and failure is important. Consider Helpless Hannah, for example; she accepts full responsibility for her failures, believing that they result from her low ability. But she believes that her rare successes are caused by external factors such as luck. Hannah has an internal locus of control with regard to failure and an external locus of control with regard to success. Some students have the opposite pattern of causal beliefs; they accept responsibility for success but assume that some external factor (e.g., a biased or unfair teacher) caused failure.

Connell (1985) has developed a measure of locus of control which makes even finer distinctions than the IAR. Children respond to questions concerning their perceptions of control with regard to cognitive, social, and physical outcomes. Within each of these domains, subscores provide information on the degree to which they believe they or powerful others (e.g., parents, teachers, popular peers) control outcomes and the degree to which they do not know why certain outcomes occur.

Skinner, Chapman, and Baltes (1988; Little, Oettingen, Stetsenko, & Baltes, 1995; Schmitz & Skinner, 1993; Skinner, Zimmer-Gembeck, & Connell, 1998) have developed a measure that reflects their own conceptualization of perceived control regarding school performance. Five types of means to achieve success or avoid failure are included: effort, ability, powerful others, luck, and unknown causes. For each of these five means there are questions about strategy beliefs (assumptions about the effectiveness of these strategies in bringing about desirable outcomes) and agency or capacity beliefs (perceptions of personal access to the means).

Classroom Contexts and Beliefs About Control

Although students arrive with dispositions, the immediate classroom context is also important. Some classroom conditions are more likely to result in an external LOC than others. For example, students are most likely to develop an external locus of control in situations in which rewards (e.g., grades, acknowledgement) are not closely tied to skills or performance. If very lenient or very difficult standards are used, so that different levels of performance result in similar rewards, or if rewards are variably given in conjunction with the same performance (e.g., three errors result in an "A–" one time and a "B" the next), students may perceive rewards to be unrelated to their performance. This is why consistency and clarity in grading and giving rewards is critical to students' perceptions of control.[1] The

---

[1] I discovered the hard way how easily students' beliefs in their ability to control rewards can be undermined. In an effort to reduce graduate students' obsession with grades, I discouraged inquiries about grading criteria for my seminar—promising that if they focused on mastering the material good grades would follow. My intentions were good, but I underestimated the strength of good grades as a valued reinforcement. Among the many unintended consequences of my reluctance to discuss grading criteria were high anxiety and resentment. By leaving students unclear about the contingencies of reinforcement—about the means to their desired end (an "A")—I got less effort from them than I would have if I had I provided clear contingencies.

social climate of the classroom may also be important. In a longitudinal study of children aged 8–12 years, Skinner, Zimmer-Gembeck, and Connell (1998) found that students who experienced their teachers as warm had more positive beliefs about their control over academic outcomes.

Clarity of the means to classroom rewards does not guarantee perceptions of agency or capacity. Some students who are very clear about the criteria for good grades still believe that they do not have the capacity to achieve the criteria. Some structure is, therefore, necessary but not sufficient to promote feelings of personal control.

Weiner's Attribution Theory

Although in some respects attribution theory is a refinement and elaboration of Rotter's locus of control theory, it differs in significant ways. A primary difference is that attribution theorists, unlike social learning theorists, assume that humans are motivated primarily to understand themselves and the world around them— to "... attain a cognitive mastery of the causal structure of [the] environment" (Kelly, 1967, p. 193).

Attribution theorists assume that people naturally search for understanding of why events occur, especially when the outcome is important or unexpected (Moeller & Koeller, 1999; Weiner, 1992). Thus, the student who expects to do well but does poorly on a test will seek information to answer the question: "Why did I fail that test?" In a sense, attribution theory turns locus of control theory on its head. Whereas LOC theorists study people's expectations related to future events, attribution theorists study perceptions of the cause of events that occurred in the past.

Perceptions of the cause of outcomes are referred to as **causal attributions.** Performance on tasks or tests are the outcomes typically studied in achievement contexts. The most common attributions for performance outcomes are *ability* ("I did well because I'm smart"; "I did poorly because I'm dumb") and *effort* ("I did/ did not study"; Weiner, 1992). But people make many other attributions: "I was lucky"; "The task was easy"; "The teacher explained things badly"; "My friend or parent helped me prepare"; "I didn't feel well"; "I was tired/hungry"; and so on. Some perceived causes are highly idiosyncratic. Indeed, I have heard very creative attributions for poor performance ("I was distracted by the coughing of the girl in front of me"; "I got hit on the head at football practice and I had trouble concentrating").

Weiner (1986, 1992, 1994, 2000) claims that the specific causal attribution is less important than the underlying dimension of the attribution. The causal dimensions he describes represent an elaboration and refinement of Rotter's internal-external locus of control dimension. Weiner points out that whether a cause is perceived as "internal" or "external" does not tell the full story, especially if our goal is to predict behavior in achievement situations. He claims, for example, that effort and ability attributions, which are both internal and treated equivalently by Rotter, have different behavioral implications. Most people see effort as under the control of the individual, whereas most do not see ability as controllable. Ability is also generally perceived as a relatively stable cause, whereas effort can vary from situation to situation. Consequently, Weiner distinguishes between different kinds of internal causes of achievement outcomes with regard to their stability and controllability. The control and stability dimensions that Weiner added to Rotter's original internal-external dimension allow much more specific behavioral predictions from beliefs about the cause of reinforcement (i.e., success, high grades). (See also Graham, 1994.)

Thus, Weiner has developed out of Rotter's single internal-external locus of control dimension three separate dimensions: locus, stability, and control. As in Rotter's theory, *locus* refers to the source of the cause, i.e., whether the outcome is contingent on a person's characteristics or behavior ("internal") or on some "external" variable unrelated to the person. The *stability* dimension differentiates causes on the basis of their duration. Ability, for example, is usually considered relatively stable over time, whereas effort, luck, or mood can vary from moment to moment. The *control* dimension concerns the degree of control a person has over the cause. We control how much effort we exert, whereas presumably we have no control over how lucky we are.

A person's own interpretation, not the attribution theorist's, influences his or her behavior in an achievement situation. Luck, for example, could be perceived by some people as a relatively stable quality (i.e., "I am a lucky/unlucky person"). Keeping in mind such possible person-to-person or even situation-to-situation variations, the most common placement for a few frequently used attributions on Weiner's causal dimensions is summarized in Table 5.1.

Antecedents to Attributions

Researchers have identified several factors that affect people's perceptions of the cause of achievement outcomes. *Consensus* information (about how well others performed) is associated with the locus dimension of causal attributions. If everyone in a class receives the same high grade, students are most likely to make an

TABLE 5.1 Dimensions of Common Attributions for Achievement Outcomes*

	Causes	
Causal Dimensions	**Ability**	**Effort**
Locus	Internal	Internal
Stability	Stable	Unstable
Controllability	Uncontrollable	Controllable

*From Graham & Weiner, in Tommy M. Tomlinson, *Motivating Students to Learn: Overcoming Barriers to High Achievement,* copyright 1993 by McCutchan Publishing Corporation, Richmond, California 94806. Used by permission of the publisher.

external attribution (e.g., easy task or easy-grading teacher). If only one student receives a good grade, that student is likely to make an internal attribution for his or her performance (e.g., high ability, studied hard).

Consistency is associated with the stability dimension. People usually attribute outcomes that are consistent with previous performance (e.g., "I have always failed in the past, and I failed again this time") to stable causes, such as ability. Conversely, outcomes that are inconsistent with previous outcomes are most likely to be attributed to unstable causes, such as effort, luck, or an unusually hard or easy task.

Weiner's focus on the situational factors that affect students' attributional judgments is one of the major differences between his and Rotter's analysis of achievement-related cognitions. Rotter emphasizes generalized beliefs that develop over time with experience in achievement settings and that are assumed to hold regardless of situational factors.

Attribution Dispositions

A few attribution researchers, however, have studied relatively stable individual differences in tendencies to attribute achievement outcomes to one cause versus another (e.g., Fincham, Hokoda, & Sanders, 1989; see Graham, 1991). These researchers conceptualize attributions, as Rotter conceptualized LOC, as a generalized set of relatively stable beliefs that evolve from previous experiences and socialization.

Researchers have examined several factors that appear to contribute to attributional dispositions. Below is a summary of studies that have examined past performance, culture, gender, and teachers' attitudes and behaviors.

Many studies have shown that students who have a *history of poor performance*, like Helpless Hannah, are more likely to attribute success to external causes and failure to a lack of ability than students who have a history of good performance (Marsh, 1984; Vlahovic-Stetic, Vidovic, & Arambasic, 1999). Children with retardation and children with learning disabilities, who presumably experience frequent failure, are much more likely to blame themselves for their failure than are normally developing or achieving children (see Dev, 1998; Licht, 1992).

Past performance also affects attributional dispositions indirectly, through the perceptions of competence that students develop. Thus, students who, as a result of repeated failures develop a perception of themselves as academically incompetent, interpret achievement outcomes consistent with this view. Failure is attributed to their lack of ability and success is attributed to some external cause (e.g., an easy task; Marsh, Cairns, Relich, Barnes, & Debus, 1984). In essence, they interpret a new failure as further evidence of their lack of competence. This reasoning is why it is often difficult to convince children who have failed in the past that they could succeed in the future.

There is also evidence for *cultural differences* in beliefs about the causes of achievement outcomes. Japanese and Chinese students attribute outcomes more to effort and less to ability than do American students (Chen & Stevenson, 1995; Lee, Ichikawa, & Stevenson, 1987; Stevenson, Lee, & Stigler, 1986; Stevenson & Stigler, 1992; Tuss, Zimmer, & Ho, 1995). The emphasis on effort is consistent with traditional Asian philosophy, which assumes malleability in humans and stresses the importance of striving for improvement. Cultural differences in beliefs about the causes of achievement outcomes suggest that these perceptions are, to some degree, socialized. Parents and teachers within our culture, therefore, may influence children's perceptions of the cause of achievement outcomes.

Gender differences are also commonly found in attribution research. Females are less likely than males to attribute success to their own high ability and more likely to attribute failure to low ability (e.g., Cramer & Oshima, 1992; Nicholls, 1979a, 1980; Parsons, Meece, Adler, & Kaczala, 1982; Stipek, 1984c; Vermeer, Boekaerts, & Seegers, 2000; see Sohn, 1982, for a metaanalysis; see also Eccles, Barbar, Jozefowicz, Malenchuk, & Vida, 2000; Eccles, Wigfield, & Schiefele, 1997). Gender differences are more prominent in domains, such as math and science, that are often sex-stereotyped as "male," than in other domains. In a study of fifth and sixth graders, for example, I found that girls were more likely to attribute failure in math to their lack of ability and less likely to attribute success to their ability than were boys; in contrast, there were no differences in boys' and girls' perception of the cause of achievement outcomes in spelling (Stipek, 1984c; see also Stipek & Gralinski, 1991).

Why might girls make more negative attributions? The tendency for girls to accept more personal responsibility for their failures than their successes is probably linked to a finding that will be discussed in Chapter 6; girls tend to rate their competencies lower than boys, especially in math and science. If girls don't perceive themselves to be very competent in a subject area, success in that area must have been caused by something other than high ability. If they do poorly, like students who typically achieve at a low level, they accept their poor performance as further evidence of their low competence. Girls' actual performance, however, even in math and science, is typically as high or higher than boys' performance.

Measurement

Weiner emphasizes situation-specific attributions, which can be measured by asking open-ended questions (e.g., "Why did you do well/poorly on your spelling test?") or by providing a set of options (e.g., effort, ability, task difficulty) and asking the respondent to rate the importance of each cause listed (e.g, "How much was low effort a cause of your poor performance on the spelling test?").

Other researchers have assessed students' generalized perceptions of the cause of academic outcomes. In some studies they ask students to rate the causes of an outcome experienced by a hypothetical person described to them in a story. This method assumes that students project their own beliefs about the causes of academic outcomes through their ratings. In other studies they ask students to think about their own past academic outcomes. Table 5.2 is an example of how students' beliefs about the causes of outcomes might be measured. The questions

TABLE 5.2   **Measure of Attributions for Performance on Academic Tasks**

	not at all a reason				an important reason
When you do well in school, is it usually because: (rate the importance of each explanation)					
you studied hard?	1	2	3	4	5
you studied the right things?	1	2	3	4	5
you are smart?	1	2	3	4	5
the teacher explained things well?	1	2	3	4	5
someone helped you?	1	2	3	4	5
the work was easy?	1	2	3	4	5
When you do poorly in school, is it usually because:					
you didn't study much?	1	2	3	4	5
you didn't study the right things?	1	2	3	4	5
you are not smart?	1	2	3	4	5
the teacher didn't explain things well?	1	2	3	4	5
you weren't helped by anyone?	1	2	3	4	5
the work was hard?	1	2	3	4	5

can easily be adapted to apply to a particular outcome (e.g., the student's grade on a test) or to outcomes in a particular subject area. (See Weiner, 1983, for a discussion of measurement issues.)

Consequences of Attributions

The consequences of attributions are what make the attributions relevant to a discussion of motivation in the classroom. Different dimensions are associated with different kinds of consequences.

Expectations.   Performance expectations usually rise following success and fall after failure. Motivation theorists refer to these expectancy changes as "typical shifts." Attribution theorists have shown that typical shifts occur only when a stable attribution for past performance is made (see Weiner, 1980a, 1992). This is because past outcomes attributed to unstable causes do not have clear implications for future performance. For example, if success is attributed to a substitute teacher giving an easy test, a student's expectations for success in the future may not increase. But if success is attributed to a high level of mastery of the subject area, the success should lead to higher expectations for future success. The stability dimension is, therefore, associated with performance expectations.

Effort attributions for learning are generally considered more adaptive than most other attributions because effort attributions have positive implications for expectations about future performance (Weiner, 1994). Effort is usually considered unstable. Students who attribute past failure to low effort therefore can hope for success in the future (assuming that they are willing to exert greater effort). Students who attribute past failure to low ability (in the sense of a stable trait), on the other hand, are not as likely to exert effort on future tasks because without the prerequisite ability they cannot expect success.

An effort attribution is also desirable when success occurs. The perception that effort was an important cause of success implies that the student possesses the required ability, but also acknowledges that success is not achieved without some effort. In contrast, attributing success solely to ability can have negative effects on behavior in achievement situations. When students succeed without trying very hard, they may come to believe that effort is not needed for success. Therefore they do not try very hard on future tasks, and, as a result, they perform at a level below their true capability.

Helpessness.   Attributing failure to causes that the individual does not control can lead to maladaptive behavior referred to as **learned helplessness.** Learned helplessness in animals was first investigated by Seligman and Maier (1967). Dogs were placed in a situation in which nothing they did prevented them from receiving a mild shock. The dogs soon became passive in the "helpless" situation, making no attempt to avoid being shocked, even when they were later placed in a situation in which they could avoid it. Other dogs who were previously able to prevent shock by their own behavior quickly learned the avoidance strategy. The authors claim that the animals in the helpless situation became passive because they perceived the environment to be unresponsive to (or not contingent upon) their own behavior.

Learned helplessness in achievement situations occurs when students—usually those who have experienced a great deal of failure, like Helpless Hannah—believe that there is nothing that they can do to avoid failure. When they do fail, helpless children typically attribute the failure to their low ability, which they believe is stable and out of their control (Dweck, 2000; Dweck & Goetz, 1978). These students exert little effort on school tasks and give up easily when they encounter difficulty. They are unresponsive to teachers' exhortations to try and generally seem disengaged from classroom activities. Many studies have demonstrated the debilitating effects on subsequent performance of a low-ability attribution for failure (see Weiner, 1994), which include escape or avoidance behavior (Poon & Lau, 1999) and negative emotions such as fear and anxiety (Sedek & McIntosh, 1998). Table 5.3 lists additional behaviors associated with learned helplessness and can be used to identify children who have developed such maladaptive beliefs.

TABLE 5.3   Behaviors Suggesting Learned Helplessness

The student:

- Says "I can't"
- Doesn't pay attention to teacher's instructions
- Doesn't ask for help, even when it is needed
- Does nothing (e.g., stares out the window)
- Guesses or answers randomly without really trying
- Doesn't show pride in successes
- Appears bored, uninterested
- Is unresponsive to teacher's exhortations to try
- Is easily discouraged
- Doesn't volunteer answers to teacher's questions
- Maneuvers to get out of or to avoid work (e.g., has to go to the nurse's office)

Much of the research on learned helplessness in achievement settings has been done by Dweck and her colleagues. In an early study, Dweck and Reppucci (1973) assessed connections between children's beliefs about the cause of achievement outcomes and their reactions to failure. Children who indicated on a questionnaire that they believed that controllable factors, such as effort, determined achievement outcomes tended to persist at an experimental task even after experiencing failure. The performance of children who indicated on the questionnaire that they tended to blame their failures on uncontrollable factors, such as the difficulty of the task or their lack of ability, deteriorated under failure conditions; these children gave up quickly when they encountered difficulty on the experimental task. (See also, Diener & Dweck, 1978; Dweck, 2000.) Licht and Dweck (1984) found, likewise, that the performance of children who minimized the role of effort in achievement outcomes (helpless children), unlike children who emphasized effort, deteriorated when they encountered a confusing paragraph inserted into a text. Thus, in both studies the two groups of children behaved very differently in the same achievement situation, and their behavior was directly related to their perceptions of the cause of achievement outcomes.

Diener and Dweck (1980) demonstrated that beliefs about the cause of achievement outcomes also affect children's reactions to success. They found that children who tended to attribute success to uncontrollable causes (e.g., luck or an easy test) underestimated the number of successes they experienced, overestimated the number of failures, tended not to view their successes as indicative of ability, and tended not to expect success in the future. These studies illustrate how generalized beliefs can supersede situational variables. They also explain why success doesn't always affect a child's self-perceptions or expectations. They interpret the success in a way that allows them to maintain their view of themselves as incompetent.

Licht and Dweck (1984) suggest that high-achieving girls may be particularly vulnerable to learned helplessness. They found, in the study described above, that the higher boys rated their intelligence, the less debilitated they were by the confusing paragraph. In contrast, girls' ratings of their intelligence tended to correlate negatively with their performance in the confusing condition. That is, the girls who considered themselves bright (and by objective evidence were relatively bright) were most debilitated by the confusing paragraph. The authors propose that attribution tendencies may contribute to girls' lower participation in higher level mathematics because in math, more than in most other subject areas, students encounter tasks that may, at first, be difficult or confusing. These are the conditions that are most likely to elicit helpless behavior.

Although learned helplessness is more common among low-achieving children, it is sometimes seen also in children who perform relatively well in school (Dweck, 2000). Even children identified as gifted are not immune from maladaptive attributions and feelings of helplessness (Cramer & Oshima, 1992). Indeed, gifted children may be especially vulnerable because parents, usually proud of their child's special academic talents, sometimes express exceptionally high expectations that the child feels incapable of fulfilling. Children who regard as failure any performance that is below parents' expectations, and who do not believe that they can meet those expectations, may give up trying altogether. Gifted children also can develop learned helplessness as a result of being moved to a special class for gifted children. A child who is accustomed to being the highest achiever in a regular class does not always adjust easily to performing at a comparatively lower level among other gifted children. A lower standing in the gifted class can cause feelings of failure and a belief that no amount of effort will assure success (which the child defines as being one of the best in the class; see Marsh, Chessor, Craven, & Roches, 1995). This belief presumably explains why Safe Sally dropped out of her calculus class after getting a "C+" on the first quiz.

There is also evidence that learned helplessness can be subject specific; students can develop a helpless orientation in one subject but not in another. Sedek and McIntosh (1998) developed a measure that they gave to high school students to assess feelings of helplessness in mathematics, physics and language, with questions to which they were asked to agree or disagree such as: "I feel helpless," "I have difficulty concentrating on the topic of the lesson," "I feel my thoughts are stuck in a dead end." The associations among scores in the three subject areas for this measure were very low, although all scores were strongly associated with performance in the subject matter.

Clearly, it is best to prevent children from developing an attributional pattern that results in helpless behaviors. As we saw with Hannah, such an attributional pattern is difficult to reverse. Children can fall into a self-perpetuating cycle in which they attribute failure to causes over which they have no control, do nothing to avoid failure in subsequent situations, and consequently fail again, thus confirming their perception of themselves as low in competence. And so the cycle continues.

Teachers may inadvertently contribute to maladaptive attributions and to this self-defeating cycle. Sedek and McIntosh (1998) studies found that learned helplessness was less common in classrooms in which teachers focused on understanding, stimulated creative thinking, and asked students' their opinions. In Chapter 7, we discuss further strategies for preventing attributions associated with helpless behavior and for altering maladaptive attribution patterns when they occur.

Emotions.   Weiner and his colleagues have examined the effect of different causal attributions on individuals' emotional reactions to their own as well as to others' achievement outcomes (see Weiner, 1986, 1992, 1994, 1995, 2000; Graham & Weiner, 1993). In a series of studies with adult subjects, Weiner, Russell and Lerman (1978, 1979) found that some emotions occur strictly as a function of outcome, regardless of an individual's perception of the cause of the outcome. Thus, students feel happy when they succeed and sad when they fail, regardless of their attribution for the cause of their success or failure. Other emotions are tied to specific attributions. Students claim to feel surprised when they attribute success or failure to luck, grateful when they attribute their success to someone else's help, and guilty when they attribute their failure to a lack of effort. Pride and shame occur only when an outcome is attributed to some internal cause. For example, a student who attributes success to his or her own hard work and ability is more likely to feel proud than a student who attributes success to help received from another individual. Personal failure attributed to internal causes such as lack of effort or ability is, similarly, more likely to result in feelings of shame than failure blamed on external causes (e.g., an unfair teacher, interfering noise while taking a test). Studies show that even children as young as three years show more pride when they succeed at a difficult task (for which they can take personal responsibility) than when they succeed at an easy task (which should engender an external, task difficulty, attribution; Lewis, Alessandri, & Sullivan, 1992). (See also, Mone & Baker, 1992; Niedenthal, Tangney, & Gavanski, 1994; Van Overwalle, Mervielde, & De Schuyter, 1995, for research on attribution-emotion linkages.)

Consider, for example, a situation in which a student receives the only "A" in the class versus a situation in which everyone in the class receives an "A." In the former case the student is likely to attribute the successful outcome to his or her own behavior or disposition; in the latter case the student is likely to attribute the successful outcome to an indiscriminate teacher or an easy test. The student who makes the internal attribution should feel more pride than the student who makes an external attribution. Consider next a student who knows, before he begins a multiple choice test, that he did not study for the test and has not mastered the material. He nevertheless does fairly well on the exam by guessing and he attributes his successful performance to good luck. Because an external attribution is made, he may experience relief and happiness, but not pride (unless he sees good luck as a personal characteristic or something he controls).

These emotional consequences of attributions have important practical implications. The anticipation of feeling proud can sustain a student's effort on a difficult task, just as the anticipation of feeling ashamed can inhibit a student from approaching an achievement task (Atkinson, 1964; Weiner, 1986). Weiner (1992) claims that guilt, which is associated with low effort attributions for failure, is a more desirable negative emotion than shame, because guilt engenders a desire to make amends (and therefore increase effort in the future), and shame engenders a desire to withdraw. He claims further that internal attributions for success are associated with self-esteem. The attributional analysis explains therefore why success on easy tasks, which is likely to be attributed to an external rather than an internal cause, does not engender pride or increase self esteem.

Support for some of the proposed effects of emotions on achievement behavior comes from a study by Covington and Omelich (1984b), in which college students' guilt about their performance on one midterm was associated with enhanced effort and performance on the next midterm, and humiliation for previous performance was associated with subsequent decreased effort and performance.

Interpersonal Attributions

Links between attributions and emotions also have implications for how individuals respond to *others'* behavior. Weiner (Weiner & Hareli, 2000) has developed both an intr*a*personal attribution theory—where individuals make judgments about the causes of their own outcomes—and an int*er*personal attribution theory—where individuals make judgments about the causes of others' outcomes. Attributions for others, just like self-attributions, can produce particular emotions as well as other behavioral responses.

For example, Weiner (1992, 1994, 2000) points out that a teacher who attributes a student's failure to an uncontrollable cause—such as poor health, undeveloped English language skills, or low ability—may feel sympathy, whereas a teacher who attributes failure to controllable causes, such as low effort or sloppiness, is more likely to respond with anger. Teachers can experience emotions as a consequence of their perceptions of their students' success as well (Weiner & Hareli, 2000). For example, if they attribute the success in part to their own teaching, they may experience pride.

Many studies have also shown that people's reactions are affected by their attributional judgments and concomitant emotions (Reyna & Weiner, in press; Weiner, 1986, 1992, in press), and that children know this (Juvonen, 2000). Studies have shown that children as young as six years understand that people experience anger when they attribute a negative outcome to a controllable cause, such as low effort, and by nine years they associate pity with attributions to uncontrollable causes (e.g., a disability or lack of intelligence; Graham, Doubleday, & Guarino, 1984; see also, Butler, 1994).

Teachers convey their attributional judgments through their emotional expressions and through their behavior. If a teacher believes a child did poorly because she didn't try, she is more likely to punish the child (e.g., with a bad grade or staying inside during recess to redo the assignment) than if she believes the child did the best she could but lacks the necessary skills. In the latter case, she may offer help as well as sympathy, or give the child a chance to do another assignment to make up for the low grade.

Juvonen (2000) found some interesting age differences in children's perceptions of the effect of effort and ability attributions on other's judgments of hypothetical children. Fourth, sixth, and eighth graders all believed that teachers had positive views of students who are "hard working" (e.g., do their homework and pay attention in class) regardless of their ability levels. When asked who would be popular with peers, however, fourth-graders gave the highest scores to the hard workers, sixth graders rated hard workers and "smart" students about equally, and eighth graders rated the students who were high in ability and low in effort as the most popular. The study shows important age differences in students' values and perceptions of social approval that could have important implications for their own behavior. The result suggests that an eighth grader would have to negotiate a conflict between behavior they needed to engage in to gain teacher approval (high effort) versus behavior that would win peer approval (low effort).

Children's own judgments about the cause of their performance may, therefore, be affected by the teacher's or their parents' emotional and behavioral reactions; an angry teacher response to low performance may foster a belief that the outcome was caused by low effort (a controllable cause), and a sympathetic response may foster a belief that the outcome was caused by low ability (an uncontrollable cause; Graham, 1984a, 1990; Graham & Weiner, 1993). (See Chapter 13 for a more extended discussion of ways in which teachers convey their perceptions of the cause of students' performance through their emotional expressions.)

Weiner's attribution analysis brings in clear relief the ways in which the classroom is a place in which judgments are made and conveyed (Reyna & Weiner, in press; Weiner, in press). Not only is a child's performance judged as good or bad, but the response—harsh or supportive, punishment or help—is affected by others' judgments of the cause of performance outcomes.

Summary

Like Bandura's social cognitive theory, Atkinson's, Rotter's, and Weiner's theories all represent a significant departure from strict reinforcement theory. Reinforcement theory is "mechanistic" in that it does not incorporate beliefs, values, expectations, emotions, or anything else that is not directly observable. Cognitive theorists, such as those reviewed in this chapter, consider unobservable thoughts and feelings to be important factors in understanding achievement behavior. Reinforcement theory concerns the environment, specifically the contingencies of reinforcement. Cognitive theorists are concerned with people's *interpretation* of the environment.

The next chapter focuses on individuals' beliefs about their competence. This particular judgment underlies, to some degree, the cognitions (e.g., expectations for success, perceptions of control, and perceptions of the cause of outcomes) emphasized in the achievement motivation theories discussed above.

TABLE 5.4   Summary of Terms

Term	Definition
Expectancy x Value Theory	
Motive for success (Ms)/ Need to achieve (Nach)	Unconscious disposition to strive for success
Motive to avoid failure (MAF)	Unconscious disposition which directs individuals away from achievement tasks
Perceived probability of success (Ps)	Individuals' expectations regarding the probability of success on a task
Incentive value of success (Is)	Amount of pride anticipated—inversely related to the perceived probability of success
Perceived probability of failure (Pf)	Individuals' expectations regarding the probability of failure on a task
Incentive value of failure (If)	Amount of shame anticipated—inversely related to the perceived probability of failure
Resultant tendency to approach or avoid an achievement activity (TA)	The strength of the tendency to approach minus the strength of the tendency to avoid a task
Locus of Control Theory	
Locus of control (LOC)	Beliefs about whether reinforcement is contingent upon one's behavior or characteristics
Strategy (means-ends) beliefs	Beliefs about the extent to which certain strategies or means are sufficient to cause particular ends
Capacity (agency) beliefs	Beliefs about the extent to which a person has access to those means
Attribution Theory	
Causal attributions	Perceptions of the cause of outcomes
Learned helplessness	Not trying as a consequence of a belief that rewards are not contingent upon one's behavior

CHAPTER

6

Perceptions of Ability

Perceptions of ability play an important role in all cognitive theories of achievement motivation. People usually need to have confidence in their ability to be high on self-efficacy, which is a central construct in Bandura's social learning theory. In Atkinson's theory, the higher people rate their competencies related to a task, the higher they rate the probability of their success. In Rotter's locus of control theory, people who believe they are academically competent are more likely to believe they control rewards associated with academic success. That is, they believe they have the capacity to achieve the performance upon which rewards are contingent. And in Weiner's attribution theory, people who believe they are competent at a task tend to attribute success to their ability and effort, and failure to some other cause; in contrast, those who believe they are incompetent will attribute failure to their lack of ability and will search for an external explanation for success.

At a practical level, and consistent with these theoretical analyses, perceptions of competence affect achievement-related behavior. Many studies have shown that perceptions of ability influence task choice, course choice, intended effort, persistence, thoughts and feelings while working on tasks, evaluations and attributions about one's performance, and ultimate achievement (see Byrne, 1996; Eccles, Wigfield, & Schiefele, 1997; Marsh, Byrne, & Yeung, 1999; Marsh & Yeung, 1997a, 1997b; Muijs, 1997; Miserandino, 1996).

Two new theories in which perceptions of ability also play a central role will be introduced in this chapter. Deci, Ryan, Connell, and their colleagues, for example, propose that people universally are born with a *need* to see themselves as competent, and they function poorly in contexts in which this need is not met (Connell, 1991; Connell & Ryan, 1984; Deci & Ryan, 1985). Focusing on American culture, Covington (1992, 1998) claims that because children see that competencies are valued and rewarded in school and elsewhere, their own sense of self-worth becomes partly based on their perceptions of their intellectual competencies. Consistent with his claim, researchers have found that self-esteem is strongly associated with children's perceptions of their academic competence (Wigfield, Eccles, & Pintrich, 1996).

Given the importance of being competent in our culture, researchers have found that people often exert a fair amount of effort to *look* competent, or at least to avoid looking incompetent. Social psychologists refer to such efforts as

impression management (Midgley, Arunkumar, & Urdan, 1996; Midgley & Urdan, 1995; Urdan, Midgley, & Anderman, 1998). To some degree the most effective way to look competent is to *become* competent. In this respect, students' efforts to look competent to others can promote productive learning behaviors. But some behaviors directed at this purpose ironically inhibit the development of genuine competencies. Obvious examples are not asking questions in class to avoid revealing ignorance or cheating rather than studying for a test.

This chapter describes some of the self-defeating strategies students use to look competent in situations in which they risk looking incompetent. Gender and age-related differences that have been found in research on self-perceptions of ability are discussed, as well as the effects of school practices, such as ability grouping and tracking, on perceptions of competence. Finally, strategies for assessing students' self-perceptions related to their competencies are provided.

First, however, we need to consider carefully what we mean by "ability."

What Is "Ability"?

Most people distinguish between *ability*, in the sense of capacity, and *achievement*, i.e., how well someone actually performs. If effort is high, a student's achievement should reflect that. But if a student doesn't pay attention, or doesn't put much effort into a task, his achievement may be below what it could have been with maximum effort. The term "underachiever" is often used to refer to students whose achievement is believed to be below their ability.

Dweck and Elliott (1983) claim that adults actually have two different concepts of ability, which they have measured using the questionnaire shown in Table 6.1 (see also, Cain & Dweck, 1989; Dweck, 2000, in press; Dweck & Bempechat, 1983; Dweck & Leggett, 1988; Molden & Dweck, 2000). According to the **entity** (capacity) concept, ability is a stable trait. An entity theory, like the notion of an intelligence quotient (IQ), also includes the beliefs that ability is distributed unevenly among individuals (some have more of it than others), and that it is a general trait that affects learning and performance in a variety of domains.

According to the **instrumental–incremental** concept, ability consists of ". . . an ever-expanding repertoire of skills and knowledge . . . that is increased through one's own instrumental behavior" (Dweck & Bempechat, 1983, p. 144). Ability, using this definition, is more task specific and is developed through study or practice. A person's ability in one area is not necessarily relevant to his or her ability in another area.

Most adults use both conceptions, sometimes with regard to the same skill area. For example, occasionally when I play tennis and I feel especially discouraged from my poor performance, I believe that I am constitutionally uncoordinated and incapable of ever learning to play tennis or any other game that requires physical coordination. I am convinced that no amount of practice will result in any significant improvement. But when I am feeling more optimistic,

TABLE 6.1   Implicit Theories of Intelligence

Response options: 1 = strongly agree, 2 = agree, 3 = mostly agree, 4 = mostly disagree, 5 = disagree, 6 = strongly disagree

1. You have a certain amount of intelligence, and you really can't do much to change it.
2. Your intelligence is something about you that you can't change very much.
3. You can learn new things, but you can't really change your basic intelligence.
4. No matter who you are, you can change your intelligence a lot.
5. You can always greatly change how intelligent you are.
6. No matter how much intelligence you have, you can always change it quite a bit.

Source: From Dweck (2000), page 177. Copyright 2000 from *Self-theories: Their role in motivation, personality, and development* by C. Dweck. Reproduced by permission of Routledge, Inc., part of The Taylor & Francis Group.

perhaps encouraged by an unusually patient opponent, I believe that if I just practice, my game will improve. The former view is an example of an entity theory of tennis ability; the latter illustrates an instrumental-incremental theory.

Dweck and her colleagues claim that students' concepts of intellectual ability have important implications for their behavior in achievement contexts. Consider students who see ability as an entity that you either have or don't have. If, as Covington claims, they also believe that being competent is highly valued in their culture and relevant to their self-worth, they will want to demonstrate their competence. (See Chapter 10 for further discussion of student goals.)

The implications this desire to look competent will have on behavior will depend substantially on students' perceptions of their ability. Students who are fairly confident about their ability seek opportunities to demonstrate it. But, like Safe Sally, they tend to select tasks in which there is no risk of failure, so the limits of their ability are never revealed. Students who have an entity concept of ability but lack confidence in their ability avoid achievement situations, especially those in which their lack of ability would become public. If they are given a choice in tasks, they may select either very easy tasks, to ensure success, or very difficult tasks, so that failure can be attributed to task difficulty rather than low ability. If they have no choice in tasks, as is usually the case in school, like Hannah, they often develop learned helplessness (Burhans & Dweck, 1995). Children with learning disabilities such as ADHD may be particularly vulnerable in achievement situations because they are more likely to adopt an entity theory of intelligence and they often have relatively low perceptions of their academic competencies (Dunn & Shapiro, 1999).

The goal of children who have an instrumental–incremental concept of ability is not to look smart, but to *be* smart by increasing their skill level. If they fail, they assume that practice and effort will increase their chances of future success. They select moderately difficult tasks because they are more likely to produce learning than very easy tasks, which require little effort, or very difficult tasks which may be impossible to complete. Rather than becoming helpless when they encounter difficulty, they intensify their effort and try new strategies (see Burhans & Dweck, 1995).

Dweck's distinction between a concept of ability as a stable trait versus as a skill that can be developed also has implications for how effort is viewed. According to an entity definition, effort has limited potential for increasing ability, and under certain circumstances it can undermine one's image of being capable. This is because effort and ability are assumed to be inversely related; if two people achieve the same level of performance, the person who exerted less effort is seen as more able. If you are an entity theorist, claiming you didn't study for a test is a good way to look smart; if you don't do well, you can attribute your poor performance to low effort rather than low ability. If you do well despite not studying, you look really smart.

In general, people who have an entity theory of ability have a diminished view of the role of effort in learning and performance. They do not see effort as playing a role in their successes, and they are less likely to attribute difficulties or failure to a lack of effort (and more likely to attribute it to a lack of ability; see Dweck, in press).

People who view ability as stable and not much affected by effort are particularly vulnerable when they encounter difficulty. They are not likely to maintain a sense of self-efficacy in the face of challenge, or to increase their self-efficacy over time as learning proceeds. Research finds that they are also more likely to show defensive or self-defeating behavior in the face of challenge, and that their intrinsic interest in a task declines, especially when they perceive that task to be an assessment of their ability (Butler, 1999).

Teachers, like students, differ in the degree to which they see intellectual ability as stable or as malleable and expanding (Dweck, in press), and their beliefs appear to affect the way they judge students and even the way they teach. Teachers or other adults with an entity theory have been shown to render judgments more quickly, on the basis of initial or preliminary performance (Butler, 2000; Plaks, Stroessner, Dweck, & Sherman, 2001), and not change their judgments easily in the face of contradictory evidence. Midgley, Feldlaufer, and Eccles (1988) found also that teachers who believed that math ability was fixed perceived themselves to be less efficacious and had a stronger need to control student behavior than teachers who believed that math ability was amenable to change. Teachers clearly need to monitor their own beliefs and the effects their beliefs have on their instructional strategies.

The desire to "look smart" promoted by an entity theory of ability can have serious negative consequences for learning-related behavior. Covington and his colleagues have vividly described the self-defeating strategies that students sometimes use to avoid looking incompetent in efforts to preserve their self-worth.

Covington's Self-Worth Theory

Self-worth concerns people's appraisal of their own value. It is similar to such concepts as self-esteem and self-respect. A fundamental assumption of Covington's self-worth theory is that human beings naturally strive to maintain a sense of self-worth (Covington, 1984, 1992, 1998; Covington & Beery, 1976). This desire explains why people often take more responsibility for their successes than for their failures (McAllister, 1996; Miller & Ross, 1975), as well as why they behave maladaptively when their self-worth is threatened, especially in public contexts.

Outcomes that make people look competent or incompetent in achievement situations have important implications for their emotional experiences as well as their sense of self-worth (Covington & Omelich, 1981). Failure engenders greater shame and distress when it is seen as a reflection of low ability than when it can be attributed to some other cause. Shame may be stronger for entity than for incremental theorists because a judgment of low ability has more profound and long-term implications for the former than for the latter ("It's something about *me* that I cannot change").

When failure is expected or experienced, the student's task is to avoid having the failure interpreted as evidence of incompetence. As mentioned above, one strategy to avoid revealing incompetence and the accompanying negative emotions is to not try. Failure can then be attributed to low effort rather than to low ability.

But, alas, it's not so easy because not trying has its own negative consequences. Children like Defensive Dave, who expect failure, are in a real bind. If they try but fail, they provide unambiguous evidence that they lack ability. If they don't try, they have an alternative explanation for their failure, but because effort is also valued and rewarded in most classrooms, they risk disapproval and punishment (Blumenfeld, Hamilton, Bossert, Wessels, & Meece, 1983; Urdan, Midgley, & Anderson, 1998; Weiner, 1994, 1995). Thus, although failure with high effort engenders more shame or humiliation for students, failure with low effort elicits the most disapproval from teachers. This is why Covington and Omelich (1979a) refer to effort as a "double-edged sword."

What happens to children who decide that no amount of effort is ever going to promote either their own or others' perceptions of them as academically competent? How do they preserve their self-esteem?

One strategy for poor achieving students to maintain self-worth is to discount the importance of academic success. A study by Harter, Whitesell, and Junkin (1998) suggests the effectiveness of this strategy. They found that high school students high in self-worth were able to discount areas of weakness better than students with a relatively low sense of self-worth. Some adolescents, like Alienated Al, develop antiacademic values and shift their attention to developing competencies and seeking recognition in nonacademic domains. In the best cases they may turn to sports or the arts; too often the alternative domain involves gangs and criminal behavior. The antiacademic success values that some adolescents develop is a defensive strategy of last resort, not a genuine choice. It represents an almost desperate effort to maintain a sense of acceptance and worthiness. We return to this issue in Chapter 9.

The strong link between self-perceptions of academic ability and self-worth in our culture can be problematic for all students, even those who perform fairly well. In most American classrooms, rewards that symbolize success (e.g., good grades) are based on relative performance, thus guaranteeing failure for some students. Success is usually defined by the teacher and because some students face standards that are too difficult for them to achieve, they know their effort will not pay off. Even if the teacher attempts to individualize standards for success, because of the competitive nature of most classrooms, students attend to their classmates' accomplishments and often strive to keep up with them—whether or not their classmates' achievements represent realistic goals.

The emphasis on ability as an important attribute in this culture and the impossibility of all students' succeeding force some students, like Defensive Dave, to protect themselves from the negative implications that failure usually has for one's ability. Most of these strategies undermine learning. This is why some theorists refer to them as "self-handicapping" (Riggs, 1992; Urdan, Midgley, & Anderman, 1998). A few of the more common strategies are described below. (See also Covington & Beery, 1976; and Covington, 1998.)

Avoiding the Negative Implications of Failure

Students can avoid school failure, to some degree, by *minimizing participation*. Being absent, especially on the day of a big test, is not uncommon. Not volunteering answers to questions in class is less drastic.

But students in most classrooms cannot escape some level of participation. Thus they have to resort to more subtle methods to avoid failure, or in those cases in which failure is unavoidable, to prevent the teacher and classmates from interpreting their failure as evidence of low competence, to attribute to some other cause that does not have implications for self-worth.

As mentioned above, one strategy is to not try—or at least to make people *think* you didn't try. Performance with no effort provides no information regarding a student's ability because it is impossible to determine what he would have accomplished if he had tried harder. Some students publicize their refusal to work and publicly devalue the importance of studying. Teachers are often frustrated and puzzled by such behavior, but students' obstinate refusal to exert any effort has its own logic. It achieves the short-term goal of avoiding a low ability attribution for the failure.

There are risks, of course, when such strategies are employed. As mentioned above, teachers expect students to try and they reward and punish students accordingly. Students must therefore simultaneously deal with the knowledge that failing with high effort suggests low ability, and that not trying often results in punishment and has its own negative implications for self-worth. Students who anticipate failure are in a no-win situation. If they try hard and fail, they look stupid; if they do not try, they get into trouble with the teacher. The evidence is clear, however, that when faced with a choice between the teacher's wrath for not trying and the feelings of humiliation and incompetence associated with trying and failing, many students will choose the former (Covington, Spratt, & Omelich, 1980).

Some students are clever enough to find some middle ground to avoid punishment for not trying. They try just enough to stay out of trouble, but not so hard that failure unambiguously implies lack of ability. They know that to maximize the desired image of a hard worker it is best to look eager, and then pray that the teacher calls on someone else. Extreme attention to note-taking, with my head bowed so as not to catch the teacher's eye, is a technique I used as a college student. Sitting in the back of the room, positioned out of view of the teacher, is another useful technique.

Covington and Beery (1976) give examples of similar strategies which they refer to as *"false effort"*—feigning attention during a class discussion, asking a question even though the answer is already known, or giving the outer appearance of thinking by adopting a pensive quizzical expression. These behaviors do not reflect a real attempt to learn. Rather, they are designed to look attentive and stay out of trouble.

There are other ploys used to maintain a perception of ability while avoiding censure for not trying. *Excuses* are probably the most typical strategy used to avoid the negative sanctions associated with low effort, although clearly, to be effective, excuses must be used sparingly.[1]

Procrastination is another common strategy used to avoid the negative implications of failure. Creating a personal handicap by studying at the very last minute provides the student with a ready, nonability-related explanation for subsequent failure. As mentioned above, successful students occasionally use this technique to enhance their image as highly competent. They are careful to announce before a test that they did not begin studying until midnight the night before and are concerned about their performance. Then, their good performance can be attributed to extremely high ability, since effort has been ruled out as an explanation. This technique is also a useful safeguard for students who are uncertain about their performance; if they do poorly they have a ready excuse that has ambiguous implications for their ability.

There are other strategies used by students to avoid the implications of failure for ability. One paradoxical strategy is to *set unattainable performance goals*. Failure is assured, but failure at an extremely difficult task does not necessarily imply low ability, whereas failure at a task that is considered to be very easy inescapably results in a judgment of low ability. Perhaps this is why Sears (1940)

---

[1]College students in my classes are exasperated by my refusal to listen to their excuses. My leniency in allowing a student to retake an examination or rewrite a paper seems to be less important to them than my hearing out the nonability-related reasons for their previous poor performance. An opportunity for success on the second round, apparently, is less effective in preserving a perception of competence and self-worth than the opportunity to make sure I attribute their previous failure to external causes (e.g., "My child was sick all weekend and I wasn't able to study").

found that children who had a history of success in school set their academic goals at a realistic level, but students who had experienced considerable failure often overestimated, sometimes by extreme degrees, how well they would perform on various arithmetic and reading tasks. For some of the failure-prone students, the poorer their performance, the higher they set their aspirations. Sears speculated that the unrealistic goal setting might also result from the poor-performing students' hope that they could win approval by merely claiming to have ambitious goals, even if they know they cannot achieve them.

Related to setting unrealistic goals is selecting very difficult tasks. Even though failure may be assured on a very difficult task, the failure provides little information on the student's competence.

There is evidence that simply describing a task as highly difficult can improve the performance of those who are concerned about performance and chronically worry about failure (Karabenick & Youssef, 1968). Presumably, performance is less debilitated by anxiety because if they fail they can attribute the failure to the extreme difficulty of the task rather than to their own incompetence.

Miller (1985) provides a compelling demonstration of how describing a task as difficult can alleviate students' performance concerns and enhance effort. He gave sixth-grade children a series of matching tasks that were constructed in such a way as to ensure failure. Following this failure children were given an anagram task to work on while their behavior was carefully observed. Children who were told that the subsequent task was moderately difficult completed fewer anagrams than children who were told that the anagram task was very difficult. Simply telling children that the next task was very difficult apparently alleviated the concerns about competence that the previous failure experience created. Presumably this message allowed children to try hard without risking demonstrating low competence on yet another task. (See also Miller & Hom, 1990.)

There is some evidence that boys may be more concerned about their public image than girls. In Miller's (1985) study, the positive effect of referring to the task as difficult was especially prominent for boys. Other studies have found that boys also report using more self-handicapping strategies than girls (see Table 6.2; Midgley & Urdan, 1995; Urdan et al., 1998).

Success without Learning

Another approach to maintaining an image of ability is to *ensure success*, but not necessarily by developing the required competencies. Perhaps the most common method of ensuring success without learning is cheating. Butler (1998) found that boys who believed that asking for help revealed incompetence favored cheating over asking for help.

Another method, mentioned above, is to attempt only very easy tasks. Success is ensured, but little learning results. This is Safe Sally's strategy. She avoids challenging tasks to preserve her image as an able person. A related strategy is to have very low aspirations. A student may announce to friends before a test that he or she would be delighted just to be able to pass the test. Anything above a

TABLE 6.2   An Assessment of Self-Handicapping Strategies

Response options: 1 = not at all true, 2, 3, 4, 5 = very true

- Some students put off doing their work until the last minute so that if they don't do well on their work they can say that is the reason. How true is this of you?

- Some students purposely don't try hard in school so that if they don't do well they can say it is because they didn't try. How true is this of you?

- Some students fool around the night before a test so that if they don't do well they can say that is the reason. How true is this of you?

- Some students purposely get involved in lots of activities. Then, if they don't do well on their schoolwork, they can say it is because they're involved in other things. How true is this of you?

- Some students let their friends keep them from paying attention in class or from doing their homework. Then, if they don't do well they can say their friends kept them from working. How true is this of you?

- Some students look for reasons to keep them from studying: not feeling well, having to help their parents, taking care of a brother or sister, and so on. Then, if they don't do well on their schoolwork, they can say this is the reason. How true is this of you?

Source: From Urdan, Midgley, & Anderman (1998, p. 120). Copyright 1998 by the American Educational Research Association. Reprinted with permission.

passing grade, therefore, can be construed as a success. In any new skill situation, it is useful to announce beforehand: "I'm not very good at this." This lowers the expectations of observers. Then, even mediocre performance is perceived as evidence that the person is "actually pretty good." (I do this every time I play tennis against a new opponent.)

A strategy to ensure success in a group question-and-answer period is to rehearse answers to the question that one is likely to be asked.[2] If teachers ask predictable questions, or if they question students in a predictable order, it is often possible to rehearse or plan a response to one's own question. Although this strategy precludes learning from other students' questions and answers, it maximizes the probability of giving a correct answer.

Related to these kinds of success-ensuring (but not necessarily learning-ensuring) tactics is what Covington and Beery (1976) refer to as *"overstriving."* The overstriver is driven by an intense desire to succeed, but more importantly, to

[2]Years ago I took a Spanish class in an adult evening program. The teacher frequently gave us a printed set of questions and proceeded around the table in order, asking students to answer the questions. I expertly avoided the public humiliation of giving a wrong answer by counting around the table to figure out which question I would be asked. I concentrated all my effort on figuring out how to answer that question before the teacher reached me. This classic technique achieved my immediate goal—to be successful and avoid looking incompetent; but the positive consequences were short-lived. By not attending to questions that other students answered, I minimized the amount I learned. My strategy temporarily allowed me to preserve an image of competence, but I still can't speak Spanish.

avoid failure. Again, Safe Sally is a good example. Her schoolwork is characterized by over-preparedness and excessive attention to detail. Because of the tremendous effort exerted, successes are attributed to effort. Thus, she continues to harbor doubts about her real abilities. Covington and Beery point out that overstrivers' uncertainty about their abilities make them extremely vulnerable in the event of failure. As a consequence, they develop a "loathing of failure far out of proportion to its importance" (p. 57).

In summary, the strategies presented in this chapter can reduce anxiety or humiliation in the short run. But all of them inhibit real learning and, in the long run, make real success impossible. Evidence suggesting incompetence will mount, despite all efforts to avoid such a conclusion, and self-serving explanations become less and less plausible. Children who are uncertain about their competence and, as a result, expend their energies on avoiding "looking dumb" rather than on learning, eventually become convinced of their incompetence and give up the game. Such a child is transformed from a failure-avoiding student (like Dave) to a failure-accepting student (like Hannah or Al). Defensive Dave's approach to schoolwork is hardly conducive to learning, but it does preserve some semblance of competence. Helpless Hannah gave up altogether and instead of making an effort to give the impression that she knows what she is doing, she is resigned to her incompetence. Alienated Al doesn't even bother to come to school much of the time. While Dave is able to maintain some—albeit fragile—sense of self-worth in school, at least for the time being, Hannah and Al must either exclude academic ability as a factor related to self-worth, which is not easy to do in American culture, or they must devalue their own worth, which is a tragedy.

Gender Differences in Self-Perceptions of Ability

The evidence is inconsistent, but many studies find that girls rate their competencies lower than do boys, even when their performance is equally good or better (see Cole, Martin, Peeke, Seroczynski, & Fier, 1999; Eccles, Wigfield, Harold, & Blumenfeld, 1993; Freedman-Doan, Wigfield, Eccles, Blumenfeld, Arbreton, & Harold, 2000; Licht & Dweck, 1984; Meece & Courtney, 1992), especially in math and science (Hackett & Betz, 1992; Kahle & Damnjanovic, 1994; Meece et al., 1990; Marsh & Yeung, 1998; Rennie, Parker, & Kahle, 1996; Stipek & Gralinski, 1991; Wigfield & Eccles, 1994; Wigfield, Eccles, Harold, Blumenfeld, Arbreton, Freedman-Doan, & Yoon, 1997; see Eccles, Barbar, Jozefowica, Malenchuk, & Vida, 2000; Eccles, Wigfield, & Schiefele, 1997). Even gifted and very high-achieving girls tend to underestimate their competencies (Eccles et al., 2000).

The gender differences in perceptions of competence are important because they appear to affect people's confidence in being able to succeed in gender-stereotyped occupations (see Eccles, Barbar, Jozefowica, Malenchuk, & Vida,

2000). Girls' relatively low perceptions of competence in math and science, for example, probably contributes to females' underrepresentation in these stereotypically male professions (Eccles, Barber, & Jozefowicz, 1998; Hackett & Betz, 1992; Mooce & Courtney, 1992).

The reasons for the gender differences are no doubt deeply embedded in cultural stereotypes and the messages that teachers and parents subtly convey to boys and girls. Perhaps this is why perceptions of ability become more sex-role stereotyped as children get older (Eccles, Barbar, Jozefowica, Malenchuk, & Vida, 2000).

There is some evidence that girls may be more influenced by parental evaluations than are boys (Eccles et al., 1983), and also that parents tend to view boys as more competent in math and science. Eccles (1993; Jacobs & Eccles, 1992), for example, reports that the mothers in her studies who had stereotyped beliefs about math competency (i.e., believed that boys are naturally more talented than girls), rated sons' competencies higher than daughters' competencies. Parents also reported less time working or playing on the computer with girls than with boys, and they report that they encourage girls less than boys to do math or science activities (Eccles, 1993).

It is difficult to determine who drives the gender differences in experiences—children or their parents. Girls also report more enjoyment from and spending more time on reading and writing activities than do boys, with boys preferring scientific, math-related, and electronic hobbies more than do girls (Eccles, Barbar, Jozefowica, Malenchuk, & Vida, 2000). Thus parents are probably both responding to and reinforcing interests that they perceive in their children.

Whatever the roots of girls' tendency to rate their competencies lower than boys in some domains, the challenge for teachers is to overcome such biases that could undermine girls' actual mastery. Chapter 13 discusses strategies for conveying high expectations to both boys and girls.

Age-Related Changes in Perceptions of Ability

Helpless Hannahs and Defensive Daves are more common in the higher grades than in the first few grades of school. This is because children's concepts of ability change and because their judgments of their own ability decline, on average, with age.

When asked about their academic ability, most kindergarten-age children claim to be the smartest students in their class. In many studies of self-perceptions of academic ability, children's ratings are near the top of the scale through the early elementary grades and decline, on average, thereafter (e.g., Eccles, Roeser, Wigfield, & Freedman-Doan, 1999; Eccles, Wigfield, Midgley, Reuman, Mac Iver, & Feldlaufer, 1993; Schuster, Ruble, & Weinert, 1998; Wigfield & Eccles, 1994; see Stipek & Mac Iver, 1989; Wigfield et al., 1996; Wigfield, Eccles, Yoon, Harold, Arbreton, Freedman-Doan, & Blumenfeld, 1997). Similar declines have been found in self-efficacy beliefs (Shell, Colvin, & Bruning, 1995). As they decline, self-perceptions of ability become more accurate in the sense that they correlate more strongly with external indices (e.g., teacher's ratings; see Harter, 1999; Marsh, 1993; Marsh, Craven, & Debus, 1998; Nicholls, 1978, 1979a; Schuster, Ruble, & Weinert, 1998).

The typically strong positive bias in young children and the ensuing decline in perceived competence can be explained, in part, by changes in children's conceptions of academic competence and the criteria they use to assess competence. Children in preschool (and to some degree in the first year or two of elementary school) have a broad concept of ability that includes social behavior, conduct, work habits, and effort (Blumenfeld, Pintrich, Meece, & Wessels, 1982; Stipek & Daniels, 1990; Stipek & Tannatt, 1984). Over the elementary years, children's definitions of academic ability become more narrow and more differentiated by subject matter (Marsh, Barnes, Cairns, & Tidman, 1984; see Marsh & Hattie, 1996).

Systematic age differences have also been found in the type of information regarding competence that children attend to most, in how they process different types of information, and in their propensity to make judgments based on intra-individual versus inter-individual comparisons. Interview studies suggest that preschool-age children and children in the first few grades of elementary school focus on effort expended (Harter & Pike, 1984), personal mastery (Blumenfeld, Pintrich, & Hamilton, 1986), and social reinforcement (Spear & Armstrong, 1978) in their ability assessments. Emphasis on these sources of information declines with age, and the way children interpret this kind of information also changes.

Consider effort, for example. Young children assume that people who try hard are smart and people who are smart try hard. Nicholls and Miller (1984b) describe a study in which children were shown a videotape of two actors, one who obviously did not try and the other who tried hard. Both actors were shown to receive the same high score. Many of the younger children simply refused to believe that one of the actors succeeded without working hard. Some claimed that this actor must have started earlier or "must have been thinking while fiddling" (p. 195). (See also, Miller, 1985; Nicholls, 1978, 1983, 1990; Nicholls, Jagacinski, & Miller, 1986; Nicholls & Miller, 1984a, 1984b.)

Not until about the age of 11 or 12 do children fully differentiate performance, effort, and ability—what Nicholls refers to as a differentiated, or "mature" concept of ability. Only adolescents in the study described above perceived an inverse relationship between effort and ability, claiming that the actor in the videotape who worked very hard was not as smart as the actor who did not work hard but achieved the same level of performance. This understanding may explain why eighth graders, but not sixth and fourth graders in Juvonen's (2000) study, rated hypothetical students who were high in ability and low in effort as the most popular.

While effort and mastery decline in importance as indicators of academic competence and change in their implications, children pay increasing attention to grades (Blumenfeld et al., 1986; Nicholls, 1978, 1979a), and they become more sensitive to differential treatment by teachers (see below). However, the most important developmental changes in the ability–assessment process concern the use of social comparative information.

Children as young as preschool age make social comparisons and competitive, "besting" verbal statements (Mosatche & Bragonier, 1981). By the age of 3-1/2 years children also react differently to winning and losing a competition (Heckhausen, 1984). The evidence suggests, however, that although preschool-age children may make simple comparisons with one other individual, they do not use group normative information (i.e., their own performance compared to the performance of a group of age-mates) to assess their competence until later (Aboud, 1985; Boggiano & Ruble, 1979; Nicholls, 1978; Butler & Ruzany, 1993; Ruble, Grosovsky, Frey, & Cohen, 1992).

The evidence on whether children use normative information to evaluate their competence in the first few grades of school is inconsistent (Morris & Nemcek, 1982; Ruble & Frey, 1991). It is clear, however, that dramatic changes occur between kindergarten and about second or third grade (Butler, 1989; Stipek & Tannatt, 1984). By third or fourth grade, children's ability judgments are consistently affected by normative information, and they begin to explain their judgments of their ability in social–comparative terms. Older children are also more skilled than younger children at interpreting social–comparative information (Aboud, 1985; Ruble, 1983). For example, in one study fifth graders took into consideration the differences in the amount of time they and a peer were given to work on a test when judging their performance relative to the peer, while second graders did not (Aboud, 1985).

Students' attention to social comparison information increases even more when they enter junior high school (Feldlaufer, Midgley, & Eccles, 1988). Furthermore, during the junior and senior high school years students place their achievement into an increasingly broader social context. Elementary school students compare themselves primarily with classmates. In junior high students begin to pay attention to track placement and grade point averages, which can be compared schoolwide. By the final years of high school, outcomes of scholarship competitions, college admissions, and other indicators of achievement relative to national norms figure into some students' judgments of their competence. Analogous changes are likely to apply to athletic and other spheres of performance. While younger children most likely compare their performance to teammates, as they get older children begin to assess their own competence in comparison to children on other teams, and eventually for some, to national records.

The shift toward using normative criteria to judge ability is a major factor in the average decline in children's ratings of their ability from the early grades to high school. Children's own competencies, in an absolute sense, are constantly improving. Focusing on mastery and accepting praise at face value assures most young children of positive judgments of their competence. In contrast, social comparison inevitably leads to some negative judgments because half of the students in a class must, by definition, perform below average.

Classroom Practice Effects

Age-related changes in students' definitions of competence and perceptions of their ability are to some degree a consequence of shifts in the organizational, instructional, and evaluation practices that students are exposed to in school (see Anderman & Maehr, 1994; Eccles et al., in press; Stipek & Mac Iver, 1989).

In early childhood children receive little information that challenges their inflated view of their competencies. Preschool teachers usually accept a child's product as satisfactory as long as the child has worked on it for a reasonable amount of time, and most children end up receiving positive feedback on tasks they complete (Apple & King, 1978; see also Blumenfeld et al., 1982). Tasks are typically done individually or in small groups, and comparative information about classmates' performance is not readily available. Under these circumstances it is not surprising that preschool-age children rarely compare their performance with peers and are able to maintain positive perceptions of their competence.

But children are not protected for very long from the potentially harsh effects of academic competition. The nature of tasks, competence feedback, and student-teacher relationships all change gradually over the early elementary school years, and sometimes dramatically when students enter junior high.

Several changes in school tasks and evaluation practices presumably contribute to a more differentiated concept of ability. Throughout the early elementary grades, teachers tend to emphasize effort and work habits, even in report card grades (Blumenfeld et al., 1983; Brophy & Evertson, 1978). Effort figures less prominently in report card grades as students move through elementary school (Entwisle & Hayduk, 1978), and by junior high, grades tend to be based more narrowly on test performance (Gullickson, 1985). Tasks, too, become more focused on intellectual skills as students advance in grade, and in middle school teacher-student relationships become much more formal and centered on school performance (Eccles et al., 1993; Eccles & Wigfield, 2000, in press; Midgley et al., 1988, 1989b; Midgley, Anderman, & Hicks, 1995). Accordingly, children's concept of ability shifts from a poorly differentiated construct that includes effort, work habits, and social skills to a more narrowly defined construct which focuses more exclusively on performance on academic tasks.

Many changes in the nature of instruction and evaluation also foster student interest in social comparison. Over the elementary school years students are increasingly given tasks that involve a single right answer (Eccles, Midgley, & Adler, 1984; Higgins & Parsons, 1983). They also encounter ability grouping (Hallinan & Sorensen, 1983) and other public evidence (e.g., star charts) of their own and their classmates' skills (Higgins & Parsons, 1983). Assignments become more uniform among students as they advance through the school grades (Eccles & Midgley, 1989), and older students experience more whole-group and less individualized and small-group instruction than younger students (Brophy & Evertson, 1978).

Social comparison is more salient as a result of these changes, because uniform task structures reduce intra-individual variation in performance across time and make it easier to compare inequalities in performance across students. When tasks do not vary much from day to day, students perform more consistently than when the format and nature of tasks vary. When all students do the same task at the same time, performance is more comparable, more salient, and more public than when tasks vary or are individualized.

The amount of positive social reinforcement also declines as students advance in school (Pintrich & Blumenfeld, 1985) and as grades are given more frequently and emphasized more (Harter, Whitesell, & Kowalski, 1992). Partly because grades are increasingly based on relative performance (i.e., a normal curve)—a criterion which requires some students to do poorly—grades decline, on average. Because grades are easily comparable, these changes in evaluation practices no doubt contribute to students' interest in social comparative information, as well as to the decline in average self-ratings of ability.

In summary, the nature and diversity of tasks, evaluation practices, and relations with teachers change systematically as students progress through school. These changes occur in ways that increasingly emphasize individual differences in performance on academic tasks, making it difficult for average- and below-average students to maintain positive perceptions of competence.

Changes in instructional and evaluation practices occur, however, in conjunction with changes in students' information processing abilities. We do not know, therefore, to what degree increased emphasis on social comparison and declines in ability judgments are an inevitable consequence of cognitive development, or primarily caused by shifts in school practices that children experience as the progress through grades.

Some motivation theorists propose that the changes that typically occur when children transition to middle school are the opposite of what young adolescents need (Anderman & Maehr, 1994; Eccles et al., 1993; Eccles & Midgley, 1989; Eccles & Wigfield, 2000, in press; Wigfield et al., 1996). They point out that the increased competition and emphasis on evaluation occurs at a time when students are developing the cognitive capacity to process social comparative information and are unusually self-conscious and concerned about peer approval. Thus, social comparison information becomes particularly salient just when students are most vulnerable to its negative effects.

A common change students experience when they move from elementary to middle school is a shift from within-class ability grouping to between-class ability grouping—sometimes for individual courses (e.g., honors versus regular English), sometimes for all courses (e.g., honors versus regular track). The next section discusses the implications of such groupings on students' perceptions of their ability.

Grouping and Tracking

Grouping and tracking have important implications for students' perceptions of their competence. Students base their self-judgments to some degree on their group assignment (e.g., honors or college preparatory). Teachers worry that students who are placed in "low" groups will develop low perceptions of their competence and the accompanying feelings of shame and self-defeating behavior described above. But group assignment also limits the peers students compare themselves with on a daily basis. Thus, students in the "low" group have only relatively low-achieving classmates with whom they can compare their daily performance. This could bolster their self-confidence.

Marsh (1987) explains that students primarily use their immediate social context as a standard, which he refers to as the "big-fish-little-pond-effect." In one study, for example, he found that students rated their academic competencies relatively low in schools that enrolled relatively high-ability students (Marsh, Kong, & Hau, 2000). This suggests that students' judgments of their competencies were influenced by the performance levels of students in their own school. In another study, the competency ratings of students in gifted and talented programs declined over time, whereas the self-ratings of equally high-performing students in heterogeneously grouped classes did not (Marsh, Chessor, Craven, & Roche, 1995; see also Fuligni, Eccles, & Barbar, 1995; Hoge & Renzulli, 1993). Presumably when the gifted children were grouped with other gifted children they began to assess their competencies relative to their classmates'.

If students use the immediate social context as their frame of reference, relatively high-achieving students should have lower perceptions of their academic competence in a high-achieving group, track, or school (because they compare themselves to high-achieving peers) than they would if they were heterogeneously grouped (giving them low- as well as high-achieving peers to compare themselves to). Conversely, low-achieving students should have higher perceptions of their competence in a low group, track, or low-achieving school than in a more heterogeneous group or setting. Thus, on average, ability grouping should have a positive effect on relatively low-performing students' and a negative effect on relatively high-performing students' perceptions of competence.

Research indicating that self-ratings of ability are also based on group membership, however, suggests the opposite (Felson & Reed, 1986). To the degree that students base their perceptions of their ability on their group membership, students placed in relatively high groups should rate their academic ability higher than students placed in relatively low groups, regardless of their performance within the group. Thus, students in the high group should rate their competencies high and students in the low group should rate their competencies low.

Eder (1983) provides ethnographic evidence indicating that as early as first grade students use both frames of reference—their own performance compared to members of the immediate group and the relative standing of their group. The effect of grouping or tracking, therefore, should vary according to how salient performance differences are within and between groups. To the degree that differences among students in the immediate social context are salient, students' performance relative to other students in their group should affect their perceptions of their own ability. If differences among groups in a classroom or in a school are salient, students' group placement should affect their perceptions of competence. Consistent with this assumption, research suggests that students' self-perceptions are more affected by their group assignment when the ability groups are constituted *within* the classroom (making the groups very visible) than when the groups are constituted *between* classrooms (Reuman, 1989). Variations across studies in how grouping is implemented may explain why research on the effects of ability group placement on students' perceptions of their competence is not consistent (see Fuligni et al., 1995; Goldberg, Passow, & Justman, 1966; Weinstein, 1976).

A study by Renick and Harter (1989) demonstrated that students do not necessarily choose a frame of reference that will result in the most positive judgment. They found that most of the mainstreamed students with learning disabilities that they studied spontaneously compared their academic performance to the nondisabled students in their regular classroom. This was found even though they rated themselves higher when they were specifically asked to rate their competence relative to students in the learning disabled class they attended for part of the day. Their global self-worth ratings were also better predicted by their perceptions of their competence relative to their nondisabled classmates than by their perceptions of their competence relative to their learning disabled peers.

In addition to comparing their performance to classmates, students use a personal frame of reference to judge their competence; that is, they compare their own performance in different subject areas. Although the evidence is not entirely consistent, some studies suggest that judgments about competence in one domain are based partly on a person's perception of his or her performance in that domain relative to other domains (see Byrne, 1996; Skaalvik & Rankin, 1990, 1995; Williams & Montgomery, 1995). A student who is particularly good in math may self-rate lower in English than would be expected on the basis of her performance in English relative to classmates. An example of the use of a personal frame of reference to judge competence is the straight-"A" student who claims to be terrible in a subject in which he or she once received a grade of "B."

Taken together, the research suggests that within-class ability grouping is likely to have the most negative effects on relatively low-achieving students' perceptions of their competence. But the evidence is not overwhelming and the effects of grouping practices need to be assessed in particular contexts. Chapter 7 makes specific suggestions for minimizing the negative emotional and behavioral effects of low ability judgments.

Assessing Ability Perceptions

Most students reveal through their behavior a fair amount of information about their confidence in their ability. Behaviors like those listed in Table 6.3 are usually associated with high- and low self-confidence in ability. It is important to observe even high-achieving students because many, like Safe Sally, have very fragile confidence in their academic abilities (Kolb & Jussim, 1994; Phillips, 1984), and thus achieve less than they could (Miserandino, 1996). Dweck (2000) proposes that people who hold an entity view of their ability are particularly vulnerable to losing their self-confidence easily when they encounter difficulty.

TABLE 6.3   Behaviors Reflecting Perceptions of Ability and Self-Efficacy

Students who are self-confident in their ability to succeed:

- approach tasks eagerly
- persist in the face of failure
- seek help after they have tried on their own
- enjoy and choose challenging work
- volunteer to answer questions and provide answers when called on
- help other students
- show pride in their work

Students who lack self-confidence in their ability to succeed:

- say things like, "I can't" and "It's too hard"
- attribute success to external causes, such as help or luck
- prefer easy work that can be done without much effort
- are easily discouraged or distracted
- give up easily
- seek help without trying, or don't seek help even when they need it
- don't volunteer answers to questions
- volunteer to answer questions and then "forget" their answer
- change assignments to something they can do
- claim that the work is boring
- make excuses for not completing work
- procrastinate, then claim that they didn't have time
- "overstrive," that is, review over and over; rewrite and rewrite
- obsess; have difficulty "letting go" of work

Although observations are important, they are usually not sufficient for detecting low perceptions of ability. The same behavior can reflect different kinds of problems. A student might procrastinate because he is afraid he will fail and needs a nonability-related explanation, or simply because he finds the work uninteresting. A child may say she "can't" because she genuinely believes she can't, or because she just doesn't want to do an assignment. The claim that an assignment is "boring" is sometimes used to disguise a lack of confidence in being able to complete it. It is, therefore, useful to supplement observations with other diagnostic methods.

Researchers have measured students' perceptions of their academic competence both at a general level and for specific subject areas (see Byrne, 1996 and Keith & Bracken, 1996, for reviews of scales). Harter (1982) developed a measure for students above second grade that has been used in many studies. Students are asked to identify which of two statements applies most to them (e.g., "Some kids often forget what they learn" versus "Other kids can remember things easily"), and then to indicate whether the selected statement is "really true for me" or "sort of true for me." The 36-item measure includes three subscales which measure self-perceptions of cognitive, social, and physical competence, and a fourth general self-worth subscale. Harter and Pike (1984) developed another version of the measure for children in preschool through second grade which includes pictures and has four subscales: cognitive competence, physical competence, peer acceptance, and maternal acceptance. (See, however, Fantuzzo, McDermott, Manz, Hampton, & Burdick, 1996, for a challenge to its validity for low-income children.)

Marsh and his colleagues (Marsh, Barnes et al., 1984; Marsh & Gouvernet, 1989; Marsh & Holmes, 1990; Marsh, Smith, & Barnes, 1983) developed a measure of perceived competence that differentiates between subject areas. The 66-item Self-Description Questionnaire (SDQ) includes subscales for perceived competence in reading, mathematics, and all school subjects, as well as subscales in four nonacademic areas: physical abilities, appearance, relations with peers, and relations with parents. Research using the measure suggests the importance of assessing perceptions of competence in specific domains, even for children in the early elementary grades (e.g., Byrne & Gavin, 1996; Eccles, et al., 1993; Simpson, Licht, Wagner, & Stader, 1996; Wigfield et al., 1996).

Many researchers have asked a smaller set of questions to assess students' perceptions of their academic competence in school (in general) or in particular subjects. Table 6.4 provides the questions Eccles (1980) and her colleagues asked, usually using a 7-point Likert scale. Even a 3-item scale seems to work effectively for many research purposes.

Teachers as well as researchers can use these measures to identify students who have low perceptions of their academic ability. Teachers are often surprised to find that some high-achieving students are less confident about their abilities than would be expected from their objective performance. Students' answers to questions about their perceptions of their ability to succeed on school tasks can help explain self-defeating (e.g., not trying, giving up easily, avoiding challenge) behavior, and can help teachers to structure the curriculum and assignments in ways that maximize students' self-confidence.

Questions can be more specific than those in Table 6.4. For example, the question could be: "How good are you at multiplying fractions? writing a good paragraph? or analyzing a poem?" It is also useful to ask students whether they see improvement in their skills, whether they expect to be able to complete tasks, and how difficult they find tasks to be. Again, questions can be as general or as specific as desired. Examples of questions focused on specific tasks are given in Table 6.5.

It is useful to know whether students view ability as something that they can improve through practice and effort or as something there is little they can do to change. In addition to the questionnaire shown in Table 6.1, questions such as

TABLE 6.4   A Measure of Self-Perceptions of Academic Competence*

1. *How good are you at math?*

    not at all good   1   2   3   4   5   6   7   very good

2. *If you were to rank all the students in your math class from the worst to the best, where would you put yourself?*

    the worst   1   2   3   4   5   6   7   the best

3. *Compared to most of your other school subjects, how good are you at math?*

    much worse   1   2   3   4   5   6   7   much better

*From Eccles, 1980; note that any subject area could be substituted for "math."

those below can be used as "conversation starters" in small group or whole class discussions.

- What does it mean to be smart? (in science? in math? in English?)
- Could a student who has a lot of trouble with math ever become really good at it?
- What would a student who doesn't do well in math need to do if he or she wanted to do well?
- If a student didn't think he was as smart in science as he would like to be, is there anything he could do to become smarter? If yes, what could he do? If no, why isn't there anything he could do?

To be sure, time spent in such discussions or in completing questionnaires is time away from the regular school curriculum, but identifying problems in self-confidence can go a long way toward explaining behaviors that interfere with learning. In the long-run, teachers who know and understand their students will produce higher achievement levels than teachers who do not devote time to trying to understand the source of maladaptive behavior.

Summary

No child or adult enjoys confronting tasks that engender feelings of incompetence. And people use a variety of tactics to avoid failure, or if failure is inevitable, to avoid looking incompetent. The common tactics described by Covington and Beery (1976) may achieve the short-term goal of avoiding the implications of failure, but in the long-term they undermine learning and performance.

TABLE 6.5   **Sample Questions About Improvement, Expectations, and Task Difficulty***

1. Are you better now than you were when you started doing this kind of work? (Circle one response.)

not much better	a little bit better	quite a bit better	a lot better

2. Do you feel confident that you could do harder problems or do you need practice and help on these kinds of problems? (Circle one response.)

I'll never be able to do this	I still need help on these	I need a little more practice on these	I can do harder problems now

3. Do you think you will be able to do this assignment well? (Circle one number.)

1	2	3	4	5	6	7

I definitely won't do it well	I'll do OK	I definitely will do it well

4. Look at your math work for today. How hard do you think this work will be for you? (Circle one number.)

1	2	3	4	5	6	7

really easy	medium hard	really hard

*Adapted from MacGyvers & Stipek, *A Teacher's Guide to Assessing and Enhancing Students' Motivation*, unpublished manuscript.

Self-confidence in being able to succeed (high self-efficacy) is an essential ingredient for effective learning. Without this, students will not engage in productive learning behaviors. A general concept of oneself as being academically competent is extremely helpful, although the implications of low competence judgments vary, depending on one's definition of ability—as a stable trait or as something that can be improved through practice and effort—and depending on the social context of the classroom. The next chapter describes instructional strategies that will help maintain self-confidence in students.

TABLE 6.6   Summary of Terms

Term	Definition
Entity concept of ability	Ability is a stable trait of which individuals have a fixed amount and which is only moderately affected by practice and effort
Instrumental–incremental concept of ability	Ability, like a skill, can be increased through practice and effort
Self-worth	People's appraisal of their own value
Impression management	Making statements or engaging in behaviors with the explicit goal of influencing others' judgments of oneself

7 Maintaining Positive Achievement-Related Beliefs

Students' beliefs affect their behavior regardless of their validity. Helpless Hannah believes she is incompetent and she expects to fail. She avoids achievement situations when she can, and when she is required to do a task—even one that she could do—she works on it halfheartedly and gives up easily. Alienated Al gave up on the idea of succeeding in school a long time ago and consequently rarely exerts any effort. Defensive Dave is not totally convinced he is incompetent, but neither is he confident that he will succeed. He therefore devotes more of his energies to avoiding looking stupid than to completing school tasks. Safe Sally harbors doubts about her ability to succeed in challenging situations and, to avoid the remote possibility of failure, never tests the limits of her skills.

Contrast these four students who have negative beliefs about their competencies to students who are confident that they can perform at the level required to receive the rewards that they seek. Students with more adaptive beliefs are likely to approach academic tasks eagerly, exert effort in order to increase mastery, focus their attention on strategies to solve the problem at hand, persist on tasks when they do not immediately succeed, and experience positive emotions in achievement contexts.

Previous chapters have commented on the practical implications of research on achievement-related beliefs. This chapter is devoted to practical suggestions for fostering the positive beliefs that lead to productive learning behaviors and minimizing the negative beliefs that inhibit learning.

First, however, it is important to be clear about our goal; we do not want to try to fool all students into thinking that they are the most competent in the class. By definition, half of the students in a class are below average relative to any given skill. Regardless of what the teacher does, students become aware of differences between their classmates' skills and performance and their own by the time they reach second grade. Some students will inevitably perceive themselves as less skillful than others in particular domains.

These comparative self-assessments are not altogether harmful. Students need to know their strengths and weaknesses to make wise decisions about where to invest effort and about long-term educational and professional plans. A realistic appraisal of one's competencies does not necessarily result in the maladaptive avoidance, defensive, and helpless behaviors described in Chapters 5 and 6. However, the consequences of such appraisals depend on a student's inter-pretation. A student's perceptions of having relatively low skills is most damag-ing, for example, if the student believes that she can't do the work she is given, or if she believes that the teacher's respect depends upon her demonstration of high skills. Teachers may not be able to eliminate social comparison, but they do have considerable impact over the salience and meaning of students' judgments about their competencies and over their expectations for success on particular tasks.

A realistic and worthy goal, therefore, is for all students to believe that they are efficacious—that they have the competence required to learn and to complete the tasks they encounter in school. A second, related set of goals is for all students to believe that they have personal control over their academic outcomes and to take pride in their accomplishments. A third goal, perhaps necessary for achiev-ing the first two, is for students to have an incremental concept of academic ability—the belief that ability is something that can be improved through practice and effort. Fortunately, achievement motivation researchers have provided many clues on how to accomplish these goals.

The first section of this chapter translates theory and research on achieve-ment motivation into specific, concrete recommendations for classroom practice. Some of these recommendations are inferred from research findings on studies of achievement-related beliefs; others have been tested directly by teachers and re-searchers in real classrooms. This section is followed by a description of two com-prehensive programs designed to address motivational problems related to self-defeating achievement-related beliefs: mastery learning and cooperative in-centive structures.

Effective Classroom Practice

This section is organized into different aspects of practices that affect achievement-related beliefs: tasks, goals, evaluation, help, direct statements, and classroom structure.

Tasks/Assignments

There are many qualities of tasks that need to be considered by teachers to pro-mote maximum student learning. The focus here is on qualities that are likely to affect students' beliefs about their competencies and their expectations for success.

1. Make sure the task is clear.   Children do not believe they have control over their learning or performance when the requirements of a task are unclear. Make sure students know what they are expected to do and where they can find the resources and materials they need to complete tasks. Let them know when they will have to work, and how much time they must devote to the task, and when the task need to be completed. To promote efficiency (and a sense of personal control), make sure materials are easily accessible and kept in the appropriate places. Avoid changing the rules midstream, unless there is a good reason to do so.

2. Give tasks that are challenging but achievable for *all* students.   Easy tasks do not produce feelings of competence because no improvement in skill level or understanding is required to achieve success. Attempts to complete very difficult tasks usually do not result in success; when they do, the amount of effort required diminishes the value of the accomplishment. Tasks of intermediate difficulty, those that allow students to experience improvement in their skills, are most effective in producing feelings of competence.

a. Vary the difficulty of tasks among students according to their skill levels.   A task that one student finds easy may be impossibly difficult for another. Thus, providing tasks that are appropriately challenging for every student in a group of students whose skills vary requires individualizing the complexity of the tasks. Teachers are sometimes reluctant to vary tasks because they are concerned that students will feel embarrassed about doing assignments that are easier than those completed by their peers. To the contrary, completing assignments and being able to take personal responsibility for success are far more likely to encourage self-confidence than repeatedly failing to do the more difficult tasks that classmates are given. Moreover, all students can take pride in their success if the teacher creates a climate in which hard work and success are rewarded at whatever level each student is working.

b. Give tasks that can be completed at different levels.   Teachers can vary the difficulty of the task, in part, by providing tasks that can be completed at different levels and by conveying different expectations. The same assignment—to write a book report, a poem, or a story—can be made to be equally challenging for all students. What is important is for students to understand that they are expected to complete the task at a level that requires real effort and persistence and will thus help them develop their skills. Differential expectations can be conveyed by guiding students' choices (e.g., of the book selected to report on), and by making direct statements and evaluation ("This is technically correct, but you could have made a more compelling argument").

Different skill levels can often be accommodated in the same task. Consider a math assignment in which all children are asked to graph data based on a student poll. The teacher might ask questions, in either a whole class or a small group format, that require analysis at different levels. Some students might be asked to report differences in data sets (e.g., between boys' and girls' responses), requiring them only to interpret the graph; others might be asked questions that require manipulations of the information, such as translating frequencies into percentages. The task, in this case, looks the same for all students, but the actual level of mathematical problem-solving required is adjusted to each student's current mathematical skills.

The same math problem can also be approached in different ways by students who vary in skill level. For example, some students may be able to solve a problem with only one strategy; others will use several different strategies. Some students may analyze the symbolic meaning of a poem while other students describe the visual images created. Thus teachers can engage students at an appropriate level of challenge without having to create entirely different tasks for each student.

    c. **Make sure that the highest achievers are challenged.**   Teachers usually worry more about motivating the relatively low-achieving students than about challenging the high-achieving students. But a steady diet of success does not prepare students to deal with the difficulties they will inevitably encounter in future educational contexts and in life. Many high-achieving students who enter a new academic arena—by taking an unusually difficult course, by moving from the regular to the honors track in high school, or from advancing from high school to college or college to graduate school—are ill prepared for the challenges they face. Like Safe Sally, they have always succeeded, often without much effort, so their self-confidence is fragile and collapses easily.

3. **Organize assignments to provide frequent opportunities for students to see their skill level increase.**   In addition to being moderately challenging, tasks need to provide opportunities for regular feedback which indicates improvement in skill or understanding. Initial failures in developing a skill are inevitable, but a long period of engagement or a series of failures without this feedback undermines feelings of competency.

    a. **Order problems and assignments by difficulty level** to provide students with a sense of increasing mastery.

    b. **Break down difficult tasks into subunits** to make sure that students receive positive competence feedback before they become discouraged or concerned about the direction in which they are headed. Some children may need smaller units and more frequent positive feedback than others.

Goals

Students are less likely to become discouraged during long-term tasks when they set short-term goals. An appropriate level of challenge can be achieved by adjusting goals for students with varying skill levels.

    1. **Create short-term (proximal) goals.**   Although the long-range or **distal goal** is important for students to keep in mind, progress toward a long-term goal is sometimes difficult for students to gauge. **Proximal goals** can raise self-efficacy simply by making a task appear more manageable, and they can also enhance perceptions of competence by giving continual feedback that conveys a sense of mastery (Harackiewicz, Manderlink, & Sansone, 1992; Schunk, 1984a, 1990, 1991).

    A study by Bandura and Schunk (1981) demonstrates the advantage of proximal goals. They gave elementary-school-age children seven sets of subtraction problems to work on over seven sessions. Children were told either to complete one set each session (proximal goal), to complete all seven sets by the end of the seventh session (distal goal), or simply to work on the problems with no mention of goals. The proximal goal situation led to the highest self-efficacy and subtraction skill. Students in the distal goal condition performed no better than did students who were given no specific goal.

Some students are overwhelmed by large, multidimensional projects. These projects can easily be broken down into sections with independent due dates and feedback. If students focus their attention on the section at hand, the task will seem more manageable. As children develop skills for planning and organizing, they should take more responsibility and require less assistance from the teacher in dividing tasks up into smaller units.

2. Vary goals among students. While it may be realistic for some students to aspire to fill in a multiplication grid in 2 minutes, a 4-minute goal may be equally challenging for others. However, differential goal setting will work only if appropriately challenging goals are valued and reinforced, regardless of how one student's goals compare to other students' goals or achievements. Thus, completing the multiplication grid in 2 or 4 minutes needs to be reinforced in the same way, if these two goals represent equal levels of challenge for the students who set them. Research has shown that goal-setting has the best effects on performance when goals are specific (quantifiable or framed in terms of specific action as opposed to general terms, such as "I'll do my best"), and when feedback provides information on performance relative to the goal (Locke, Shaw, Saari, & Latham, 1981).

3. Engage students in personal goal-setting. Students sometimes undermine their own self-confidence by aspiring to unrealistic goals and failing to meet them; or they set goals that are too easily reached and do not produce any learning. Teaching students to set goals is important because they will need this skill when their achievement pursuits are not monitored on a day-to-day basis. Personal goal-setting has also been shown to raise self-efficacy (Schunk, 1985a) and enhance performance (Hom & Murphy, 1985).

There is evidence that even young children can be taught to set realistic goals. Gaa (1973) demonstrated that first and second graders can develop skills in setting appropriate goals for themselves—ones that are challenging but likely to be achieved. Some of the children in the study met weekly with an experimenter to set goals for the next week and discuss achievements relative to the previous week's goals. These children subsequently set fewer and more appropriate goals at the end of the intervention, and attained a higher level of reading achievement than children without experience setting and reviewing personal goals. Having students graph their goals and accomplishments can also help them develop skills in setting appropriate goals. (See also Tollefson, Tracy, Johnsen, Farmer, & Buenning, 1984.)

a. Provide incentives for setting challenging goals. Students will sometimes take the easy route when there is no incentive to set challenging goals. This was demonstrated in a study by Clifford (1988). She provided fourth, fifth, and sixth graders with items varying in difficulty from the Iowa Tests of Basic Skills in mathematics, spelling, and vocabulary. When told to select any six problems in each domain, students chose problems considerably below their ability level. The low-risk-taking tendency increased markedly with each grade level, suggesting that as children get older they become less inclined to seek challenging academic tasks.

Students can be offered incentives to set more challenging goals. For example, more points can be given for more difficult math problems or spelling words. The overly ambitious student quickly learns that attempting words that are too difficult results in lots of "0's," while choosing words that are too easy results in a relatively low score. The number of points are maximized by selecting the most difficult words that the student is likely to spell correctly. The effects of such a system were documented by Clifford (1991) on her problem choice task, described above. When points were linked to the difficulty level of problems (that is, more points were given for more difficult problems), children were more willing to take risks.

Evaluation

External evaluation is often necessary for students to increase their competence level. Although they may be able to determine the correctness of their spelling words by consulting a master list, they usually need assistance in judging whether the imagery in their writing is more vivid or their argument more persuasive than previously. Teachers' feedback can direct future efforts as well as point out newly developing competencies. Knowing what they need to do to improve gives students a perception of control over achievement outcomes which, as research described in Chapter 5 indicates, enhances effort and learning. However, some kinds of evaluation are more likely to accomplish these goals than are others.

1. **Make evaluation criteria clear.**   Students do not feel in control of their academic outcomes when the criteria for evaluation are vague. Rubrics are often helpful. In addition to clarifying the criteria and standards for evaluation, rubrics help students make independent judgments of their work and determine on their own when they need to make corrections or revisions.

2. **Give students different ways to demonstrate what they know.**   When students are given diverse opportunities to demonstrate their understanding, teachers gain a more complete picture of their skills and students have more chances to demonstrate competence. Understanding of mathematical concepts, for example, might be expressed by finding correct solutions to a calculation problem, explaining why a strategy for solving a problem is efficient, representing the problem and solution in a drawing, or assisting another student.

3. **Point out what is good, right, or shows improvement.**   Students need external validation of the competencies they have developed, as well as information on how to improve. This is particularly true on assignments that students are

likely to have difficulty evaluating, such as a task that is new for them (e.g., writing a book report or writing up a science experiment for the first time). Commending what is good or shows improvement lets students know that they are developing competencies.

4. **Provide clear, specific, and informative feedback.**
   a. **Avoid global, uninformative comments.** "Nice job," "well done," or "good," on the cover of a paper doesn't give a student the message that her work met clear, well-defined standards. Students do not always consider such global feedback credible (Damon, 1995).
   b. **Focus on the behavior, not the person.** Dweck (2000) and her colleagues have found that person-praise (as well as criticism) promotes an entity theory of ability and engenders concerns about demonstrating ability. Accordingly, it makes children more vulnerable to losing their self-confidence and becoming helpless when they encounter difficulty (see also Kamins & Dweck, 1999; Mueller & Dweck, 1998). This line of research suggests that teachers should avoid comments that focus on personal traits, such as, "You are so smart." It is better to focus attention on the students' effort and behavior ("You used some really creative strategies"), or their level of mastery ("You really understand this well").
   c. **Provide written, substantive comments when possible.** Specific commendations (e.g., "The paper is well organized"; "The transitions are smooth"; "Your strategy is creative and shows that you really understand the math ideas"; "Your summary of the results of the experiment is clear and concise") provide clear, credible evidence of competence. Substantive and specific feedback also helps students develop criteria that they can use to assess their own skills and identify their strengths and weaknesses.

5. **Base rewards (including high grades) on achieving a clearly-defined standard or set of criteria or on personal improvement.** Some of the decline in enthusiasm for schoolwork in junior high or middle school is probably caused by the stricter and more social comparison-based standards for grading. The decline in grades caused by the competitive standard lowers some students self-confidence and, consequently, their interest in learning. Indeed, the magnitude of a drop in grades following the transition into junior high or middle school is a major predictor of leaving school prior to graduation (see Eccles & Roeser, 1999).

Ironically, a competitive standard for rewards does not necessarily build self-confidence in the "winners." This is because some high-achieving students perform at a high level, relative to classmates, without much effort and without developing their competencies. As mentioned above, the perceptions of high competence developed by students who are constantly rewarded for their schoolwork, regardless of their effort, are very fragile and fall apart in a situation in which success or rewards do not come easily.[1]

---

[1]This "unraveling" of self-confidence is common among my graduate students who previously received perfect marks without having to work very hard. I have witnessed their self-confidence evaporate with the first critical feedback they receive on their work.

Rewards, including good grades, stars, happy faces, or privileges should therefore be based on a set of clearly-defined criteria or standards, or on improvement, rather than on relative performance.

6. Give students multiple opportunities to achieve a high grade.   Teachers can allow students to keep working (within some reasonable limit) until they have achieved a satisfactory level of mastery or performance. One teacher I interviewed developed the simple but ingenious method of marking incorrect responses on written assignments with a dot. Students continued to work on assignments until all answers were correct. Dots could easily be changed to check marks, which she used to indicate correctness without leaving any evidence of the original error. Thus errors were treated as a natural step in mastering new material. Students can also be given opportunities to rewrite papers or redo assignments to achieve a higher grade or demonstrate a higher level of mastery.

Providing substantive feedback en route to task completion is also helpful. This is a critical feature of the current popular approaches to teaching writing. Students write several drafts of their papers, concentrating on correcting different aspects of the writing (e.g., getting thoughts on paper, developing and organizing ideas, mechanics) at different points in the process. Feedback along the way provides useful corrective information and gives students a feeling of control over their performance outcomes.

7. Teach students to celebrate their classmates' successes, at whatever level they occur.   The teacher is not the only evaluator in a classroom. Classmates' reactions can be just as important, and peers can undermine the teacher's efforts to reinforce effort and improvement.

The values of the teacher, therefore, need to be internalized by every student in the classroom. This will occur, to some degree, if the teacher models appropriate behaviors. But students can also be instructed to support the teacher's goals. They can, for example, be encouraged to applaud their classmates for significant improvements, regardless of the student's relative skill level. This conveys to students that improvement, which is genuinely available to all students, is valued by everyone, and it gives students an example of concrete behaviors that communicate this value to each other.[2]

8. Minimize public evaluations.   Wall charts and other public displays of students' performance may enhance the motivation of a very small group of top performers, but they can threaten and discourage other students, especially if evaluative criteria are uniform despite varying skill levels among students. For all

---

[2]A teacher once shared with me a story about a child with learning disabilities who was reading far below the level of most of his third-grade classmates. When he announced that he had read his first chapter book, his classmates secretly asked the teacher to buy a copy that they could all sign and present to him. They wanted to celebrate this milestone with him, even though most of them had passed it long ago. This teacher had clearly created a "community of learners."

students, these public displays orient attention to relative performance rather than personal improvement or mastery.[3]

a. If evaluation is public, it must be a "fair contest." All students must have a realistic chance of "winning." This can be done by charting progress toward achieving goals that are adjusted to be realistically attainable by all students. I observed an example of this in a classroom in which paper boats with students' names on them "raced" across a blue sheet of paper on the bulletin board. The position of each student's boat was determined by how much progress that student had made in mastering an increasingly difficult set of spelling words. All students began at the same point on the sheet of blue paper, even though their actual beginning level of mastery varied considerably. Consequently, the student who won the race did not necessarily attain the highest level of mastery. Rather, the winner made the most progress from his or her personal starting point.

b. Have students keep personal progress records. A better method than public displays for helping students monitor their progress is to have them keep records, including charts, in their desks. A personal chart, unlike a class chart, focuses students' attention on their own improvement and mastery rather than on how they compare to classmates. It is also useful for communicating student goals and progress with parents.

c. Give students an opportunity for private interactions with the teacher. A classroom structure in which students' interactions with the teacher are either private or in small groups can also minimize the public quality of performance and evaluative feedback and therefore reduce the risk of embarrassment.

9. Teach students to evaluate their own work. An authority figure is not always available to give students feedback on their developing competencies. Students should be encouraged *and taught* to evaluate their own work and to monitor their own progress. This provides them with more opportunities to experience a sense of developing competencies as well as strategies to guide their own efforts to improve. Self-evaluations also have been shown to promote self-regulation skills (Perry, 1998).

a. Encourage students to use their own judgment. When students ask for feedback (e.g., "Is this good?"), encourage them to venture a judgment on their own (e.g., "What do you think, does it look good to you?") and to consider strategies for making a personal judgment (e.g., "Do you have any

---

[3]I experienced the negative effects of public displays of performance outcomes during a year in a French university. It was standard procedure to hand back papers and exams in the order of students' scores. The assumption, I am sure, was that the humiliation of being among the last to receive one's paper would foster future effort to avoid such humiliation. What I observed instead, in other students and myself, was withdrawal and discouragement. My solution, contrary to the instructor's intentions, was to miss class on the day that the next exam was returned.

ideas about how you could figure out whether it is good, besides asking me?").

b. Give students opportunities to check their own work.   Students can check their own solutions to math problems or the accuracy of their spelling words against an answer sheet or by making comparisons with a classmate. Asking classmates to resolve discrepancies provides opportunities for collaborative learning. Students can check facts by consulting a book or using the Internet.

c. Give students explicit instructions on how to evaluate their own work.   Students learn criteria for making independent judgments in part by receiving specific, substantive feedback on their work from teachers. They also need explicit instructions and reminders of evaluation techniques. Models of good work can be useful, although they need to be used carefully to minimize the potential for students developing an unnecessarily narrow view of a good product. As mentioned above, rubrics are often helpful, such as those used to assess writing samples in standardized tests.

d. Link evaluation criteria directly to instruction.   Students will not be able to assess their own progress (and thus experience a sense of mastery) if the evaluation criteria they are given are not aligned with instruction. If, for example, math instruction is focused on providing clear and persuasive explanations for solutions, students should be given a set of criteria and strategies for determining whether an explanation is clear and persuasive. If writing instruction is focused on teaching students to use paragraphs, they should be given a set of criteria for writing a good paragraph.

Help

When students work on challenging tasks they will inevitably encounter difficulties and need help. Research suggests that the students who need help the most are typically the least likely to ask for it (see Newman, 2000; Newman & Schwager, 1992), and students become less likely to seek help as they grow older. Good, Slavings, Harel, and Emerson (1987) found that low-achieving students were fairly active participants in the classroom until the end of third grade, but subsequently became relatively passive. The decline is most likely explained by age-related increases in students' desire to avoid looking incompetent (see Chapter 6). There are, however, strategies for getting students to seek help when they need it.

1. Make it safe to ask for help.   Students are more likely to ask for help in a classroom that promotes learning and mastery than in a classroom that focuses on performance and competition (Butler & Neuman, 1995; Newman, 1998b, 2000). When students construe their need for help as evidence of low ability and expect to incur negative judgments, they are not likely to ask for help (Ryan & Pintrich, 1997).

Accordingly, students should be taught that negative reactions to classmates' questions will not be tolerated, and teachers should respond respectfully and helpfully to students' questions and requests for help. Overly-dependent students can be encouraged to make an independent effort, but gently, with an expression of confidence that they can succeed on their own and a promise to help later if they are still having difficulty after making a genuine effort.

Some studies suggest that students feel more comfortable asking for help in small group than in large group contexts (Newman, 1998a, 2000). Small groups may be particularly helpful to girls for mathematics. This is suggested by a study in which many girls claimed to be concerned that the teacher might think they were "dumb" if they ask questions in math classes (Newman & Goldin, 1990).

2. Encourage students to seek help. Sometimes teachers need to remind students that having difficulty is not a reason for fear or embarrassment—that all students, even teachers, need to ask questions and seek assistance when they are developing new skills. Soliciting questions and checking for confusion and misunderstandings on a regular basis also helps. And be patient and thorough when responding to requests. Research has found that students are more likely to ask for instrumental help (e.g., hints, but not the answer) when they perceive the teacher to support help-seeking (e.g., the teacher takes time to explain something when asked; Arbreton, 1998).

a. Model help seeking. Having the teacher admit ignorance and use resources (including students in the class) to answer questions or obtain information is a powerful way to convey to students that it is OK not to know everything. This is an effective strategy for creating a classroom community of learners, which includes adults as well as children.

3. Give no more assistance than necessary. Some kinds of help are more likely to foster feelings of mastery and competence than others. Students need to be encouraged to seek the kind of assistance that helps them understand and allows them to work independently. Teachers need to recognize the difference between a real need for help and a failure to try. When help is given, it should be limited to what is really needed. The more students can accomplish on their own the better, both in terms of their learning and their perceptions of mastery.

a. Teach students how to use classroom resources to answer their questions. There are many resources in classrooms—dictionaries, encyclopedias, books, measurement instruments, charts, newspapers, and now the Internet. Students may not think of using these resources, or they may not know how to use them. Encouraging them to use classroom resources reinforces the message that they should do what they can on their own before they ask for help.

4. Encourage students to use peers for assistance. In many classrooms there are implicit norms which discourage seeking help from peers. Sometimes, getting help from a peer is even construed as cheating (Nelson-le Gall & Resnick, 1998). Such norms deny students who need assistance access to an important resource. Promoting norms of helping also liberates teachers from serving as the sole source of information and assistance and gives them more time to engage in instruction. Students also benefit from providing assistance to each other.

Explaining a task to others helps them consolidate their own understanding and develop self-confidence, empathy, and teaching skills. It also creates a climate of collaboration and mutual support—a community of learners rather than a group of competitors.

    a. Teach students *how* to give help. I observed a first-grade classroom in which the children were generous with their help, but they had only one strategy—to give the answer. These young children were so helpful, they often wrote the answers in their classmates' workbooks. Even older students need to be taught how to give instrumental help—help that fosters skills and independence rather than dependence in the help-seeker. This can be done in part by modeling effective help-giving strategies, but it usually requires some explicit instructions and monitoring.

Direct Statements

Direct statements to students about their effort and competencies can affect students' own judgments about their competencies. In general, the goal is to get students to believe that they are able to succeed if they try, and that when they fail it is because they were not trying hard enough, they need more practice, or they didn't use an appropriate strategy. Results of studies suggest the value of the following practices.

    1. Attribute "failure" to low effort or an ineffective strategy. By explicitly attributing a failure to low effort (e.g., "I don't think you were really concentrating") the teacher communicates a belief in the student's ability to succeed with sufficient effort (Schunk, 1982, 1984a, 1984b). A statement suggesting that a student performed poorly even though she tried hard (e.g., "Don't worry, you did the best you could do") may seem sympathetic, but it can inadvertently reinforce a student's doubts about her ability.

    Several researchers prefer strategy over effort attributions (Hattie, Biggs, & Purdie, 1996; Pressley, El-Dinary, Marks, Brown, & Stein, 1992). Students who do poorly despite considerable effort can be confused and discouraged if the teacher suggests that their poor performance is caused by poor effort. Commenting on the strategy they used, or suggesting that they try a different strategy, provides recognition for their effort and conveys a positive and sometimes constructive suggestion. Schunk (1989) points out that encouraging the use of different strategies can also enhance feelings of self-efficacy by giving students a perception of control over outcomes. The usefulness of strategy attributions is suggested by studies indicating that effective adult tutors are more likely to attribute outcomes to strategy than to effort (Lepper, Aspinwall, Mumme, & Chabay, 1990).

    Several researchers have demonstrated, through **attribution retraining** programs, that students' self-defeating attributions can be changed into more adaptive ones by making the kinds of explicit statements suggested above. (See Forsterling, 1985; Robertson, 2000, for reviews.) Interventions designed to promote effort attributions among children with learning disabilities have even increased intrinsic motivation (Dev, 1998).

In perhaps the first attribution retraining study, Dweck (1975) showed that the belief that failure is caused by low ability can be changed into the belief that failure is caused by low effort or insufficient practice. She identified a number of extremely "helpless" elementary school-age children. These "helpless" children showed the attributional pattern associated with learned helplessness; compared to nonhelpless children, helpless children took less personal responsibility for outcomes and tended to place less emphasis on the role of effort. Moreover, the performance of the helpless children following failure was severely impaired. During 25 daily training sessions, half of these children were given a heavy dose of success. The other half of the children received attribution retraining; they had considerable success, but several failure trials were programmed each day. When failure occurred, the experimenter explicitly commented to the child that the failure was due to a lack of effort. At the end of the training the children in the attribution retraining condition, but not the children in the success-only condition, attributed outcomes more to effort than they had previous to the training. Attribution-retraining children also showed improvement in their response to failure; they persisted, using appropriate problem-solving strategies, rather than giving up. In contrast, children who had been in the success-only treatment showed no improvement in their response to failure. Some of these children even showed a tendency to react somewhat more adversely to failure than they had before the start of the treatment. This study suggests that success experiences may not be sufficient to get a student like Helpless Hannah to try harder; instead, the teacher needs to change the students' perceptions of the cause of failure.

Teachers need to know their students' skills and monitor their behavior well to make attributions that are fair, appropriate, and constructive. An effort attribution is not fair and can be discouraging for a student who has been struggling or even for a student who doesn't try because of lacking the prerequisite skills to complete a task. Direct messages to students about the cause of their successes or failures, therefore, need to be based on close and careful observations of their behavior and skills. When effort is not effective after a reasonable amount of time, the teacher needs to acknowledge the student's efforts and adjust the task or the student's goals, so that effort will result in success.

    a. **Model adaptive attributions.** Teacher modeling can also be used to influence students' attributions. For example, in a study designed to improve learning strategies among learning-disabled students, the teacher purposefully made mistakes while giving instructions and then made explicit attribution statements focusing on effort or strategy attributions: e.g., "I need to try and use a different strategy" (Borkowski, Weyhing, & Carr, 1988).

2. Attribute success to effort and competence. Schunk suggests that teachers can also enhance self-confidence by attributing success to ability. Attributing success to external causes (e.g., "You were lucky you solved that one") denies students personal responsibility and an opportunity to experience pride, and will undermine their perceptions of their ability.

Schunk cautions against making effort attributions when success occurs, because this can actually undermine feelings of competence. This was demonstrated in a study in which, while working on subtraction problems, third graders were told either, "You're good at this," or "You've been working hard," or both (Schunk, 1983). The children who received only the ability attribution judged themselves the most efficacious and correctly solved the highest number of posttest problems. (See also Schunk, 1984b). Schunk suggests that attributing success to effort reduces students' perceptions of their ability because they believe that success requiring high effort indicates lower ability than success achieved without effort.

In a study of young children who had learning disabilities, tutors (who also had learning disabilities) made effort, strategy, and ability attributions (Yasutake, Bryan, & Dohrn, 1996). Tutors were trained to say, for example: "Try to sound out the word," or "You're getting smart because of your hard work." Both the tutors and the tutees showed increases in their perceptions of their competence as a consequence of the intervention.

Schunk's findings notwithstanding, teachers should not give successful students the impression that effort is not necessary to achieve success. Optimal motivation on any task occurs when students believe they are able to achieve success, but some effort is also required. No learning will result from success that is achieved without effort. Consequently, while teachers need to provide a learning context in which students feel competent, students must not perceive ability alone to be sufficient.

Classroom Structure

In addition to feedback directed toward individual students, there are many aspects of the classroom environment that influence students' conceptions of ability and their evaluations of their own and their classmates' ability. Two important elements of classroom structure are the salience of students' relative performance and the degree of stability in students' performance levels across tasks and over time.

1. Differentiate tasks among students and over time. Rosenholtz and Simpson (1984a, 1984b) have demonstrated that the degree to which tasks are differentiated across students and over time affects students' judgments about their own ability relative to classmates, as well as the way they conceptualize ability (see also Simpson & Rosenholtz, 1986; Rosenholtz & Rosenholtz, 1981). They claim that an **undifferentiated academic task structure**—in which all students work on the same task, using the same materials, requiring the same responses—promotes social comparison and results in students performing at the same relative level over time. Bossert (1979) points out that teachers in classrooms with undifferentiated task structures, referred to as **unidimensional classrooms,** often face managerial problems with high achievers who finish work earlier than others. Students who know they can finish regular assignments in less than the allotted time may fool around while they are working on the assignment, causing additional discipline problems.

In a **differentiated task structure,** on a given day different students may work on several different kinds of tasks, and the types of tasks vary from day to day. The differentiated task structure used in **multidimensional classrooms** makes social comparison more difficult and results in less consistency in students' relative performance from task to task and from day to day.

Rosenholtz and Simpson (1984a) explain that task structure influences classroom processes in several mutually reinforcing ways. It influences: (1) the distribution of actual performances, (2) the salience and quantity of information available to students concerning their own and their classmates' performance, (3) the comparability of information about self and others, and (4) the consistency of information concerning any one type of performance for any one student. These consequences, in turn, affect how students form perceptions of their own and their classmates' ability.

Research findings support their analysis. Pepitone (1972) demonstrated experimentally that uniformity in curricular tasks results in greater social comparison behavior ("I got fewer wrong than you") than differentiation in tasks. Studies also show that both teachers' evaluations of students and students' evaluations of themselves and their peers are more stratified (that is, there is greater dispersion in judgments) in unidimensional than in multidimensional classrooms (Rosenholtz & Rosenholtz, 1981; Rosenholtz & Simpson, 1984b), and children's self-perceptions in unidimensional classrooms correspond more strongly to teacher evaluations (Rosenholtz & Rosenholtz, 1981). Students also tend to agree with each other on their own and their classmates' relative ability in unidimensional classrooms (Rosenholtz & Simpson, 1984a). In brief, greater agreement exists between all actors in their ratings of particular students in unidimensional classrooms than occurs in multidimensional classrooms. Thus, students develop a perception of ability as stratified, measurable, and consensual—as something that has an objective reality and that can be perceived by others. This concept of ability is similar to IQ, and to what Dweck (1986) refers to as an "entity" theory (Chapter 6).

2. Point out "within-student" variation in skill levels.   When students' performance varies from task to task, teachers have the opportunity to convey to them the idea that skill development is incremental and domain-specific. They can, for example, point out to students who are having difficulty in one domain that they are doing well in another, and that with effort and persistence they will catch on in their relatively weak domain as well.

3. When instructing in a whole-class format, involve *all* students productively.   Whole-class instruction can make relative performance levels very salient. Right and wrong answers automatically become both public and comparable. It is not unusual for a few self-confident students to dominate large-group instructional periods, while children lacking in self-confidence and fearful of humiliating themselves refuse to participate.

Group instruction, whether involving a small group or the whole class, does not need to have negative effects. Sensitive teachers who integrate wrong answers into their instruction, thus giving every student a feeling of having made a constructive contribution, can engage the participation of all children and avoid making students feel embarrassed for giving wrong answers. Thus, rather than turn to another student when a student gives a wrong answer ("Does anyone know the right answer?"), pursue the question, rephrasing it or perhaps simplifying it until the student shows some understanding.

4. Use "ability grouping" flexibly and temporarily to address specific skill needs.   Studies indicate that children prefer mixed ability groups over homogeneous grouping (Elbaum, Schumm, & Vaughn, 1997; Vaughn, Schumm, Klingner, & Samuell, 1995). As explained in Chapter 6, research on the effects of skill-based grouping on students' perceptions of their competencies, however, is mixed (Fuligni et al., 1995; Mosteller, Light, & Sachs, 1996; Slavin, 1993); it is likely that *how* skill-based grouping is implemented is at least as important as *whether* it is implemented. The following recommendations, in addition to those discussed in Chapter 13, should minimize potential negative effects.

    a. **Create temporary instructional groups** designed to assist students in developing and practicing particular skills. If only a few students in the class have not understood the correct use of quotation marks, bring them together for a few days to work specifically on that skill. The same strategy might be used for a group of students who have not learned to scan information on the Internet, or who don't understand place value, or who are having difficulty reading a map. Forming temporary groups is also useful for meeting the needs of students who are further along in the curriculum than most of their classmates. For example, they may collaborate, using computer software or the Internet to enrich their regular classroom curriculum or they may read more broadly on a topic than other students and then share what they have learned with each other or with the whole class.

    b. **Allow students to volunteer for skill-based groups.**   In a classroom in which students feel safe exposing their ignorance and asking for help, skill-based groups can be made voluntary. Teachers can announce that they will provide instruction related to a particular skill for any student who needs it or would benefit from it. If the students who need the intervention do not volunteer, the teacher should reflect on whether the climate and expectations in the classroom make it risky for students to admit having difficulty or needing extra help. Teachers can also privately invite particular children who need the opportunity to work on the particular skill. All students should also be allowed to volunteer for accelerated work. Teachers are often surprised to find that they have underestimated a student's capacity, and if the activity turns out to be too difficult for some students, they will most likely drop out on their own.

c. **Avoid concentrating behavioral problems in groups.**   Children who have the poorest skills are often the most difficult to manage. Try to spread out children who have discipline problems so that no single group is likely to have substantial time taken away from instruction while the teacher deals with discipline.

5. Convey the value of different kinds of skills.   Teachers should also give students opportunities to publicly demonstrate competence in many different domains, and they should express positive values for good performance in a variety of areas, including those that are not typically part of school requirements (e.g., playing an instrument, athletics, rapping, and drawing).

6. Give relatively poor-performing students the role of "expert."   Research by Cohen and Lotan (1995, 1997) has shown that the status and participation of relatively low-performing students can be raised by calling other students' attention to their particular skills or talents, and recommending that other students use them as resources. Students who have relatively low skills can also build self-confidence (and strengthen their skills) by being given opportunities to tutor younger children (see, for example, Cochran, Feng, Cartledge, & Hamilton, 1993).

Comprehensive Programs

Some educational researchers have developed and tested the effectiveness of comprehensive programs designed to foster positive achievement-related beliefs and maximize learning. **Mastery learning programs** and **cooperative learning programs** have the most extensive research bases and are described here as examples of integrated, packaged programs that teachers could choose to implement. Even a carefully developed program, however, can be delivered in different ways. The principles described above are important to keep in mind if such a program is implemented, and adjustments often need to be made to make a program work in a particular setting with a particular group of students.

Mastery Learning Programs

Evaluation based on mastery is a central component of the various mastery-based educational programs that have been developed by Bloom (1981) and others (see Guskey, 1997). Bloom's model has been used in hundreds of classrooms throughout the United States and in as many as 20 other countries. Consequently, many variations of the original model exist. The fundamental assumption underlying mastery learning models is that all students can learn the basic school curriculum, but that some take longer than others. By providing slower-learning students with more time to master skills, all students will master the curriculum and all students will receive high grades.

Although mastery learning programs vary, they share several characteristics (see Guskey, 1990, 1997). Students are given regular, corrective feedback on their progress to help them achieve mastery. Most programs also provide enrichment activities to help students extend and broaden their learning. Guskey (1990, 1997) emphasizes the importance of congruence among the different instructional components—including what students are expected to learn, the instructional activities, feedback on learning progress, corrective activities, and procedures used to evaluate students' learning.

Mastery learning is a form of **outcome-based education (OBE),** which has been promoted by many school reformers and policy makers (Evans & King, 1994; Varnon & King, 1993). OBE emphasizes setting clear objectives and giving students multiple and different kinds of opportunities to reach those objectives. It has been implemented at the district level (e.g., Johnson City, New York) and in entire states (e.g., Utah, Missouri, and Minnesota).

Outcomes in OBE can extend beyond academic skills. They can also include motivational orientations, such as being a self-directed learner, a collaborative worker, or a community contributor (Marzano, 1994). OBE is implemented in many different ways and the effects of the general approach have not been systematically evaluated. Implementers and assessment experts are working on developing assessments of students' achievements related to identified outcomes, but much work remains to be done to develop reliable and valid performance-based assessments.

We focus on mastery learning programs rather than outcome-based education because they are more clearly defined and have been assessed in many different educational contexts. The mastery learning program developed by Bloom, and another program developed by Keller, are briefly described below to illustrate different ways that mastery-based systems have been implemented in regular classrooms. Although guidelines and commercial materials for these programs are available, it is possible (and usually preferable) for teachers to design their own program and to develop materials that are suited to their own style of teaching and the particular characteristics and needs of their students (see Guskey, 1985, 1997; Block, Efthim, & Burns, 1989, for practical suggestions).

Mastery learning approaches involve varying the amount of time students spend learning concepts or skills and evaluating them on their progress. Introducing a mastery learning program does not necessarily affect the nature of instruction. It does not preclude, for example, whole-class instruction and lecturing, although more individualized instructional techniques may be easier to use.

Whatever the mode of instruction, however, mastery learning programs require clear instructional objectives. It is necessary to break a course or subject into small, discrete units of learning to give students specific skills to work toward and to allow individualized evaluation of increments in mastery. In Bloom's Learning for Mastery (LFM) program, the teacher is instructed to develop brief, ungraded, student-scored, diagnostic-progress tests used for formative evaluation of students' levels of understanding. These evaluations provide the teacher and student with feedback about the student's progress toward achieving the educational objectives. The student is given additional instructional material ("correctives") based on his or her specific level of mastery. The correctives are used for further instruction and should differ from the teacher's group instruction. Students continue the diagnostic test and corrective instruction cycle until they have achieved mastery. Students are supposed to do the additional studying on their own time, although class time is often set aside for this purpose. In the LFM program, grading is noncompetitive in that any student who has mastered the curriculum designated for that length of instructional time is given an "A." Ideally, all but a few students should achieve the predetermined level of mastery.

Keller (1968) developed an instructional model that is compatible with the basic assumptions of Bloom's model, but in practice works quite differently (see also Guskey, 1994, 1997). In Keller's Personalized System of Instruction (PSI) students proceed through a set of written curriculum materials at their own pace. After initially attempting to complete the unit's material, a student takes the unit mastery test, given by a "proctor" (who may be the teacher, a teacher's aide, or a more advanced student or classmate). If the student passes the test, he or she advances to the next unit. Otherwise, the student uses the unit correctives to restudy the unmastered material. The cycle continues until the student demonstrates mastery on one form of the unit's test. Grading is noncompetitive, as it is in LFM programs.

The major difference between LFM and PSI programs is that in LFM classrooms, students are expected to work on their own time to master material so that the entire class can collectively move on to the next unit of study. In PSI classrooms students continue to work at their own pace throughout the school year. This difference has two important implications. Theoretically, the LFM method should reduce the variability in achievement levels among students. Students who learn more slowly take more time to achieve mastery, but some of that additional time is their own. The PSI method could actually result in increased variability in mastery because the fast learners are not delayed in their progress by the slower learners, as they are to some degree in traditional, unidimensional classrooms. An advantage of the PSI method is that fast learners can create a highly challenging and highly motivating educational program, and they are spared the boredom that can result from having to go over material they have already mastered.

Mastery learning programs such as these two have been implemented in schools throughout the world and their effects on motivation and learning have been extensively evaluated. Evaluations suggest that mastery learning programs have positive effects on student attitudes and achievement, particularly for weaker students (Guskey & Pigott, 1988; Kulik, Kulik, & Bangert-Drowns, 1990a), although whether research has demonstrated positive effects on students' standardized test performance is disputed among reviewers (Anderson & Burns, 1987; Kulik, Kulik, & Bangert-Drowns, 1990b).

Although most of the mastery learning programs that have been studied appear to have some positive effects on achievement, they are not entirely effective in achieving some motivation-related goals, such as focusing students' attention on improving their own skills as opposed to competing against classmates. Informal observations of mastery-based programs suggest that it is difficult to eliminate altogether students' interest in comparing their performance with that of classmates. Crockenberg and Bryant (1978) point out that booklets or units are usually organized hierarchically, and the level is usually indicated by a salient marker, such as color. Learners can easily determine who is more or less advanced in the curriculum, and some observers claim that many children are keenly aware of where they are in comparison to their classmates. Levine (1983) has noted that children tend to create a "race to the end of the curriculum." Other observers have noted that if left on their own, students also procrastinate and consequently make little progress (Sherman, 1992). Notwithstanding these limitations, these well tested programs provide teachers with models of evaluation that are based on a mastery standard and which can be adapted to their own teaching style and student needs.

Cooperative Incentive Structures

One way to use competitiveness constructively is to create group competition that pits groups of students of equal ability levels against each other. Educational researchers have developed and tested instructional programs that involve cooperative group learning and team competition.

Johnson & Johnson (1985b, 1989) identify four characteristics of effective cooperative group learning. First, there is interdependence among group members—students need to be concerned about the performance of other students. Second, there is individual accountability—every student's mastery of the material is assessed and "counts." Third, there is face-to-face interaction among students. Fourth, students learn the social skills (such as communication and managing conflict) needed to work collaboratively. (See also Cohen, 1994; Cohen & Lotan, 1997; Slavin, Sharan, Kagan, Hertz-Lazarowitz, Webb, & Schmuck, 1985).

Cooperative learning programs vary in terms of two principle aspects of classroom organization: task structure and reward structure. All cooperative learning programs use **cooperative task structures,** in which students work collaboratively with classmates, usually in small groups. Not all programs reward students on the basis of their group (referred to as a **cooperative incentive structure**) as opposed to their individual performance. Slavin's (1984, 1997) review of research on cooperative learning suggests that the cooperative incentive structure results in the highest level of motivation and learning.

The defining feature of a cooperative incentive structure is that a group's reward is contingent upon the performance of all group members. By combining high- and low-performing students in groups, and by making rewards contingent upon the group's performance, cooperative incentive structures can equalize opportunities for rewards. A group reward structure can, therefore, relieve motivation problems that many low-ability students have in individual competitive situations in which they have no hope of "winning."

Evidence suggests that when rewards are based on the sum of the individuals' performances, simply being a member of a successful group allows all students the advantages of success, such as high self-perceptions of ability, satisfaction, and peer esteem (Ames, 1981; Ames & Felker, 1979). Because cooperative incentive structures give all students an equal chance at being a member of the winning team, they also focus students' attention on effort as a cause of outcomes, rather than on ability (see Ames & Ames, 1984).

Johnson and Johnson (1985b) also stress individual accountability, suggesting that positive interdependence can be achieved by dividing up roles, materials, resources, or information among group members in a way that requires all students to contribute. Group size is an important consideration; as the size of the group increases it becomes more difficult to identify individual members' contributions. They suggest groups composed of 2 to 6 children. It is also important for all students to understand that their efforts are required in order for the group to succeed.

In a study of teachers endeavoring to implement reform-minded mathematics instruction, I observed many effective strategies for ensuring individual accountability. In several classes, for example, students knew that one of the members of their group would be asked to present and explain their group's strategy for solving a mathematics problem to the class. Because they didn't know which student would be called on, they had to make sure that everyone in their group understood their strategy. In one class the teacher picked names out of a bowl until everyone had presented, to ensure that all students were called on an equal number of times.

As in sports, where excellence in individual performance is encouraged by peers because it benefits the whole team, team competition in the classroom can result in greater student support of each other's achievements. By rewarding groups as well as individuals for academic achievement, peer norms favor rather than oppose high achievement (see Johnson & Johnson, 1985b; Sharan, 1980, for reviews). Studies have found, for example, that students in cooperative incentive structures are more likely than students in individual competitive situations to agree with such statements as, "Other children in my class want me to work hard" (e.g., Hulton & DeVries, 1976). This effect on norms applies as well to students with learning disabilities (Gillies & Ashman, 2000). Research has also shown that students in cooperative incentive structures are more likely to tutor, help, and encourage classmates (see Johnson & Johnson, 1985a, 1985b) and to accept students with disabilities (Cosden & Haring, 1992; Putnam, Markovchick, Johnson, & Johnson, 1996) than students in individual competitive structures. This environment can also reduce racial prejudice (Walker & Crogan, 1998).

Several programs using cooperative incentive structures—Groupwork, Team-Games-Tournaments, Student Teams and Achievement Divisions, and Jigsaw—have been well studied (see reviews by Aronson, Stephan, Sikes, Blaney, & Snapp, 1978; Cohen, Bianchini, Cossey, Holthuis, Morphew, & Whitcomb, 1997; Johnson & Johnson, 1985a; Sharan, 1980; Slavin, 1984, 1990, 1997; Slavin et al., 1985). Practical guides also exist to assist teachers as they implement cooperative learning and group evaluation structures (e.g., Burns, 1987; Cohen, 1994; Gibbs & Allen, 1978; Johnson, Johnson, Holubec, & Roy, 1984; Slavin, 1990). Recently studies of cooperative learning using technology have also found positive effects on motivation (e.g., McInerney, McInerney, & Marsh, 1997).

Although cooperative learning approaches can increase motivation and learning, their potential is not always realized. Cohen (1994) points out that students need to be carefully prepared and trained to engage in cooperative learning, and she provides many practical suggestions for such training. Webb (1984, 1985) has conducted studies which demonstrate important differences in students' interactions (e.g., the nature of help sought and given) and learning as a function of the composition (e.g., gender and ability-level mix) of the group. (See also Ross, 1995.) Cosden and Haring (1992) point out that "free riders" (students who allow their group-mates to complete most of the work) are common and some of the more capable students reduce their participation because they feel exploited. Issues such as student training and group composition need to be carefully considered before a cooperative learning approach is implemented.

Summary

It is important for students to have a realistic understanding of their skills. Without this they are not likely to select tasks that will foster learning and they will not make good decisions about where to apply their efforts. To engage productively in school tasks students need to feel efficacious—to believe that with some effort they will be able to complete the tasks at hand. And if they know they do not have the prerequisite skills to complete a task, they need to know that they can develop them. They also need to know that their efforts will be rewarded, regardless of their skill level relative to classmates.

Teachers cannot and should not want to eliminate individual differences in students' academic achievements. But they can minimize self-defeating, face-saving behaviors that inhibit learning. These are worthy goals. They lead to better learning and they make school a more pleasant and rewarding place for students.

TABLE 7.1   **Summary of Terms**

Terms	Definition
Proximal goals	Short-term goals that can be achieved relatively quickly
Distal goals	Long-term goals that may involve several steps
Attribution retraining	Making explicit statements to change a person's perceptions of the cause of failure (usually from ability to effort or strategy)
Undifferentiated task structure	Students work on the same tasks at the same time, and the nature of tasks varies little from day to day
Unidimensional classroom	A classroom with an undifferentiated task structure in which valued performance outcomes are narrowly defined and social comparison information is salient
Differentiated task structure	Students work on different tasks at the same time and the nature of tasks varies from day to day
Multidimensional classroom	A classroom with a differentiated task structure in which many different kinds of performance are valued and social comparison information is not salient
Mastery learning	A program of instruction in which students move through the curriculum at their own pace, as a function of demonstrated mastery
Outcome-Based Education (OBE)	An instructional program that is guided by a set of well-defined objectives, frequent assessment, and multiple opportunities to achieve the objectives
Cooperative task structure	Students work collaboratively with classmates, usually in small groups
Cooperative incentive structure	Students' rewards (e.g., grades) are based on their group's performance

CHAPTER

8   Intrinsic Motivation

A group of 4-year-olds sits at a table in a preschool. Two children are drawing a picture with markers; another is sorting buttons by their color into bowls. On the floor, two others explain that they are making a hotel out of blocks. The children work intensely and appear to enjoy these activities which, in addition to being fun, help them develop fine-motor, perceptual, and cognitive skills.

A strict reinforcement theorist would explain these children's efforts by their reinforcement histories: in the past, these or similar behaviors must have led to social approval, or maybe even tangible rewards. Or perhaps failing to engage in one of these teacher-sanctioned activities was punished. A social cognitive theorist would add that the children may have observed other children being reinforced for these activities, and that they expected to be reinforced for their efforts in this situation or punished for alternative behaviors.

Intrinsic motivation theorists offer another explanation. They claim that human beings are innately inclined to develop skills and engage in learning-related activities; external reinforcement is not necessary because learning is inherently reinforcing. This chapter discusses three perspectives on intrinsic motivation, all based on the assumption that human beings have natural inclinations that render some tasks intrinsically motivating. According to these three views, human beings are born disposed to seek opportunities to develop competencies, and to seek novelty—events and activities that are somewhat discrepant from their expectations. Also, people have an innate need to feel that they are autonomous and engaging in activities of their own volition.

These three perspectives on intrinsic motivation are not mutually exclusive. To the contrary, they are compatible and to some degree overlapping. Each is discussed below.

Competence Motivation

In 1959 White published a now-classic paper presenting evidence that human beings have an intrinsic need to feel competent and that behaviors such as exploration and mastery attempts are best explained by this innate motivational force. White claimed that the underlying need to feel competent explains behaviors as diverse as an infant examining an object visually, a 2-year-old building a tower out of blocks, a 9-year-old playing a computer game, and an adolescent writing a story.

White's defense of an intrinsic **competence motive** rests partly on this motive's evolutionary adaptive value, since it impels a person to deal more effectively with the environment. He points out that human beings, unlike lower animals, have few competencies innately provided and need to learn a great deal about how to deal with the environment. Thus, a drive or innate disposition to become competent has considerable adaptive value.

Piaget (1952) similarly claims that, from the first day of life, human beings are naturally inclined to practice newly developing competencies (what he calls "schemes"), and that practicing new skills is inherently satisfying. For the very young infant, the "skill" may be as simple as grabbing an object; infants usually attempt to grasp nearly any object that is close to them and, as a consequence of practicing this skill in different contexts and with different objects, they become more adept at grasping differently shaped objects.

Piaget's theory provides an explanation for children's repetitive, and occasionally annoying, behaviors that appear to serve no purpose. For example, when children begin to learn to take off their own shoes they repeatedly remove them, or they might turn door knobs without any apparent desire to go through the doorway. Older children may make the same cookie recipe over and over until they have perfected it, listen to the same record until they have "mastered" every note and word, or play the same video game until they consistently "beat the machine." As children develop, they practice different and more varied skills and consequently become more effective in their interactions with the environment. For example, toddlers can develop their spatial abilities by doing increasingly difficult puzzles. Adolescents may become more adept at thinking hypothetically by playing chess or arguing politics.

To be sure, behaviors that children engage in to increase competence can also result in tangible reinforcement. Most children enjoy eating the cookies they bake, but the feeling of competence that is derived from making a successful batch of cookies can be as rewarding as the good taste. Infants and children are also encouraged to perform some mastery activities and are praised for their successes (unless, for example, children remove their shoes just as their parents are leaving to take them outdoors). But children often practice developing skills without any external reinforcement. Indeed, they engage in some competency-developing activities even when the activity results in some form of punishment. Consider the one-year-old who is frequently punished by falls while he practices walking. I have yet to see a child stop trying to walk as a consequence of such punishment.

Principle of Optimal Challenge

Competence motivation explains children's efforts only on challenging tasks—tasks that will lead to increased competence. The motive to achieve competence does not explain participation in activities that are easy and that will not lead to increased skills or understanding. Once children have mastered a skill, they will no longer practice it, except as a means to another end. Thus, once toddlers have mastered the skill of opening doors they won't turn a knob unless they want to go into another room. The preschooler who has fully comprehended the movie she has been watching over and over suddenly becomes disinterested.

A study by Danner and Lonky (1981) demonstrated children's preference for tasks that allow them to practice newly developing skills. Children were given experience with three classification tasks varying in levels of difficulty and then told that they could spend time working on any of the three tasks. Children spent the most time with and rated as most interesting the tasks that were one step ahead of their pretested level of classification skill. McMullin and Steffen (1982) found that when the older subjects in their study worked on puzzles that became slightly more difficult with each subsequent trial, they displayed more subsequent intrinsic motivation than when the difficulty level remained constant.

Emotional Reactions to Mastery

According to White and Piaget, the increasing competence that results from practicing newly developing skills and mastering challenging tasks engenders a positive emotional experience, which White refers to as a feeling of efficacy.[1] This feeling of efficacy (mastery or competence) is evident in children's smiles when they achieve a goal—completing a puzzle or a drawing, or solving a difficult arithmetic problem. It is this positive emotional experience that makes mastery behavior self-reinforcing.

Consistent with the principle of optimal challenge, several studies have confirmed that children's emotional responses (i.e., joy, pride) are most intense when they master moderately difficult tasks. Studies of infants as young as eight weeks have shown that smiling is associated with processing novel visual stimuli (a form of mastering the environment for an infant) more than with processing familiar stimuli. As infants get older, they smile at increasingly complex stimuli, presumably because simple stimuli are no longer challenging (Shultz & Zigler, 1970).

Harter systematically studied positive emotion (smiling behavior) in elementary school-age children's responses to mastery attempts. In several studies she gave anagrams (letters that can be arranged into words) to children, and observers rated the intensity of pleasure children expressed at the moment they solved each puzzle (Harter, 1974, 1978b). When the problems were extremely difficult and required an unusual amount of time and effort to solve, children expressed little pleasure and reported feeling annoyed and frustrated. Easily

---

[1]White's *"feeling of efficacy"* is the emotional consequence of mastery. It is sometimes referred to as a feeling of competence, similar to pride. White's *feeling* of efficacy is, to a great extent, an emotional experience, and thus differs from Bandura's "self-efficacy," which is a cognitive *judgment* that a person's efforts are likely to lead to success.

solved anagrams did not produce very much smiling either. Tasks that required some effort but were not extremely difficult resulted in the most positive expressions.

Competence motivation and the principle of challenge explains why adults get little pleasure from beating someone who is much less skillful at tennis, or why people are compelled to try a steeper hill after mastering a ski run. Success at a challenging task, which is most likely to lead to improved competence, results in the most positive emotional experience.

Effects of the Social Environment

Competence motivation has been presented as a biologically-based "motive," compelling people to engage in activities that result in increased competency to deal with the environment. While there are merits to this view, it is important to recognize the role of the social environment as well.

As children get older they require more adult feedback to determine whether they have mastered tasks. Infants usually do not need an adult to tell them whether mastery has been achieved. Their mastery attempts are, for the most part, directed at affecting the environment in some way, and the feedback comes directly from the objects they manipulate; if the shoe comes off or the door knob turns, they know they have been successful. Feedback is also intrinsic to some tasks for older children. A child who makes it around the ice rink for the first time without falling will feel efficacious regardless of whether or not an adult congratulates her. But an adult or older child is often needed to inform a child that her swimming stroke has improved, or the paper she wrote for her English class is well organized or compelling, or her solutions to a set of arithmetic problems are correct. Thus, in some situations the feeling of competence requires social input.

Adults also influence standards of achievement by encouraging and praising particular outcomes. For example, a parent who praises only certain kinds of drawings might influence a young child's artistic standards, and thus which drawings engender her own feelings of competence. Differential reactions of adults to children's performance may explain, at least in part, why 85 percent correct or a grade of "B" will generate feelings of competence and pride in one child and incompetence and shame in another.

Subtle classroom practices can affect students' standards for achievement as well. Putting only papers with 100 percent of the answers correct on the bulletin board may undermine feelings of competence in children who achieve lower, albeit respectable, scores. Grading competitively (i.e., based on a normal curve) can deny feelings of competence to children who cannot outperform classmates, even when their own performance has improved. Many children don't enjoy schoolwork because it fails to provide the feelings of competence and mastery they need to sustain intrinsic interest. Redefining what constitutes mastery can give these students an opportunity to succeed and to find intrinsic value in school tasks (Stipek, 1997; see Chapter 10).

Self-Perceptions of Competence and Intrinsic Motivation

People don't enjoy working on tasks that make them feel incompetent. Just as feelings of efficacy and competence engendered by success on challenging tasks reinforce mastery efforts and enhance intrinsic motivation to engage in similar tasks, feelings of *in*competence undermine intrinsic motivation. Working on a task without achieving success destroys enthusiasm for work on similar tasks.

This link between feeling competent and intrinsic motivation is seen in specific task situations, and is evident, more generally, in associations found consistently between perceptions of academic competence and motivation to engage in academic tasks. Many studies have demonstrated that students who believe that they are competent academically are more intrinsically interested in school tasks than those who have a low perception of their academic ability (Gottfried, 1990; Harter, 1992; Mac Iver, Stipek, & Daniels, 1991; Skaalvik & Rankin, 1995). Teachers also report that high achievers in their classrooms exhibit more intrinsic motivation, and studies show that people are most interested in topics about which they have prior knowledge (see Tobias, 1994).

The study I did with two colleagues suggests a causal relationship between perceived competence and intrinsic motivation (Mac Iver, Stipek, & Daniels, 1991). We assessed, at both the beginning and the end of the semester, junior and senior high school students' perceptions of their competence and their intrinsic interest in a subject they were studying. Analyses revealed that interest changed in the same direction that perceived competence also changed. That is, students whose perception of competence increased over the course of the semester rated the subject more interesting at the end of the semester than at the beginning. In contrast, students whose perception of competence decreased rated the subject as less interesting at the end of the semester than they did at the beginning. Harter (1992) reviews further evidence, based on path analyses, suggesting that perceptions of competence engender positive affective experiences, which in turn engender intrinsic motivation. She also describes a study in which students' intrinsic motivation for academic work increased, remained the same, or decreased from elementary school to junior high, depending on whether their perceptions of their academic competence increased, remained the same or decreased (see also Harter, Whitesell, & Kowalski, 1992). Similar findings are reported for a group of gifted students who moved from a regular classroom to a program for gifted children (Harter, 1992).[2]

---

[2]For some children who experience incompetence, just a few success experiences can rekindle intrinsic interest. I observed this effect from my daughter's experience on a little league baseball team. At her first game she failed twice to make it to first base. Despite considerable praise for her efforts, she wanted to go home. Fearing that I would never get her back again (and believing that all she needed was to feel competent), I insisted that she stay. A subsequent hit and tour of the bases was all it took to create such enthusiasm that it was I who eventually had to beg her to leave.

In summary, some motivation theorists believe that people are naturally inclined to seek opportunities to develop their competencies, and they derive pleasure from the experience of increased competence that these opportunities afford. The practical implications are clear—students will not enjoy academic work that they do not feel competent doing. A student who shows little interest in schoolwork may need to have her tasks adjusted to be appropriately difficult. If she can complete the work, but doesn't believe she can, she needs her self-confidence boosted, using some of the strategies described in Chapter 7.

Teachers need to be careful not to allow the current preoccupation with standards and testing to have negative effects on their teaching. In an effort to bring students to a particular standard, I have observed teachers tying to "skip steps." They teach material that will be on the test regardless of whether their students have the prerequisite skills to master the material. Giving work that is too advanced for students does not help them achieve higher test scores, and the negative effects on motivation of being asked to do work that is inappropriately difficult undermines students' learning all the more. High standards and expectations are important, as will be discussed in Chapter 13, but they must be realistic as well, and student-centered teaching that builds on students' current skills is just as important.

Although the emphasis is different, the theoretical perspective on intrinsic motivation described next is related to the notion of competency motivation, in the sense that novel situations require more effort to process than familiar or predictable situations. Therefore, they may produce similar feelings of efficacy.

Novelty

Theorists taking the second perspective on intrinsic motivation portray human beings as information processors. Berlyne (1966), Hunt (1965), and Kagan (1972) claim that we are predisposed to derive pleasure from activities and events that provide some level of surprise, incongruity, complexity, or discrepancy from our expectations or beliefs. This predisposition may explain why infants a few months old look longer at a novel visual image than at an image they have seen before (Hunter, Ames, & Koopman, 1983), why an 8-month-old likes to look at things upside down, or why a 2-year-old will call herself by a wrong name and then laugh hysterically. It may also explain why so many children like cartoons, science fiction, and video games.

According to information processing theorists, pleasure is assumed to derive from creating, investigating, or processing stimuli that are moderately discrepant (Spielberger & Starr, 1994). Stimuli that are not at all discrepant or novel will not arouse interest, and stimuli that are too discrepant from the individual's expectations will be ignored, cause anxiety, or even provoke "terror and flight" (Berlyne, 1966, p. 30).

The information processing perspective is thus similar to Piaget's and White's competence motivation emphasis on moderate challenge. A novel stimulus offers a challenge, just as a task might. People have to exert more effort to process or understand stimuli that are discrepant from their expectations or previous experiences than they do to process expected or familiar stimuli. Competence motivation and information processing theorists also agree that once people encounter a novel event or challenging task, they are naturally motivated to reduce the discrepancy, either between their expectation and the novel stimulus or between their current skill level and the skill level required to complete the task.

Deci (1975) describes human beings as engaging in a perpetual process of seeking challenge and novelty and then "conquering" it. People seek novel situations and situations that challenge their current level of skill or understanding and then they strive to achieve mastery—to conquer the challenge and experience feelings of competence or understanding.

Again, the practical implications are clear. Think about how exciting it is to do routine tasks—for example, mowing the lawn, setting the table, or balancing your checkbook. The same kinds of tasks day after day at school are just as uninteresting for children as routine tasks are for adults. Sometimes students' academic motivation can be substantially increased by simply making sure that there is variety in the kinds of tasks they are asked to do.

Self-Determination

A third perspective on intrinsic motivation stresses autonomy. DeCharms, Deci, Ryan, and other achievement motivation theorists agree with White's theory that people are intrinsically motivated to develop their competencies, and that feelings of competence enhance intrinsic interest in activities. They add, however, another innate need—the need to feel self-determining. These theorists propose that people naturally want to believe that they are engaging in activities by their own volition—because they *want to* rather than because they *have to* (deCharms, 1976; 1984; Deci, 1975; Deci & Ryan, 1985; Ryan & Deci, 2000). They differentiate between situations in which people perceive themselves as the cause of their own behavior, which they refer to as an **internal locus of causality,** and situations in which people believe they are engaging in behavior to achieve rewards or please another person, or because of external constraints (referred to as an **external locus of causality**). These theorists claim that people are more likely to be intrinsically motivated to engage in an activity when their locus of causality is internal than when it is external.

According to the theory, the very same activity can be more motivating and pleasurable when one chooses to engage in it than when it is done for some external purpose. Consider, for example, "pleasure reading." People use the phrase when they refer to books or articles they chose to read, not when they refer to a class assignment. The phrase implies that books read to meet course requirements do not engender pleasure. Consider roommates reading the same book. One chose to read it in her leisure time, and enjoys it; the other is reading it because it was assigned, and finds the same book to be pure drudgery.

Many factors affect the perceived locus of causality, including both the level of control exerted by others and the availability of rewards. Despite the important effects of these and other external variables, theorists stress that a person's *perception* of causality is more important than any objective measure of causality. Thus two people in the same situation can have different perceptions of their reasons for engaging in a particular behavior or activity. Consider, for example, two students in the same class and assigned the same book to read. One student perceives herself to have had a choice. Perhaps she took the course because of the particular books it covered. The other student took the course because she needed one more literature course to complete her major and it was the only one she could fit into her schedule. She, accordingly, feels coerced to read the book.

Although White was the first to popularize the concept of competence motivation, the notion that people are innately wired to strive for increasing competence and to take pleasure in its achievement is critical to Deci and Ryan's theoretical formulation of intrinsic motivation as well (e.g., Deci, 1975; Deci & Ryan, 1985). But they add that people also need to feel self-determining. Activities and situations that promote feelings of self-determination, as well as feelings of competence, are the most intrinsically motivating.

Returning to the practical implications, Deci, Ryan, and their colleagues point out the value of giving students some choice and minimizing external constraints or monitoring that would undermine their feelings of control. They recommend activities that foster students' perception that they are doing something because they want to rather than because they have to. Teachers clearly need to play an active role in directing students' learning, but there are many ways, described in Chapter 11, to minimize students' feelings of being controlled, and thus maximize their intrinsic motivation to learn.

Advantage of Intrinsic Motivation

Theory and research suggest that there is considerable value to trying to maximize intrinsic motivation. Below are advantages that have been demonstrated empirically.

Learning Activities Outside of School

Intrinsically motivated achievement behavior is desirable, in part, because external reinforcement is not always available. Students like Safe Sally, who become dependent on external rewards for learning, will not engage in intellectual activities outside of school where grades and other forms of recognition are less available. If learning is perceived as an activity that one does only to obtain rewards and avoid punishment, there is no reason to do it when no rewards are available and punishment is not likely.

Preference for Challenge

Studies have also shown that people are more likely to select challenging tasks when they are intrinsically motivated than when they are motivated to obtain an extrinsic reward. Pearlman (1984), for example, found that when a reward (+3 points on the next test) or penalty (–3 points on the next test) was made contingent on whether students' solutions to a problem were correct or incorrect, they selected easier problems than when no reward or penalty was at stake. In a study by Pittman, Emery, and Boggiano (1982), the preference for a simple version of a task in a situation in which an extrinsic reward was offered carried over even to a situation in which the original reward contingencies were no longer in effect. (See also, Flink, Boggiano, Main, Barrett, & Katz, 1992.)

Conceptual Understanding

There is considerable evidence suggesting that people learn more when they read material that they rate as intrinsically interesting (see Shirey, 1992; Wade, 1992; Tobias, 1994). The enhanced learning occurs, at least in part, because people are more attentive to text that interests them, and this attention helps them process and remember what they have read (see discussion below). Research further suggests that the conditions that produce interest and enjoyment (i.e., that foster intrinsic motivation) are more valuable for promoting understanding and conceptual learning than for promoting rote learning (e.g., Benware & Deci, 1984; Ryan, Connell, & Plant, 1990; see Utman, 1997).

Creativity

Studies have found that the conditions supporting intrinsic motivation also foster greater creativity (see Hennessey, 2000). In a study reported by Amabile (1983), female college students who expected to be graded produced less creative art work than those who did not expect to be evaluated. Butler and Nisan (1986) found that when evaluative feedback was given in the form of grades, students' performance on a quantitative task subsequently improved and their performance on a task assessing divergent (creative) thinking declined; written comments, in contrast, resulted in improved performance on both tasks. Amabile and Hennessey (1992) report studies in which researchers were able to increase children's creativity by focusing their attention on their intrinsic interest and away from the extrinsic rewards related to tasks.

The reasons for these negative effects of extrinsic motivation on conceptual and creative thinking are not clear. Amabile (1983) suggests that extrinsic contingencies can create an instrumental focus that narrows attention to the quickest and easiest solution (see also Flink et al., 1992). It is also possible that students are used to being evaluated on rote learning rather than on conceptual understanding; as a consequence, those who expected to be evaluated in the studies described above focused their attention primarily on facts that could be memorized.

Pleasure and Involvement

Intrinsic motivation is also associated with greater pleasure and more active involvement than extrinsic motivation (Harter, 1992; see also Tobias, 1994). Miserandino (1996) found that students who engaged in schoolwork for intrinsic reasons reported more involvement, persistence, participation, and curiosity along with less boredom in school activities than students who reported being extrinsically motivated. Intrinsically motivated students also reported feeling less anxious and angry, more confident, and less likely to avoid schoolwork or to fake diligence (Vallerand, 1997; see also Patrick et al., 1993).

In summary, because of these many benefits to intrinsic motivation, it is important to take advantage of this motivational system. Chapter 11 summarizes classroom practices that have been shown to maximize intrinsic motivation. We will next discuss links between intrinsic motivation and rewards.

Intrinsic Motivation and Extrinsic Rewards

Intrinsic motivation and motivation based on extrinsic rewards are, to some degree, in competition with each other. Research has shown that under certain circumstances, offering extrinsic rewards for engaging in tasks actually undermines intrinsic motivation. Two classic studies illustrate this effect. Deci (1971) enlisted college students to participate in a problem-solving study over three sessions. In the first session, all of the students were asked to work a series of interesting puzzles. In the second session, half of the students were told that they would be given an extrinsic reward (money) for correctly solving a second set of puzzles; no mention of a reward was made to the other half of the students. During the third session the experimenter left all of the students with the puzzles, telling them that they could work on the puzzles if they wanted, or they could look at current issues of *Time*, *The New Yorker*, and *Playboy*, which were placed near the students. In this last session, like the first, no students were offered extrinsic rewards.

Students were observed through a one-way mirror, allowing experimenters to assess the effect of the reward on the amount of time they chose to work on puzzles. In the second session, students who were offered a reward for working on the puzzles spent more time working on them than students who were not offered a reward. Thus, the extrinsic reward had the immediate effect of increasing the amount of time subjects engaged in the task. In contrast, in the third session, when no reward was offered to anyone, students who had previously been rewarded spent less time working on puzzles than did students who had never been offered a reward. The rewarded students lost interest in the task when the reward was withdrawn.

Lepper, Greene, and Nisbett (1973) conducted a similar study with preschool-age children, in which children who had been offered a reward for playing with Magic Markers subsequently spent less free time on the activity than children who were never given a reward. As many as 100 studies have used a paradigm similar to these two studies to examine the effects of reward on subsequent engagement in various activities (see reviews by Cameron & Pierce, 1994; Deci, Koestner, & Ryan, 1999; Deci & Ryan, 1985; Kohn, 1993; Lepper & Henderlong, 2000; Ryan & Deci, 2000; Tang & Hall, 1995). These studies suggest that external rewards can undermine intrinsic interest in a task, and the larger the reward, the more negative the effect on intrinsic interest.

This observed effect of extrinsic rewards contradicts reinforcement theory. According to reinforcement theory, a reward made contingent on a behavior *increases* the frequency of the behavior. When it is withdrawn the behavior should return to baseline (its level of frequency before the reward had been given), but it should not dip below baseline, as was found in many studies.

Intrinsic motivation theorists assume that the negative effect rewards have on the target behavior after they are withdrawn can be explained by cognitive or affective processes. "Self-attribution" theorists propose that when a reward is offered, people perceive the reward as the reason for engaging in the activity, even though intrinsic interest might have been a sufficiently strong reason for them to do the task. But because of their perception of the reason for doing the task, they cease the activity when the reward is withdrawn.

This effect of rewards on motivation is related to what theorists refer to as the discounting principle. According to the **discounting principle,** if one possible explanation for a person's behavior is salient, all other explanations will be "discounted." An external reward for performing an activity is usually more salient than intrinsic reasons. Consequently, when a desired extrinsic reward for a behavior is offered, intrinsic interest is discounted and the more salient extrinsic reward is perceived to be the cause.

The discounting principle and the undermining effect of rewards are illustrated by an anecdote about an old man who was bothered by the noisy play of boys in his neighborhood (from Casady, 1975). The old man called the boys together, told them he was deaf and asked them to shout louder so he could enjoy their fun. In return he would pay each of them a quarter. The boys were delighted and on the first day the old man was provided with a considerable amount of noise for his money. On the second day, he told the boys that he could only afford to pay twenty cents. The pay rate dwindled day by day and eventually the boys became angry and told the old man that they certainly were not going to make noise for nothing!

While self-attribution theorists focus on people's interpretation of events after they have occurred, cognitive evaluation theorists believe that the effect of rewards involves processes that occur at a deeper level than thoughts and prior to or during, as well as after, task engagement. Deci and Ryan (1985) claim that rewards cause people to shift from an internal to an external locus of causality; rewards create a feeling of being controlled and interfere with a feeling of self-determination. Cognitive evaluation theorists conceptualize motivation on a continuum rather than in terms of an internal–external dichotomy. Thus, intrinsic motivation is proportional to the degree to which people perceive their behavior as self-determined or volitional rather than controlled by others, by rewards, or by intrapsychic forces (like guilt or a sense of obligation; Deci, Vallerand, Pelletier, & Ryan, 1991; Ryan & Connell, 1989; Ryan & Stiller, 1991).

Whether locus of causality is conceptualized as a dichotomy or as a continuous dimension, there is good evidence that it is affected by the availability of rewards and other aspects of the social context. Rewards, however, can be used in different ways and for different purposes; studies suggest that the effects of rewards on locus of causality, and thus on intrinsic motivation, are determined by *how* they are used as much as by *whether* they are used.

Controlling Versus Information Function of Rewards

Lepper (1981), Deci (1975), and Bandura (1982) all distinguish between two uses of rewards in classrooms—(1) as an incentive to engage in tasks (that is, to control behavior), and (2) as information about mastery (see also Deci & Ryan, 1985). Intrinsic motivation is undermined by rewards used to control behavior, as well as by other instructional practices that shift students away from a perception of autonomy and personal causation and toward a perception of external causation (e.g., close monitoring of performance). Rewards used to provide information vary in their effect, depending primarily on whether the information is positive (suggesting competence) or negative (suggesting incompetence).

When the teacher makes recess (a reward) contingent upon students' finishing their math assignment, the reward contains no information about students' level of mastery. In this situation the reward is being used to control students' behavior. It will create an external locus of causality, and students will complete their math assignments only if a reward is expected, even if they were previously intrinsically interested in the task.

Task-contingent rewards (based on engaging in the task), such as the example above, are nearly always experienced as controlling (Deci, Koestner, & Ryan, 1999; Ryan & Deci, 2000). Other practices that can create a feeling of being controlled, and thus undermine intrinsic interest, include close *monitoring* (Plant & Ryan, 1985), *deadlines* (Amabile, DeJong, & Lepper, 1976), *external evaluation* (Hughes, Sullivan, & Mosley, 1985), *imposing goals* (Manderlink & Harackiewicz, 1984), and *competition* (Vallerand, Gauvin, & Halliwell, 1986). (See Ryan & La Guardia, in press, for a review.) Extrinsic rewards, therefore, constitute one among many classroom practices that can promote the belief that behavior is externally controlled, and therefore interfere with intrinsic motivation.

The effect of any of these practices on motivation, however, varies depending on the context and emphasis. Goals might actually enhance intrinsic motivation if students' own views are solicited and if the goals allow the student to experience developing levels of mastery. Competition can make a task more exciting without undermining intrinsic motivation if all students have an equal chance of winning (and experiencing a feeling of competence), and if the emphasis is on what is being learned rather than on who wins or loses.

Performance-contingent rewards, based on a specified level of performance, provide information about levels of mastery and are less likely to undermine interest than are task-contingent rewards. They may even enhance it (Boggiano & Ruble, 1979; Deci, Koestner, & Ryan, 1999; see Deci & Ryan, 1992; Ryan & Deci, 2000; Lepper, Keavney, & Drake, 1996). The competence feedback implicit in social reinforcement may explain why praise does not usually reduce intrinsic motivation, even though it is external (Deci, 1971; see Cameron & Pierce, 1994; Deci, Koestner, & Ryan, 1999; Ryan & Deci, 2000, for reviews).

Deci and Ryan (1985) caution, however, that even performance-contingent rewards can be perceived as controlling rather than informational, depending on the interpersonal context or the message that is conveyed. Praise, for example, can be worded so that it will be experienced as informational ("Nice work, your argument is clear and compelling") or controlling ("Good job, you're doing it exactly the way I asked you to"). Research suggests that praise that is interpreted as informational supports intrinsic interest, but praise interpreted as controlling does not (Pittman, Davey, Alafat, Wetherill, & Kramer, 1980; Ryan, 1982).

In summary, the evidence is clear that offering a reward for engaging in activities that people already find intrinsically motivating, or making people feel controlled in some other way, such as by monitoring their behavior or focusing their attention on evaluation, will undermine their intrinsic interest. Their attention shifts to the external reason for engaging in the activity, and when that extrinsic reason is withdrawn, they no longer have a reason to do it.

The effects of rewards, however, vary substantially as a function of how they are given and how they are perceived. The distinction between task-contingent and performance-contingent rewards illustrates the complexity of the teacher's job in monitoring the use of rewards in the classroom. Rewards are effective and advisable in many situations, but careful attention needs to be given to whether they are likely to be interpreted as controlling or informational. Even if they provide information, they only support interest and motivation if the information is positive—if it communicates mastery and competence.

Below is a summary of the practical implications of research on the undermining effect of rewards.

1. Use tangible extrinsic rewards as little as possible. Studies demonstrating that rewards undermine intrinsic interest have involved tasks that appealed to the subjects. Consequently, the reward was superfluous. In real classrooms, rewards are sometimes necessary to prod students into engaging in tasks in which they have little initial interest. Some students may not have been socialized to value a particular skill, may find a particular task uninteresting, or may not at first believe that they will be able to master it. Although rewards should be used as little as possible, they are acceptable in circumstances where they are appropriate, effective, and can be given in ways that do not have detrimental effects.

2. Use the most modest reward possible.   A reward is less likely to undermine intrinsic motivation if it is not so dramatic or salient that it becomes the sole focus of attention.[3] So if a pat on the head and a few words of praise work, there is no need for candy, trinkets, or added recess time.

3. Make rewards contingent upon the quality of work or a standard of performance, not simply on engaging in an activity.   Ames and Ames (1990) describe an actual example of the effects of rewards contingent only upon engaging in a task. Children in a classroom they observed received a certificate for a special treat at a local restaurant for writing four book reports in a month. Because quantity rather than quality was rewarded, they chose short, easy, and often uninteresting books rather than longer or more challenging ones.[4]

Rewards based only on engagement focus students' attention on their controlling function and thus undermine whatever intrinsic interest they may have had in the activity. They also convey the message that the activity is not worth doing without the reward. Rewards that are contingent on a particular level of performance focus students' attention on their information function. By conveying competence or mastery, rewards can increase intrinsic motivation. Make sure, however, that all students can achieve the level of mastery on which the reward is based.

4. Withdraw external rewards as soon as possible.   When rewards are offered as a means of getting students started on a task, an attempt should be made to shift their attention to the intrinsic or utility value of the task or to their developing competence as soon as possible. This, of course, can work only if the task is interesting, the skill useful, and students experience success fairly soon after attempting the task. If these conditions are met, the teacher may be able to maintain students' interest in completing tasks without continuing to offer external rewards.[5] Thus, just as students can turn their attention to extrinsic reasons for engaging in activities that they were previously intrinsically motivated to do, they can shift their attention from extrinsic to intrinsic reasons for engaging in an activity.

---

[3]When I was a child my parents gave me a dollar for every "A" on my report card. Even in those days this was a modest reward for a semester of hard work. I don't know to what degree I can attribute my strong academic values to the dollar rewards, but I suspect that a much larger amount of money would have interfered with the internalization process described in Chapter 9.

[4]I remember my third-grade teacher putting wheels on a bulletin board, which were filled in by colored paper for each book report we wrote in various categories. I can't remember what the ultimate reward was for filling in our wheel, but I do remember getting very good at filling in the book report forms without actually reading the books.

[5]Occasionally students get "hooked" quickly and forget about the reward. In an effort to get my daughter to try ice skating (after spending several sessions hugging the wall), I promised an ice-skating outfit for circling the rink without touching the wall. By the end of that session she accomplished the task. She was so delighted by her sense of developing competence, and intrinsically motivated to continue to develop her skills, she forgot about the promised reward. It was at least a year later when she remembered.

Individual Differences

If motivation to learn is innate, why do some students approach new tasks with enthusiasm and seem to genuinely enjoy learning, while others seem totally uninterested? The answer can be found directly in the theories discussed above. Recall that people are assumed to be driven by needs for competence, novelty, and autonomy. Therefore, their intrinsic motivation will vary according to the degree to which settings provide opportunities to meet these needs. A classroom that engenders feelings of incompetence or of being controlled, or in which activities are familiar and repetitive, will not promote intrinsic motivation.

Even within a classroom there will be individual differences in intrinsic interest in academic tasks because the same circumstances can be experienced differently by different students. A task that is optimally challenging (and therefore can engender feelings of mastery and competence) for some students may be too easy or impossibly difficult for others. Only those students who find tasks moderately difficult will experience competence motivation. Teachers occasionally treat students in a classroom differently—for example, by granting more autonomy to some students (usually those who are already highly motivated) than to others.

Despite the innate origins of competence motivation, how and how much it is manifested are influenced by the social environment. Relatively stable individual differences in mastery behavior can develop as a consequence of differences in the behavior of parents and other significant adults. Harter (1978a) has speculated that social reinforcement from early infancy is necessary to sustain a child's mastery attempts. She proposes that social reinforcement for attempting or for mastering tasks enhances mastery behavior, whereas punishment for attempting or failing to master tasks inhibits intrinsic interest in achievement tasks. Students may develop a preference for easy work because their parents (or previous teachers) punished failure and they do not want to risk the failure that sometimes occurs when initially attempting a moderately difficult task. Children who have overintrusive parents, and thus fail to develop self-confidence in their own ability to complete tasks, may be overly dependent on the teacher for help. Previous experiences in achievement contexts can have enduring effects on students' behavior that can be resistant to teachers' efforts to change.

Measures of Individual Differences in Motivation

In most experimental studies, intrinsic motivation is measured either by whether people voluntarily choose to engage or persist in an activity or by their ratings of their interest in or enjoyment of a particular activity. Several researchers have developed questionnaires to assess relatively stable individual differences in students' intrinsic motivation to engage in academic work. Harter (1981), for example, developed a measure designed to assess five dimensions related to intrinsic motivation: (1) preference for challenging work versus preference for easy work, (2) learning that is motivated by curiosity versus learning done to please the teacher, (3) desire to work independently versus dependency on the teacher for help, (4) independent judgment about selecting tasks versus reliance on the teacher's judgment, and (5) internal criteria for success or failure versus external criteria (e.g., grades, teacher feedback). For each dimension, the measure pits responses that are presumed to reflect an intrinsic orientation toward academic work against responses presumed to reflect a more extrinsic orientation. Table 8.1 provides examples of statements students are asked to respond to when they fill out the questionnaire.

By forcing a choice between intrinsic and extrinsic responses, Harter's scale artificially creates a dichotomy that does not necessarily exist. When children are allowed to rate the items separately the intrinsic and extrinsic ratings are negatively correlated, but very weakly (Lepper & Henderlong, 2000; Lepper, Sethi, Dialdin, & Drake, 1997). These recent findings suggest that intrinsic and extrinsic motivation are not always in conflict with each other.

Gottfried (1985, 1990) developed the Children's Academic Intrinsic Motivation Inventory (CAIMI), which assesses intrinsic interest in specific subject areas (reading, math, social studies, and science), and in school in general. One version is for children in the lower-elementary grades and the other is for children above third grade. Measures designed specifically to assess motivation for reading also exist (e.g., Baker & Wigfield, 1999).

It is useful to assess intrinsic interest in different academic domains because there is considerable variation in students' interest in various school tasks. In addition to using the questionnaires discussed above, teachers can assess students' intrinsic motivation for tasks by observing their behavior in different task situations. Behaviors that are associated with high intrinsic interest are summarized in Table 8.2.

Perhaps the most straightforward and, ironically, the least-used strategy is to simply ask students how interested they are in various school tasks or how much they like different school subjects. Teachers can create brief, anonymous questionnaires that ask students to rate their interest in some of the work they have been doing in their classroom (see Table 8.3 for an example), or they can ask open-ended questions in a group discussion about which activities students enjoy and what they do not enjoy in school. Just asking the question gives students the important message that their views are valued (although asking and ignoring their responses can engender cynicism).

Age-Related Changes

In addition to individual differences at any one age, there appear to be systematic differences in these dispositions associated with age. Harter (1981, 1992) found that scores on her subscales measuring preference for challenge, curiosity and interest, and independent mastery all declined from third to ninth grade, while scores on the independent judgment and internal criteria subscales increased with age and experience in school. Students apparently tend to become less motivated to engage in academic activities for their own pleasure, but become better able to judge the quality of their performance. (See also Anderman & Maehr, 1994; Hidi

TABLE 8.1   Sample Items from Harter's Intrinsic Motivation Scale*

Really true for me	Sort of true for me			Really true for me	Sort of true for me
		Preference for challenge	**Preference for easy work**		
4	3	Some kids like to go on to new work that's at a more difficult level	Other kids would rather stick to assignments that are pretty easy	2	1
		Pleasing the teacher/ getting grades	**Curiosity/interest**		
1	2	Some kids do extra projects so they can get better grades	Other kids do extra projects because they learn about things that interest them	3	4
		Dependence on the teacher	**Independent mastery**		
1	2	When some kids get stuck on a problem they ask the teacher for help	Other kids keep trying to figure out the problem on their own	3	4
		Reliance on teacher's judgment	**Independent judgment**		
1	2	Some kids think the teacher should decide what work to do	Other kids think they should have a say in what work they do	3	4
		Internal criteria	**External criteria**		
4	3	Some kids know whether or not they're doing well in school without grades	Other kids need to have grades to know how well they are doing in school	2	1

*From Harter (1981). A copy of the scale and a manual for scoring and interpreting results is available from Professor Susan Harter, Department of Psychology, University of Denver, 2155 S. Race, Denver, CO 80210. Copyright © 1981 by the American Psychological Association. Reprinted with permission.

TABLE 8.2   Behaviors Associated with Intrinsic Motivation

Students who are intrinsically motivated:

- initiate learning activities on their own
- prefer challenging tasks or pursue challenging aspects of tasks
- spontaneously make connections between school learning and activities or interests outside of school
- ask questions that go beyond the specific task at hand in order to expand their knowledge beyond the immediate lesson
- go beyond the requirements
- are reluctant to stop working on tasks they have not completed
- work on tasks whether or not extrinsic reasons (e.g., grades, close teacher supervision) are salient
- smile and appear to enjoy working on tasks
- express pride in their achievements

TABLE 8.3   An Example of a Teacher-Developed Measure of Students' Intrinsic Motivation

Instructions to students:

Please rate how much you enjoy doing the following activities in this class:

	not at all				a lot
Doing problems in the arithmetic workbook	1	2	3	4	5
Doing arithmetic word problems on the board	1	2	3	4	5
Making up your own arithmetic problems	1	2	3	4	5
Reading stories from reading books	1	2	3	4	5
Answering questions at the end of chapters in reading books	1	2	3	4	5
Making up and writing your own stories	1	2	3	4	5
Working on science projects	1	2	3	4	5
Listening to the teacher read stories	1	2	3	4	5
Working on the class newspaper	1	2	3	4	5

& Harackiewicz, 2000; Lepper, Sethi, Dialdin, & Drake, 1997; Wigfield, Eccles, Yoon, Harold, Arbreton, Freedman-Doan, & Blumenfeld, 1997).

We can only speculate about the reasons for these shifts. Research on the undermining effect of external reinforcement on intrinsic motivation suggests that young students' interest in engaging in tasks for the sake of developing mastery may be replaced by an interest in obtaining external rewards, such as high grades. A second explanation concerns the consistent trend, discussed in Chapter 6, for students' perceptions of their competence to master academic tasks to decline with age. Because low perceived competence dampens intrinsic motivation, it is not surprising that intrinsic interest in academic tasks declines along with perceptions of competence.

A third explanation is that the achievement context changes as a function of grade level. For example, evaluation may be emphasized more in higher grades and failure may be tolerated less. As discussed in Chapter 6, school becomes more formal, more evaluative, and more competitive (Anderman & Maehr, 1994; Eccles et al., 1984, 1993; Midgley et al., 1995). A longitudinal study (Harter et al., 1992) of children who were transitioning to junior high confirmed that with each grade students perceived a greater emphasis on evaluation, performance, and social comparison. Moreover, those students who perceived a relatively greater emphasis on these external factors scored higher on a scale of extrinsic motivation. These and other changes in educational practices therefore may contribute to the age-related declines in intrinsic motivation.

Interest

Related to intrinsic motivation is the concept of interest. Most researchers distinguish between personal and situational interest (Hidi, 2000; Krapp, 1999, 2000; Renninger, Hidi, & Krapp, 1992; Tobias, 1994). **Personal interest** is an enduring (or dispositional) evaluation of a domain (Bergin, 1999). For example, a student might be interested in airplanes, or animals, or eastern religions. **Situational interest** concerns emotions aroused by specific qualities of a task or activity. Satisfied Santos may get very enthusiastic about a particular science experiment, but he is typically inattentive.

The two types of interest are not entirely unrelated. In fact, arousing situational interest can lead to personal interests. A student reading about achievement motivation initially because it was a class requirement may become very engaged, and as a consequence read other books about motivation or pay particular attention to motivational issues in her classroom. Gradually, a brief, externally imposed topic becomes an enduring personal interest. Eventually, the student goes to graduate school and becomes a national expert on the subject.

Interests involve feelings ("I feel eager and excited when I have a chance to learn about animals"), but they also reflect values. Thus one student might be interested in rain forests because he values preservation of the environment, while another student might have less socially sanctioned domains of interest, such as sex, drugs, and rock-and-roll, which are embedded in a larger set of values.

Studies have shown that when students read text related to their interests, they comprehend it and process the information at a deeper level (e.g., recall main ideas more coherently) than when they read text unrelated to their domains of interest (Krapp, 1999; Renninger et al., 1992; Schiefele & Krapp, 1996). Studies suggest that the advantages of material that is personally interesting come from increased attention, use of effective learning strategies, and positive affective states (Krapp, 1999; Renninger, 2000).

The practical implications of research on interest is straightforward. Students' engagement in tasks can be increased by giving them material that is relevant to their interests. For example, teachers might take advantage of an unmotivated student's interest in baseball, ballet, or rockets by finding books on those topics.

Summary

Although there is no doubt that external rewards can motivate achievement-related behavior, people engage in many activities for which no tangible reinforcement is expected or likely. Intrinsic motivation theorists explain this behavior by positing innate motives to develop competencies, experience novelty, and be self-determining. Educational contexts that provide students opportunities to achieve these objectives promote motivation. Intrinsic motivation is worth promoting because it fosters creativity, conceptual learning, challenge-seeking, and enjoyment.

It is possible for a person to have both intrinsic and extrinsic motives for engaging in the same activity, but many studies suggest that the availability of extrinsic rewards can undermine intrinsic interest in tasks—especially if people perceive the rewards as controlling rather than as providing information about their competencies. There are also individual differences in the degree to which intellectual tasks promote intrinsic interest because students have different socialization histories, different perceptions of their academic competencies, and because they experience or perceive the same context differently.

So far we have described two motivational systems that teachers can tap into to engage students in the process of learning. The next chapter discusses a third motivational system which, like intrinsic motivation, is experienced as self-determining, but which does not require tasks to be intrinsically motivating.

TABLE 8.4   Summary of Terms

Term	Definition
Intrinsic motivation	Motivation to engage in an activity in the absence of any extrinsic reward or purpose
Competence motive	Natural disposition to engage in tasks and activities that contribute to learning and development
Internal locus of causality	Perception of engaging in an activity by personal preference
External locus of causality	Perception of engaging in an activity for some external reward or for some reason other than personal preference
Discounting principle	Discounting a reason for engaging in an activity because another reason is more salient
Task-contingent rewards	Rewards based on engaging in an activity or completing a task
Performance-contingent rewards	Rewards based on achieving a specified level of performance
Individual interest	Relatively stable evaluative orientation toward certain domains
Situational interest	Emotional state aroused by specific features of an activity or task

CHAPTER

9

Values and Relationships

People rarely choose to do tasks they don't think they can do. But an affirmative answer to the question "*Can* I do this?" is only one prerequisite to approaching and persisting with an academic task. Another prerequisite is an affirmative answer to the question "Do I *want* to do this?" Satisfied Santos does not have a problem with self-confidence. His problem is that he doesn't value school tasks. He knows the way but lacks the will. Alienated Al no longer thinks he can succeed in school and, not coincidentally, doesn't care any longer whether he succeeds. His answer is negative to both the "Can I?" and the "Do I want to?" questions.

Santos might be willing to put more effort into his schoolwork, at least in the short run, if a highly desirable reward were made contingent on his effort. But as Chapters 3 and 8 indicate, salient extrinsic rewards have important limitations. Engaging students' intrinsic interest has advantages over using extrinsic rewards, but it is not realistic to make every school task intrinsically interesting for every student.

Fortunately, some students seem to work hard on assigned tasks that are not intrinsically interesting and for which no reinforcement is expected; they simply do what the teacher asks—even if the task is boring or unchallenging. What produces this behavior? Neither reinforcement theory nor intrinsic motivation theory offers a satisfactory explanation.

This chapter proposes internalized values as an explanation for such achievement efforts. Two different theoretical frameworks for the study of values are discussed. One evolved from the self-determination branch of intrinsic motivation theory (Chapter 8); the other is based on Atkinson's expectancy x value theory (Chapter 5).

Self-determination theorists (e.g., Ryan, Connell, Deci) claim that children begin to value the behaviors for which they and others in their social surroundings are reinforced. When these values are **internalized** (accepted as their own), students *choose* to engage in activities that are consistent with them, whether or not the behavior is reinforced. They consequently feel self-determining, even though they may not enjoy the activity.

Eccles and her colleagues study values in the context of an expanded expectancy x value theory. Like Atkinson, they assume that people choose to engage in tasks that they value and in which they expect to succeed, but Eccles conceptualizes values more broadly than Atkinson, and she makes distinctions among types of values that are not made by self-determination theorists.

Relationships are also discussed in this chapter because students' relationships with their teachers affect whether they adopt their teachers' values. Furthermore, classrooms are very social places. Students form relationships with each other as well as with the teacher, and although researchers often study social relationships separately from motivation and learning, the two domains are inextricably linked.

Self-Determination and Internalized Motivation

According to self-determination theorists, children learn from parents and other significant adults that achievement behaviors are valued in our society. Some children internalize these values as their own and behave in ways that are consistent with them.

The more people accept the values of their social surroundings as their own, the more they experience socially sanctioned behavior as self-determined. People who have internalized socially accepted values function more effectively and are better assimilated in their community (Ryan & La Guardia, in press). Studies of classrooms have shown that students who value learning and doing well in school are more curious and mastery oriented, less angry and bored, more persistent, more likely to use learning strategies aimed at deep (rather than superficial) processing, and they achieve at a higher level than students who have not internalized academic values (Miserandino, 1996; Sheldon & Elliot, 1998; Sheldon & Kasser, 1998; Yamauchi & Tanaka, 1998).

As mentioned in Chapter 8, Ryan, Deci, Connell, and their colleagues conceptualize motivation as a continuum from extrinsically controlled to self-determined. At one end of the continuum are externally-controlled behaviors (to get a reward) and at the other end are intrinsically-motivated behaviors (for pleasure). In the middle of the continuum are behaviors that were originally regulated by external contingencies (**extrinsically regulated**) but came to be experienced as self-determined (**self regulated**); that is, they came to be adopted by the self as valuable and worth doing (Connell & Wellborn, 1991; Ryan & Connell, 1989; Ryan et al., 1985; Ryan, Connell, & Grolnick, 1992; Ryan & Deci, 2000; Ryan & Stiller, 1991; Ryan & La Guardia, in press).

Self-regulation of achievement behavior is believed to result from a process of internalization in the same way that all other behaviors valued in a child's social environment come under self-regulation, including moral behavior (e.g., not stealing) and social behavior (e.g., sharing; Bandura, 1991; Aronfreed, 1969; Mussen & Eisenberg, 2001). At first, children need to be externally reinforced for certain behaviors that are not intrinsically interesting. Thus, a child may initially do homework assignments only to earn a star on a public chart or to avoid punishment. Gradually, as he learns to anticipate the reactions of others he begins to judge himself for engaging or not engaging in a behavior in the same way that his parents or teachers had judged him in the past. This internalized judgment results in emotional reactions to compliance and noncompliance—what Ryan and colleagues call **introjected regulation.** At this point, our student may finish his homework because he will feel anxious or guilty if he doesn't, or he may spend time with his grandmother because it makes him feel good. Even though external forces (the promise of a reward or the threat of punishment) are not present, introjected regulation is associated with feelings of being controlled or coerced more than with feelings of self-determination.

Ultimately, our child accepts as his own some of the values underlying the behaviors for which he was previously reinforced—a motivational level referred to as **identification.** Now behavioral regulation has been integrated into his self; he experiences volition without a sense of pressure or coercion. For example, he might explain that he studies vocabulary words because he wants to be able to write and speak well—because he *values* these qualities. He experiences himself as self-determining, engaging in the activity because he wants to, even though he may not find the activity interesting or enjoyable and he is not externally reinforced for it. Thus, identified regulation is extrinsic in the sense that the child is not intrinsically interested in the activity, but it is experienced as volitional. Research suggests that "identifying with" academic values has some of the same positive benefits as intrinsic motivation to engage in academic tasks, such as higher levels of engagement and more positive emotional experiences (e.g., Patrick et al., 1993).

The least coercive and salient forms of extrinsic reinforcement are the most likely to facilitate identification with adults' values (as opposed to introjected regulation). Thus, children are more likely to integrate parents' and teachers' values if they are socially reinforced (e.g., praised) than if they are given tangible reinforcement (e.g., money, toys, candy). Both social and tangible reinforcements give the message that the activity is valued, but tangible reinforcement is more salient and gives children the additional message that they are not expected to engage in the activity unless they get something for it. This **"minimal but sufficient" principle** applies to punishment, too. Studies have found that mild rather than severe threats of punishment are more effective in promoting children's ability to inhibit themselves from engaging in prohibited activities (Lepper, 1973). Salient rewards, like severe punishment, focus children's attention too much on the external reasons for a behavior.

This internalization process applies to any domain of activity. Thus, the student who internalizes his parents' value of athletic skills may demonstrate considerable effort on the athletic field, but little in the classroom. The student who learns to value the performing arts may practice an instrument every day, but barely glance at her textbook when it comes to learning about the Civil War. Other students may put their effort into being tough or popular or funny. One student is not necessarily less motivated than the other. Rather, they value competency and success in different domains.

Students who have an internalized "schoolwork ethic" are the easiest to teach. Teachers are not obliged to make tasks intrinsically interesting for such students, nor do they need to offer an external reward for effort or threaten punishment for not working. But such internalized values cannot be relied on alone. It is unlikely that valuing academic work can sustain effort in the absence of occasional rewards on a long series of tasks that are not at all intrinsically interesting and do not result in feelings of competence.

Measures of Internalized Motivation

Harter (1992, 2000) developed a questionnaire containing a subscale that assesses internalized motivation. The questionnaire contains 24 items to assess three motivational orientations (extrinsic, intrinsic, internalized). The scale is introduced to children as a questionnaire asking them about their reasons for doing their schoolwork. An item assessing internalized motivation ("I do my schoolwork because I've learned for myself that it's important for me to do it") can be contrasted with an intrinsic reason ("I do my schoolwork because what we learn is really interesting") and an extrinsic reason ("I do my schoolwork because my teacher will be pleased with me if I do").

Ryan and Connell (1989) created the Self-Regulatory Style Questionnaire, which assesses external, introjected, identified, and intrinsic motivation. Respondents are asked to rate the validity of various explanations for their behavior (see Table 9.1). Research has shown that students who score relatively high on external regulation also perceive that they have relatively low support for autonomy in their classroom, and they claim to be relatively high on anxiety and low in enjoyment of schoolwork. Identified and intrinsic motivation are associated with perceptions of high support for autonomy in the classroom and greater enjoyment.

In summary, according to self-determination theorists, people sometimes choose to engage in activities that they do not enjoy; the more they have internalized values related to the task or activity, the more they feel that that they are self-determined. Many of the benefits of intrinsic motivation can therefore be achieved by instilling values. Although conceptualized somewhat differently, internalized values are also critical to Eccles' elaboration of expectancy x value theory, described next.

Values in Eccle's Revised
Expectancy x Value Theory

Recall that Atkinson conceptualized incentive values in terms of the pride or shame a task is expected to generate. Achievement situations that are expected to generate feelings of pride have positive value (make a person want to approach the task) and those that are expected to produce feelings of shame are presumed to have negative value (make a person want to avoid the task). This is a very narrow conceptualization of values especially considering that levels of pride and

TABLE 9.1　**Sample Items from the Academic Self-Regulatory Style Questionnaire***

Why do I do my homework?

Response options: 1 = not at all true, 2 = not very true, 3 = sort of true, 4 = very true

External (rule following; avoidance of punishment)

- ❐ Because I'll get in trouble if I don't
- ❐ Because that's what I'm supposed to do
- ❐ So that the teacher won't yell at me
- ❐ Because that's the rule
- ❐ So others won't get mad at me

Introjection (self- and other-approval; avoidance of disapproval)

- ❐ Because I want the teacher to think I'm a good student
- ❐ Because I will feel bad about myself if I don't
- ❐ Because I'll feel ashamed of myself if I don't
- ❐ Because I want the other students to think I'm smart
- ❐ Because it bothers me when I don't
- ❐ Because I want people to like me

Identification (self-valued goal; personal importance)

- ❐ Because I want to understand the subject
- ❐ Because I want to learn new things
- ❐ To find out if I'm right or wrong
- ❐ Because I think it's important to

Intrinsic (enjoyment, fun)

- ❐ Because it's fun
- ❐ Because I enjoy it

*Adapted from Ryan & Connell (1989). The full scale is available from Richard Ryan, Department of Psychology, University of Rochester, Rochester, New York 14627. Copyright © 1989 by the American Psychological Association. Reprinted with permission.

shame are entirely determined, in theory, by a person's perception of the probability of success or failure.

More recent theorists, most notably Eccles and her colleagues, have offered broader conceptualizations of the value component of expectancy x value theory. Eccles, Adler, Futterman, Goff, Kaczala, Meece, and Midgley (1983) propose three kinds of values relevant to achievement (see also Jacobs & Eccles, 2000; Wigfield & Eccles, 1992).

Attainment value is determined by how the task or the domain fulfills a person's needs; it concerns the relevance of an activity to a person's actual or ideal self-concept. According to the theory, people engage in activities and develop competencies that are consistent with their real and desired concept of themselves (as feminine, musically talented, popular, socially deviant, or hard working, for example). Of the three kinds of values in Eccles' theory, attainment value is the most closely related to internalized motivation in self-determination theory. Thus, if I see myself as scholarly, I might value writing books and engaging in intellectual conversation; if I wanted to see myself as athletic, I might value more my efforts on the tennis court.

Utility value concerns the usefulness of a task as a means to achieve goals that might not be related to the task itself. For example, understanding chemistry and biology would have considerable utility value for a college student planning to attend medical school. In the context of school tasks, utility value usually requires some future time perspective, and an understanding of the links between immediate tasks and long-term goals (Husman & Lens, 1999).

Intrinsic value is the immediate enjoyment one gets from doing a task. When a task has intrinsic value it is engaged in for its own sake, rather than for some other purpose. This component of values in Eccles' theory is essentially the same as the notion of intrinsic motivation discussed in Chapter 8.

Eccles and her colleagues point out that values need to be considered in the context of *costs*—in energy, psychological risks (e.g., of humiliation if failure occurs), and alternative activities (Wigfield & Eccles, 1992). For example, college students who do not work hard in a particular class are not necessarily lazy or unmotivated. They have more likely chosen to exert their effort in other domains. They may put their energy into other courses or nonacademic domains (e.g., work, athletics, social organizations, families, relationships, and so on). Students who face the difficult task of apportioning their time among different courses as they prepare for final exams are painfully aware of the costs of achievement-related choices.

Where Do Achievement Values Come From?

As mentioned above, self-determination theorists have described a process of internalization that begins with minimally sufficient external reinforcement for particular behaviors (e.g., effort on academic tasks), moves toward self-reinforcement or punishment (feeling good or bad about exerting or not exerting effort on schoolwork), and results in total acceptance of a value (e.g., it is important to work hard in school).

Extrinsic reinforcement is not the only way adults can promote their values regarding hard work and learning. They can model academic values by engaging in intellectual activities themselves (Eccles, 1993; Jacobs & Eccles, 2000). They can also make direct statements, e.g., "It's really important to be able to write well," or "Don't worry about math, I was never good in it and I make a good living." Adults also instill values subtly, by indicating with what they pay attention to or the facial expressions they make in reaction to children's successful or failed mastery attempts. The father who ignores his son's recounting of the difficulties he is having with algebra but becomes attentive when he mentions the field goal he missed at football practice makes a clear statement about what he thinks is more important.

Perceptions of competence may also affect the attainment and even the utility value of academic work, just as they affect intrinsic value (Chapter 8). Studies have found, for example, that achievement values in mathematics are positively related to self-perceptions of competence (Covington, 1999) and to students' history of performance (Eccles, 1984); values are inversely related to anxiety about mathematics performance (e.g., Meece et al., 1990). Because the research is cross-sectional, we don't know whether children begin to value activities in which they feel confident (as intrinsic motivation theory suggests), or that they engage in activities they value and consequently develop competencies and self-confidence. Most likely, both causal directions are true.

Eccles et al. (1983) proposed that people's concept of themselves—their self-schema—also affects their values. For example, a student who thinks of himself as a nonconformist may devalue all schoolwork. This issue is discussed in more detail below in the context of social class and ethnic differences in academic values.

Sex Stereotyping

Most of the research on self-schema and values has focused on gender differences. There is evidence that some academic domains are sex-typed as "masculine" or "feminine" (see Eccles et al., 1983). Math and science, for example, are often considered male domains. Eccles and her colleagues (1983) propose that the attainment value of mathematics achievement is relatively low for females who perceive mathematics courses as a masculine activity and for whom femininity is central to their self-schema (see also Eccles, 1984; Eccles, Barber, & Jozefowicz, 1998; Eccles, Barber, Jozefowicz, Malenchuk, & Vida, 2000; Wigfield et al., 1991; Wigfield & Eccles, 1994).

Studies suggest that occupations requiring mathematics are more sex-stereotyped than are math courses. Eccles points out, however, that if females are less likely to aspire to a profession in mathematics, mathematics courses will have less utility value for them than for males. Differences in goals related to occupational choices may also affect males' and females' perceptions of the value of certain occupations. One study found, for example, that adolescent girls tended to value helping others in the context of an occupation more than boys (see Eccles, Barber, Jozefowicz, Malenchuk, & Vida, 2000). These kinds of gender differences in career aspirations can have implications for the attainment as well as the utility value of academic courses.

Ethnicity and Social Class

Social scientists have tried to explain ethnic and social class differences in values related to school achievement and attainment. A study by Mickelson (1990) suggests that some African American students do not value academic achievement because they believe that their efforts in school will have little economic or social payoff. Van Laar (2000) similarly proposes that African American students disidentify with academic values in part because they make increasingly external attributions for academic outcomes—they come to believe that academic outcomes are determined by forces over which they have no control. (See also Murdock, 1999.) Interpreted in the context of Eccles' model, attaining academic skills has low utility value for some African American students.

Ogbu (1992, 1997) has similarly proposed that African American students are aware that they are members of a caste-like minority and thus have limited social and economic opportunities. He goes further, claiming that they cope with this harsh reality by developing "oppositional identities"; they become indifferent or even contemptuous of mainstream values, including academic achievement. Ogbu coined the phrase "acting White" to refer to any display of valuing hard work and school success. Osborne (1997), Steele (1997), and others (e.g., Major, Spencer, Schmader, Wolfe, & Crocker, 1998) have also discussed African Americans' **disidentification** with academic achievement values.

There is evidence that disidentification applies to high- as well as low-achieving minority students. Covington (1998) describes the ways in which high-achieving African American adolescents try to conceal their academic prowess by making jokes or strange faces in class or feigning ineptitude or disinterest while privately working hard and doing well. McFarland (2000) similarly describes how some high-achieving students maintain peer respect by answering teachers' questions correctly, but with a tone of defiance or disrespect. He gives an account of one adolescent, who pretended not to be paying attention and refused to take notes, then embarrassed the teacher by correctly answering a question that the teacher obviously asked to catch him off guard.

Steele (1997, 1999) describes another way in which high-achieving minority students are at risk. His studies, primarily with Stanford college students, show that when a test is introduced as a test of ability, African American students do not perform as well as Caucasian students, even when the ability of the two groups is held constant. Differences in performance are not found when the same test is introduced as a study of how certain problems are generally solved rather than as a test of abilities. Steele explains this finding with the notion of **stereotype threat.** He claims that African American students are anxious when the test is presented as a test of ability because they are concerned about confirming the stereotype that African Americans have inferior intelligence. This anxiety interferes with their performance. Analyses of their problem-solving strategies support his interpretation. Under stereotype threat conditions, African American students seemed to be trying too hard. They reread questions and multiple choices, checked and rechecked answers. As a consequence they were less efficient.

The very high-performing African American students in Steele's studies appeared to be working to overcome the stereotype of being intellectually inferior. In contrast, the typically low-performing middle-school students that Graham et al., studied had apparently given up on disconfirming the stereotype. To maintain some sense of self-worth in a mainstream culture that values academic success, they ceased caring. Unfortunately, both groups suffer, albeit in different ways.

The evidence on oppositional identities as an explanation for devaluing school is indirect and mixed. For example, studies have found that the more African American students perceived discrimination, the less they valued school, the less engaged in school they were, or the more maladaptive emotional functioning (e.g., depression, anger) they evidenced (Roeser, Eccles, & Sameroff, 1998, 2000; Taylor, Casten, Flickinger, Roberts, & Fulmore, 1994). But in the Taylor et al. study, a stronger ethnic identity actually predicted higher engagement in school.

While the evidence for oppositional identities is weak, there is clear evidence that many students develop antiacademic values, and a disproportionate number are nonwhite. Graham, Taylor, and Hudley (1998) used a clever strategy for assessing students' achievement values. They were concerned that self-report measures would not be answered honestly. Instead, they asked adolescents in the study to nominate peers whom they most admired, respected and wanted to be like. Students also identified classmates who fit descriptions of: (1) trying hard and getting good grades, (2) not trying and receiving poor grades, (3) following or (4) not following school rules, (5) being good at sports, and (6) wearing nice clothes. Teachers rated all students on how well they were achieving in school. The researchers found that African American and Hispanic American girls and Caucasian girls and boys primarily nominated a high-achieving student when asked who they most admired, respected, and wanted to be like. African American and Hispanic American boys, in contrast, were more likely to nominate low-achieving boys than high-achieving students. The results suggest that minority boys, but not minority girls, are the most likely to reject achievement-related values.

Middle-class Caucasian children are not immune from developing negative values related to school. Indeed, Roeser, Eccles, and Sameroff (1998, 2000) identified a group of adolescents (14 percent of their sample) from mostly middle- and high-income families who expressed considerable doubt about the importance and utility of school, even though they were performing at an average level and had confidence in their abilities. Their antiacademic values seemed to be rooted in the school and classroom climate. The alienated youth in this study rated the competitiveness of their school environment high, and compared to the students who valued school more, they claimed that the teachers in their school were not very supportive and had low regard for them, the curricula was not very meaningful, and they had little autonomy. To be sure, even within the same school students vary in their academic values. But these findings suggest that school practices themselves can be a factor in students' beliefs about the value of schooling.

Effects of Values

Values are important because they affect choices in activities as well as level of effort and persistence. Values also influence students' intentions and decisions about course enrollment, and even career choices (Eccles, 1984, 1994; Meece et al., 1990; Meece & Courtney, 1992). Gender differences in utility value, for example, appeared in one study to explain why girls were less likely than boys to take honors math courses in high school (see Eccles, Barbar, & Jozefowicz, 1998).

Values also mediate the effect of perceptions of competence on self-esteem (Harter, 2000). In a study reported by Harter (1987), for example, low perceptions of competence had more negative effects on self-esteem in domains children valued highly than in domains they valued less.

Pintrich and Schrauben (1992) report in their review of research that values also affect how students approach learning. When students are working on tasks in valued domains they are more likely to use active cognitive strategies, such as rehearsal, elaboration, and organization strategies, and they are more likely to report that they were thinking critically about course material.

Age-Related Changes

The developmental trajectory of academic values appears to parallel those of perceptions of competence and intrinsic motivation; academic values decline with age, although the evidence is not as consistent as it is for perceived competence and varies by domain (see Eccles et al., 1983; Eccles & Midgley, 1989; Eccles, Wigfield, Harold, & Blumenfeld, 1993; Wigfield, Eccles, Mac Iver, Reuman, & Midgley, 1991; Wigfield & Eccles, 1994; Wigfield, Eccles, Yoon, Harold, Arbreton, Freedman-Doan, & Blumenfeld, 1997).

Although children as young as first grade appear to have distinct beliefs about what they are good at and what they value (Wigfield et al., 1997), young children may not differentiate among subjects or among the components of the Eccles model (attainment value, utility value, and intrinsic value) as much as do older children (Wigfield & Eccles, 1992; Eccles & Wigfield, 1995). Wigfield and Eccles (1992) propose that for young children, the subjective value of a task is primarily determined by the amount of pleasure they get from the task. Perhaps as children get older, and as they internalize social norms, attainment and utility values begin to figure more significantly into their assessment of tasks.

Measures of Values

Eccles and her colleagues have done most of the research on achievement-related values. The measure they have used in a number of studies, shown in Table 9.2, has good reliability and validity, and can be used with children as early as first grade.

In summary, there are at least two reasons—in addition to obtaining a reward or finding enjoyment—why students might choose to exert effort and persist at an academic activity. They may value the activity because high academic achievement is part of their self-concept, or they may believe certain academic skills have some utility in their lives outside of school or for their long-term career plans. Values thus play an important role in student behavior and performance.

TABLE 9.2   **Assessment of Achievement-Related Values***

*All items are answered on a 1–7 scale, with the anchors shown in parentheses.
Any subject matter can be substituted for math.*

Importance *(Attainment Value)*

- ❐   For me, being good in math is (not at all important, very important)
- ❐   Some kids find what they learn in one subject or activity more important than what they learn in another. Compared to most of your other activities, how important is it to you to be good at math?

Usefulness *(Utility Value)*

- ❐   Some things that you learn in school help you do things better outside of class—that is, they are useful. For example, learning about plants might help you grow a garden. In general, how useful is what you learn in math? (not at all useful, very useful)
- ❐   Some kids find what they learn in one subject or activity more useful than what they learn in another. Compared to most of your other activities, how useful is what you learn in math?

Interest *(Intrinsic Value)*

- ❐   In general, I find working on math assignments (very boring, very interesting [fun])
- ❐   How much do you like doing math? (not at all, very much)
- ❐   Some kids find that they like one subject or activity much more than another. Compared to most of your other activities, how much do you like math? (not at all, very much)

*From Wigfield, Eccles, Yoon, Harold, Arbreton, Freedman-Doan, & Blumenfeld (1997). Copyright © 1997 by the American Psychological Association. Reprinted with permission.

Next, we turn to a topic that has implications for how well students internalized their teachers' academic values, as well as for their comfort and adaptive behavior in academic settings.

Relationships

Children who fare poorly in school are burdened with more than the frustration and humiliation of their failure. Often they are not treated as well by their teachers and peers—not just as learners, but as people. Many children who fail in school have consistently negative interactions with their teachers. They are frequently in trouble—for not completing assignments or not paying attention, or for goofing off or acting out. Often they deserve being sanctioned, but the classroom becomes a very unpleasant place for children who have mostly conflict and discipline-related interactions with their teachers.

Contributing to some poor achieving students' distress are peers, who can be very cruel. The negative peer relationships occur partly because poor achievers also often become troublemakers. Peers sometimes exclude low-achievers from play and birthday parties, resist being placed in work groups with them, and make fun of their academic problems. It is not surprising that many students' perception of themselves as being academically incompetent evolves into a perception of themselves as being unworthy human beings.

Only recently have researchers begun to examine the effect a student's relationships with teachers and peers have on motivation. Self-determination theorists coined the term **relatedness**—the need to feel securely connected to people in the social context and ". . . to experience oneself as worthy and capable of love and respect" (Connell & Wellborn, 1991, p. 51). They claim that relatedness is a basic human need, along with feelings of competence and self-determination (Connell & Wellborn, 1991; Ryan & Deci, 2000; Ryan & La Guardia, in press). People do not function effectively in environments in which the need for relatedness, as well as feelings of competence and self-determination, is not met.

McCombs (1994) similarly includes social support as one of three critical components in her model of motivation (along with "will" and "skill"). She describes social support as a ". . . culture of trust, respect, caring, concern, and a sense of community with others . . ." that provides opportunities for ". . . individual choice, expression of self-determination and agency, and freedom to fail or take risks" (p. 54).

Wentzel (1997) examined students' perspective on the qualities of good relationships with their teacher. She asked middle-school students: "How do you know when a teacher cares about you?" and "How do you know when a teacher does not care about you?" Common responses, shown in Table 9.3, suggest that attentiveness to students as human beings is important. One noteworthy finding is that students considered teachers' instructional behaviors in assessing how much their teachers cared about them. Their responses suggest that teachers can convey that they care by making serious efforts to promote learning and by holding students to appropriately high standards.

Boys are at greater risk of developing negative relationships with teachers than are girls. Studies consistently show that teachers rate relationships with boys as less close than they rate relationships with girls (Howes, Phillipsen, & Peisner-Feinberg, 2000; Ramey, Lanzi, Phillips, & Ramey, 1998), and girls report closer relationships with teachers (Valeski & Stipek, 2001). It is likely that the more distant and conflictual relationships with boys are related to boys' higher levels of disruptive behavior. But negative relationships also exacerbate the misbehavior as well as undermine learning, creating a downward spiral that is difficult to escape.

Consequences of Relationships

Students in schools with caring and supportive interpersonal relationships have more positive academic attitudes and values, and are more satisfied with school (Baker, 1998, 1999; Battistich, Solomon, Kim, Watson, & Schaps, 1995). Eccles (1993), for example, reports that the value of math increased for those students in

TABLE 9.3   **Students' Descriptions of Teachers Who Care**

	Teachers Who Care	**Teachers Who Do *Not* Care**
Teaching behaviors	Makes an effort to make class interesting; teaches in a special way	Teaches in a boring way, gets off task, teaches while students aren't paying attention
Communication style	Talks to you, pays attention, asks questions, listens	Ignores, interrupts, screams, yells
Equitable treatment and respect	Honest, fair, keeps promises, trusts me, tells the truth	Embarrasses, insults
Concern about individuals	Asks what's wrong, talks to me about my problems, acts as a friend, asks when I need help, takes time to make sure I understand, calls on me	Forgets name, does nothing when I do something wrong, doesn't explain things or answer questions, doesn't try to help me

Summarized from Wentzel (1997). Copyright © 1997 by the American Psychological Association. Reprinted with permission.

her study who moved from an elementary school teacher whom they perceived to be low in support to a junior high school teacher whom they perceived to be high in support. In contrast, the value of math decreased for those students who moved from a highly supportive to a relatively unsupportive teacher.

Negative relationships might help explain why some African American students develop antiacademic values. In a study by Murdock (1999), low-income African American students were more likely to perceive teachers as disinterested. Moreover, the more disinterested students perceived their teachers to be, the more noncompliant behavior they exhibited.

Students who feel that they have caring, supportive teachers are also more engaged in academic work in school than those who do not (Connell & Wellborn, 1991; Ryan & Deci, 2000; Ryan & La Guardia, in press). In contrast, students who describe their teachers as disinterested, disrespectful, or unfair are typically not very engaged. Indeed, they are more likely to drop out of school altogether (see Murdock, 1999).

A study by Skinner and Belmont (1993) is illustrative of research showing the positive effects of good relationships on student learning behavior. They assessed teachers' perceptions of their involvement with their students, using a measure which asks about their *affection* (how much they like, appreciate, and enjoy the student), their *attunement* (their understanding, sympathy, and knowledge about the student), and their *dependability* (their availability in case of need). Using similar items, students rated their own involvement with their teacher. Teachers' ratings of their involvement with students in the fall strongly predicted students' relatedness to their teacher and their feelings of autonomy in the spring, which in turn predicted students' engagement in classroom activities.

The Skinner and Belmont (1993) study revealed an important reciprocal effect between teachers' and students' behavior. Teachers' level of involvement with students was positively influenced by high levels of student engagement at the beginning of the year, which in turn enhanced students' feelings of relatedness to the teacher. The study demonstrates the bidirectional nature of student-teacher relationships, and the importance, for teachers, of recognizing the negative trajectories that can spiral into maladaptive interactions.

Research by Connell and Wellborn (1991) has also shown that the more emotionally connected students feel they are to their teacher and classmates, the more they are cognitively, emotionally, and behaviorally engaged in classroom activities, and the more willing they are to seek help when they need it (Ryan, Gheen, & Midgley, 1998). (See also, Connell, 1991; Connell, Spencer, & Aber, 1994; Connell & Wellborn, 1991; Deci, Vallerand, Pelletier, & Ryan, 1991; Goodenow, 1993; Pianta, 1999; Pianta & Nimetz, 1991; Pianta & Steinberg, 1992; Skinner, Zimmer-Gembeck, & Connell, 1998; Skinner & Wellborn, 1994.)

A few theorists have speculated about why students are more engaged in classrooms in which they have developed a positive, secure relationship with their teacher. A positive relationship may lead students to want to please their teacher by doing what their teacher expects of them, or they may internalize (accept as their own) their teachers' values more readily if they like and respect them. This latter explanation is suggested by comments made during a study of females who had been successful in careers requiring mathematics (Zeldin & Pajares, 2000). Reflecting on how they overcame gender stereotypes, the women interviewed often referred to the encouragement of adults whom they respected and trusted. They explained that the confidence these caring adults had in their competencies helped them develop their own self-confidence.

Harter (1987) suggests that the sense of self-worth fostered by a sense of belonging and being socially supported engenders a generally positive affective and motivational state. Certainly, it is difficult for anyone to get interested in activities while feeling anxious, humiliated, or ashamed. Students who believe that the teacher will continue to care about them, even if they perform poorly, should feel more comfortable taking risks—for example, by volunteering answers, asking questions when they are having difficulty, or selecting challenging work. Consistent with her proposal, Harter and her colleagues have shown empirically that adolescents rate their feelings of self-worth higher and feel freer to speak up and express their opinions in contexts in which they feel supported and validated as individuals (Harter, Waters, & Whitesell, 1998; Harter, Waters, Whitesell, & Kastelic, 1998).

Assessing Teacher-Student Relationships

All of the items from the measure used in the Skinner and Belmont (1993) study are shown in Table 9.4. Teachers can probe their own relationships with their

TABLE 9.4 Teachers' and Students' Ratings of Their Relationship

Response options: 1 = not at all true, 2 = not very true, 3 = sort of true, 4 = very true

Teacher Questions	Student Questions
Affection	
■ This student is easy to like. ■ I enjoy the time I spend with this student. ■ Teaching this student isn't very enjoyable for me. ■ This student is difficult to like.	■ My teacher likes me. ■ My teacher really cares about me. ■ My teacher doesn't seem to enjoy having me in class.
Attunement	
■ I know a lot about what goes on for this student. ■ I know this student well. ■ I don't understand this student very well. ■ I don't know very much about what goes on for this student outside of school.	■ My teacher spends time with me. ■ My teacher talks with me.
Dependability	
■ When this student does not do as well as she/he can, I make time to help him/her find ways to do better. ■ This student can count on me to be there for him/her. ■ Sometimes I feel like I can't be there for this student when s/he needs me. ■ I can't always be available to this student.	■ My teacher is always there for me. ■ I can count on my teacher to be there for me. ■ I can rely on my teacher to be there when I need him/her. ■ I can't count on my teacher when I need him/her. ■ I can't depend on my teacher for the important things. ■ My teacher is never there for me.

Reprinted from Skinner and Belmont (1993). (This scale can be obtained from Professor Ellen Skinner, Department of Psychology, P.O. Box 751, Portland OR 97207-0751.)

students by completing these questions for some of the students in their class. The student items parallel the teacher items.

Pianta and his colleagues have developed a measure for teachers of preschool and early elementary-age children, called the Student Teacher Relationship Scale (STRS; Pianta & Steinberg, 1992). The measure has five subscales: (1) conflict/anger (e.g., "This child and I are always struggling"); (2) warmth/closeness (e.g., "I share a warm, affectionate relationship with this child"); (3) open communication (e.g., "This child shares information about him/herself with me"); (4) dependency (e.g., "This child is always seeking my help when it's not necessary"); and (5) troubled feelings (e.g., "Despite my best efforts, I'm uncomfortable with how this child and I have gotten along"). Pianta and his colleagues and other investigators have found that scores on this measure are fairly consistent over the early grades, and they predict teachers' future relationships with children, children's classroom behavior in future grades, teachers' retention decisions, and children's adjustment to kindergarten (see, for example, Pianta, 1994; Pianta & Steinberg, 1992; Pianta, Steinberg, & Rollins, 1995).

Age-Related Shifts.   The increase in alienation toward school and devaluing of school achievement, often seen in adolescence (Anderman & Maehr, 1994), may be due partly to a shift in the nature of relationships between teachers and students. Students tend to report less positive relationships with their teachers when they transition from elementary school to middle school. The more formal, academically-focused relationships have, in turn, been shown to lead to a decline in interest in academic work (Eccles, 1993; see also Lynch & Cicchetti, 1997; Midgley & Edelin, 1998; Midgley, Feldlaufer, & Eccles, 1988). Even outside observers have rated junior high school teachers as less friendly, less supportive, and less caring than elementary school teachers (Feldlaufer, Midgley, & Eccles, 1988; Eccles, 1993). Ironically, relationships between teachers and students typically become much less personal and caring just when children may be in the greatest need of a supportive, attentive adult (see Eccles & Wigfield, 2000, in press).

Fostering Positive Relationships

Teachers who genuinely care about their students' welfare and learning will convey this to students in their interactions with them. But the entire classroom climate is important. The suggestions below are designed to help teachers make sure that students' social-emotional needs are met and social relationships support rather than undermine their ability to learn in their classroom. The goal is to make classrooms psychologically safe places for students to learn without fearing rejection.

   1. Respect and value students as human beings.   Carl Rogers (1951), a very well known clinical psychologist, urged parents to give their children "unconditional positive regard." This dictum applies just as well to teachers. Defensive Dave would not have to engage in such dysfunctional behavior if he believed that the teacher would accept and value him regardless of his level of performance. Students who trust that the teacher respects and cares about them can take academic risks with impunity. Students who believe that their value in the teacher's eyes depends on their academic success risk more than a low grade: they risk humiliation and rejection.

   Respect may be the most important ingredient in supporting students' motivation to learn. It is conveyed in the most subtle ways—whether the teacher looks directly into the eyes of a student who is speaking; how long the teacher waits for a student to respond to a question; the teacher's facial expression when a student reveals poor understanding. Teachers' respect for students can affect students' respect for themselves, their motivation to engage in academic tasks, and even their attitudes and perceptions of the intrinsic value, perceived usefulness, and impor tance of academic subjects (Midgley, Feldlaufer, & Eccles, 1989b).

Although respect can be described in behavioral terms it needs to come from the heart. Teachers who do not genuinely respect and value their students will have a difficult time convincing them otherwise. It helps to get to know students whom teachers find difficult to like. (They exist, and teachers usually agree on who they are.) Often a student's behavior that seems indefensible and bothersome can become more understandable, and even tolerable, when the cause is better understood. Getting to know students, their home circumstances, and other aspects of their lives can promote greater understanding and more positive feelings. When the teacher conveys these feelings, difficult-to-like students sometimes improve their behavior and become easier to respect.

a. Be attentive and interested in students—as human beings as well as students. Solicit and be attentive to students' ideas and opinions in class discussions. Show them that you take their ideas seriously by building on their comments or asking them follow-up questions.

Although the focus must remain on learning, it doesn't hurt to express interest in students' lives outside of school—to congratulate them for their efforts on the soccer field the night before, inquire how they are feeling after being out sick, or wish them a happy birthday. Teachers can also create a supportive climate by sharing their own feelings and values and encouraging students to do the same. It is important that students are accepted and supported when they disclose their ideas and feelings.

b. Hold students to high standards. One of the best ways to show respect for students is to hold them to high standards—by not accepting sloppy, thoughtless, or incomplete work, by pressing them to clarify vague comments, by encouraging them not to give up, and by not praising work that does not reflect genuine effort. Ironically, reactions that are often intended to protect students' self-esteem—such as accepting low quality work—convey a lack of interest, patience, or caring. "Tough love" can be given with support and compassion, and it shows students that you really care about their future.

c. Avoid ridiculing or embarrassing students, publicly or in private. Engendering fear of ridicule or humiliation can control students' behavior, but at a great cost. Fear of humiliation engenders avoidance, not approach. It makes students want to withdraw and play it safe, not to engage actively in learning tasks and take risks. Being humiliated in public may be worse than it is in private, but teachers are authority figures and need to be mindful that an offhand comment, even in private, can have tremendous impact on a student's feelings of self-worth and respect.

d. Avoid sarcasm. Again, teachers need to recognize their importance—even for students who appear (most likely, pretend) not to care. A sarcastic remark that might be considered humorous by another adult, or even by a child in another context, can be devastating in a context in which the adult has power and authority. Young children are particularly vulnerable because they are more likely to take teachers' comments at face value.

   2. Create a risk-free environment.   Students need to feel that they can take risks, make mistakes, and reveal a lack of understanding—without losing the positive regard of the teacher or classmates.
   a. Take all questions seriously.   Unless a question is intentionally asked to disrupt or reflects repeated lack of attention, it should be taken seriously, regardless of how elementary it may seem.
   b. Follow up on wrong answers.   A wrong answer should not be ignored or criticized, and simply supplying the correct answer can be humiliating. The best response to a wrong answer—for saving face and for promoting learning—is to guide the student with follow-up questions and hints, to help her discover and correct her error or misunderstanding. If this requires more time than context allows, let the student know at the time that she's a little off the target and you'll help her later to get back on track.
   c. Praise students' efforts to do challenging tasks, even when they fail.   By doing this, teachers convey to students that approaching challenging tasks is valued, and there is no risk of disapproval or rejection when failure occurs.

   3. Assist students in developing positive relationships with each other.   Relationships among students affect their enjoyment and their ability to concentrate on academic tasks, as well as their feeling of being safe and supported in the classroom.
   a. Teach students to be respectful of each other.   To a considerable degree, students take their cues from the teacher. A teacher who is abusive toward students will foster disrespect among students; a teacher who is accepting, supportive, and respectful will engender the same. Explicit discussion of what is acceptable and respectful classroom behavior and what is not is also usually needed. In one elementary school where I worked, children were taught to differentiate between "put-ups" and "put-downs" from the first week of school, and reminded that only put-ups are acceptable. In the upper grades students engage in extended discussions of issues of respect and integrity, and the effects their behavior and remarks have on others.
   b. Help students develop positive relationships with each other.   Conflict among peers can interfere with students' motivation and ability to engage in academic work. Although not usually seen as part of the "basic" curriculum, explicit instruction and discussion of social conflicts and problem-solving strategies are critical to a psychologically safe classroom climate, as well as to students' social–moral development. Discussions about resolving social conflicts can be based on real situations that emerge at

school (Stipek, de la Sota, & Weishaupt, 1999). A fight that occurred on the playground because a child was called a derogatory name, or laughter in response to a student's answer to a question in the classroom provide meaningful material for social problem-solving lessons.[1]

In summary, theorists who have studied social relationships in school settings all assert the fundamental importance of nourishing respect and worthiness in students. A social context that is accepting and supportive, in which each student is valued regardless of his or her academic skills or performance relative to others, should go a long way toward diminishing the negative consequences of relatively poor performance. Being a slow learner or having difficulties with schoolwork should not get translated into feelings of being unvalued or unworthy as a person. My own observations suggest to me that the social climate of the classroom is at the heart of effective education. I have never seen a successful teacher who did not care about and respect students as people, and who did not create a classroom in which all children were encouraged and supported as human beings as well as learners.

Positive relationships, however, are not sufficient to produce high levels of learning. Midgley and Edelin (1998) observed that middle schools which have shown dramatic improvements in the social climate do not always show student academic gains. They propose that in their effort to be warm and caring, teachers sometimes express overly sympathetic attitudes and acceptance of work that does not reflect serious effort. Studies discussed in Chapter 14 provide further evidence for the importance the combining of a positive social context with high academic expectations.

Summary

Motivation theory and research have come a long distance from the early, rather simplistic view of behavior as based entirely on external consequences. To be sure, extrinsic reinforcement plays a critical role in achievement-related behavior. But there are other motivational systems that teachers can exploit to engage students' interest and effort in academic work. In addition to obtaining rewards, people also engage in activities because they are fun, because they have internalized values associated with them, and because they serve purposes beyond the classroom.

---

[1]My daughter's kindergarten teacher was an astute observer of the friendship networks and conflicts that developed among her students, and she organized instruction and activities to support positive relationships and to minimize tension among children. When my daughter and two other girls developed a problematic triangle, she engaged the entire class in a discussion about the problems that arise when two children exclude another and possible solutions. The teacher addressed the problem directly and sensitively, without referring to the particular children involved in the conflict, always showing respect for students' feelings. As a consequence, she contributed to a supportive classroom climate that fostered feelings of security while helping students develop social problem solving skills.

The teacher's task is to create an environment that takes good advantage of all of these motivational systems. As the work on relationships suggests, this can be best accomplished in a social context in which all students feel respected and valued by the teacher and classmates.

TABLE 9.5   Summary of Terms

Term	Definition
Self-Determination Theory	
Internalized motivation	Motivation that was originally based on external figures (extrinsically regulated) that becomes self-regulated
Extrinsic regulation	Behavior is controlled by external consequences
Self-regulation	Controlling one's own behavior without external rewards or constraints
Introjected	Behaving as the result of emotions (e.g., pride or guilt) associated with previously experienced parental responses (e.g., reward and punishment)
Identification	Caretakers' values are fully internalized
Minimal but sufficient principle	The less salient the extrinsic reward, the more likely the rewarded behavior will become valued by the individual
Expectancy x Value Theory	
Attainment value	The subjective importance of doing well on a task or in an achievement domain
Utility value	Perceived usefulness of a task as a means to achieve goals that might not be related to the task itself
Intrinsic value	The immediate enjoyment from doing a task
Disidentification	Ceasing to identify with a set of values that are perceived to be unattainable to protect a sense of self worth
Stereotype threat	The threat of being viewed through the lens of a negative stereotype or fear of doing something that would inadvertently confirm that stereotype
Relationships	
Relatedness	The need to feel securely connected to individuals in the social context and to experience oneself as worthy and capable of love and respect

CHAPTER

10 Goals

Goal theorists believe that all reasons for doing schoolwork are not equal; the nature of students' goals affects how they approach tasks and what they learn. Goals are related to values, but goals and values involve different levels of analysis. Values pertain to general feelings or beliefs about domains of activities in relation to the self. Goals concern the reasons one has for engaging in a particular activity. Although goal theorists measure general dispositions to be oriented toward one set of goals versus another, they are primarily concerned with people's immediate, subjective experience in task situations.

Most goal theorists distinguish between **learning goals** (referred to by some researchers as "mastery" or "task" goals) and **performance goals.** Learning goals concern mastery and developing understanding and skills; performance goals concern performing better than others, demonstrating more intelligence, and winning approval (Ames, 1992; Ames & Archer, 1988; Harackiewicz & Elliot, 1993; Linnenbrink & Pintrich, 2000; Nicholls, 1983; Maehr, 1984; Meece, 1991, 1994). Students are more likely to have learning goals when they are doing a task that they find intrinsically interesting, because they have internalized values related to the task, or because they see some utility in the skill that the task is designed to teach. Students are more likely to have a performance goal in the absence of these other reasons for working, and when extrinsic rewards are salient.

Researchers have also found that some children often have neither learning nor performance goals. They appear to be motivated primarily to avoid academic work. Nicholls, Cobb, Wood, Yackel, and Patashnick (1990) refer to this inclination as a **work-avoidance goal.** There is some evidence that children's learning goals and performance goals decrease and their work-avoidance goals increase with time in school (see Eccles, Wigfield, & Schiefele, 1997).

Implications of Task Goals

Dweck (1986) has described the different behaviors of students with learning goals and those with performance goals. Believing that ability can be achieved through effort, the student with learning goals seeks challenging tasks that provide opportunities to develop new competencies and persists when she encounters difficulty. She bases her judgments of competence on the amount of effort she expends and the real learning or mastery she achieves. In contrast, the student with performance goals holds an entity view of ability and therefore, like Safe Sally, wants to look competent or, like Defensive Dave, avoid looking incompetent. She judges her competence on how well she performs relative to others or on external feedback, not on real gains in understanding or mastery. (See also Dweck & Elliott, 1983; Dweck & Leggett, 1988; Elliott & Dweck, 1988; Lepper, 1988; Nicholls, Cobb, Yackel, Wood, & Wheatley, 1990; Dweck & Sorich, 1999).

These important implications for how students with different goals define and understand academic contexts are summarized in Table 10.1. Most of Dweck's general claims about the effects of goal orientations on behavior, as well as on their of achievement contexts, are well supported by evidence, to which we now turn.

Risk Taking and Challenge-Seeking

Studies have shown that a task- or mastery-orientation is associated with moderate risk-taking and willingness to engage in challenging tasks. In one study, students who were task-oriented tended to select a task described to them as difficult but that would promote skill development, whereas performance-oriented students selected a task they were told would not teach them anything new, but on which they could demonstrate their competence (Elliott & Dweck, 1988). In another study students who perceived their classroom as relatively mastery-oriented claimed that they would prefer a science project that would be difficult but result in new learning over an easy project (Ames & Archer, 1988; see also

TABLE 10.1   Learning and Performance Goals

	Learning	Performance
Success defined as:	Improvement, progress, mastery, innovation, creativity	High grades, high performance compared to others, winning, recognition
Value placed on:	Effort, persistence, attempting difficult tasks	Avoiding failure, succeeding with low effort
Reason for effort:	Intrinsic and personal meaning of activity, learning, mastery	Demonstrating ability/one's worth
Evaluation criteria:	Absolute criteria (standard), evidence of progress	Norms, social comparisons, another individual
Errors viewed as:	Part of learning process, informational	Failure, evidence of lack of ability or worth
Competence viewed as:	Increasing through effort, "incremental"	Inherited, fixed, an "entity"

Adapted from Maehr & Midgley, p. 36 (1996). Copyright © 1996 by Westview Press, Member of Perseus Books Group. Reprinted by permission of Westview Press.

Burhans & Dweck, 1995; Fuchs, Fuchs, Karns, Hamlett, Katzaroff, & Dutka, 1997; Nicholls, 1984; Smiley & Dweck, 1994; Meyer, Turner, & Spencer, 1997; Turner, Thorpe, & Meyer, 1998).

Focus of Attention

Research also suggests that learning versus performance goals have implications for students' attention while they work on tasks. When students are motivated to learn or master they focus more on the process of completing the task (i.e., they are **task-oriented**). When they have performance goals they are more focused on the self, especially on external evaluations of the self (i.e., they are **ego-oriented;** Nicholls, 1979b, 1983; see also, Butler, 1992, 1995, 1999; Thorkildsen & Nicholls, 1998).

An ego orientation is illustrated by a child in Peterson and Swing's (1982) study, mentioned in Chapter 2, who, when asked what she thought about during a math lesson, commented: ". . . I was nervous, and I thought maybe I wouldn't know how to do things . . . I was mostly thinking . . . I was making a fool of myself" (p. 486). In contrast, a task-oriented child responded to the same question by describing in detail the strategies she used to solve the problems.

Csikszentmihalyi (1975, 1988; Moneta & Csikszentmihalyi, 1996) refers to the intense involvement associated with a task-orientation as **flow.** People experiencing flow are so intensely attentive to the task at hand they may lose awareness of time and space. Most great artists and scholars report that they experience flow when working in their field. And people who are known for their creativity have reported that they were in a flow state when they did their best work (Nicholls, 1983).

Learning Behavior

Learning goals promote the use of effective problem-solving strategies. In one study, for example, students scoring high on a measure of mastery-orientation in science reported relatively greater use of active metacognitive strategies (e.g., reviewing material not understood, asking questions as they worked, making connections between current problems and past problems), and less use of "superficial engagement" (copying, guessing, skipping questions) than children who claimed to be relatively more performance-oriented (Meece, Blumenfeld, & Hoyle, 1988). Learning goals have been associated with other active learning strategies, such as planning, organizing material, and setting goals (Ames & Archer, 1988), and to "deep" processing strategies (e.g., discriminating important information from unimportant information, trying to figure out how new information fits with what one already knows, and monitoring comprehension (Nolen, 1988; Yamauchi & Tanaka, 1998).

Observations of children in classrooms confirm what has been found in survey studies. Meyer, Turner, and Spencer (1997), for example, describe two mastery-oriented children they observed working on a math project as being particularly flexible in altering plans that fell short of their goals. "Both students explained how they monitored, evaluated, and used self-explanations to block discouragement and to support persistence. They seemed to have developed ways to give themselves time, to make mistakes work for them . . ." (p. 515). (See also Middleton & Midgley, 1997; Pintrich, 1999; Pintrich & Schrauben, 1992; Young, 1997).

Researchers have also compared students behavior in classrooms in which the teacher focuses more on learning than on performance. In one study, fifth- and sixth-graders who perceived their classroom to be more learning-oriented reported relatively more positive coping skills (trying to figure out what they did wrong so it won't happen again). The more performance-oriented students perceived their classroom to be, the more they claimed to blame difficulties on others (e.g., the teacher) and the more they claimed they would just deny the importance of the outcome ("I tell myself it didn't matter"; Kaplan & Midgley, 2000). The positive coping strategies, in turn, were associated with positive emotions (excitement, enthusiasm, enjoying school), and the negative coping strategies were associated with negative affect (frustration, anger, anxiety).

Performance goals undermine effective problem solving for children who have doubts about their competence more than for self-confident children. This was shown in a study by Elliott and Dweck (1988). They experimentally induced performance or learning goals by emphasizing either the benefits of learning or the importance of performance in their instructions. They also manipulated children's perceptions of their own skill on a task. When performance-oriented children who perceived themselves to be low in skills encountered difficulty, their problem-solving strategies deteriorated. This did not occur for performance-oriented children with high perceptions of their skills. Learning- or mastery-oriented children's strategies were not affected by whether they had high or low confidence in their ability. (See also Brockner, 1979; Butler, 1999; Smiley & Dweck, 1994.)

The best problem-solving strategy, in some cases, involves asking for help. When students' goal is to master or understand, they are more likely to be autonomous help seekers. For example, they request hints that enable them to complete a task on their own rather than ask how to complete a problem (Butler, 1998). Children who are concerned about their performance and how smart they look, especially those who also lack confidence in their competencies, are reluctant to ask for help, even when they need it (Arbreton, 1998; Ryan, Gheen, & Midgley, 1998). They view asking for help as tantamount to publicizing their incompetence, rather than as a tool or strategy for increasing their understanding or skills. The strategies they use to avoid looking incompetent are not likely to promote learning. Indeed, in one study boys who claimed they didn't ask for help because they wanted to avoid negative ability judgments were more likely than other students to cheat (Butler, 1998).

Many studies have shown that students' willingness to ask for help is influenced substantially by the classroom climate. When the focus is on demonstrating ability, students are reluctant to ask for help. When the teacher focuses students' attention on learning and understanding, they are more willing to ask for help when they need it (Dembo & Eaton, 2000; Newman, 1998a, 1998b, 2000; Middleton & Midgley, 1997; Ryan, Gheen, & Midgley, 1998; Ryan, Hicks, & Midgley, 1997; Ryan & Pintrich, 1997, 1998).

Attributions

Learning goals are also associated with more constructive beliefs about what causes success or failure (Nicholls, 1992). In the study by Ames and Archer (1988), mentioned above, students who perceived their classroom to be mastery-oriented tended to attribute success to high effort and effective learning strategies, while students who perceived their classroom to be more performance-oriented tended to attribute failure to low ability. The latter students are disadvantaged because students who attribute failure to low ability have no reason to exert effort in the future (see Chapter 5; see also Nicholls, Cobb, Wood, Yackel, & Patashnick, 1990; Thorkildsen & Nicholls, 1998).

Studies also suggest that for students with mastery goals, more effort is associated with greater feelings of competence. Students with performance goals measure success in normative terms, by their performance relative to classmates (Jagacinski & Nicholls, 1984; see Chapter 5), and are particularly interested in obtaining normative information related to their performance (Butler, 1992).

Emotions

Students also experience greater interest, pleasure, satisfaction, and emotional involvement when they have mastery goals (see Harackiewicz, Baron, & Elliot, 1998; Harackiewicz, Barron, Tauer, Carter, & Elliot, 2000; Linnenbrink & Pintrich, 2000; Roeser, Midgley, & Urdan, 1996; Thorkildsen & Nicholls, 1998), and more anxiety and negative feelings about failure when they have performance goals (Middleton & Midgley, 1997; Turner, Thorpe, & Meyer, 1998). One study found a positive association between students' reports of mastery goals in their classes and their emotional functioning (Roeser, Eccles, & Sameroff, 1998). In the Ames and Archer (1988) study, the more students perceived their classroom as supporting mastery goals, the more they liked the class. Several other studies have reported more positive emotions in classes perceived as having mastery goals than in classes perceived as stressing performance goals (Ames & Archer, 1988; Kaplan & Maehr, 1999; Kaplan & Midgley, 2000; Meyer, Turner, & Spencer, 1997; Roeser et al., 1996).

Elliott and Dweck (1988) report that many of the children in a performance-oriented condition who had low perceptions of their ability spontaneously expressed negative feelings about the task with comments like, "After this (problem), then do I get to go?" "This is boring," or "My stomach hurts" (p. 10). Children who were task-oriented rarely made such comments, whether or not they believed that they were competent at the task.

Ryan (1982; Ryan & Stiller, 1991) explains why performance goals might be unpleasant. He proposes that ego involvement is experienced as a kind of internal control or pressure that people apply to themselves. Being pressured by these internal constraints (i.e., a feeling that it is necessary to do well to prove one's self-worth) undermines intrinsic motivation and pleasure in the same way as do external pressures (e.g., a salient reward, emphasis on evaluating, close monitoring).

Learning

Finally, goals affect *what* as well as *how much* students learn (see Fuchs et al., 1997; Jagacinski, 1992; Schunk, 1996; Utman, 1997). One study, for example, manipulated whether fifth- and sixth-grade students were performance oriented (by claiming that performance on the task was diagnostic of problem-solving ability) or task oriented (by claiming that the task would be challenging and fun). Compared to subjects who were primarily concerned with mastering the task, subjects who were performance-oriented showed poorer word recall at deep processing levels (having to do with meaning), but not at shallow processing levels (having to do with the sound of the word; Graham & Golan, 1991; see also Benware & Deci, 1984; Utman, in press).

Are Performance Goals All Bad?

In much of the achievement-motivation literature, mastery goals and performance goals are described as though they compete with each other—as though students have either one or the other. Actually, studies often find either no correlation or a positive correlation between the level of students' mastery goals and performance goals (Harackiewicz, Baron, Tauer, Carter, & Elliot, 2000; Midgley et al., 1995; Nicholls, 1992; Stipek & Gralinski, 1996; Young, 1997).

Although studies generally support the benefits of mastery goals when compared to performance goals, not all studies find negative effects of performance goals. In a study a colleague and I conducted, for example, students who had relatively high performance goals claimed to employ both active and superficial learning strategies more than students who were low in performance goals (Stipek & Gralinski, 1996). In another study both performance and learning goals were positively associated with self-efficacy for middle school students (Midgley et al., 1995). And one study showed that enjoyment was actually enhanced by performance-orientating instructions for individuals who have a strong need for achievement (described in Chapter 5; Harackiewicz & Elliot, 1993).

Recently, goal theorists have made a distinction between two forms of performance goals: one directed toward demonstrating competence (labeled by different theorists as "performance-approach," "self-enhancing," or "ability-approach" goals), and one directed toward avoiding the demonstration of incompetence ("performance-avoidance," "self-defeating," or "ability-avoid" goals;

Elliott, 1999; Elliot & Harackiewicz, 1996; Elliot, McGregor, & Gable, 1999; Middleton & Midgley, 1997; Midgley, Kaplan, Middleton, Maehr, Urdan, Anderman, Anderman, & Roeser, 1998; Skaalvik, 1997). The distinction is similar to the one Covington (1999) makes, described in Chapter 6, between "failure avoiders" and "success strivers" (see also Covington & Beery, 1976).

The research making this distinction finds that when students have the goal of demonstrating competence, they are not as likely to show the negative effects of performance goals that they show when they are trying to avoid demonstrating incompetence. Indeed, studies have shown that performance-approach goals are positively associated with intrinsic motivation and effective cognitive and metacognitive strategies, and negatively associated with anxiety. Performance-avoidance goals, in contrast, appear to have negative effects (Pintrich, 2000; Wolters, Yu, & Pintrich, 1996; see also Middleton & Midgley, 1997).

Not surprisingly, students who are trying to demonstrate their competence are more confident about their abilities than are children who are trying to avoid demonstrating incompetence (Skaalvik, 1997b). This line of research therefore provides additional support for the notion that the combination of low self-confidence and performance goals is highly undesirable. But for children who are self-confident, although mastery goals have clear benefits, performance goals are better than no goals at all.

I recommend some prudence, therefore, in the rush to condemn performance goals or other goals that are not directly linked to learning and mastery. Learning goals do not preclude other goals, and although there are good reasons to minimize performance goals, the evidence does not suggest that students would benefit from their total demise.

Beyond Learning and Performance Goals

Most goals theorists focus on learning and performance goals, but Wentzel (1992, 1993a, 1993b, 1994, in press) points out that students, particularly high-achieving students, have other goals that are unrelated to mastery or performance, but that have positive effects on learning. For example, students in her studies rate looking responsible, dependable, helpful, and compliant as significant goals in their achievement strivings. (See also Ainley, 1993; Meece & Holt, 1993; Urdan & Maehr, 1995.) These **social responsibility goals** are extrinsic and similar to performance goals in the sense that the goal is unconnected to the learning purposes of school tasks. Another goal that is not directly related to learning or mastery is the goal of bringing honor to the family or community.

Social responsibility goals could be conceptualized as internalized values—work hard in school, be conscientious, and so on. If they are genuinely internalized, such that students experience themselves as being self-determining. and if they do not involve excessive concern with social approval, they may enhance productive achievement behaviors without negative consequences. Students who manifest these behaviors are also preferred by teachers (Wentzel, 1993a).

Beyond Achievement

Students may engage in tasks for reasons entirely unrelated to those studied by goal theorists (Urdan & Maehr, 1995). Making or maintaining friendships may be the primary goal for working on tasks involving peer collaboration. Some students may work hard in school to maintain their social status in the high-achieving peer group. A high school boy may participate in a class discussion to attract attention from a girl in the class, or in an effort to convince his teacher that he should be allowed to leave class early on Fridays for soccer games. These nonachievement-related goals might be considered in any effort to increase student engagement with academic tasks.

Teachers also need to be aware of goals that interfere with task engagement. Some adolescents, for example, are striving to maintain status in a peer group that devalues academic achievement. For these students, teacher *dis*approval is the goal. Because most parents and teachers do value academic achievement, students whose peer group has different values and goals are caught in a conflict. As discussed in Chapter 9, they may work erratically or try to balance peer and teacher approval by working hard but pretending not to, or demonstrating competence in class while being disrespectful to the teacher.

Ethnicity, Culture, Values, and Goals

Goals need to be viewed through a broad cultural lens. And there is some evidence for systematic variations within the United States in cultural values and goals related to academic achievement.

Consider for example the goal of demonstrating antiachievement values that Ogbu (1992) describes. As discussed in Chapter 9, he proposes that African American students have this as a goal to avoid "acting White" to maintain cultural connections. Studies of Hispanic American families suggest other goals related to culture—which although constructive, might conflict with the goal structure of many schools. For example, Delgado-Gaitan (1993) and Laosa (1982) propose that goals of family cohesion and responsibility, found to be particularly strong among many Hispanic American families, may be inconsistent with a focus on individual effort and achievement in schools.

An understanding of cultural differences related to goals can help teachers interpret students' behavior. A child who asks for or gives help to a classmate on a test may not realize he is cheating; he may not have fully understood that the purpose of the activity is to assess his own understanding or skill. Also, this individualistic goal may not make sense to him. Some children may work poorly in competitive situations because they have been socialized to value collaboration and thus are not comfortable with the goal of outperforming others.

It is important to avoid stereotyping students by ethnicity, given the considerable variation in goals, values, and cultural beliefs within ethnic groups. But understanding cultural differences in the goals and values students internalize in their family context can guide teachers' efforts to assist students to work effectively in their classroom. As the discussion on relationships in Chapter 9 indicates, this needs to be done in a way that respects students' home culture.

Assessing Students' Achievement-Related Goals

Several researchers have developed measures of students' goals. As can be seen from the items on Ryan and Connell's (1989) measure (Table 9.1), their conceptualization of introjected and identified motivation overlaps substantially with what other researchers have referred to as performance goals and mastery goals, respectively. Thus, engaging in a task to achieve social approval (introjected regulation) is conceptualized as a performance goal, and engaging in a task to develop understanding or skills (idenfitifed motivation) is conceptualized as a learning or mastery goal.

Nicholls and his colleagues developed a measure to assess students' task- versus ego-orientation to schoolwork, and their "work avoidance" goal (Nicholls et al., 1990). The items are given in Table 10.2. Another measure, used in many studies by Midgley and her colleagues (e.g., Midgley et al., 1998) assesses task goal orientation ("I like schoolwork best when it really makes me think"), ability-

---

TABLE 10.2   Assessment of Students' Goals*

Response scale is: YES = 1, yes = 2, ? = 3, no = 4, NO = 5

I feel really pleased in school (math) when:

Task Orientation

- ❐ I solve a problem by working hard
- ❐ The problems make me think hard
- ❐ What the teacher says makes me think
- ❐ I keep busy
- ❐ I work hard all the time
- ❐ Something I learn makes me want to find out more
- ❐ I find a new way to solve a problem
- ❐ Something I figure out really makes sense
- ❐ Something I figure out makes me want to keep doing more problems

---

Ego Orientation

- ❐ I know more than the others
- ❐ I am the only one who can answer a question
- ❐ I finish before my friends
- ❐ I get more answers right than my friends

Work Avoidance

- ❐ I don't have to work hard
- ❐ All the work is easy
- ❐ The teacher doesn't ask hard questions

---

*From Nicholls, Cobb, Wood, Yackel, & Patashnick (1990). Reprinted with permission from *Journal for Research in Mathematics Education*, copyright 1990 by the National Council of Teachers of Mathematics. All rights reserved.

approach ("I want to do better than other students in my classes"), and ability-avoidance ("One reason I would not participate in class is to avoid looking stupid") goal orientations.

Skaalvik (1997) also developed a measure that differentiates between self-enhancing and self-defeating performance goals, shown in Table 10.3.

Ames and Archer (1988) developed a measure of students' perceptions of their classroom goals, which presumably would influence their own goals (see Table 10.4). Some of the questions refer to teacher or classroom practices that support mastery or learning goals (e.g., "In this class, making mistakes is a part of learning"). Other questions refer to practices that are more likely to foster performance goals (e.g., "In this class students compete to see who can do the best work"). Giving this measure to students can provide feedback on specific behaviors and instructional strategies which give students messages different from those the teachers intend.

Students also reveal their goals through their behavior. Table 10.5 lists behaviors that are typically associated with performance goals. Students who manifest these behaviors may be more concerned about doing well or looking good than they are about developing skills or mastering problems.

TABLE 10.3   Assessment of Self-Enhancing and Self-Defeating Performance Goals*

Response scale is: true, mostly true, mostly false, false

Self-Enhancing Performance Goals

❐   I feel successful at school when I do the work better than other students.
❐   At school I try to score higher than other students.
❐   At school it is important for me to manage tasks that other students do not manage.
❐   I always try to do better than other students in my class.
❐   I answer questions in class in order to show that I know more than other students.

Self-Defeating Performance Goals

❐   When I answer questions in class I am occupied by how I am perceived by other students.
❐   When I am working on the blackboard I am concerned about what my classmates think about me.
❐   At school I am concerned not to make a fool of myself.
❐   When I give a wrong answer in class I am most concerned about what my classmates think about me.
❐   The worst thing about making mistakes at school is that other students may notice.
❐   At school it is important for me to avoid looking stupid.
❐   At school I try not to be among the poorest students.

*From Skaalvik (1997). Copyright © 1997 by the American Psychological Association. Reprinted with permission.

TABLE 10.4   Classroom Achievement Goals Questionnaire

Response scale: 1 = strongly disagree, 2, 3 = neutral, 4, 5 = strongly agree

In this class:

Mastery-oriented items

- Making mistakes is a part of learning.
- Students don't care about the grades other students get.
- The teacher wants us to learn how to solve problems on our own.
- It's important to keep trying even though you make mistakes.
- Students are encouraged to find answers to their questions on their own.
- The teacher tries to find out what each student wants to learn.
- The teacher wants us to try new things.
- Students are given a chance to correct their mistakes.

Performance-oriented items

- Students compete against each other to get high grades.
- Only a few students can get top marks.
- Students try hard to get the highest grade.
- Students feel badly when they do not do as well as others.
- Students compete to see who can do the best work.
- The teacher favors some students more than others.
- Students know if they're doing better or worse than other students.
- Students want to know how others score on assignments and tests.

Selected items used in Ames and Archer (1988).

TABLE 10.5   Behaviors Associated with Performance Goals

1. Uses shortcuts to complete tasks (tries to get them done without going through steps that would contribute to learning)
2. Compares scores/grades with classmates
3. Seeks attention for good performance
4. Only works hard on graded assignments
5. Is upset by low scores/grades
6. Chooses tasks and courses that are most likely to result in a positive evaluation
7. Is uncomfortable with assignments in which criteria for evaluation are not very clear
8. Repeatedly asks for teacher evaluation (e.g., "Is this what you meant?")
9. Obsesses (e.g., copies papers over several times; overstudies for tests)
10. Copies classmates' papers
11. Cheats

Summary

The work by goal theorists is important because it makes it very clear that the teacher's task is not just to "get students working." Different strategies for motivating students to work are likely to have different consequences, in part because the reasons students engage in academic tasks have so many implications for how and what they learn. Most studies suggest the value of a mastery or learning orientation, and indicate that a concern about performance can be debilitating, especially for children who doubt their ability. It may not be realistic or even desirable to try to eliminate performance goals altogether, but they can seriously undermine learning for children who lack confidence in their skills.

TABLE 10.6   Summary of Terms

Term	Definition
Learning/task mastery goals	Goals involving learning, mastery, or developing competencies
Performance goals	Goals are to demonstrate competence, to avoid demonstrating incompetence, or to gain social recognition or approval
Performance-approach goals	Goals directed toward demonstration of competence
Performance-avoidance goals	Goals directed at avoiding demonstrating *in*competence
Task-oriented	Attention is focused on strategies needed to complete a task or to develop understanding or skill
Ego-oriented	Attention is focused on the self, especially others' evaluation of the self
Flow	Intense task involvement; unaware of environment
Social responsibility goals	Looking responsible, dependable, helpful, or compliant

11 Maximizing Intrinsic Motivation, Academic Values, and Learning Goals

Teachers who want to enhance learning in the classroom have a variety of motivation systems to engage. The shortcomings of extrinsic rewards suggest the desirability of maximizing alternative systems of motivation. The three previous chapters discussed the value of promoting intrinsic motivation to learn, internalized academic values, and learning and mastery goals. This chapter makes specific, practical suggestions for enhancing these three motivational outcomes.

The Teacher's Task

Often teachers' first task is to reawaken a motivational system that may be barely operative when students enter their classrooms. After the first few grades in school, few students show the same determination and persistence on school tasks that they demonstrated in infancy and early childhood or that they may still show outside of school. Being able to read, solve math problems, or write a good essay should engender the same feelings of competence in a student that being able to walk, take off a shoe, or complete a puzzle engenders for the very young child. But the intrinsic motivational system, which has such a powerful effect on children before they enter school and in activities outside of school, seems to disappear when they enter the classroom. Teachers can, however, rekindle and exploit this powerful motivational force.

A related task for teachers is to refocus students' attention on understanding and developing their competencies and to reduce their concerns about external evaluation, especially grades. Grades are important; they have long-term implications for students' opportunities. But, like Safe Sally, many students' concerns about grades and social approval prevents them from taking advantage of opportunities (e.g., working on challenging tasks or taking advanced placement classes) that might expand their future options.

Strategies for engendering academic values will vary according to students' ages and backgrounds. Often the task for teachers of young children, who are used to choosing their own activities, is to get them to want to complete teacher-assigned work. Middle school teachers may need to convince students that academic success is as important as being popular or getting on the soccer team. In secondary school, some teachers have to work hard to overcome the effects of a peer culture that devalues academic work. In other contexts, teachers need merely to reinforce the values that children are exposed to at home.

The basic goal is to create an instructional program which capitalizes on students' intrinsic desire to learn, focuses their attention on understanding and mastery, and fosters academic values. This does not mean that extrinsic rewards have no place in the classroom. It is unrealistic to expect students to exert effort voluntarily and enthusiastically on every school task. Some extrinsic incentives for schoolwork are necessary. Therefore, the practical issue is how to create a context in which a focus on learning and understanding prevails, and in which extrinsic rewards and concerns about performance do not undermine intrinsic motivation and attention to understanding and mastery.

Critical to achieving all of these goals is engendering in students confidence in their academic competencies and high expectations for success with school tasks. Accordingly, every recommendation made in Chapter 7 is relevant to achieving the objectives described above. The practical recommendations in this chapter, which overlap somewhat with recommendations made previously, are divided into four areas of classroom practice—tasks, evaluation, control, and climate. The recommendations reflect a mixture of general principles that should apply most, if not all, of the time (e.g., emphasis on effort and learning), and suggestions for specific practices that might be used occasionally (e.g., collaborative work).

Tasks

1. Explain the demands and purposes of tasks and the real-world significance of the skills they are designed to teach.   Students usually don't have learning as a goal when they don't know what a task is supposed to teach or why it is important. Students need to be told the purposes of a task—what skills it is designed to teach, and how those skills are important outside of school. The value of making sure that students understand the purpose of what they are learning is illustrated in a study by Mitchell (1993). Students' beliefs about the real-world significance of what they were learning in math was the second strongest predictor of how much they enjoyed and were interested in their math class (Mitchell, 1993).

Evidence from classroom research suggests that this principle is commonly violated. Anderson (1981, 1984) reports that the children he has interviewed rarely knew why they were asked to complete particular assignments. Most explained simply that "It's just our work." The children's inability to explain why they were doing a task was not surprising; the teachers he observed discussed the purpose or the content being taught for only 1.5 percent of the assignments they gave!

In the 317 presentations of new tasks that Brophy (1983) observed, not one teacher commented that the task would help children develop skills that would bring them pleasure or enjoyment. Only a few (3 percent) expressed personal enthusiasm for the task, or tied the task to the personal lives or interests of the students. Most comments would contribute little to students' motivation to work on a task. For example, many teachers indicated that students were not expected to like the task or to do well on it (8 percent); some reminded students that their work would be checked or that they would be tested on it (6 percent); others said that there would be negative consequences for poor performance (4 percent); and some indicated that students had a limited amount of time (6 percent). Most of the teachers' remarks concerned procedural demands or evaluation (Brophy, Rohrkemper, Rashid, & Goldberger, 1983). And the most negative comments (e.g., "Get your nose in the book, otherwise I'll give out writing assignments" or "This test is to see who the really smart ones are") were associated with relatively low student engagement on tasks (Brophy, 1987, p. 204).

Real-world significance can sometimes be achieved by providing tasks that are similar to those encountered outside of school. Stigler and Stevenson (1991) note that in American classrooms, teachers typically teach rules for mathematical operations first, and then, occasionally, they point out the real-world applications of the rule. Asian teachers, in contrast, begin a lesson with a real-world problem, which they often ask students to solve, and in doing so, construct for themselves the mathematical rule. An example is a lesson in which a teacher begins by asking students how many liters of colored water were contained in a large beaker shown to the class. Students then generated the concept of fractions by pouring the water into smaller beakers. The lesson ended with a discussion of rules for writing fractions to represent the parts of a whole.

2. Give challenging tasks.   Recall that intrinsic interest derives primarily from the feelings of competence that are associated with working on and completing tasks, and that only moderately difficult tasks engender feelings of competence when they are completed. Information processing theorists claim that optimal arousal and interest are generated by a moderate discrepancy between an external stimulus (or task) and an individual's representations (or skill level; see Chapter 8).

Consistent with these theories of intrinsic motivation, research on teaching and learning has shown that engagement rates, as well as achievement gains, are enhanced when teachers give students assignments that they can complete successfully only if they invest some real effort. Assignments that are completed without much effort or that are confusing or frustrating result in low engagement (see Brophy & Alleman, 1991; Good & Brophy, 1986).

Many studies have shown that students prefer and are more motivated to complete appropriately challenging tasks. One study, for example, showed that people were more motivated to persist on tasks when there was an increasing standard of success than when the standard was constant (e.g., McMullin & Steffen, 1982). In another study, adolescents rated the classes that made them think hard as the most interesting (Newmann, 1992; see also, Danner & Lonky, 1981; Boggiano, Pittman, & Ruble, 1982; Shapira, 1976; Turner, 1995; Turner, Meyer, Cox, Logan, DiCintio, & Thomas, 1998).

Challenging doesn't just mean difficult, however. Students are not motivated to complete tasks that they do not believe they have the skills to complete. The importance of both challenge and self-confidence was demonstrated in a study of upper elementary school-aged students who were asked to keep a daily log for their math instruction (Turner et al., 1998). They answered two questions: "How challenging was math class today?" and "How were your skills in math today?" For each question they circled a number from 0 (low) to 9 (high). They also reported how they felt (e.g., bored, proud, ashamed, confused, happy, alert, apathetic, relaxed, involved, uninvolved) on a set of scales. Students were most engaged and reported the most positive emotions and interest in math instruction in the classrooms in which challenge and skills were *both* rated high. Self-confidence alone was not enough. When level of challenge was rated as lower than skills, students were less engaged, had less positive emotional experiences (e.g., less relaxed), and were less intrinsically motivated.

The researchers also observed instruction (Turner et al., 1998). They found that teachers in the high-challenge, high intrinsically-motivating classrooms were more likely to hold students accountable for understanding, for example by asking them to explain the strategy they used to get an answer. They assisted students (thus giving them a sense of confidence) by scaffolding questioning, e.g., "Let's break this problem into parts"; "What information is needed to solve this problem?" And they provided encouragement: "This may seem difficult, but if you stay with it, you'll learn more than you bargained for!"

As mentioned in Chapter 7, it is not easy to provide tasks that are appropriately challenging (that can be completed, but only with real effort) in a classroom of students who vary substantially in skill levels. The suggestions made in that chapter for adjusting the difficulty level of tasks should enhance interest directly and indirectly, by giving them opportunities to see their competencies developing.

High-achieving students are sometimes the least likely to be challenged. In many classrooms there is a group of students who repeatedly finish assignments in less than the allotted time and with few mistakes. Because most tasks are not at all challenging and do not offer good opportunities for them to improve their understanding and skills, they are not intrinsically motivated to engage in schoolwork and they usually become more focused on getting right answers and good grades than on learning and achieving mastery. Below are some strategies for engaging these students' interest and focus on learning.

a. **Allow students to go at their own pace some of the time.** The general approach used in the mastery learning programs described in Chapter 7 can be integrated into many classroom structures. A middle school math program I observed is an example of a practice that provides opportunities for fast learners to challenge themselves without pushing the slower learners too fast. During two days each week students worked in workbooks individually or in small groups at their own pace. The teacher moved around the classroom, assessing students' understanding and providing individualized and small-group instruction. During the other three days students worked together in heterogeneous groups on real-life projects in which they applied their math skills. The projects were sufficiently multidimensional (e.g., designing a library to scale) to allow students to contribute to the work at their own level of math understanding. These students, thus, had opportunities to develop their skills at their own pace and to participate in collaborative and project learning.

   b.   **In whole-class instruction, include problems and questions that challenge students with the highest levels of mastery.**   Stigler and Stevenson (1991) observed that most math instruction in Asian classrooms is done in a whole-class format, even though variation in student skill levels is as high as it is in American classrooms. Teachers gave problems that could be solved at different levels of mathematical understanding. Students were encouraged to attempt solution strategies that reflected their level of understanding. These different strategies were subsequently discussed and compared by the class.

   c.   **Include very challenging questions on assignments and tests.** Stevenson and Stigler (1992) also observed that in China assignments and tests usually included some very easy problems, which every student in the class could solve, and some very difficult problems, which *no* student in the class could solve. All students, therefore, began a test expecting to solve some but not all of the problems. This is a clever method of challenging the fast learners and encouraging them to strive for a higher level of understanding without discouraging the slower learners from trying. After all, no one in the class will get all of the problems right.

   d.   **Provide enriching activities for students who have completed their work.**   Give students an opportunity to work on a class newspaper, write and put on a play, keep a diary, build a model of a bridge, communicate with a real scientist or a child in another city or country over the Internet, or engage in any number of other enriching activities that will allow them to challenge themselves. It is important that all children have an opportunity to engage in these enriching activities, but some students who complete their regular work more quickly than others can take greater responsibility or spend more time on individual or small group projects.

   3. **Create tasks that allow students to engage in substantive, intellectual work.**

   a.   **Give tasks that require higher-order or divergent thinking and active problem-solving.**   These are more intrinsically interesting than tasks that involve memorizing or applying simple rules or procedures. I observed a compelling demonstration of this principle in a fifth-grade class. The teacher allowed students who finished their math worksheets (a page or two of calculations in their textbook) to work on a math puzzle—usually a complicated word problem. Students rushed through their textbook problems for the *opportunity* to work on this more difficult problem. Seeing this day after day made me wonder what these students' motivation to do math and their math competencies would be if their math curriculum included more "puzzles" and fewer sets of repetitive calculations. Indeed, the problems given to students who completed their mathematics assignments were precisely the kinds of authentic mathematical tasks—requiring students to "explore, conjecture, and reason logically"—that the National Council of Teachers of Mathematics (2000) and other math reformers promote (see, for example, Stein, Grover, & Henningsen, 1996).

Blumenfeld, Puro, and Mergendoller (1992) describe ways in which a science teacher provided opportunities for students to be deeply engaged in substantive scientific thinking. The teacher built lessons so that the main idea was evident in presentations, demonstrations, discussions, and in tasks; she posed high level questions and pressed students to explain and justify their answers. (See Ball, 1993; Resnick et al., 1991 for descriptions of strategies that teachers can use to engage students in substantive mathematical thinking.)

b. Give tasks that revolve around "big ideas" rather than focus on small, fragmented skills or concepts.   Tasks related to a theme make schoolwork more meaningful and gives students a sense of competence. Zahorik (1996) interviewed teachers about the "big ideas" they used to engage students in a variety of academic tasks, including reading, writing, and discussion. Here are some of the examples they gave: "One theory of why dinosaurs became extinct is that volcanic eruptions eliminated their food supply"; "No country exists that does not need another country for something"; "Plants and animals exist in a symbiotic relationship" (p. 559). Such broad issues force students to consider connections among various concepts they are learning and to analyze and reflect more deeply than they do when they are asked to learn about isolated topics (e.g., the effect of volcanoes on vegetation; the economic policy of the Soviet Union before World War II; the diet of giraffes).

c. Give open-ended tasks.   Open-ended tasks that require some creativity are more interesting than tasks that require simple, right-or-wrong responses. Analyzing a story or comparing two poems, for example, is usually more interesting than answering factual questions about a story or memorizing a poem. One study found that young children used more reading strategies, persisted longer, and were more attentive when they were given open-ended tasks (emphasizing meaning and higher-order thinking) than closed tasks (requiring primarily memory and recognition; Turner, 1995)

4. Give multidimensional tasks.   Multidimensional tasks that require sustained effort and result in a product are intrinsically motivating because they provide variability and opportunities to experience pride in a tangible accomplishment. Examples are math assignments that require problem solving, explanations of strategies, and visual representations of the solution; reports that require research and written summaries and possibly some design or artwork; and experiments that require planning, manipulation of materials, observation, analysis, and summarizing.

Some assignments can be embedded in long-term projects. A class newspaper, for example, gives students an opportunity to do math (determining how much it will cost to produce and how much they should charge for it), social studies (writing on current political events), art (designing a logo), and tasks that develop other practical skills (e.g., using the computer to do word processing and spreadsheets). Other examples of long-term projects that I have seen include a model city, a class book of poems, and a map of the school drawn to scale. (See Blumenfeld, Soloway, Marx, Krajcik, Guzdial, & Palincsar, in press, for a discussion of the motivating effect of project-based learning.)

5. Provide tasks that require active student participation, exploration, and experimentation.   Tasks that involve a high degree of student participation and activity promote curiosity and are more enjoyable than tasks that put students into a more passive mode (Guthrie, Wigfield, & VonSecker, 2000; Mitchell, 1993). Manipulation of materials and role playing can also generate a deeper understanding of the concepts and issues than more passive learning activities, such as listening or reading. Thus, learning measurement in the process of building a model or making a map is more interesting and more effective than doing a workbook page of measurement problems. A multiplication game using playing cards is more fun than reciting the multiplication tables. Acting out a real debate between loyalists and separatists in the New England colonial period is more fun and develops a better appreciation of the issues than reading about the conflict in a textbook. Doing a science experiment is usually more engaging than watching a teacher carry out an experiment.

Even when a teacher uses a whole class format, active participation can be achieved by encouraging students to ask questions, offer opinions, share personal observations and experiences, debate with each other, and engage in critical discussion. As Bruner (1966, p. 117) explained, "There are games not only with objects, but with ideas and questions."

a. Make sure that "hands-on" activities involving exploration and experimentation also involve substantive learning.   Manipulation, exploration, and dramatization are highly motivating and *can be* extremely effective teaching tools, but only if they are used effectively. Well-meaning teachers endeavoring to enhance their students' intrinsic interest often create tasks that are fun but do not teach anything. Zahorik (1996) found in his interviews of teachers that many treated "hands-on" activities more as ends than as means; they created activities that may have actually distracted attention from the concepts they were supposed to teach and thus did not promote student learning.

To engender learning, hands-on activities need to be accompanied by some teaching, and the best activities focus students' attention on the concepts they are designed to teach. Instruction I once observed in a fourth-grade classroom is an example of what often occurs when this principle is violated. To introduce the concept of probability, the teacher had children play a dice game in which they predicted and recorded outcomes of a series of throws. Student enthusiasm for the game was extremely high, but informal interviews with children after the game revealed that they had not extracted any mathematical principles at all. When the teacher began instruction on probability the next day, students made no connection between what they were learning that day and the "game" they had played the day before. The activity could have been an effective strategy for giving students an intuitive notion of probability theory if the teacher had directed students' attention to particular patterns, and if individual results had been combined and discussed with the whole class. Unaccompanied by instruction, the game had no value.

Dramatization designed to increase understanding of historical events is another common example of motivation in the absence of learning. In the class plays that I have observed, more attention was usually given to costume and set than to the political or social issues the teacher wanted students to understand. There are surely benefits (e.g., developing artistic talents, developing skills in cooperation) derived from costume and set design. But more efficient productions and simulations might produce better understanding of social history. If dramatization is used, it must be embedded in instruction and discussion related to the learning goals.

6. Provide some tasks that are complex, novel, and have an element of surprise or fantasy.   Recall that one theoretical perspective on intrinsic motivation stresses novelty, incongruity, complexity, and surprise. Children usually like tasks that involve fantasy or simulation (including role-playing), incorporate game-like features, or involve elements of uncertainty about the outcome, such as suspense or hidden information.

Suspense and curiosity can be induced by asking students a question before beginning a lesson—"What was the 'iron curtain?'" "Why is blood blue under your skin and red outside?" "What proportion of the U.S. mainland would Alaska cover?" "Why do people in Mexico speak Spanish?" "What will happen when two chemicals are mixed?" Instruction can begin with speculations and questioning that forces students to confront contradictions and errors in their thinking.

Studies using computer-assisted instruction (CAI) have demonstrated some positive effects on motivation of fantasy or other embellishments such as color, noise, or surprise outcomes (see Cordova & Lepper, 1996; Lepper & Cordova, 1992; Lepper & Malone, 1987; Parker & Lepper, 1992). Cordova and Lepper (1996) found that embedding fantasy into a CAI math task contributed to students' level of involvement, the complexity of the problems they attempted, and their learning, as well as to their enjoyment.

Some theorists warn, however, that such embellishments can also interfere with learning (see Blumenfeld, 1992; Lepper & Malone, 1987). Their concerns are supported by research in which personalized anecdotes and vivid details unrelated to the main ideas are added to texts. Studies have found that details added for interest value actually can have detrimental effects on learning (Garner, Alexander, Gillingham, Kulikowich, & Brown, 1991; Wade, 1992). Young children, in particular, have difficulty differentiating nonessential information from important elements of text (see Shirey, 1992). If embellishments such as color, fantasy, surprise outcomes, music, or anecdotes are used to increase intrinsic interest in school tasks, care needs to be taken that they do not distract students' attention from the learning goals and that whatever value they have for generating enthusiasm is not lost in actual learning.

7. Give tasks that are linked to students' interests. Students are also more motivated when the topics are personally interesting. There is considerable evidence that when students read materials they find interesting, they comprehend and remember the material better (Anderson, Shirey, Wilson, & Fielding, 1987; Garner, Alexander, Gillingham, Kulikowich, & Brown, 1991). Meece (1991) found, also, that students reported a high level of motivation to increase their knowledge of science in classrooms in which teachers adapted instruction to their personal interests.

Personalizing tasks can have the added advantage of allowing students to explore issues that are emotionally troubling. Rueda and Moll (1994) describe a teacher who asked students to write about recent violent incidents in their community. The teacher reported improved writing as well as an exceedingly high level of motivation to complete the task, with many students recounting personal experiences with great emotion. Writing assignments can also be linked to social conflicts that arise—not as punishment, but as an opportunity for students to express their feelings or explore solutions while they are developing their writing skills.

a. Allow students some choice in topics. Teachers often choose books or stories for children to read or topics for writing assignments, even though a child's choice—perhaps among a set of appropriate options—will work just as well. Teachers should give students as much discretion as possible. The more choice students have, the more likely they are to be intrinsically interested in the task or learning activity.

For a social studies unit on Native Americans, for example, some students may prefer to do research and write on agriculture or food, others on dress, and others on religion and ceremonies. Similarly, during silent reading periods, a wide range of books can be offered so that all students may read a book on a topic that appeals to them. Sometimes students can be grouped around interests. I have seen book clubs, for example, in which students meet to discuss a book with the other students in the class who are reading the same book.

b. Integrate students' interests and experiences into lessons and discussion. When giving examples or applications of concepts being learned, teachers can refer to people (TV characters, rock stars) or events that are likely to catch their students' attention. Abstract concepts or new material can be made meaningful by giving examples or analogies which refer to familiar concepts or events. Brophy (1987) describes a history lesson on Roman society in which the teacher encouraged students to consider possible parallels between Roman gladiators and modern tolerance for violence in sports.

c. **Invite students to express opinions, or respond personally to the content.** I have rarely observed much enthusiasm for history and politics in classes that were taught in a matter-of-fact and unemotional way, with neither the teacher nor the students expressing opinions. Classes in which students debate controversial subjects openly are much livelier. Rather than avoid controversial issues, teachers can encourage students to express and support their opinions, thus helping them to appreciate the complexity of the issue at hand and the diversity of perspectives.

Teachers can also incorporate students' questions and comments into instruction. I observed a wonderful example of this in a kindergarten class where a child announced in the middle of a lesson on measurement that he was wearing new shoes. The teacher asked him and other students what size shoe they wore and launched into a lively discussion, with considerable student input, on size as a form of measurement.

d. **Connect new or abstract concepts to familiar or concrete ones.** Teachers can also use the kind of role-playing and manipulations described above to increase the meaningfulness of concepts or information that are distant from students' own experience or to make abstract concepts more concrete. Students who are learning about money can, for example, play store, each taking a turn at being in the role of the shopper (who has to decide how much to give to the vendor) and that of the vendor (who has to calculate change). High school students can explore economic principles by playing the stock market. Each member of the class might be given $1,000 in play money to buy stocks, and asked to follow and chart their earnings. Class discussions could be devoted to the American economy, balance of trade, world events, and other factors that are influencing students' own stock prices. Stocks could also be bought and sold by small groups of students. This might engender some lively discussion of factors that influence the value of the stocks.

8. Give students an opportunity to collaborate. Students tend to find cooperative learning groups more enjoyable than working independently (see Johnson & Johnson, 1985b; Mitchell, 1993). Some studies suggest that girls respond particularly well to math and science instruction when it is taught in a cooperative manner (Eccles & Roeser, 1999; Eccles, Wigfield, & Schiefele, 1998). As discussed in Chapter 7, individual accountability is important, and cooperative learning activities need to be planned and implemented thoughtfully to ensure that all students are actively participating in substantive intellectual work. Students can collaborate in pairs for a few minutes to solve a single math problem during whole-class instruction, as they often do in Japanese classrooms (Stigler & Stevenson, 1991), or they can collaborate for many weeks on a multidimensional task, like developing a business which requires them to create a marketing plan, use spreadsheets, and calculate profit and loss.

9. Vary tasks and format from day to day.   Avoid predictable, unvarying formats. A common practice for elementary level math instruction, for example, is to begin with 15–20 minutes of whole-class instruction, during which the teacher and occasionally students do a few problems on the board. This is followed by 25–30 minutes of seatwork, typically a page of problems out of a text or workbook. This is what Brophy (1986) describes as "the daily grind"—". . . a steady diet of routine and predictable lessons followed by routine and predictable assignments" (p. 34). Variation in instruction and assignments is associated with higher levels of motivation (Blumenfeld, Puro, & Mergendoller, 1992; Meece, Blumenfeld, & Puro, 1989) as well as lower levels of problem behavior (Munk & Repp, 1994).

Often the same skills can be promoted with alternative formats—such as integrating whole-class instruction with seatwork or breaking students into small groups or dyads to work on problems, as Japanese teachers do. Minor changes can sometimes have significant effects. A fifth-grade teacher once complained to me that her students worked halfheartedly on their daily reading assignment—answering a series of questions at the end of a story they were asked to read. She changed the task one day by asking students to generate their own questions and to exchange them with a friend in the class. This minor modification in the assignment sparked considerable enthusiasm, which was sustained by other, equally modest modifications made thereafter.

In summary, the questions provided in Appendix 11-A can be used to help teachers assess the motivational value of their tasks. It is always important to ask oneself what students are likely to learn and whether the likely achievement gains are worth the amount of time and energy that the activity requires. Sometimes modest changes, such as weaving more instruction into the activity or asking students to record and reflect on their observations can substantially increase student learning from an activity.

Careful observation and assessment of student learning is essential. When students are working individually or in small groups a teacher can assess understanding by engaging students in conversation and asking questions while moving around the room. Postactivity discussions are also useful for assessing the value of a task, and they increase the instructional value of the activity. It is useful for teachers to keep a notebook in which they make comments regarding student motivation and learning on particular activities—in part as a reference to consult later and in part to force assessment and reflection. Whatever the strategy, it is extremely important to assess how much students actually learn from tasks, and to adapt tasks when learning goals are not realized.

Evaluation

The salience and nature of evaluation have profound effects on students' intrinsic interest in tasks and their goals while working on a task. The most engaging activity can be made oppressive by focusing students' attention on external evaluation, particularly if the standards for evaluation are unclear or if a positive evaluation is perceived to be unattainable. Below are suggestions for using evaluation to support rather than undermine motivation.

1. De-emphasize external evaluation.   Stressing evaluation (e.g., by continually threatening bad grades or reminding students that if they engage in a particular behavior they will be rewarded with a good grade) focuses attention on performance goals, engenders a feeling of being controlled, and kills whatever intrinsic interest students might have had in a task. Emphasizing external evaluation has other negative effects on motivation and learning. Research suggests, for example, that students tend not to select challenging tasks when they are concerned about external evaluation. This is illustrated in a study by Harter (1978b), in which elementary school children were asked to solve anagrams at four difficulty levels. Half of the subjects were instructed that the task was a game and half were instructed that it was a school-type task for which they would receive a letter grade. Under the game condition, children chose optimally challenging problems. Those children working for grades chose significantly easier anagrams; they also expressed less pleasure (smiling) when they solved a problem, and verbalized more anxiety. (See also Deci, 1992; Hughes et al., 1985.)

The current emphasis on using standardized tests to evaluate teachers and schools has the same negative effects on teachers that a focus on external evaluation has on students. The salient evaluation can undermine teachers' own intrinsic interest in teaching. Teachers pass their concerns about standardized tests on to their students, thus undermining students' intrinsic interest to learn as well. The salience of tests in high schools that focus on college preparation can have similarly negative effects on motivation. I have seen advanced placement courses be conducted in a way that makes them seem more like a test preparation course than an opportunity to learn about history, science, or math. It is not easy in the current political environment, but teachers need to try to focus on learning rather than test performance. Focusing on learning and understanding will have all the positive effects on motivation described in this book, and ironically, it will result in higher test performance.

2. When grades or other forms of evaluation are given, base them as much as possible on effort, improvement, and achieving a standard, rather than on relative performance.   Most schools require grades, and the best teachers can do is minimize their negative effects on students' motivation. Research provides some clues about how this can be accomplished.

Ames and her colleagues (Ames, 1984, 1986; Ames & Ames, 1984) have found that the criteria for evaluation affect students' goals (to perform versus to learn), their perceptions of the cause of success and failure, and the kind of information they attend to in evaluating themselves. Research indicates, for example, that competition (focusing students' attention on relative performance) tends to foster performance goals. In one study, students working in a competitive goal structure were more likely to claim that they were concerned with their ability and less likely to claim that they engaged in self-monitoring and self-instructions related to the task than students who were simply asked to challenge themselves (an individual goal structure; Ames, 1986). Another study found that evaluation reduced intrinsic interest in a task when it was based on comparisons among students, but actually increased intrinsic interest when it was based on achieving a predetermined score (Harackiewicz, Abrahams, & Wageman, 1987).

Researchers have also shown that in competitive contexts students emphasize ability (and sometimes luck) when interpreting their performance. In situations in which evaluation is based on group performance, personal improvement, or meeting a preestablished standard, students are more likely to attribute their performance to effort (Ames, 1981; Ames & Ames, 1981; Rheinberg, 1983).

A study by Ames and Ames (1981) suggests that the criteria teachers use for evaluation also affects the information students use to evaluate themselves. Children were given an opportunity to establish a personal performance history on a task (success or failure) and then were given either a competitive (with another child) or individual (challenge yourself) goal. When subsequently asked a series of questions, children's self-reward and feelings of satisfaction in the competitive situation were based on whether they won or lost, and not on the quality of their performance. Children in the individual goal structure focused on their personal history with the task (i.e., whether they improved).

Evaluating students on personal improvement or in terms of a predetermined standard is preferable for both high- and low-achieving students. High-achieving students always have a higher standard of excellence to aspire to when the objective is to surpass their own previous level of performance. Low-achieving students benefit because success defined in terms of improvement or achieving a realistic standard is attainable and effort should always have some payoff. By fostering the belief that effort leads to success, noncompetitive evaluation also engenders a perception of ability as something that improves with effort; it should increase low-achieving students' expectations for success, and it may also contribute to a perception of fairness.

Some of these benefits were demonstrated in a study of college students by Covington and Omelich (1984b). They found that undergraduate psychology students who were graded using a mastery standard (i.e., grades were determined by what score the student attained) perceived the grading system to be more fair and more responsive to effort than students who were graded using a competitive, norm-referenced standard (i.e., who were graded on a curve). The students in the mastery condition also aspired to a higher grade and had more self-confidence about being able to achieve a high grade.

3. Emphasize the information contained in grades.   Rather than congratulate a student for getting an "A" on a test, as though the "A" itself was the goal, comment on the high level of competence the "A" signifies. For some students a

"B" or even a "C" might represent improvement. This too can be pointed out. Low grades, similarly, should not be presented as punishment, but as information—an indication that the student needs to exert more effort or get assistance.

Focus on the informational purpose of tests as well. Researchers who have manipulated subjects' goals in experiments have shown that the way a test is introduced can affect students' behavior. Researchers have easily induced performance goals by simply introducing experimental tasks as a measure of intelligence or competence (e.g., Ryan, 1982; Stipek & Kowalski, 1989). Explaining to students that a test will provide information about students' level of understanding or skill—information that can be used to guide individual student's subsequent efforts and the teachers' curriculum planning—engenders a task focus.

4. Make grading criteria clear and fair.   Students who understand the criteria used in grading feel that they have control over school outcomes. Involving students in discussions about grading criteria can sometimes foster better understanding and acceptance of the criteria and can inform teachers of perceptions of unfairness that need to be addressed.

5. Provide substantive, informative feedback, rather than grades or scores on assignments.   Avoid giving global evaluations, such as letter grades, as much as possible because students typically attend only to the grade, even when it is accompanied by more useful information. Global performance feedback also fosters global self-evaluations (e.g., "I'm a 'C' or an 'OK' student"), which serve no purpose. In contrast, specific and informative feedback on assignments helps students make judgments about their strengths and weaknesses and focuses their attention on what they need to do to improve.

Several studies have demonstrated the advantages of substantive evaluation. In a study by Butler and Nisan (1986) sixth-grade students received either substantive comments on their papers with no grade or they received numerical (normatively distributed) grades with no comments. Students who received comments rated the task as more interesting than did students who did not. Students in the comment group were also more likely to attribute their effort on the task to their interest, and their success to their interest and effort, than children who received grades, and they performed better on a subsequent task requiring creativity. In a later study by Butler (1988), students who received written comments with substantive suggestions for improvement maintained high interest in a task, whereas grades, with and without comments, undermined both interest and performance. In an experiment with fifth and sixth graders, evaluation in the form of global praise (e.g., "very good") and normatively distributed grades resulted in higher ego involvement, and lower task involvement, interest, and desire to engage further in the activity, than evaluation involving comments that included both reinforcement and goal-setting (e.g., "You thought of quite a few ideas; maybe it is possible to think of more unusual, original ideas"; Butler, 1987). Mac Iver (1990) found evidence that even retention and dropout rates were improved by including handwritten comments on report cards. He suggests that in addition to providing useful information, handwritten notes convey to low-achieving students that teachers are paying attention to them.

In summary, students need to be held accountable for their work and they need evaluative feedback to plan future efforts. Evaluation does not necessarily undermine students' motivation to engage in school tasks, and can even increase motivation if the information function is emphasized, if it is viewed as fair, and if positive evaluations are genuinely achievable. Appendix 11-B can be used to help teachers evaluate their own evaluation practices.

Control

Recall that some motivation theorists believe that a feeling of personal control or self-determination is a basic human need (Chapter 8). Whether or not people are born with this need, it is clear that they enjoy and are more motivated to engage in activities that they believe they are doing because they *want* to do them than they are to engage in activities that they believe they *have* to do.

Sarason (1993) distinguishes between teachers who *boss* and teachers who *lead*. Teachers who lead create a clear framework for learning in the context of options. Achieving a balance between giving appropriate limits and direction, and allowing students some discretion and control is difficult, and implementing the recommendations below requires consideration of a variety of variables, such as the age of the students, and their experience and skill in making decisions. Efforts to implement the principles discussed below, however, should enhance students' motivation to engage in school tasks.

1. Give students as much discretion as they can handle productively.   Students are most motivated when they are given choices and have some control over their academic work (Cordova & Lepper, 1996; Deci, Nezlek, & Sheinman, 1981; Deci, Schwartz, Sheinman, & Ryan, 1981; Guthrie & Alao, 1997; Guthrie, Wigfield, & VonSecker, 2000; Gutman & Sulzby, 2000; Iyengar & Lepper, 1999; Perry, 1998; see Ryan & La Guardia, in press). Likewise, students who have more autonomy-supportive teachers are more curious, have a greater desire for challenge, a more independent learning style, less anxiety, more confidence and even higher self-worth (Black & Deci, 2000; Deci et al., 1981).

Student choice was a particularly important feature of the highly motivating science class Meece et al. (1989) observed. In small-group activities, for example, students had some choice in their work partners, the materials they used, and how to complete the activity. Moreover, feedback was inherent in many of the small group tasks, minimizing students' dependence on the teacher. In contrast, in the classroom in which students expressed relatively low interest in learning science, the teacher determined the groups and specified all aspects of the materials and procedures. Choice has even been found to reduce disruptive behavior, presumably because it enhances students' interest in sanctioned activities (Munk & Repp, 1994).

A modest amount of choice may be all that is needed. Zuckerman, Porac, Lathin, Smith, and Deci (1978) increased intrinsic motivation by simply giving some of the subjects in their study an opportunity to select which three of six puzzles they worked on during an experiment. (See also Cordova & Lepper, 1996).

Increased student choice has been shown to enhance student learning as well as motivation. In Matheny and Edwards' (1974) study of 25 elementary classrooms, teachers were trained to (1) give students some flexibility and responsibility for determining when they completed assignments; (2) allow students to score most of their own written work and use individual conferences to evaluate student progress; (3) contract with students for long-range assignments; and (4) set up independent learning centers. Successful implementation of these strategies produced greater intrinsic motivation and greater gains in reading achievement. DeCharms (1976, 1984) reports that students who were trained to be "origins" rather than "pawns"—who were given more autonomy and responsibility for their learning—had better achievement scores and even better graduation rates than students in control classrooms.

Corno and colleagues (1989; Corno & Rohrkemper, 1985) suggest another value of providing students some control over their academic lives. They point out that students who are always told what to do and how and when to do it do not develop a sense of personal responsibility and strategies for regulating their own behavior. They do not learn how to use internal resources to solve problems and engage in deliberate planning and monitoring.

This benefit of giving children some, but not too much, discretion in their activities is illustrated by a classic study by Lewin, Lippitt, and White (1939). In an examination of the effect of adult control on children's productivity, they compared three organizational climates on the behavior of 10-year-old boys who were members of after-school "hobby clubs." In the three different conditions, the adult either controlled virtually every activity (autocratic condition), let the children do as they pleased (laissez-faire condition), or took an active role in the group's activities, but encouraged the children to participate in decision making (democratic condition). The authoritarian and democratic groups were equally productive, and more productive than the laissez-faire group, when an adult was present. The difference between the two productive groups became apparent when the adult leader left the room. Children in the democratic group were little affected by the absence of the leader. They worked at the same level whether an adult was present or absent. In contrast, productivity decreased markedly when the adult was absent from the autocratic group.

Providing students some control may be particularly important as children enter adolescence. Ironically, research suggests that at this developmental stage, when children are most concerned with issues of autonomy, school and classroom structures typically become more structured and teacher controlled (Eccles & Midgley, 1989; Eccles, Wigfield, Midgley, et al., 1993). The value of providing autonomy was demonstrated in a study of middle school students in which the less autonomy students claimed they were given at school, the more alienated they were from school (Eccles, Early, Fraser, Belansky, & McCarthy, 1997).

There are many ways to provide some student choice without creating chaos in a classroom. And if students are not overly concerned about negative consequences of poor performance, the evidence suggests that they will choose challenging tasks that will promote learning. Below are strategies for increasing student autonomy and feelings of self-determination.

Note that these principles need to be applied to *all* students in a classroom. Ryan and Grolnick (1986) found that upper-elementary school-aged students in the same classrooms varied considerably in the degree to which they thought they could be "origins" (responsible, instrumental, and having an internal locus of causality), versus "pawns" (reactive, with little sense of personal causation). Moreover, the students who felt they were in control had relatively high perceptions of competence and global self-worth.

The most disaffected students, who have the greatest need of classrooms that enhance motivation, are given the least amount of autonomy. Teachers need to be careful not to be satisfied with implementing practices that are motivating to only some students (usually those who need it least).

a. **Allow students to participate in the design of their academic tasks.** For example, rather than the teacher drawing up a list of vocabulary words to accompany a book students are reading, students can be asked to generate their own list. In one class I visited, each student contributed a word to a class list and became the "expert" for that word. This practice had the additional advantage of giving relatively low-achieving students an opportunity to be consulted by their peers for their expert knowledge.

b. **Give students choices in how tasks are completed.**   After reading a story students might choose from among several assignments—to write a summary of the story, to write a sequel to the story, or to write about a similar experience of their own. The teacher's goal for students to practice writing is accomplished regardless of each student's choice, but by being given some freedom, students have more control and a greater sense of responsibility.

c. **Give students some choice in the difficulty level of assignments or tasks that they work on.**   This kind of choice has to be implemented cautiously because, as mentioned above, students often select school tasks that assure a positive evaluation rather than tasks that challenge their current skill level.

DeCharms (1976) describes an activity with a built-in incentive for selecting the appropriate difficulty level. Students play a spelling game that involves teams, as in a spelling bee. Each student is asked whether he or she wants to try an easy word (worth 1 point for the team), a moderately hard word (worth 2 points), or a hard word (worth 3 points). The difficulty level of the words is individualized as a function of each student's performance on the pretest. An easy word is a word the student previously spelled correctly, a moderately hard word was spelled incorrectly, but the student had two days to study it. A hard word is from a new list tailored to the student's ability. When DeCharms tested this game, he found that the number of moderately hard words children chose increased over a five-week period, indicating that they learned to set realistic but challenging goals for themselves. This technique could be adapted to many different kinds of tasks.

d. Give students some discretion about when they complete particular tasks.   Some people like to get the most difficult or least appealing tasks out of the way first. Others prefer to do a few easy tasks to give them a feeling of accomplishment before they tackle the hard ones. Practices like giving students a homework packet on Monday to be turned in on Friday, rather than giving homework on a daily basis, gives students more discretion and an opportunity to develop skills in managing and organizing their time.

e. Allow students to correct some of their own assignments.   Students might check their solutions to math problems or their spelling words with an answer sheet. Or they can be given rubrics or a set of questions to help them assess their work. They might, for example, be asked to answer a series of questions after writing a paragraph: "Is there a topic sentence?" "Are there at least three sentences that support or elaborate on the topic sentence?" "Does the final sentence provide a transition to the next paragraph?" Ultimately, students' mastery has to be assessed by the teacher. But on a day-to-day basis students benefit greatly from instruction and experience in evaluating their own work.

f. Involve students in personal goal setting.   As suggested in Chapter 7, goals should be near (proximal), specific, and challenging. Students can, for example, set such goals as the number of spelling words they will get right on the next spelling test, or the number of arithmetic problems they will solve each day, and record whether or not they meet their goal.

2. Monitor learning and understanding more than student behavior.   Constant monitoring of student behavior and reminding students of deadlines make them feel controlled rather than self-determining. Clearly, deadlines need to be given and enforced, and teachers need to monitor students closely to be able to provide assistance and instruction. But deadlines should not become the teacher's central focus. And teachers should avoid monitoring when it has no instructional value and may be experienced as repressive. Looking over students' shoulders without engaging them in an instructional conversation, or walking around the room asking students how many problems they have completed, or telling students to get to work are experienced as controlling and unhelpful. Walking around the classroom checking students understanding and engaging them individually in instructional conversations focuses their attention on understanding and mastery and facilitates motivation. It can get distracted students to focus on the task, but by asking students about their understanding rather than admonishing them for not working conveys the message that the teacher cares about students' learning, not just about obedience.

3. Give help in a way that facilitates students' own accomplishments.   As mentioned in Chapter 7, when a child received unnecessary help, his or her success does not engender feelings of competence and intrinsic motivation. The negative effect of "overhelp" on intrinsic motivation has been demonstrated in studies of young children. Farnham-Diggory and Ramsey (1971), for example, found that when an experimenter frequently offered help during a play session, five-year-old children persisted half as long on a subsequent achievement task as did children who had previously played uninterrupted for the same amount of time. Fagot (1973) and Hamilton and Gordon (1978) provide further evidence suggesting that children in classrooms in which teachers are directive and intrusive display relatively low task persistence. Students perceived by the teacher to have behavioral or learning problems are particularly vulnerable to being offered more help than they actually need.

4. Hold students accountable.   Students need to understand that with control comes responsibility. They need to know *what* they will be held accountable for and *when*, and that there will be *consequences* for failure to meet their responsibilities. If their work is not completed when it is due, for example, they may need to lose some recess time or be required to complete it at home. I am not recommending severe punishment, but freedom without accountability promotes neither motivation nor learning. Choice often needs to be introduced gradually and teachers may need to provide some assistance to help students use their freedom productively.

In summary, allowing some student choice fosters intrinsic interest in school tasks and has the added advantage of teaching the self-management skills required for success in higher grades and in the workplace. It is impossible for students to develop a sense of personal responsibility and the ability to regulate their own learning behavior if they are always told what to do, and how and when to do it. A summary of the strategies for supporting student autonomy is found in Appendix 11-C.

As with most principles of good instruction, more is not necessarily better. As the Lewin et al. (1939) study demonstrated, there is such a thing as too much autonomy. Teachers need to experiment to find out how much autonomy students can handle, and they usually need to teach students strategies for taking productive advantage of the choices they are given.

Classroom Climate

It is important to think beyond tasks to the general climate of the classrooms. Research has revealed particular qualities of classrooms that promote intrinsic motivation and a focus on learning and mastery. Specific suggestions for making students feel respected, valued, and emotionally secure were discussed in Chapter 9. Below are additional suggestions for creating a classroom climate that allows students to become intellectually engaged.

1. Treat errors as a natural part of learning.   Outside of school, errors are considered a natural part of learning a skill. No one would expect to make perfect serves when learning how to play tennis or to bake a perfect soufflé on the first attempt. But in most classrooms errors are viewed negatively—as something to avoid. Red checks next to answers are reasons for distress, and 100 percent at the top of a paper is cause for celebration. In school, students learn to devalue errors, even on assignments based on new material.

Bulletin board displays of papers with no errors or that have stars, smiling faces, and "A's" on them can discourage the students who rarely achieve such high levels of performance. They also cause some high-achieving students, like Safe Sally, to be distressed when they receive anything less than a perfect score. Students deserve praise for attempting hard tasks, even if their efforts result in more errors than they would have made on an easier task. Safe Sally might take more risks if her teachers praised effort on difficult tasks with a few or even many errors as much as they praised perfect papers.

Classroom teachers should behave as expert tutors have been found to behave. Effective tutors rarely label a student's mistake as incorrect or as an error, and they do not suggest answers (Lepper et al., 1990). Instead, they rely on indirect strategies; they direct a students' attention to the source of the difficulty, offer hints, and give them a second chance. Thus, errors are treated as part of a process on route to achieving a correct solution.

  a. **Emphasize the information value of errors.**   In one fifth-grade classroom I observed, the teacher asked children to try to identify a pattern to the errors they made on math problems, and then to make up and try to solve similar problems. In this way she stressed the information conveyed in errors and their use for directing future efforts. Requiring students to correct errors on assignments forces them to try to remedy misunderstandings, and is preferable to simply indicating how many errors students made.

  b. **Incorporate wrong answers into discussions as productive contributions.**   In the American classrooms, Stigler and Stevenson (1991) observed, teachers tended to look for the "right" answer, dismissing rather than taking advantage of errors. The teachers they observed in Asia treated errors as topics for discussion from which all students can learn, thus turning every student's participation into a contribution to the larger goal of developing understanding. Meece et al. (1989) report that rather than turn to another student when one student failed to provide a satisfactory answer to a question (a common practice in American classrooms), the highly motivating science teacher they studied reworded the question or prompted students who responded incorrectly. Sometimes that teacher asked the student to explain or justify an incorrect response, so he or she would independently become aware of the problem. Thus, the teacher took advantage of rather than dismissed wrong answers.

2. Create a community of learners, which includes teachers as well as students.   Teachers instill academic values and engender interest in learning by modeling being learners themselves. They can talk to students about their own learning activities—a course they are taking, or a book they are reading. Teachers should also freely admit their own lack of knowledge and model using resources, including students, to address the gaps in their knowledge and skills.[1]

3. Model enthusiasm. Students take their cues from the teacher. If the teacher seems bored or complains about the curriculum, students are likely to feel the same way. The teacher who expresses his or her own interest and excitement about learning and enthusiasm for particular content and activities is likely to promote this same enthusiasm in students. In fact, Covington (1999) found that teacher enthusiasm was often mentioned by the students he interviewed as a source of their own motivation.

Summary

Students are more intrinsically motivated and focused on learning and mastery when tasks are moderately challenging, novel, and relevant to their own lives than when tasks are too hard or too easy, repetitive, or perceived to be irrelevant. Students are intrinsically motivated to work when they feel self-determining rather than controlled, when the threat of negative external evaluation is not salient, and when their attention is not focused on extrinsic reasons for completing tasks. They will also feel more competent and proud, and thus more intrinsically interested in tasks when they can take responsibility for their success.

None of the recommendations made in this chapter will be effective if they are not implemented in a climate of support and respect that makes students feel secure and valued. Students will not be motivated to engage in even the most intrinsically interesting tasks or under optimal conditions of autonomy if they fear humiliation or rejection by the teacher or peers.

---

[1]Students often have more expertise than teachers in the area of technology. By seeking assistance from expert students, teachers can convey to students that lack of skill is not a reason for embarrassment.

12 Achievement Anxiety

Achievement anxiety is not all bad. A small amount of anxiety does not undermine performance and may even facilitate it, especially if the task is not very difficult (Ball, 1995; Luthar, 1995; Sieber, O'Neil, & Tobias, 1977; Zeidner & Nevo, 1992). But for some students, anxiety debilitates performance in achievement settings by interfering with learning and retrieving previously learned material. This chapter examines the measurement, effects, and origins of achievement anxiety and makes specific recommendations for minimizing the negative effects of anxiety on learning and academic performance.

Most students who are highly anxious in achievement situations have low perceptions of their academic competence (e.g., Abu-Hilal, 2000; Bandalos, Yates, & Thorndike-Christ, 1995; Harter, 1992; see Hembree, 1988) and low self-efficacy (Bandura, 1988; Pajares & Miller, 1994; Pintrich & De Groot, 1990; Sapp, 1999; Wolters & Pintrich, 1998); they are most anxious in situations that threaten their self-esteem (Schwarzer & Jerusalem, 1992). In their early work on test anxiety, Sarason, Davidson, Lighthall, Waite, and Ruebush (1960) described the test-anxious child as one who has "self-deprecatory attitudes, anticipates failure in the test situation in the sense that he will not meet the standards of performance of others or himself, and experiences the situation as unpleasant" (p. 20). Because high-anxiety students are fearful of failure they avoid highly evaluative situations when they can, and they choose easy tasks on which success is fairly certain (Hill, 1980, 1984; Hill & Wigfield, 1984; Tobias, 1992; Sarason & Sarason, 1990). When they must perform in evaluative situations, they are overly concerned about evaluation of their performance, and these concerns interfere with their performance on the task.

A distinction is usually made between **trait anxiety,** a relatively stable personality characteristic, and **state anxiety,** a temporary emotional state (Spielberger & Vagg, 1995). People who are generally more prone than others to experiencing a state of anxiety in achievement settings do not experience anxiety all of the time. Trait anxiety is believed to interfere with learning and performance only when the achievement conditions create a *state* of anxiety. Thus, even students who are prone to be anxious (i.e., who are high on trait anxiety) may feel very relaxed in nonthreatening situations, such as when they are self-confident and expect to succeed, or when their performance will not be evaluated. Therefore, debilitating anxiety can be minimized, even for anxiety-prone students, by creating conditions that do not engender a state of anxiety.

Anxiety in achievement contexts is commonly referred to as "test anxiety." However, "test" is used broadly in this literature, and the research is usually applicable to all situations in which a student's intellectual abilities are being evaluated—ranging from formal testing situations to simply being asked a question by the teacher.

There are two components to achievement anxiety: a *cognitive* component (worry), and an *emotional* component (Anderson & Sauser, 1995; Pajares & Urdan, 1996; Sapp, 1999; Sarason & Sarason, 1990; Spielberger & Vagg, 1995; Zeidner, 1998). The cognitive, worry component of test anxiety involves negative expectations for success and concerns about one's performance, and is believed to interfere most directly with learning and task performance (see Sarason & Sarason, 1990; Tobias, 1992; Zeidner & Nevo, 1992). The emotional component refers to the autonomic (physiological) reactions that are evoked by evaluative stress, such as sweating and an accelerated heart rate.

Measuring Anxiety

Several self-report instruments have been developed to measure students' propensity to experience anxiety in evaluative situations. (See Anderson & Sauser, 1995, for a summary and discussion of anxiety measures; see Bedell & Marlowe, 1995, for evidence on validity; see also Sapp, 1999.) The original instrument given to children, the Test Anxiety Scale for Children (TASC), was developed by Sarason et al. (1960). Students respond to questions, such as "Do you feel nervous while you are taking a test?" or "Do you think you worry more about school than other children?"

A positively-worded revision of the TASC (called the TASC-Rx) was developed by Feld and Lewis (1969). An example of a question is "Do you feel relaxed while you are taking a test?" The authors found that students' responses to the questionnaire fell into four categories: (1) specific worry about tests; (2) physiological reactions to evaluative pressure; (3) negative self-evaluation; and (4) worry about school while at home. Children who scored high in one category were not necessarily high in other categories. Anxiety seems to be experienced by children in different ways and in different situations.

The results of research on anxiety have potential implications for the classroom. Remedies for high anxiety may be different, depending on which kind of anxiety a student experiences. For example, the student who has unpleasant physiological reactions in test situations may need a different kind of intervention than a student who has a negative view of his or her ability to succeed. The first student may need instructions on test-taking or relaxation strategies, or simply more experience taking tests. The second student may need success experiences and other interventions, like those described in Chapter 7, designed to build self-confidence.

Harnisch, Hill, and Fyans (1980) selected seven items from the TASC-Rx, primarily from the test-worry category, to create the Test Comfort Index (TCI). This scale has been used extensively in classrooms for diagnostic and research purposes. Hill (1984) reports that school personnel like the TCI because it is quick and easy to administer and is worded positively. The seven questions are given in Table 12.1. The student responds "yes" or "no" to each question. According to research by Hill and his colleagues, it is highly likely that the test performance of students who respond "no" to these items does not provide an accurate assessment of their true competence. Their anxiety probably interferes with their performance in ways that are described below.

A number of test anxiety scales have been developed for adults, including Sarason's (1978) Test Anxiety Scale, and Spielberger's (1980) Test Anxiety Inventory. Sarason (1984) created the 40-item Reactions to Tests (RTT) measure, with four subscales. Two of the subscales are associated with the emotional component of achievement anxiety, *tension* (e.g., "I feel distressed and uneasy before tests") and *bodily reactions* (e. g., "My heart beats faster when the test begins"); the other two subscales are associated with the worry component, *worry* (e.g., "During tests, I wonder how the other people are doing") and *test-irrelevant thought* ("Irrelevant bits of information pop into my head during a test").

It is useful to measure students' anxiety directly because teacher observations are not always reliable. Sarason et al. (1960) found that when asked to rate student anxiety, teachers often underestimated the anxiety of high-performing students. The researchers suggest that anxiety in bright, high-performing students is the most likely to be overlooked by teachers because their problems are usually not as obvious as hostile children who act out, or extremely shy, withdrawn children.

Safe Sally is an example. Although anxiety does not appear to interfere with her performance in the achievement situations she limits herself to, it does inhibit her from achieving her full potential. Anxiety about performing poorly leads to

TABLE 12.1   Test Comfort Index (TCI)*

When the teacher says that she is going to give the class a test, do you feel relaxed and comfortable?

1. Do you feel relaxed before you take a test?
2. Do you feel relaxed while you are taking a test?
3. Do you feel relaxed when the teacher says that she is going to ask you questions to find out how much you know?
4. When the teacher says that she is going to give the class a test, do you usually feel that you will do good work?
5. While you are taking a test, do you usually think you are doing good work?
6. Do you like tests in school?

*Harnisch, Hill, and Fyans (1980).

obsessive studying and preparation, time which could be used for activities that would contribute more to her intellectual development. Also, the anxiety causes her to avoid challenging achievement situations. Because she performs well her teachers are not likely to perceive, or at least to be concerned about, her anxiety about performing well.

Anxiety and Achievement

Considerable evidence indicates that students who report high anxiety in achievement situations perform poorly compared to students who report relatively low anxiety (e.g., Everson, Smodlaka, & Tobias, 1994; Pintrich & De Groot, 1990; see Hembree, 1988). Demonstrating a link between achievement and anxiety, however, does not establish the causal direction of the association. Do students who have not mastered the material become anxious when they are being evaluated? Do anxious students have difficulty learning new material? Or do anxious students have difficulty demonstrating what they know in evaluative situations?

Research suggests that the association between anxiety and achievement is complex (Covington & Omelich, 1988; Everson, Smodlaka, & Tobias, 1994), but all of the above are true to some degree. Anxiety interferes with learning and with demonstrating understanding, and students who are poorly prepared and who expect to fail are more likely to feel anxious than students who are well prepared and self-confident. Anxiety is, therefore, a cause as well as a consequence of poor preparation.

Tobias (1992) suggests that anxiety interferes with learning and performance at three levels. First, anxiety inhibits the efficient *preprocessing* of new information, that is, of registering and internally representing instructional input. For example, the student may have difficulty attending to and organizing the material presented. Second, anxiety interferes with *processing*—applying new understanding to generate a solution to a problem. The student understands the new material, but when asked to apply the new knowledge to a specific problem, he or she is unable to remember what has been learned or is unable to use effective problem-solving strategies. Third, Tobias suggests that anxiety interferes with the *output* of a response. The correct answer may be grasped and then lost before the student verbalizes or records it. Or the student may be able to demonstrate understanding immediately after the material is learned, but has difficulty reproducing it on a summative test given later. When we claim that our mind "went blank," or that we are "blocking on a name," we are referring to the output level of a response.

Preprocessing and Processing

There is considerable evidence for the effect of anxiety on these three levels of learning and performance. Consider first the preprocessing and processing levels. Researchers have found that high-anxiety students have less effective study skills than students lower in anxiety (Naveh-Benjamin, McKeachie, & Lin, 1987; Topman, Kleijn, van der Ploeg, & Masset, 1992), and are more prone to avoidance as a coping strategy (Zeidner, 1994; see Zeidner, 1995). In a study by Benjamin, McKeachie, Lin, and Holinger (1981), for example, high-anxiety college students reported spending more time studying for an exam than low-anxiety students reported, but the high-anxiety students had more problems learning the material. High-anxiety students also did worse on a take-home exam, which presumably tested the students' ability to analyze and organize information that was in front of them rather than to retrieve previously-learned material.

Research evidence also suggests that high-anxiety students are easily distracted when they are learning new material (Dusek, Mergler, & Kermis, 1976; Eysenck, 1991; see Hembree, 1988) and can be assisted by being given strategies that help focus their attention (Dusek, Kermis, & Mergler, 1975). In the Dusek et al. study, for example, children were asked to memorize the position of animal drawings in a stimulus array; the performance of high-anxiety, but not of low-anxiety children improved considerably when they were asked to label the drawings as they were placed in the stimulus array. Presumably, the labeling helped the high-anxiety children focus their attention on the central stimuli.

Output

Anxiety is believed to interfere in several ways with students' ability to demonstrate their knowledge. Wine (1980) claims that attention in testing situations is divided between task-relevant and task-irrelevant thoughts. People with a high level of anxiety devote a significant amount of attention to task-irrelevant thoughts, leaving only small amounts of attention for task-relevant responses.

Some task-irrelevant thoughts may not be directly related to concerns about inadequacies or performance. But most test-anxiety theorists believe that people high in anxiety are preoccupied with "worry" about their performance, and that this interferes with their ability to retrieve and demonstrate skills and knowledge (see Hembree, 1988; Sapp, 1999; Sarason & Sarason, 1990; Schwarzer & Jerusalem, 1992; Tobias, 1992; Zeidner, 1998). Bandura (1988) proposed that people low in self-efficacy, in particular, dwell on their deficiencies and envision failure scenarios in threatening situations, diverting their attention away from the task. Both the thoughts themselves and their physiological effects (e.g., trembling) can interfere with performance. Demster and Corkill (1999) suggest that everyone is vulnerable to irrelevant and interfering thoughts, but some people are more effective at resisting the interference than others.

Highly anxious students may also become obsessed with unimportant aspects of the task, such as their handwriting. Or, in severe cases, they may attend to entirely irrelevant aspects of the task. I once observed a child who was supposed to be answering a set of questions based on a brief story. Rather than reading the story, he busily counted and recounted the number of words it contained. This activity seemed to offer some relief; at least he was doing something. And by giving the teacher the impression that he was engaged in the task at hand, it delayed her inevitable negative reaction to his failure to complete the assignment. This is the kind of behavior that one might expect of Defensive Dave—designed in part to promote, if only temporarily, a perception of competence.

Deficiencies in test-taking skills are also believed to account for poor perfor mance (Bruch, Juster, & Kaflowitz, 1983). Students who are anxious in test situations seem to lack abilities such as accurately interpreting instructions, pacing themselves appropriately, or doing the easy questions first.

In summary, the research on anxiety and achievement provides strong evidence that anxiety interferes with both learning and performance. Thus, students who are highly anxious in achievement contexts have difficulty learning new material and demonstrating what they have learned. Before discussing possible ways to minimize the debilitating effects of anxiety on learning and performance, we will consider some explanations that have been offered for the development of high achievement anxiety.

Origins of Achievement Anxiety

It has already been suggested that low confidence can cause anxiety in evaluative situations. Nevertheless, some students who usually perform well on tests experience severe anxiety, while some students who generally do poorly show little evidence of anxiety. Other factors are clearly involved.

A few theorists have suggested that anxiety has its roots in parent-child relationships. Sarason et al. (1960), for example, proposed that parents of highly anxious children hold unrealistically high expectations and are overly critical. The children internalize the parents' negative evaluations and consequently feel inadequate in evaluative situations regardless of their performance. The unconscious hostility toward the parent for being so critical is internalized in the form of anxiety, rather than externalized in overt aggressiveness.

Child-rearing explanations for the cause of achievement anxiety have not been well researched, although there is a little supportive evidence. One study found that high anxiety in children was associated with negative parental feedback (blame and punishment), inconsistency in child rearing, and parents' tendency to control and restrict the child (Krohne, 1992). Another study found that parents who expressed relatively more annoyance, anger, or disappointment and tried to restrict their children's behavior (e.g., urging the child to hurry up, giving instructions in a preemptory tone) while the child was working on homework assignments had more anxious children. Case studies of college students high in anxiety, by Anton and Lillibridge (1995), however, indicate that child rearing varies considerably among highly anxious students.

Early school experiences may also affect anxiety. The amount of success versus failure is undoubtedly important. Although not all students who consistently fail become highly anxious, students high in achievement anxiety are more likely to have a history of failure than students low in anxiety. Thus it is possible that early school failures affect later performance in part because students who fail develop a propensity to experience anxiety in evaluative situations, which interferes with their future learning and performance. Given that perceptions of academic ability decline with age, and an understanding of ability as capacity is not fully developed until early adolescence (Chapter 6), it is not surprising that anxiety increases with age (Wigfield & Eccles, 1989, 1990).

But some highly anxious students have a history of academic success. The origins of anxiety may be different for high-achieving students. Wigfield and Eccles (1989) suggest that while low-achieving students develop anxiety as a result of repeated failures and low expectations for success, relatively high-performing students may become anxious because of unrealistic parental, peer, or self-imposed expectations that they should excel in all academic areas.

Classroom climate and other school-related factors may also be important. Zatz and Chassin (1985) found that high-anxiety students performed more poorly on tests than low- or middle-anxious students only in classes in which students perceived the threat of evaluation to be high. Similarly, Helmke (1988) found that anxiety was especially debilitating in classrooms in which success and failure were very salient.

Wigfield and Eccles (1989) suggest that the transition to junior high may engender anxiety because the uncertainty of a new school context, including a larger school and many teachers, is compounded with stricter grading, less autonomy, and more formal relationships with teachers. Standardized testing is another feature of school environments that can engender anxiety, especially if strongly emphasized. In high school, standardized tests, such as the Scholastic Aptitude Test (SAT), play a major role in students' long-term educational and occupational options, and are no doubt a major source of anxiety for some students.

Gender differences are also commonly found in studies of test anxiety (e.g., Everson, Millsap, & Rodriquez, 1991; Hembree, 1990; Hill & Sarason, 1966; Randhawa, 1994; Wigfield & Meece, 1988; Zeidner & Nevo, 1992; see Hembree, 1988, for a review; also Eccles et al., 2000). Females are usually found to have higher scores on measures of test anxiety than males, and the difference increases with age and time at school. Sarason et al. (1960) suggest that boys may score lower than girls on measures of test anxiety because they are more reluctant to admit anxiety, not because they actually experience it less. Relatively higher anxiety among girls could also result from their lower perceptions of their ability (see Chapter 6).

Subject Matter Anxieties

Most studies on achievement anxiety do not differentiate by subject matter. But some people develop anxiety about performance in specific subject areas or with regard to particular skills. They may be comfortable in most academic contexts, but have great difficulty performing in one domain. Two domains that have been studied are mathematics and writing.

Mathematics

Anxious Alma is in good company. Mathematics anxiety, or "mathophobia," is widespread. College students report much more anxiety about mathematics than they do about English, social science (Everson, Tobias, Hartman, & Gourgey, 1993), or even writing (Sapp, Farrell, & Durand, 1995). It is estimated that about one-third of college students suffer from some level of mathematics anxiety (Anton & Klisch, 1995; see Mitchell & Collins, 1991).

A commonly used measure of mathematics anxiety is the Mathematics Anxiety Scale (MAS) shown in Table 12.2 (Betz, 1978). The scale includes 10 items and studies of middle school, high school, and college students suggest that it taps the same two dimensions of anxiety often found in more general test anxiety measures—a general sense of worry about mathematics and negative feelings and emotional reactions (Pajares & Urdan, 1996).

Mathematics does not generate as much anxiety in young children as in older children and adults. In Goodlad's (1984) study of over 17,000 young students, mathematics was rated about the same as reading in a list of "liked" subjects (after art and physical education). In the National Assessment of Educational Progress, nine-year-olds ranked mathematics as their best-liked subject; thirteen-year-olds ranked it second best, but in contrast to the younger children, seventeen-year-olds claimed that mathematics was their least liked subject (Carpenter, Corbitt, Kepner, Lindquist, & Reys, 1981). Significant declines in positive attitudes toward mathematics have also been shown over the adolescent years (Wigfield, Eccles, Mac Iver, Reuman, & Midgley, 1991; Wigfield & Eccles, 1994). Apparently children are not born with mathematics anxiety. Rather, negative attitudes toward mathematics develop over time, especially during adolescence.

TABLE 12.2   Mathematics Anxiety Scale

Items are answered on a 1–5 Likert scale.

The first five items are reverse coded, so that high scores indicate high mathematics anxiety.

---

1. It wouldn't bother me at all to take more math classes.
2. I have usually been at ease during math tests.
3. I have usually been at ease in math courses.
4. I usually don't worry about my ability to solve math problems.
5. I almost never get uptight while taking math tests.
6. I get really uptight during math tests.
7. I get a sinking feeling when I think of trying hard math problems.
8. My mind goes blank and I am unable to think clearly when doing mathematics.
9. Mathematics makes me feel uncomfortable and nervous.
10. Mathematics makes me feel uneasy and confused.

Why does mathematics, in particular, cause so much anxiety in older students and adults? One can only speculate. Lazarus (1975) points out that mathematics anxiety has a ". . . peculiar social acceptability. Persons otherwise proud of their educational attainments shamelessly confess to being 'no good at math'" (p. 281; see also Sapp, 1999).

The way mathematics is usually taught may also explain why mathematics anxiety is common. Lazarus (1975) suggests that the cumulative nature of mathematics curricula is one explanation; if you fail to understand one operation, you are often unable to learn anything taught beyond that operation.

From observations of mathematics and social studies classes, Stodolsky (1985) proposed that mathematics instruction fostered in students the belief that mathematics is something that is learned from an authority, not figured out on one's own. She found that mathematics classes were characterized by (1) a recitation and seatwork pattern of instruction; (2) a reliance on teacher presentation of new concepts or procedures; (3) textbook-centered instruction; (4) textbooks that lacked developmental or instructional material for concept development; (5) a lack of manipulatives; and (6) a lack of social support or small-group work. The instructional format, the types of behavior expected from students, and the materials used were also more similar from day to day in mathematics than in social studies classes. This lack of variety may contribute to anxiety because students who do not do well in the instructional format used in mathematics are not given opportunities to succeed using alternative formats. Later studies by Stodolsky also suggest that mathematics teachers see their subject area as more sequential and static than teachers of other subjects (Stodolsky & Grossman, 1995; see also Wolters & Pintrich, 1998). Sapp (1999) speculates that mathematics teaching often focuses on memorization of procedures, which doesn't prepare students for more conceptual, advanced mathematics. Thus, they feel ill-prepared and become anxious when rote procedures are no longer sufficient.

Stodolsky (1985) also suggests that mathematics is an area in which ability, in the sense of a stable trait, is believed to play a dominant role in performance—either one has the ability or one does not. And if one lacks ability in mathematics, nothing can be done about it. (This is what was defined as an "entity" theory of ability in Chapter 6.) By contrast, people generally believe that performance in other subjects, like reading or social studies, can be improved with practice and effort; they hold an "incremental" theory of ability.

There is consistent evidence that females suffer more from mathematics anxiety than do males (Hembree, 1990; Pajares & Urdan, 1996; Randhawa, 1994; Wigfield & Meece, 1988). Some researchers have proposed that mathematics anxiety contributes to observed gender differences in mathematics achievement and course enrollment, but the one study that actually assessed anxiety and enrollment plans found no relationship (Meece, Wigfield, & Eccles, 1990).

There is little agreement on the reasons for such gender differences. Ability differences, socialization differences, differences in the level of self-confidence, and the number of mathematics courses taken have all been proposed as explanations. Whatever the reasons for the frequency and intensity of mathematics anxiety, particularly among females, it is a problem that warrants special attention by educational researchers and practitioners.

The good news is that interventions to reduce math anxiety have been successful. Sgoutas-Emch and Johnson (1998) found that writing in a journal about frustrations and feelings reduced college students' anxiety in a statistics course.

Writing

Perhaps everyone, at one time in their lives, experiences a certain amount of panic facing a blank piece of paper or computer screen, especially if the due date for a written product—a paper for a class or a report for work—is close at hand. "Writer's block" is so debilitating for some that they avoid courses and professions that require writing. (See Daly & Miller, 1975b; Daly, Vangelisti, & Witte, 1988; Rose, 1985; Selfe, 1985.)

Although psychoanalytic explanations have been suggested (Barwick, 1995; Grundy, 1993), the few studies that have been done suggest that writing anxiety reflects some of the same dynamics that explain general achievement anxiety. Writing anxiety, like general achievement anxiety, is associated with relatively low expectations for success as well as lower writing quality (Daly, 1985; Pajares & Valiante, 1997). Rose's (1985) research on writer's block makes it very clear that the causes are usually multifaceted, and that although they may have their roots in early familial experiences, later and current experiences in writing contexts are also important.

Researchers have developed a measure of writing anxiety (Daly & Miller, 1975a), which has been shown to be more strongly associated with writing performance than a more general measure of achievement anxiety (Richmond & Dickson-Markman, 1985). Studies using the measure have found some gender differences, with females showing somewhat less writing anxiety than males. People high in writing anxiety were also high on reading anxiety and anxiety about public speaking and interpersonal communication, but relatively low on math anxiety (Daly, 1985).

Research has also examined associations between *teachers'* feelings about writing and their teaching strategies. Studies have found, for example, that highly apprehensive female teachers assign fewer writing assignments and are more likely to be concerned with issues of form and usage and less likely to emphasize personal or creative expression and effort than less apprehensive teachers (see Daly, 1985; Daly et al., 1988). Associations between teachers' own anxiety about writing and their teaching methods were strongest in upper elementary school, when many important writing skills are supposed to be taught.

Studies of interventions find that simply taking writing courses decreases writing anxiety, at least temporarily (Basile, 1982; Fox, 1980). Zimmerman and Silverman (1982) report that the writing apprehension of fifth-grade students could be reduced by emphasizing prewriting activities, expressive writing, and positive evaluation (see Daly, 1985; Schweiker-Marra & Marra, 2000).

The instructional context can exacerbate concerns about competencies that feed anxiety, and they contribute to trait anxiety both over time and collectively. One study found that high school students who were relatively high in writing anxiety reported having experienced more criticism for their writing and less encouragement and support, and they reported seeking help for writing problems less than students low on writing anxiety (Daly, 1985).

Daly (1985) proposes that writing anxiety will be greatest under the following circumstances:

- evaluation is salient
- the task is ambiguous
- the writer feels conspicuous
- task difficulty is perceived to be high
- the writer feels lacking in prior experience relevant to the task
- the task is personally salient
- the setting or task is novel
- the writer perceives the audience as uninterested but evaluative

Teachers may be able to reduce writing anxiety by minimizing students' concerns about evaluation, making assignments and criteria for grading clear, and making sure that students have the prior experience and familiarity they need to complete the writing task. Writing tasks, like all tasks, should be challenging but not so difficult or different from what students have experienced in the past as to provoke a sense of incompetence or low expectations for success. A genuine and supportive audience (e.g., classmates, parents) might also help. Most of the strategies discussed in the next section are designed to minimize anxiety of all types in achievement contexts and should reduce writing anxiety as well.

Minimizing the Negative Effects of Anxiety

Different problems related to anxiety require different solutions, so it is important to analyze the nature of the problem before planning an intervention or changing classroom practices. Benjamin, McKeachie, and Lin (1987) distinguish, for example, between anxious students who have good study habits but cannot handle evaluative pressure (whose anxiety interferes with performance in the output phase) and students who do not master the material presented to them (whose anxiety interferes in the preprocessing and processing phases). More relaxed testing conditions and training in test-taking strategies would be appropriate for the former group, while study-skill training would be more appropriate for the latter.

Teachers also need to be aware that the recommendations made for highly anxious students are not necessarily good for students who are low in anxiety. Indeed, conditions that maximize performance for highly anxious students may undermine performance for students who are low in anxiety. This is because for some students, a mild amount of anxiety actually facilitates performance.

Preprocessing

Interventions involving training in study skills have been successful in reducing anxiety and increasing performance among students who have difficulty learning new material (see Dendato & Diener, 1986; Naveh-Benjamin, 1991). Naveh-Benjamin (1991), for example, found that study-skills training benefited highly anxious students with problems in processing information; **desensitization** was more effective for high test-anxious students who had problems retrieving already learned information. (See also Algaze, 1995; Vagg & Spielberger, 1995.)

There are other ways to assist students whose anxiety interferes with their ability to process new information or material. First, highly anxious students can be helped by having opportunities to reinspect material. If new information is being presented in a lecture, it is important for the teacher to pause frequently and encourage questions, and to review the material. If the material is presented in a film, highly anxious students might be allowed to review the film. If it is presented in written form they can be encouraged to reread the material.

Clear, unambiguous instructions and a fair amount of structure also seem to facilitate the processing of new information for anxious students. Teachers can also give explicit instructions for strategies for learning material. In one fifth-grade class I visited the teacher gave students a list of written instructions designed to help them learn spelling words (e.g., "look at the word; say the letters to yourself; close your eyes and picture the word; write the word; check accuracy"; and so on). Note-taking, making memory aids, and strategies for assessing understanding and planning and organizing tasks can also be taught (see also the section on self-regulation, Chapter 4).

A self-paced curriculum can be helpful to highly anxious students, especially those who are achieving poorly. Having to keep up with the group can create anxiety. Knowing that new material and demands for performance will be regulated according to the student's own mastery should relieve some anxiety.

Processing and Output

Much of the research on alleviating anxiety in the output or production phase has involved desensitization and relaxation techniques (Algaze, 1995; Dendato & Diener, 1986; Gonzalez, 1995; Naveh-Benjamin, 1991; see Sapp, 1999; Wigfield & Eccles, 1989). Students typically work through a desensitization hierarchy, usually in a group setting. For example, they begin by imagining the teacher announcing a test, and continue to imagine more threatening situations, such as taking home a test with a poor grade. The evidence suggests that desensitization can reduce anxiety, in some cases with resulting improvement in performance (see Hembree, 1988).

Cognitive therapies are designed to diminish the worry component of test anxiety—to alleviate preoccupation with performance, ability, or adequacy. Students reflect upon and analyze their anxiety-provoking and other task-irrelevant thoughts, and develop coping strategies, such as concentrating on positive thoughts before a test and instructing themselves to attend to the task while studying or taking tests. The strategies are based on the cognitive behavioral modification approach (described in Chapter 4) and have been shown to be effective, especially in combination with other treatments (Algaze, 1995; Fletcher & Spielberger, 1995; Sapp, 1999; Vagg & Spielberger, 1995).

There are other strategies teachers can use to alleviate the effects of anxiety at the processing and output stages that are more easily integrated into the classroom curriculum than desensitization or cognitive therapy. One approach is to introduce tasks in a nonthreatening way. I. Sarason (1973, 1975; Sarason & Sarason, 1990) reports that task-irrelevant, self-deprecatory thinking among high test-anxious individuals is especially likely when tasks are introduced as a test of ability, or when attention is focused on the evaluative aspect of a task. In one study he gave a group of both high- and low-test anxiety college students a serial learning task of meaningless words (I. Sarason, 1961). Some students were simply given instructions necessary to respond to the task. Other students were told that the task was a measure of intelligence. High-anxiety students who were told that the task measured intelligence performed significantly worse than high-anxiety students who were given neutral instructions. The instructions had no effect on the low-anxiety students' performance. The instructions Sarason compared in this study are the same as those currently used in experimental studies designed to manipulate a learning versus performance orientation (see Chapter 10).

Sarason (1958) demonstrated in another study that instructions specifically designed to allay concerns about ability can enhance the performance of high-anxious students. He eliminated performance differences between high- and low-anxious students by simply suggesting to the high-anxious students that they should relax, even if they do not learn the task immediately, because it is a very difficult task. The low-anxious students actually performed better without the reassuring introduction, presumably because their own motivation was heightened when they assumed that their performance provided information about their ability.

Reminding students to focus their attention on the task or giving them reassuring directions ("Don't worry," "You will do just fine") has been shown to improve the performance of individuals high in anxiety (Sarason & Sarason, 1990). Similar to the findings of the study described above, however, the reassuring instructions seemed to undermine the performance of students low in anxiety—perhaps because they took them at face value and thus exerted less effort.

These studies illustrate how the same instructions can have different effects on different students, depending on the level of anxiety they bring to the task. In general, Sarason and others have found that when preliminary instructions have an evaluative or achievement-orienting flavor, high-test-anxious subjects tend to perform at a relatively low level, whereas a modest evaluation or achievement orientation seems to have a positive effect on the performance of low test-anxious subjects.

Giving students opportunities to correct errors can also alleviate anxiety. Students can be allowed to correct their own papers in some situations, and to redo incorrectly solved problems before their responses are turned in to the teacher. Permitting students to improve written products before a final grade is given will also alleviate anxiety.

Individualized interventions are also useful for students like Alma, who are severely debilitated by anxiety. In such extreme cases, a teacher may need to implement an individual anxiety-reduction plan, preferably one that is discussed and developed with the student. In Alma's case, for example, the teacher might suggest a book on relaxation techniques. The teacher may also make arrangements, privately, to give Alma extra time on tests, or an opportunity to retake a test on which she believes she had not shown what she knew. Alma's teacher might also help Alma build her self-confidence by having her assist a student having difficulty with assignments. Whatever individual arrangements are made, they will only be effective if the classroom climate is generally positive and supportive.

Alleviating Test Anxiety

Several techniques have been developed to alleviate the debilitating effects of anxiety in testing situations. Tests should be presented as a means to assess current understanding, help students plan future efforts, and guide the teacher's instructional plans. When possible, tests should not be presented as the final assessment of students' competence.

Having to rely entirely on memory in a testing situation can create unnecessary anxiety, and memory supports have been shown to be helpful in alleviating anxiety (Gross & Mastenbrook, 1980; Sieber et al., 1977). Thus, a highly anxious student might perform better on a mathematics task if allowed to refer to a sample problem. Or, a student might do better on a set of questions related to a reading assignment if allowed to review the text on which the questions are based. Even when questions are constructed in such a way that having books and notes available is not very helpful, students often feel more secure knowing that they have access to them.

Providing an opportunity to retake a test can enhance motivation and improve test scores, in part because it relieves anxiety. Covington and Omelich (1984c) found that undergraduate psychology students who were allowed to retake their midterm after several days of study were more self-confident and ultimately received significantly higher scores than students who were not given this option.

Hill and his colleagues have done many studies on the effect of the conditions of testing on the performance of anxious children (Hill, 1980, 1984). In all of his studies, the high-anxious students' performance was considerably improved by optimal testing conditions. Three features of testing have consistently been shown to affect the performance of high-anxious students: (1) time limits; (2) difficulty of the test material; and (3) test instructions, question-and-answer formats, and other mechanics (e.g., computerized responses).

Hill and Eaton (1977) investigated the effects of time pressure on the performance of upper-elementary grade students on an arithmetic computation test. When students were pressured for time, the high-anxious students took twice as long to do the problems and made three times as many errors as the low-anxious children. When there was no time pressure, high-anxious students worked almost as fast as low-anxious students and made only a few more errors. Several subsequent studies provide further evidence that relaxing time pressure improves the performance of high-anxious students (Plass & Hill, 1986; see Hill, 1984, for a review).

Since anxiety interferes with learning only on relatively difficult subject matter, the order of easy and difficult problems may affect performance. One study found that students prone to anxiety performed better on tasks that began with easy problems that became progressively more difficult than on tasks in which some difficult problems were placed early in the test (Lund, 1953, cited in Phillips, Pitcher, Worsham, & Miller, 1980). Zigler and his colleagues (see Zigler & Harter, 1969) found that children's IQ test performance could be improved by simply adjusting the order of questions so that an easy question followed several consecutive incorrect responses.

Finally, test instructions and the test format can affect the performance of highly anxious students. Unfamiliar question formats, computerized answer sheets, and other unfamiliar aspects of standardized achievement tests can be especially intimidating to students who are prone to anxiety. Anxiety can be relieved by making sure that students understand instructions and know how to use the answer sheets.

Summary

Not all anxiety is debilitating. For some students, a modest amount of anxiety can motivate optimal performance. But anxiety can also interfere with learning and performance. One of the teacher's many tasks is to minimize the debilitating effects of anxiety. A general principle is to remove, as much as possible, the threat failure can be to the student's ego. The strategies to diminish anxiety discussed in this chapter are summarized in Appendix 12-A.

The current political pressure and high stakes associated with standardized achievement tests are likely to have important implications for students' test anxiety. Teachers need to be aware that conveying their own concerns about students' performance on standardized tests can actually undermine their students' performance by promoting debilitating anxiety.

TABLE 12.3   Summary of Terms

Term	Definition
Trait anxiety	Proneness to a state of anxiety in evaluative contexts—a relatively stable personality characteristic
State anxiety	A temporal state of anxiety in a particular evaluative context
Desensitization	Gradual introduction of increasingly threatening images and thoughts along with images and thoughts related to overcoming the threat

CHAPTER

13 Communicating Expectations

Teachers' expectations about students' learning can have profound implications for what students actually learn. Expectations affect the content and pace of the curriculum, the organization of instruction, evaluation, instructional interactions with individual students, and many subtle and not-so-subtle behaviors that affect students' own expectations for learning and thus their behavior.

The effect of teacher expectations was first demonstrated experimentally in a classic study by Rosenthal and Jacobson (1968). Elementary-school teachers were told that some of the students in their class had shown on a written test that they had remarkable potential for academic growth. These students had actually been selected randomly, but eight months later the students in the early grades for whom teachers were led to hold artificially high expectations showed greater gains in IQ than other students in their grades. These students, in a sense, fulfilled their teachers' prophecies. This study has spawned hundreds of studies on teachers' **"self-fulfilling prophecies"** (see Brophy, 1983b; Cooper & Tom, 1984; Dusek, 1975, 1985; Jussim, 1991; Wigfield & Harold, 1992, for reviews).

Additional evidence for the effects of teacher expectations on student learning come from studies of variations in teachers' academic expectations for the students in their class. In some studies, for example, teachers expectations at the beginning of the year predicted students' performance at the end of the year, even holding constant students' beginning-of-the-year performance and motivation (Jussim & Eccles, 1992; see also Jussim & Eccles, 1995; Jussim, Madon, & Chatman, 1994). Such findings suggest that teachers' expectations somehow affected how much students learned.

Studies of effective teachers and schools also find that teachers' expectations for student learning are strongly associated with the amount students actually learn. Students in schools in which teachers expect *all* students to learn achieve at a higher level than students in schools in which teachers do not hold uniformly high expectations (Baker, Terry, Bridger, & Winsor, 1997; Evans, 1997; Lambert & McCombs, 1998; Hoy & Sabo, 1998; Newmann, 1992; Marks, Doane, & Secada, in press; Wharton-McDonald, Pressley, & Hampstron, 1998).

Expecting all students to learn does not mean expecting the exact same pace of learning or the same level of achievement for all students. Good teachers make fine-tuned, well-informed judgments about the appropriate content and pace of instruction for individual students. But they also expect all students to master the basic curriculum.

This chapter summarizes research on the bases and stability of teachers' expectations, how expectations affect teacher behavior, and how students perceive differential teacher behavior. It also suggests strategies for making sure that appropriate and well-informed judgments, rather then erroneous expectations based on stereotypes or inaccurate information, are used to plan instruction.

What Are Teachers' Expectations Based on?

Teachers' expectations about individual students are based primarily on students' past academic performance (Brophy, 1983b; Jussim & Eccles, 1992; Jussim, Eccles, & Madon, 1996). Previous performance is usually the least biased and most appropriate information available. Its value in guiding instructional decisions is, however, limited. Many of the approaches to assessing students' competencies that are used in schools (e.g., multiple choice tests) do not give students sufficient opportunities to demonstrate what they know, and thus underestimate their skills. Even when performance assessments provide an accurate picture, assessments may lead a teacher to underestimate the pace of instruction or the difficulty level of the material a student could handle in a more effective instructional program. This is why teachers continually need to create opportunities for students to disprove their assumptions about what and how quickly they can learn.

Irrelevant factors such as siblings' performance (Thurlow, Christensen, & Ysseldyke, 1983), physical attractiveness (Ritts, Patterson, & Tubbs, 1992), and gender and racial stereotypes have also been shown to play a role in teachers' expectations about student learning (see Jussim et al., 1994, for a review). There is evidence, for example, that teachers tend to perceive boys as having more talent in mathematics than girls, and girls as exerting more effort (e.g., Jussim & Eccles, 1992). More research has been done on the effects of racial stereotypes on teacher expectations than on gender bias. One methodology that has been used is to give teachers written descriptions of students. The race of the student is manipulated by using a photograph, a videotape, or an audiotape varying the dialect of the speaker. Most of these studies find that teachers express higher expectations for the Causasian child, despite all relevant information being equivalent (Baron, Tom, & Cooper, 1985). Survey studies which ask teachers about their expectations for their own students find similar disparities in teachers' judgments of African American and Caucasian students, although the differences are similar to differences in objective measures of performance (e.g., Jussim, Eccles, & Madon, 1996; Pigott & Cowen, 2000).

African American males may be particularly vulnerable to low teacher expectations. African American males were the least likely to be praised by most of the first grade teachers in a study by Grant (1985). Irvine (1990) found that teachers' initial impressions of African American males were also more persistent than were their initial impressions of other students. Findings of a study by Garibaldi

(1993) suggest that teachers may underestimate what African American males can and *want* to achieve academically. Half of the African American high school students in his New Orleans study claimed that their teachers did not set high enough goals for them and that they wished their teachers would push them harder.

Murdock (1999) found that African American seventh-grade students believed their teachers had relatively low expectations for their academic achievement, even when their actual achievement was statistically the same as Caucasian students'. Moreover, the lower students' perceptions of teachers' expectations were, the less engaged with academic work and the more noncompliant they were.

Studies also suggest that teachers have relatively low expectations for children from low-income families (Comer, 1993), even after IQ scores are controlled (Alvidrez & Weinstein, 1999). Winfield (1986) describes teachers who did not believe that their high-risk, inner-city students could learn *at all*; some teachers gave up altogether or tried to shift responsibility away from themselves by referring students for psychological testing or special education.

Because race and social class are strongly associated, it is difficult to identify the variable most affecting teachers' expectations. Nevertheless, in a meta-analysis of studies assessing the role of stereotypes in teachers' expectations, Dusek and Joseph (1983) concluded that social class was more powerful than ethnicity, and also more powerful than gender and physical attractiveness.

There is substantial variation in the degree to which teachers have differential expectations based on gender, race, or class stereotypes; in addition, the size of differences based on race and social class in teacher judgments correspond closely to the magnitude of differences found in objective measures of performance (Jussim et al., 1996). To a significant degree, teacher judgments reflect a reality that exists for other reasons. When actual effects of teacher expectations are demonstrated, they are usually modest.

Modest effects can nevertheless be important. First, there is some evidence that girls, African Americans, and low-income students may be more susceptible to teacher expectation influences than boys, Caucasians, and higher-income students (Jussim et al., 1996). Also, modest effects may become large if they accumulate over time. Finally, classroom teacher expectancy effects are often supplemented by the effects of larger institutional practices, such as the distribution of resources among schools and opportunities within schools created by such practices as tracking and access to college counselors. Teachers, therefore, need to be vigilant about stereotypes and other irrelevant information that might affect their judgments about students.

Teachers' Self-Efficacy

Another factor that affects teachers' expectations for their students' learning is their belief about their own competencies and control over how much their students learn. New teachers who feel overwhelmed and unprepared sometimes believe that teachers (in general) can teach children effectively, but that *they* lack the skills required to help students master the curriculum. Some teachers have low expectations for students' learning because they perceive parents as unable or unwilling to support students' academic efforts (Ashton & Webb, 1986; Gibson & Dembo, 1984; Guskey & Passaro, 1994). Many of the teachers in an intervention study by Weinstein, Madison, and Kuklinski (1995) did not believe that changes in their own practices would be sufficient to overcome negative parent and student factors outside of their control. A major task in their intervention designed to raise teachers' expectations for student learning was getting teachers to shift the locus of blame and responsibility from low-achieving students and families to an analysis of their own teaching practices.

Teachers may also have low expectations because they believe school resources (e.g., support personnel, curriculum materials, space, administrative support, or opportunities for professional development) are not sufficient for them to teach students effectively, or that class size is too large, or the district requires them to teach in ineffective ways (Marks et al., in press). The broader community context, including the availability of health and other services, can also affect teachers' self-efficacy and their expectations for students' learning. Regular encounters with students who are on drugs, students who are victims, witnesses, or perpetrators of violence, who are emotionally distraught or hungry, or who have chronic health problems, can challenge the self-confidence, resolve, and expectations for success of the most competent teacher.

Teachers' beliefs about the malleability of students' ability can also affect their self-efficacy as well as their expectations about their students' achievement potential. Teachers, like students, vary in the degree to which they see ability as a fixed, inherited trait that students (and teachers) cannot do much about (an "entity" theory) versus a set of skills that can be developed by good teaching and practice (an "incremental" theory). Teachers who believe that students' native ability limits their potential for mastering the curriculum may not believe they can do much to help them learn.

For most teachers, self-efficacy varies among different subject areas. For example, some teachers believe they can teach any child to read, but are not so confident in their ability to teach math. Being asked to teach in a new way can also undermine self-efficacy, at least in the short-term. Researchers have found, for example, that some teachers lose confidence in their ability to teach math when they move from a more didactic approach which focuses on rules and operations, to the more open-ended, student-inquiry approach recommended by most mathematics experts. Considerable support and opportunities for teachers to hone their skills is needed to help them regain their self-efficacy. There is also evidence that middle school and junior high school teachers feel less effective as teachers than elementary school teachers (see Eccles & Roeser, 1999; Wigfield & Eccles, in press).

Teachers' self-efficacy is important because it affects their behavior. Teachers who are high in self-efficacy are relatively more willing to try new instructional techniques, to involve all students in discussions (not just those who volunteer), to engage children in more self-directed activities and small-group discussions, and to persist with students having difficulty (see Tschannen-Moran, Woolfolk, Hoy, & Hoy, 1998). Teachers with high self-efficacy have also been observed to be less overtly controlling of student behavior in the classroom (Woolfolk & Hoy, 1990) and more effective in leading students to correct responses in classroom discussions (Gibson & Dembo, 1984). A lack of self-efficacy appears to contribute to negative emotions, stress, and burn-out, as well as to less effective teaching practices (Tschannen-Moran et al., 1998).

There is also evidence that differential treatment of high and low achievers may occur more in teachers with relatively low self-efficacy. In a study by Ashton and Webb (1986), for example, low self-efficacy teachers called on low-achieving students relatively less often, assigned more busy work to low-achieving students, and more frequently interacted with and gave more appropriate praise and feedback to high-achieving students.

Many measures of teacher self-efficacy exist, including one which focuses on efficacy in the context of special education (Coladarci & Breton, 1997). Teachers can use the measure shown in Appendix 13-A to assess their own sense of efficacy.

In summary, teachers' expectations for student learning come from many sources, including their own sense of efficacy, which vary substantially in their validity. The problem is not that teachers have expectations, but rather that expectations are sometimes based on erroneous or incomplete information, instructional decisions and other teacher behaviors can be based on these invalid judgments, and, as the next section shows, expectations are resistant to change.

Stability of Expectations

Teacher expectations are fairly stable from the beginning to the end of the school year, despite substantial changes in children's skill levels. Teachers who make relatively more differentiated judgments of students' intellectual competencies have been shown to be less likely to see improvement (Donohue, Weinstein, Cowan, & Cowan, 2000).

Inaccurate expectations are often not corrected because teachers create situations in which only confirming evidence is possible. For example, teachers sometimes develop strong "theories" about students and then structure the learning environment in a way that does not allow information contrary to their theory to emerge. Thus, students assigned to the lowest reading group may never have an opportunity to demonstrate that they could manage more difficult text and assignments.

Students' opportunities can be severely limited by teachers' unchallenged assumptions. I once observed a first grader who had made no progress in six months of reading instruction. The teacher knew that the child had been exposed to drugs prenatally; she was convinced that the drugs caused brain damage and that his difficulty in learning to read was inevitable. Consequently, she made no effort to experiment with alternative approaches to instructing him and, therefore, denied him any opportunity to disprove her theory. The school psychologist eventually intervened and gave the child a sixth-grade student tutor. In two months he was reading at the same level as his classmates in the lowest reading group. He did not excel, but he did learn to read and he might not have if the psychologist had not intervened.

Expectations also bias what teachers see and how they interpret it. Consequently, a teacher might not notice information contrary to his or her theory. Classrooms are busy places; Jackson (1968) claims that an elementary school teacher may engage in more than a thousand interpersonal exchanges with students each day. Under such conditions certain biases are likely to affect what the teacher notices. For example, teachers are more likely to monitor closely students who they expect to be fooling around than students who they expect to be working diligently on task. They are, therefore, more likely to notice the off-task behavior of the former than of the latter children, and thus maintain their perception of the former children as easily distracted.

Expectations can also bias interpretations of students' behavior. For example, researchers have shown that observers tend to interpret people's behavior in terms of a stable disposition ("She is misbehaving because she is a difficult/poorly-adjusted child"), whereas participants are more likely to focus on the specific aspects of the situation as causes ("I pulled my classmate's hair because she took my favorite pencil"). This bias is referred to as the **actor-observer effect** (Ross & Nisbett, 1991).

Given this tendency to attribute behavior to stable traits, teachers can be expected to interpret behavior in ways that are consistent with their prior beliefs. Thus, if a student who the teacher believes is very bright gives a wrong answer, the teacher is likely to attribute the wrong answer to a nonability-related cause, such as inattention. The same answer from a student perceived to be less bright may be interpreted as confirmation of the student's limited ability. Biases in how teachers interpret student behavior, like biases in what teachers notice, contribute to the stability of teachers' judgments about students.

In addition to being fairly stable, teachers' judgments affect their own behavior toward students—sometimes in appropriate ways that enhance learning, sometimes in ways that inhibit students' academic growth. Studies have found that even teachers' perceptions of students' motivation affect their interactions. Pelletier and Vallerand (1996), for example, gave teachers either no information about the motivation of a student they were asked to teach or told them that the student was highly intrinsically motivated or highly extrinsically motivated. Teachers who were told they were teaching highly intrinsically motivated students were rated by their students as more autonomy supportive.

The next section summarizes research on teacher behavior that is associated with their expectations and is likely to affect student learning.

How Do Teachers' Expectations Affect Student Learning?

The term "self-fulfilling prophecy" is apt because once an expectation develops, even if it is wrong, people behave as if the belief were true. By behaving this way, they can actually cause their expectations to be fulfilled. Self-fulfilling prophecies occur only if the original expectation was erroneous and a change was brought about in the student's behavior as a consequence of the expectation.

Researchers have studied the ways in which teachers' beliefs about students affect their behavior toward students. Some kinds of differential behavior toward students who vary in their mastery of the curriculum are appropriate and productive. Giving some students more advanced material than others is clearly necessary when there is variability in student skill level, and students need different amounts and kinds of teacher assistance and attention. Nevertheless, most of the teacher behaviors described below, which have been shown to be associated with high versus low expectations, cannot be defended as appropriate accommodations to individual student needs.

Teacher Behavior Toward High- and Low-Expectation Students

Rosenthal (1974) divided teacher behavior associated with high or low expectations into four categories: socioemotional climate, input, output, and affective feedback. Examples of each of the four categories are described below (see also Good, 1987).

Socioemotional Climate
- smiling and nodding
- friendliness

Input
- distance of seat from teacher
- amount of teacher interaction
- amount of information given to learn or problems to complete
- difficulty and variability of assignments

Output
- calling on during class discussions
- providing clues, and repeating or rephrasing questions
- wait time for student response to teacher question
- level of detail and accuracy of feedback

Affective Feedback
- amount of criticism
- amount (and basis) of praise
- pity or anger expressed for low performance

Some of these differential behaviors have direct effects on learning, and consequently widen the gap between relatively low- and high-achieving students. For example, students who are given more opportunities to learn, more clues, and who are called on more frequently should learn more than students who are given fewer such opportunities. Other teacher behaviors, such as those affecting the social–emotional climate or affective feedback, influence learning indirectly by affecting students' own beliefs about their competencies, their expectations for success, and consequently their effort and other achievement behaviors.

Teachers may also develop closer relationships with children who are high-achievers. Students like Safe Sally are often seen as easier to teach; they typically present fewer behavioral problems, and they may be more oriented toward pleasing the teacher. As discussed in Chapter 9, a positive, respectful relationship with the teacher gives students the sense of security they need to be active participants in class, ask questions, and seek challenges—which in turn promote learning. Teachers are less likely to develop a close relationship with Alienated Al, even though such a relationship might make a substantial difference in his attachment to school.

Teachers vary greatly in the degree to which they treat low- and high-expectancy students differently, and also in the nature of their differential treatment. Some teachers pay more attention to high-expectancy students, and some teachers engage in "compensatory" behaviors, focusing more on low-expectancy students (see Babad, 1992).

Even behaviors designed to provide extra support for low-expectancy students, however, can undermine learning. First, such compensatory behavior is sometimes accompanied by subtle negative behaviors or expressions. Babad (1992) found that teachers often displayed negative emotions (e.g., hostility, tenseness, anxiety, condescension), while they invested greater time and attention to relatively low-achieving students. Second, low-performing students can interpret teacher behavior that is meant to protect their feelings or to help them learn as evidence of their low competence, and this in turn lowers their own expectations and effort. Behavior reflecting teachers' best intentions, ironically, can do the most harm.

Well-Meaning But Counter-Productive Teacher Behaviors

Consider, for example, the research on pity and anger mentioned in Chapter 5. Recall that children as young as six years understand that anger is aroused when another's failure is attributed to controllable factors, such as lack of effort, and by about the age of nine years children understand that pity is aroused when another's failure is perceived to be caused by uncontrollable causes (see also Graham, 1990, 1994; Graham & Weiner, 1993). Graham (1984a) demonstrated in an experiment that expressing pity or sympathy, which is usually meant to protect students' feelings about themselves, can actually have the opposite effect. In her study an experimenter expressed either mild anger or sympathy to children who had experienced failure. Children who had the sympathetic experimenter were more likely to attribute their failure to a lack of ability than children who had an angry experimenter. The latter were more likely to attribute their failure to a lack of effort. Children who received sympathy also had lower expectations for success in the future than children who received an angry response from the experimenter. By simply expressing an emotion, the experimenter influenced children's perceptions of the cause of their failure and their expectations regarding future outcomes. And the sympathetic emotion had the more negative effects.

This process can be illustrated by a teacher's likely responses to Santos and Hannah for turning in a math assignment that is only half completed. Santos' teacher, believing that he is capable of finishing the task, attributes the incomplete paper to his typical halfhearted effort. With an exasperated voice, the teacher threatens Santos with punishment: "If you don't finish your assignment tomorrow, you'll stay after school until it is finished." Santos knows that the teacher is angry because she assumes that he didn't exert much effort and could have finished the assignment if he had tried. The teacher's emotional response, therefore, serves to reinforce Santos' confidence in his ability.

A different reaction might occur in Hannah's case. Her teacher is likely to believe that she is unable to do any better, and might sympathetically tell her not to worry about not being able to complete that task. Hannah interprets the teacher's sympathy as evidence of the teacher's low perceptions of Hannah's competence, thus reinforcing her own doubts about her ability to do the assigned work.

Findings on the effect of teachers' emotions are particularly relevant to student populations that are often viewed as having low competencies, such as learning-disabled students. In fact, one study found that teachers expressed more pity and less anger for children described as having a learning disability than for children who exerted the same effort and had the same outcome but were not given the LD label (Clark, 1997).

A related counter-intuitive finding concerns the effect of *praise*. In some circumstances there appear to be negative side effects of praise, at least for older children and adults. As mentioned in Chapter 3, praise for successful performance on an easy task can be interpreted by a student as evidence that the teacher has a low perception of his or her ability. As a consequence, it can actually lower rather than enhance self-confidence. Criticism following poor performance can, under some circumstances, be interpreted as an indication of the teacher's high perception of the student's ability.

Praise and criticism can have these paradoxical effects because of their link with effort attributions, and because, as mentioned in Chapter 6, people perceive effort and ability to be inversely related. Recall that if two students achieve the same outcome, the one who tried harder is judged by children over the age of about eleven years as lower in ability (Nicholls & Miller, 1984a). Research has shown, accordingly, that children approximately (but not below) the age of 11 rate a child who was praised by the teacher as lower in ability than a child who was not praised, and they rate a child who was criticized as higher in ability than a child the teacher did not criticize (Barker & Graham, 1987; Miller & Hom, 1997).

The potential for negative effects of praise and positive effects of criticism on children's self-confidence was also shown in a naturalistic study by Parsons et al. (1982). They found in the 20 fifth- to ninth-grade mathematics classrooms they observed that the amount of criticism of the quality of students' work was positively related to students' self-perceptions of their math ability and future expectations, unless the criticism was in reaction to a student-initiated question. Praise related to work was positively associated with math self-concept for boys but not for girls. The researchers concluded that teachers who believe they should avoid criticism and give praise freely overlook the power of the context and of students' interpretations of the meaning of the message. They suggest that well-chosen criticism can convey as much positive information as praise.

Helping behavior can also give students a message that they are perceived as low in ability, and it can undermine the positive achievement-related emotions associated with success. Meyer (1982) describes a study by Conty in which the experimenter offered unrequested help either to the subject or to another individual in the room working on the same task. Subjects who were offered help claimed to feel negative emotions (incompetence, anger, worry, disappointment, distress, anxiety) more, and positive emotions (confidence, joy, pride, superiority, satisfaction) less than subjects who observed another person being helped. Graham and Barker (1990) report that children as young as six years rated a student they observed being offered help as lower in ability than another student who was not offered help.

Again, an attributional analysis explains the effect of help on ability judgments and emotional reactions. Research has shown that in a variety of contexts people are more likely to help others when their need is perceived to be caused by uncontrollable factors, such as low ability, than when their need is attributed to controllable factors such as insufficient effort (see Weiner, 1986, 1992; see Bennet & Flores, 1998, for an attributional analysis of peer helping). This was shown in a classroom study by Brophy and Rohrkemper (1981), in which teachers expressed a greater commitment to helping "problem" students when the causes of need were presumed to be uncontrollable, such as low ability or shyness, than when the problems were attributed to controllable factors, such as lack of effort.

There are many other ways teachers can unintentionally communicate low expectations. Good and Brophy (1978) describe the behavior of a physics professor who believed that females have difficulty with physics. To avoid embarrassing them, he never called on them to answer a mathematical question or to explain difficult concepts. He also showed his concern by looking at one of the girls after he introduced a new point and asking, "Do you understand?" (p. 75). Such "helpful" behavior undoubtedly gave the females in the class a clear negative message about the teacher's perception of their competencies. I observed another example of a teacher unintentionally conveying low expectations in a fifth-grade classroom. The teacher exclaimed happily to a student who completed a math problem at the board, "Scott, I didn't think you'd get that!" I believe she meant the comment as praise, but the message that she expected him to fail was clear.

Ability Grouping and Tracking

Although ability grouping can help teachers differentiate instruction, simply assigning a student to a group can create a self-fulfilling prophesy. Even though teachers are usually responsible for students' reading group placement, there is evidence that by the end of the year the placement itself predicts teachers' as well as parents' perceptions of students' competencies, over and above the effect of students' initial skills (Pallas, Entwisle, Alexander, & Stluka, 1994; see also Pallas, Entwisle, Alexander, & Stluka, 1994). Weinstein (1976) found that the reading group to which students were assigned explained 25 percent of the variance mid-year achievement over and above the students' initial readiness score. Henk and Melnick (1998) found also that reading group assignment was frequently referred to by elementary school age children when asked questions about how they evaluated their reading ability. That ability grouping is used more frequently for reading than for math instruction may explain why some studies find that teacher expectations have a stronger impact on reading achievement than on math achievement (Smith, 1980).

Ability group placement affects learning in part because teachers often perceive all members of a group as equivalent, despite the considerable variation that usually exists within groups. Because teachers' expectations are influenced by group placement itself, they often do not monitor individual progress as much as they should, and they do not adjust instruction or move a student to another group when the student would benefit from different instructional input.

A second problem with ability grouping is that teachers vary the nature and pace of instruction between groups more than is necessary or appropriate. In general, studies find that students in high level reading groups receive more effective instruction than students in low level reading groups. Reading lessons for higher groups have been observed to be more loosely structured, to involve more meaningful questions and opportunities to connect reading to personal experiences, and to be more fun. Decoding skills, rather than meaning, are often stressed more with the "low" group (Borko & Eisenhart, 1986; McDermott, 1987).

Similarly, there is evidence indicating that students in low tracks are taught differently than students in high tracks. Again, some differences, such as the pace of the curriculum, may reflect appropriate accommodations to students' learning styles. But many differences in teacher behavior toward students are unnecessary and constrain the achievement of students in the low track.

Consider, for example, Oakes' (1990) analysis of survey data from 6,000 math and science classes in 1,200 elementary, junior high, and senior high schools in the United States. Teachers of low-ability math and science classes claimed to emphasize students' own interests less than other teachers. They also put less emphasis on developing inquiry skills and problem solving, developing skills in communicating math and science ideas, and preparing students for further study in math and science. She reports, furthermore, that in secondary schools, students in low-ability track science and math classes spent more time engaged in solitary seatwork, doing worksheets and taking tests or quizzes, than did students in high-ability track classes. In science classes they spent less time engaged in hands on activities and more time reading. In a previous study, Oakes and Goodland (1985) found that teachers of high-track classes more often included competence and autonomous thinking among the most important curricular goals for students.

Further research suggests that students in different tracks experience differences in teachers' behavior. Vanfossen, Jones, and Spade (1987), for example, report from national survey data that college-track students were more likely than other students to describe their teachers as patient, respectful, clear in their presentations, and enjoying their work. These differential behaviors are not necessary, and they undoubtedly exacerbate the existing differences between high and low achievers.

Do Teachers Treat Girls and Boys Differently?

Differences in teachers' expectations may underlie the differences in their behavior toward boys and girls that have been observed in some studies. Differential teacher behavior may, in turn, contribute to girls' lower perceptions of their competence and lower expectations for success in math and science (see Chapter 6), as well as their substantially lower participation rates in higher level mathematics and science courses and careers (Kahle, 1996a).

Classroom observation studies suggest that differential treatment of girls and boys in math and science is common. Researchers have found in some observation studies that teachers talk to, call on, praise, and give more corrective feedback to boys than to girls (e.g., Becker, 1981; Leinhardt, Seewald, & Engel, 1979; Morse & Handley, 1985; Stallings, 1985; Tobin, Kahle, & Fraser, 1990). Becker observed, for example, that although there was no difference in student-initiated interactions with teachers in a sample of geometry classes, 63 percent of the teacher-initiated academic contacts were with boys. Girls received 30 percent of the encouraging comments and 84 percent of the discouraging comments. Morse and Hadley report that female student-initiated interactions with science teachers declined from 41 percent to 30 percent of the total from seventh to eighth grade. (See Kimball, 1989, for a review.) Some differential teacher behavior can be very subtle; ethnographies describe teachers leaning forward, looking into eyes, and nodding and smiling to boys more than to girls in science classes (see Kahle, 1996a).

Parsons et al. (1982) found that student gender was only modestly related to student-teacher interaction patterns in the grade 5–9 mathematics classrooms they studied, but gender differences in teacher treatment and in math self-concept were more prominent among the students for whom teachers had relatively high expectations. Among the relatively high-achieving students, girls were praised less and they had lower perceptions of their math competence than boys. These may be the very girls who otherwise would have aspired to a career involving mathematics or science.

Brophy (1985) points out that some differential behavior toward boys and girls may reflect teacher reactions to differences in boys' and girls' behavior (e.g., volunteering to answer questions). For example, one source of gender differences in classroom interaction that has been observed is boys' domination of discussion (Kahle, 1996b).

Eccles and Blumenfeld (1985) suggest that gender differences in the subjective meaning of teacher behavior may be as important as differences in teacher behavior per se. They found, for example, that girls tended to be more reactive to criticism and less reactive to praise than were boys. Equal amounts of praise and criticism, therefore, could engender gender differences in performance expectations.

The same instructional approach may have different effects on girls and boys. Eccles and Blumenfeld (1985) report that in classrooms in which there were considerable differences between girls' and boys' own expectations, teachers were unusually critical, often using sarcasm to "put a student in his or her place" (p. 108). Teachers in classrooms in which gender-differentiated expectations were not found engaged in more private, conference-like interactions, and they called on all students rather than relying on volunteers during public question-and-answer sessions.

There is also evidence that boys are not always the beneficiaries of gender-related expectations. Palardy (1969), for example, studied five first-grade teachers who thought that boys could learn to read just as successfully as girls, and five who thought that boys could not learn to read as successfully as girls. Although students were comparable on reading readiness scores taken in September, by March boys in the classrooms in which teachers expected girls to read better than boys actually performed more poorly on a reading achievement test than did girls; in the other classrooms no difference was found in boys' and girls' reading achievement scores.

In summary, there is evidence that some teachers behave differently toward girls and boys, but it is not clear to what degree their differential behavior is in reaction to differences in boys' and girls' behavior in class. It is also possible that the same behavior and instructional practices can have different effects on boys and girls so that equal treatment leads to different outcomes.

Students' Perceptions of Teacher Expectations

"I can basically do whatever I want because they just figure I'm doing something for the school," claims a high-status high school student in an ethnography by Eckert (1989, p. 115). The student was clearly aware that he was given favorable treatment as the result of teachers' positive expectations. Presumably other students, Alienated Al for example, were equally convinced that they would *not* be given the benefit of doubt.

Research has shown that students are aware of teachers' differential behavior toward high and low achievers, and that their perceptions of their teachers' behavior affect their own expectations (Weinstein, 1985, 1989, 1993; see also Babad, 1990, 1992). Whether students were called on to read aloud and to answer questions was mentioned as a criterion for judging reading ability by nearly 40 percent of the elementary school-aged children in a study conducted by Henk and Melnick (1998). Below are examples of other kinds of differential treatment students in one study claimed to observe in their own class (Weinstein & Middlestadt, 1979):[1]

- High achievers are granted special privileges.
- High achievers are allowed to make up their own projects.
- The teacher is more concerned that low achievers learn something than enjoy themselves.
- The teacher asks high achievers to suggest or direct activities.
- The teacher lets high achievers do as they like as long as they complete the assigned work.
- High achievers spend more time discussing outside student activities than class-related materials.
- The teacher gives high achievers enough opportunity to respond before calling on someone else.
- The teacher trusts high achievers.
- The teacher collects work before low achievers have had a chance to finish.
- Low achievers are not expected to complete their work.

Teachers are not necessarily aware of such differential treatment. Babad (1992) found in the classrooms she studied that students and teachers usually agreed that low-expectancy students received more learning support and less pressure than high-expectancy students. But while teachers claimed that they provided more emotional support for high-expectancy students, students perceived the opposite.

The classrooms Weinstein and her colleagues studied varied greatly in the degree to which students perceived the teacher as behaving differently toward high and low achievers (see Weinstein, 1985, 1989). The more teachers were perceived as treating high and low achievers differently, the closer the students' expectations for themselves aligned with their teacher's expectations for them (Brattesani, Weinstein, & Marshall, 1984). Therefore, perceived differences in teacher treatment appeared to affect students' self-perceptions.

The kinds of differential behavior students perceive toward relatively high- and low-achieving students certainly have the potential of widening performance

---

[1]A copy of the questionnaire can be obtained by writing Professor Rhona Weinstein, Psychology Department, University of California, Berkeley, CA 94720.

gaps. Consider, for example, differences in autonomy and respect. The evidence in Chapter 11 points to the importance of these two variables in students' motivation. If the classrooms Weinstein and her colleagues have studied are typical, high-achieving students are provided with an instructional context that is more supportive of motivation than that given to low-achieving students. Added to the above evidence on different instructional input, it is not surprising that high- and low-achieving students' achievement differences increase with time in school.

Can the negative effects of teachers' expectations be avoided? Good and Brophy (1986) describe three types of teachers with regard to expectations. The first group is *proactive*. Such teachers do not allow expectations to undermine effective interactions with children and appropriate instructional activities. The second group is *reactive*. They allow existing differences between high and low achievers to influence their own behavior in ways that can undermine the learning of relatively low-achieving students. For example, high achievers have more response opportunities simply because they raise their hands more often than low achievers. In the third group, *overreactive* teachers provide qualitatively and quantitatively different instruction as a function of their expectations. Below are a few suggestions to help teachers be proactive, and avoid negative consequences of teacher expectations.

Avoiding the Negative Effects of Expectations

1. Communicate high expectations.   Teachers should communicate positive beliefs, expectations, and attributions in their interactions with students. They can do this explicitly, by telling students that they know they will be able to achieve a particular outcome, or implicitly, by providing opportunities to work on challenging tasks, by encouraging them to persist when they encounter difficulty, by calling on *all* students, not just those who can be depended on for the right answer, by praising only performance that truly deserves praise, and in countless other subtle ways of conveying confidence in students' ability to succeed in classroom tasks.

2. Maintain high standards.   Teachers often set low standards to protect students' self-esteem. Trying to build self-esteem in the absence of genuine skill development is not productive in the long run. Too many teachers, in my view, request and accept performance below what students are capable of achieving, asserting that more challenging work will threaten their self-confidence.

As a result of these well-intentioned but misguided practices, students adopt low standards for themselves, and the fragile self-confidence they develop is shattered in the first situation in which they are held to higher standards. Students take their cues regarding acceptable performance primarily from their teacher, and at best will work to (and not above) whatever standards are set.

Genuine and robust self-esteem and self-confidence come from encountering, persisting, and ultimately meeting challenges. To make sure that students can realistically achieve classroom standards, the teacher needs to carefully monitor students' efforts, understanding, and task completion. Protecting them from failure is not an effective strategy for building enduring self-esteem.

3. Base judgments of student's skill level on valid and reliable information. Some educational specialists recommend that teachers purposefully remain ignorant of all past information about students' academic performance to avoid self-fulfilling prophecies. I would not make that recommendation because such information can be useful. Comments from previous teachers can help a new teacher initially structure an appropriate instructional program for a student. Test scores and other information in students' records can also be informative. But the new teacher should carefully assess the reliability of all existing information. This information should not be seen as the "truth," but rather as hypotheses that the student is given ample opportunities to disprove.

Information suggesting poor past performance should be interpreted as a problem to be solved, not as a prediction for the future. As mentioned above, low achievement may be the result of poor teaching or inadequate opportunities to demonstrate competencies. Students who have previously performed poorly may flourish in a new educational context, if given a chance.

Teachers must also guard against allowing irrelevant information, such as race, social class, or gender, from influencing their expectations for a student. The basis for expectations of students must be examined carefully. It is useful for teachers to reflect upon their own gender, race, and social class stereotypes, and then consider, for specific children, whether stereotypes might be influencing their perceptions.

4. Continually re-examine judgments about students. Even judgments about students based on teachers' own observations should be thought of as hypotheses that need to be continually reevaluated. It is natural for expectations to bias what teachers see as well as their interpretation of what they see. Teachers, therefore, need to seek disconfirming evidence, in case their "working theory" is no longer accurate. This requires careful observation and some experimentation. For example, the teacher may give a student more autonomy or more difficult material to find out how well he or she handles it.

Goldenberg (1989, 1992) illustrates the importance of such experimentation in his ethnography of a teacher whose *high* expectations were not adjusted in time to provide a student with the needed instruction. Despite positive indicators at the beginning of first grade, including reading-readiness scores, Sylvia had some difficulty in completing her assignments and fell behind. Making excuses for Sylvia's poor performance, the teacher maintained high expectations for her reading achievement and did not make needed changes. When an observer forced her to attend to Sylvia's difficulties in reading, the teacher adjusted Sylvia's reading instruction. Her reading improved at a much faster rate, but the intervention came too late. By the end of the year Sylvia was among the poorest readers in the class.

Goldenberg (1989) compares Sylvia to Marta, who began first grade with a poor prognosis. The first-grade teacher originally predicted that Marta's reading achievement would be among the lowest in the class, partly because of her attitude and behavioral problems. But after the first few months of school she noticed some improvement in Marta's behavior, and tried her out in a higher reading group. From the moment she was placed in the higher group her reading skills began to improve much more rapidly than they had before. The contrast between Sylvia and Marta clearly demonstrates the value of careful teacher observation, of altering expectations as a function of those observations, and of adjusting educational interventions accordingly.

Sometimes teachers are not fully aware of the assumptions they make about students. It is helpful for teachers to make explicit the assumptions about individual students that are guiding their curriculum decisions. One method is to write down beliefs about a particular student and evaluate their validity. How good is the evidence for each assumption? Have alternative assumptions or explanations for the student's behavior been tested? What experiments might be tried to test the validity of the assumption?

5. Don't differentiate behavior toward low- and high-performing students unless there are good reasons for doing so.   Teachers should constantly monitor their own behavior and assess the degree to which they may be behaving differently toward different children. Good and Brophy (1986, p. 501) suggest asking questions such as those in Appendix 13-B to help monitor behavior toward students varying in skill levels. It is important to monitor subtle as well as more obvious differential behaviors—such as emotional reactions to students' performance, the conditions under which help is provided, the degree to which warmth and humor is directed toward students, or the responsibility given to students for self-evaluation.

It is not easy to manage a classroom, teach, and monitor one's own assumptions and subtle behavior simultaneously. Being aware of the potential ways in which one may communicate low expectations is an important first step. There are many strategies teachers can use to become more aware of their behavior. For example, it is sometimes useful to make a diagram of the seating in the classroom to check whether the high-expectancy students are more likely to be toward the front of the classroom than the low-expectancy students. It is also helpful to have another individual—an aide, a student teacher, or even a parent—observe and point out differential behavior that a teacher may not realize he or she is exhibiting.

Another method of evaluating teacher behavior toward high- and low-expectancy students is to directly assess the students' perceptions of differential behavior. Weinstein and her colleagues have developed a questionnaire that can be used for this purpose (Weinstein & Middlestadt, 1979; see footnote, page 223).

There are other strategies that can be employed to ensure equitable treatment of students. In one classroom I observed, for example, the teacher pulled students' names out of a fish bowl to call on them, ensuring an opportunity for everyone, without having to keep track mentally of whom she had already called on. Alternating boy-girl-boy-girl when calling on students helps avoid gender bias and is simple to implement.

6. Never give up on a student. Finally, although there are tremendous differences in the rate at which students learn, all students who have not been identified as having a learning handicap can master the basic curriculum. Some students do not, but it is not for lack of ability. Most students' failure to learn is caused by problems such as poor motivation or inappropriate instruction. The teacher who continues to expect each and every student in a class to learn will invariably be more successful in achieving that goal than the teacher who designates certain students as "impossible to teach" or who blames the parents or the community. To be sure, some children present more challenges than others, but even under the most difficult circumstances, teachers can make a profound difference in how much children learn.

Collective School Efficacy

Individual teachers' expectations for students are affected by (and affect) the school climate. School climate is more difficult to measure, and to some degree, different people in a school experience different climates. But most schools have a character that is perceptible to anyone who spends some time in the school. One important dimension on which school climates vary is in whether all or just some students are expected to reach high standards. Bandura (1997) refers to this dimension as "collective school efficacy" (see also Goddard, Hoy, & Hoy, 2000).

The climate is evident in a variety of explicit policies as well as in more subtle social interactions. Consider, for example, School A. Parents are called immediately when a student gets a grade below a "C" on an important test. Counselors make an effort to make sure that all students know about college entrance requirements and interventions are designed for students as soon as a student shows evidence of learning problems. Careful records of student progress are kept and examined regularly to identify problems. In School B, parents aren't called until a student has become a serious behavior problem or only after many months of a pattern of unexplained absences. Counselors provide information on college requirements only to those students in a clearly defined college track, and special services are provided only after parents intervene or when a student faces retention. Policies in general do not guard against students slipping though the cracks. These two schools give very different messages to teachers, students, parents, and the community about their expectations for student achievement.

To be sure, such policies are affected in part by the amount of resources available. Some teachers don't even have easy access to a phone to call parents when a student is having difficulty. But often these policies reflect an attitude as well as resources—that everything within the school's power is going to be done to make sure that every child succeeds (School A) or that it won't make that much difference what the school does because some students are bound to fail no matter what is done (School B).

Principals play a central role in setting the tone, in part by the kinds of policies they create to support student learning and in part by how they treat teachers. Studies show, for example, that collective efficacy is relatively high in schools where principals use their leadership to provide resources for teachers and protect them from disruptions in their teaching (Lee, Dedick, & Smith, 1991). A strong sense of community, broad participation in decision making, and opportunities for collaboration among adults are also associated with high collective school efficacy (see Tschannen-Moran et al., 1998).

Introducing new curriculum and instructional approaches to a school can initially lower collective school efficacy. This is why it is important to provide ongoing support and encouragement. Warning teachers that they are not likely to feel as effective as they usually do when they try new strategies can also buffer the effects of initial feelings of inefficacy.

The student population can also affect collective efficacy. Low collective self-efficacy is common in schools that serve students who have disadvantages believed to interfere with learning (e.g., poverty, limited English proficiency, and poor academic skills). This is probably why Chester and Beaudin (1996) found a decline in self-efficacy, even among experienced teachers, when they began teaching in an urban district.

Some schools develop what might be called differentiated collective efficacy. The collective belief is that some students (for example, those from more affluent families) can be prepared for college, and others (such as those from low-income families) cannot achieve even modest academic standards. Tracking is often used to provide entirely different curricula, thus ensuring the fulfillment of these differential expectations (Raudenbush, Rowen, & Cheong, 1992; Ross, Cousins, & Gadalla, 1996). Low-income and minority children are disproportionately assigned to the "hopeless" category.

Cultural differences may also play a role. Teachers, who are more likely to be Caucasian, may feel less efficacious in schools serving children with cultural backgrounds that are different from their own. Clearly teachers who are in the difficult situation of teaching children with whom they do not even share a language (which occurs regularly in urban or other areas with high levels of immigration) may experience serious doubts about their ability to teach effectively.

Low collective efficacy is not, however, inevitable in schools serving economically disadvantaged students. Even under difficult circumstances some schools are able to maintain a climate of high expectations for all students. In unusually effective schools, poor performance is not excused as an inevitable consequence of family circumstances or low intelligence. The pervasive beliefs in successful schools are that all children can achieve high academic standards regardless of students' home or language backgrounds, and that teachers can make a real difference (Bandura, 1993; Hoy & Sabo, 1998; Newmann, 1992).

Assessing Collective Self-Efficacy

Goddard et al. (2000) developed a measure of collective self-efficacy which can be used to assess the general level of expectations for student achievement in a school. Teachers answer questions related, for example, to the level of preparation and skills of teachers in the school to teach the subjects they are assigned to teach (e.g., "Teachers here don't have the skills needed to produce meaningful student learning"), how well the school community ensures all students opportunities to learn (e.g., "If a child doesn't want to learn teachers here give up"), and whether the conditions and supports for effective teaching are in place (e.g., "The quality of school facilities here really facilitates the teaching and learning process"). The 21 items form one factor, indicating that the scale measures a coherent set of beliefs and perceptions. One study found that teachers' scores on this scale predicted differences in students' math and reading achievement among schools better than did the proportion of low-income students in the schools. In fact, collective teacher efficacy explained over half of the between-school variance in student achievement.

Summary

Teachers' expectations for students' academic performance are based primarily on their own experience with their students' behavior and performance. But they are also influenced by group stereotypes and various beliefs—e.g., about the importance of innate ability and parent behavior, and about their own competencies as teachers. Erroneous expectations are difficult to change because they affect the opportunities teachers give students to demonstrate their competencies, and they bias teachers' perceptions and interpretations of student behavior.

Teacher expectations are important because they influence teacher behavior in ways that can undermine student learning. Teachers need to evaluate, carefully and continually, the assumptions they make about students to reflect critically on how these assumptions affect their behavior and instructional strategies. They should give students an opportunity to disconfirm their theories, and to adjust instruction and tasks accordingly. And they need to make sure that the kinds of accommodations they make are appropriate and necessary, and that they do not give subtle cues that convey low expectations that could undermine students' own confidence in their ability to learn.

TABLE 13.1   Summary of Terms

Term	Definition
Self-Fulfilling Prophecy	Initial erroneous expectations cause targets to act in a way consistent with those expectations, which in turn causes the expectations to be realized
Actor-Observer Effect	Observers' tendency to interpret people's behavior in terms of a stable disposition

CHAPTER

14 Real Students, Real Teachers, Real Schools

Students have been divided into psychological pieces by discussing independently the many factors that influence their behavior in achievement settings. But teachers deal with whole children. So now, like all the King's horses and all the King's men, we will try to put the pieces back together (with greater success, I hope).

To do this we consider possible strategies for addressing the problems posed by the six children introduced in Chapter 1. This is followed by a discussion of some of the difficulties teachers sometimes encounter in their efforts to increase students' motivation. We then move beyond the classroom to the broader school and community context to discuss additional variables that affect students' motivation directly, and indirectly by supporting or undermining teachers' efforts.

Our Six Children

Dave

Defensive Dave does everything a student might do to avoid looking stupid. He relies substantially on classmates for answers to assignments and he pretends that he can't find his assignments when he believes his answers might be wrong. He has elaborate excuses for unfinished work or poor performance. He pays little attention to directions and sometimes flaunts his low level of effort.

Dave is a classic example of Covington's "failure-avoiding" student (Chapter 6), or a student with "performance-avoidance" goals (Chapter 10). He has performance rather than learning goals, but he is not confident that he could actually perform well by legitimate methods, such as learning the material and completing tasks on his own. Consequently, although he completes most of his assignments, he uses strategies (e.g., copying or getting answers from classmates) that don't contribute to learning. His behavior is logical in the sense that it achieves his short-term goal of not looking stupid, and by advertising his inattentiveness he persuades others to attribute poor performance, when it occurs, to his lack of effort rather than to a lack of ability. Despite its internal logic, his behavior is, in the long-term, highly maladaptive. Poor performance will become increasingly inevitable and difficult to explain away.

What does a teacher do with a student like Dave? Dave must begin to believe that he can achieve real success on his own, and that learning is more important than performing. Any negative consequences of failure (as long as effort was exerted) need to be removed so Dave can focus on achieving success rather than on avoiding failure.

Making Dave believe that success is a realistic goal may require changing the definition of success. Dave will never expect to succeed if success is based on normative criteria. Success needs to be redefined in terms of personal improvement or in terms of achieving some predetermined, realistic standard of excellence. Making success achievable may also require adapting the difficulty level of tasks. For example, if the standard for a "B" on a spelling test is 80 percent correct, the difficulty of the spelling words will need to be adjusted so that this is a feasible goal. Dave's confidence in his ability to achieve success can be reinforced by explicitly attributing his successes to effort and ability, pointing out that other students who he is likely to perceive to be like him have achieved particular goals, and using some of the other strategies for maintaining self-confidence described in Chapter 7.

To alleviate Dave's concerns about failure and focus his attention on learning rather than performance, the teacher needs to accept initial poor performance, as long as he makes an effort. She needs to convince him that it is all right to make mistakes, while encouraging him to keep trying, thus conveying the message that she expects him to improve. If Dave gives a wrong answer in a public context (in a group or class discussion), the teacher needs to find something valuable in the answer, and continue to engage him in conversation until he has demonstrated to himself, and to the class, that he was able to reach some meaningful level of understanding. He might also be given several opportunities to obtain a reasonably good grade. Thus, if he misses too many problems on a mathematics test, he could be given a "preliminary" grade (in pencil) and an opportunity to study and retake the test until his performance is acceptable—to him and to the teacher.

Such practices should reduce Dave's need to avoid failure, and thus his maladaptive, avoidance behavior. Indeed, in some sense they should eliminate the notion of "failure" altogether, replacing it with something more like initial difficulties.[1]

Hannah

It is not easy to increase the effort of a student like Dave, but finding solutions to the motivation problems presented by Helpless Hannah is even more challenging. While Dave has not totally given up trying to look competent, Hannah is steadfastly convinced that she lacks ability and will inevitably fail. She has conceded defeat.

---

[1]I give three grades on graduate students' papers, "not there yet," "OK," and "really good." They cannot have any "not-there-yet" grades and receive an A for the course, but they can rewrite papers as many times as there is time for me to review them before the end of the course.

Many of the Hannahs that I have seen are substantially behind their class-mates academically, and they are often out of the mainstream socially. Although some students who are very easily discouraged perform adequately, albeit less well than they could, students like Hannah, who have given up altogether, con-sistently perform poorly.

Hannah needs considerable individual attention, which is extremely diffi-cult for a teacher of 25 to 35 students to provide. I have seen teachers engage older children, high-school students, and retired individuals in the community to help students like Hannah. If parents or older siblings are willing and able, they may also be enlisted to help Hannah at home. These "tutors" need to be given instruc-tions on being accepting and encouraging and they need to be taught specific strategies for helping her develop her skills. Close teacher supervision of tutors is essential.

Tasks need to be developed carefully so that they are appropriate for Hannah's skill level. Initially the material may need to be easy, even for her, to provide her with the success experiences she needs to build her self-confidence. Increases in difficulty should be very gradual because she is likely to become eas-ily discouraged.

Obviously, an hour or two a day of individual tutoring is the most that can be realistically expected. Consequently, Hannah's teacher must also find ways to incorporate Hannah into the classroom. All of the suggestions made to help De-fensive Dave would also be appropriate for Hannah, although it may take even greater efforts to involve Hannah in classroom activities. Hannah could also be given responsibilities (e.g., leading the line to recess, taking the lunch money to the principal's office) to give her some social prestige and to publicize the teacher's faith in Hannah's ability to carry out a task. The strategy that Cohen and Lotan (1995) developed—finding something that a student is good at it, remark-ing on it publicly, and putting the student in an expert role for an activity—could be particularly useful to enhance Hannah's status in her own as well as in her classmates' eyes. (See Chapter 7.)

Such superficial demonstrations of valuing Hannah, however, will not be effective unless she also experiences real improvement in her own skills. The best way to help a student like Hannah is to make sure that she learns to increase her skill level so that she is able to enjoy the same motivating feelings of developing competencies that the other students experience.

Sally

In contrast to Dave and Hannah, most teachers enjoy having students like Safe Sally in their classroom. Sally's elementary school teachers probably praised her for her work, which she completed precisely according to their instructions, put her many papers with 100 percent correct on the bulletin board, and gave her spe-cial privileges. Sally became hooked on these social rewards and is afraid to try anything that may cause her to lose them. Her self-worth has become dependent on others' approval and symbols (e.g., grades) associated with that approval.

In the long-run an appropriate goal would be for Sally to develop more independent standards for judging her work. But in the short-term her teachers can capitalize on her responsiveness to external contingencies and make their approval contingent on a new set of behaviors. Thus, for example, the teacher can make good grades contingent, at least in part, on her doing work that challenges her current competency level. They can praise her for attempting tasks that require considerable effort and persistence, regardless of how well she performs. Her teachers might refrain from congratulating her for getting the highest grade in the class or for completing exams with no errors. There are also more subtle ways that her teachers can convey that they value risk-taking. For example, they can make smiles and sustained interactions contingent on risk-taking rather than on "good" or correct performance.

If the long-term goal is to reduce Sally's dependency on extrinsic approval and rewards, another motivational system needs to be built up in its stead. This will not be easy because the motivational system in place has served her well for many years. Her teachers need to try to awaken her interest and curiosity. This can be accomplished in part by modeling their own intrinsic interest in the subject they teach. Students know early in the semester which of their teachers really love their subject, and their own views are affected by their teachers'.

Sally's teachers can also encourage her to engage in learning activities outside of the class requirements. Time could be set aside in an English class for Sally and other students to discuss plays they have seen or books they have read "for fun." Teachers can provide opportunities for students to share their own journals, short stories, or poems with their classmates. Newspaper articles read at home can be discussed in social studies classes. In science classes students could share their own observations of scientific phenomena.

Changes in the way tests and grades are discussed may reduce Sally's excessive need to do well on tests and her obsession with grades. Focusing on the information tests provide might diminish Sally's view of test performance as an index of her self-worth as a human being. Being clear about the criteria for good grades but not continually calling students' attention to grades might reduce Sally's focus on external evaluation as the reason for working.

The goal is not to eliminate Sally's concerns about performance altogether, but to reduce them so that they do not interfere with her enjoyment of learning and her willingness to approach challenging learning situations in which high performance is not guaranteed. Implementing the suggestions above might help Sally begin to relax and allow herself to enjoy learning for its own sake, rather than seeing it only as a means to a high grade and teacher admiration.

Santos

Satisfied Santos is, in nearly every respect, the opposite of Safe Sally. He eagerly seeks out intellectual challenges and enjoys developing his skills. The problem is that the challenges he seeks and the skills he develops rarely coincide with the school curriculum. Indeed, nearly all of his intellectual activities (computers or science projects) occur outside of the classroom.

Santos is motivated to stay out of trouble and therefore to obtain minimally respectable grades, but not to excel in school subjects. His threshold for acceptable grades is about a "C+." But he could easily be a "straight-A" student if he exerted some effort on school tasks.

Despite Santos' many intellectual achievements, he is not mastering material that wise adults believe is important to know in our society. Santos' teachers have a difficult task. They need to get Santos to attend to the school curriculum without dampening his curiosity and enthusiasm for intellectual challenge.

The first step is to gain some knowledge of Santos' own intellectual interests. The second step is to try to take advantage of these interests and to incorporate them into his school assignments. For example, if his English teacher is teaching students about biography, the teacher might encourage Santos to read a biography of a scientist. His geometry teacher might ask him to design a miniature city from another planet in which all buildings have to be built to scale and conform to certain unusual shapes. His interest in space and the pleasure he gets out of building things might make the mastery of geometry and measurement more meaningful and fun. It is unrealistic to expect Santos' teachers to find creative ways to engage Santos' interest in every school task. But occasional attempts, such as the examples given above, might help convince Santos of the practical value of mastering the school curriculum.

In general, there are two principles that need to be kept in mind for students like Santos. First, teachers should give such students as much choice as possible. The more choices students have to select the specific tasks they approach, the more likely they are to find something that interests and engages them. Why assign the same biography to every student in the class, for example, when there are many excellent biographies that would appeal to students' diverse interests?

Second, an effort must be made to demonstrate the usefulness of "school knowledge." If students are learning composition skills, why not have them write personal journals, letters to the president, or stories for a school newsletter? Certainly these approaches to engaging the enthusiasm of a bright but uninterested student like Santos will be more effective than repeatedly warning him that he will receive a bad grade.

Santos' teacher might also capitalize on his "threshold," requiring greater effort and task completion than he is currently putting forth to achieve the "C+" he seems to need. This clearly has to be done carefully, to avoid an appearance of unfairness that could alienate Santos altogether. But if grades are based to some degree on effort and improvement, the teacher certainly has license to penalize Santos for performing below his capacity.

Alma

Anxious Alma can learn the math concepts taught, but she has difficulty demonstrating her knowledge and is extremely uncomfortable in math learning contexts. Alma's mathematics teacher needs to help Alma develop strategies for reducing her anxiety in evaluative situations, and she needs to eliminate the risk Alma envisions that failure might bring.

Given the severity and uniqueness of the problem, Alma's teacher might begin by discussing his or her observations directly with Alma, explaining a concern that Alma's anxiety in evaluative situations interferes with her enjoyment of mathematics and will make her unwilling to take challenging mathematics courses in the future. Although Alma may be at first reluctant to talk about her anxiety, she might ultimately be convinced to begin a personalized program to try to alleviate it. A program might have the following components:

- Alma reads a book from the library on relaxation techniques and shares a few techniques that she found useful with the teacher.
- Alma commits to volunteering once each day to contribute to class discussion; in exchange, the teacher promises not to call on her when she doesn't volunteer.
- To build Alma's self-confidence, the teacher assigns her to assist another student who is having difficulty with the homework.

Other strategies could also be used to make tests less frightening. Alma could, for example, be given more time to finish tests. It might also be helpful to give her a few sample problems to refer to, or to allow her to refer to her textbook during a test. The questions in the test should require understanding of the mathematical concepts involved, but she may be reassured by having access to examples. She might also be told that she can take a test over if she believes that anxiety interfered with her performance. This alone might relieve anxiety enough to make it unnecessary to fulfill the promise.

Special accommodations for students who suffer from debilitating anxiety can be made in a particular class. But teachers also need to address the underlying problems, to prepare students to function effectively in classes in which the teacher may be less accommodating, or situations in which accommodations are not possible. Self-confidence is usually at the root of anxiety. Thus, any strategy a teacher might use to build self-confidence, such as those suggested for Dave and Hannah, also apply to students like Alma.

Al

Alienated Al psychologically checked out of school a long time ago. He feels, like many students who eventually drop out of school, that nobody really cares whether he is there or not, so why should he care? School has little to offer. It does not give him feelings of competence, control, or social connectedness. To the contrary, he usually performs poorly when he does the academic work, his teachers don't trust him to use autonomy productively, and aside from a few like-minded friends, he is not socially integrated.

Usually a very nurturing and attentive adult is needed to reconnect a student like Al back to an academic setting. A teacher or school counselor needs to spend time with him and to try to understand his perceptions of himself and his feelings toward school. That person needs to convey that he or she cares about Al. This can be done by listening sympathetically to Al, conveying high expectations, making sure he has the help he needs to achieve those expectations, and holding him accountable to them.

A call should be made to Al's home before noon on a day he misses school. Teachers might be asked to give progress reports regularly to a counselor working with Al, or to talk to Al directly as soon as he begins to fall behind or fail to complete work. The idea is not to make him feel like his every move is being monitored, but to let him know that people at the school care.

All of his teachers need to convey to him that they expect him to do the work and to do it as well as he can. It is difficult for teachers to keep plugging away with a student who seems to care so little. They get weary and lower their expectations to the point that they are delighted when a student like Al turns in any half-hearted attempt at an assignment. This simply reinforces Al's own view that he's not capable of genuine success, and nobody cares anyway.

Sometimes students like Al can be hooked into school through activities, like plays, music, or sports. Coaches and music directors are often the most respected adults in a school, and thus in a good position to serve as a "critical friend." But the goal is to use the activity to draw the student into the intellectual life of the school, not as an end in itself. Recognizing particular talents and interests can also help. For example, Al's skills in rap might be featured in an English class doing a poetry unit.

A caring adult who takes an interest in Al is necessary to start to bring Al back, but this won't be sufficient. No individualized effort to reconnect Al to school will be successful if the instructional program is too difficult for him, or is irrelevant to his interests. The instructional program needs to be engaging and relevant, and embedded in a school climate in which all students are expected to learn.

It's Harder Than It Sounds

Successfully implementing the suggestions made above, and others made in previous chapters, is not easy for a number of reasons. Students can sometimes be their own worst enemies, slow to respond to practices that are different from those that they are used to, and the same practice often affects students in the same class differently. Also, many of the practices that have been recommended require shifting substantial control from teachers to students, which is difficult for many teachers. The practices described also require enormous skill and commitment; teachers need to be very knowledgeable of their students' competencies and interests and attentive to their own behavior toward students. Finally, the recommended practices usually cannot stand alone; they work only if they are embedded in a complex set of mutually reinforcing practices. This section elaborates on these challenges.

The Undermining Effect of Students

Teachers' efforts to increase student motivation can fail miserably if they do not take into account the dispositions and expectations of their own students. Below are examples of problems that can arise with teachers' initial attempts to apply a few of the principles of motivation discussed in this book.

Minimize extrinsic rewards.   Students accustomed to working for grades and other rewards may cease working altogether if extrinsic rewards become less salient or available. Students need to be weaned slowly from their dependence on external rewards, and this extrinsic motivational system needs to be replaced with an alternative system that will motivate them to be engaged in school tasks.

Provide challenging tasks.   If tasks suddenly become much more challenging than what students are used to, they may become discouraged rather than more intrinsically interested. The level of challenge needs to be increased gradually, and students need to feel comfortable and safe experiencing initial difficulties.

Assign open-ended tasks.   Students who have had mostly close-ended tasks with one right answer are accustomed to clear, unambiguous feedback. Open-ended tasks that provide opportunity for creative, substantive problem solving involve more risk because the standards for evaluation are more difficult to understand, and there is greater uncertainty about what constitutes a "good" performance. To deal with the anxiety about performance such tasks sometimes provoke, students often try to turn open-ended assignments that have considerable potential for creativity into more prescribed and boring procedural tasks.[2]

Provide opportunities for collaboration.   Giving students who are used to working alone an opportunity to collaborate with classmates is initially just as likely to result in dependency (one or two children completing the task while the others fool around) or conflict (disagreements among students) as it is to promote productive collaboration. Most students need to be given explicit instruction in effective strategies for help-seeking, help-giving, and collaboration.

As ineffective as some traditional instructional approaches are, they are predictable, and students will sometimes resist change. Even if students welcome a

---

[2]When I assign a paper in my graduate courses, students invariably ask many questions to decrease the ambiguity: "How many pages?" "Double-spaced or single-spaced?" "Do we need to use sources outside of class readings?" "How many references should we have?" "Is it all right to use quotations?" I find myself making up answers to relieve students' anxiety, even though my answers end up limiting students' options in ways that I did not intend, thus reducing the intrinsic motivational value of the task.

change, they often lack the skills they need to make good use of new kinds of learning opportunities. But if implemented gradually and with careful planning, students should eventually thrive on the kinds of changes recommended in this book. Even when changes are implemented carefully and slowly, teachers need to be prepared for some false starts and slippage. Sometimes the current system needs to fall apart a little before it comes back together in a new, improved form.

Although it is important to make changes carefully and to monitor their effects, it is also important not to overreact to student resistence or to underestimate students' ability to adapt to a new approach. Teachers are often amazed at the quality of children's thinking and the creativity of their problem solving when they "let go" and give their students some freedom to show what they can do. They are surprised at how engaged their previously unmotivated students are when they are given tasks and instruction that is challenging, connected to their experience, and that allows them to become actively involved.

Different Students, Different Needs

To complicate matters further, an educational environment that is good for one student is not necessarily good for another. The principles discussed in this book need to be adjusted somewhat to students' individual needs.

For example, although it is true that challenging tasks are generally more intrinsically interesting, students who have a long history of failure, like Hannah, or who lack self-confidence, like Dave and Al, may initially need tasks that they can complete easily, with a heavy dose of praise for their efforts. Slowly, more difficult problems or tasks can be interspersed among those that they can do fairly easily. Sally, on the other hand, although she may complain at first, should be able to rise quickly to the challenge of more demanding tasks. Santos should also thrive on the challenge immediately, if the tasks are at all related to his interests.

Students also vary in their goals, so that the same goal structure will affect some students positively and others negatively. A student like Santos, who is primarily intrinsically motivated, will not work hard in a classroom in which the teacher stresses extrinsic goals, but may thrive in a classroom in which the teacher emphasizes the intrinsic value in school tasks. Students like Sally, in contrast, may not initially work hard in a class in which the teacher stresses learning and mastery.[3] Teachers do not need to capitulate to students' goal orientations, but they should be aware of them and of possible conflicts between their classroom practices and their students' orientations. They may need to individualize somewhat the messages they convey to different students.

[3]I found this to be true when I first began teaching college students. In an effort to orient students' attention toward the joy of learning about child psychology, I did not give grades for class participation or papers. I found very quickly that my own goal orientation was initially incompatible with the goal orientation of most of the students. Rather than studying to understand child development, they studied to get good grades in their other classes and came to my class unprepared.

Giving Up Control

Giving up some control to provide students more autonomy is difficult for most teachers. When faced with a group of students who appear to be unmotivated, the natural response is to be more rather than less controlling: "If these kids don't want to learn, I'll have to make them." This is perhaps why teachers in middle school tend to be more controlling than teachers in elementary school.

Perhaps teachers perceive adolescents to be less intrinsically motivated to engage in academic activities, and believe that they need to be more controlling to get students to work. Or perhaps teachers feel more constrained by the curriculum, and believe they need to exercise more control to make sure they get through all the requirements.

Monitor these impulses carefully, because many studies have shown decisively that imposing greater control and relying on extrinsic reasons for working will have the opposite of the intended effect, undermining rather than promoting students' interest and desire to complete schoolwork. Have faith that students who do not appear to be interested in academic work will come around on their own to work that has the qualities shown to promote student interest in a social context that supports their autonomy, gives them opportunities to develop their competencies, and makes them feel secure and valued.

Deci, Schwartz, Sheinman, and Ryan (1981) developed a measure of teachers' tendency toward controlling behavior in which teachers are asked to choose responses to vignettes describing problem situations. For example:

> Jim is an average student who has been working at grade level. During the past two weeks, he has appeared listless and has not been participating during reading group. The work he does is accurate, but he has not been completing assignments. A phone conversation with his mother revealed no useful information. The most appropriate thing for Jim's teacher to do is:

They are then given four possible teacher responses and asked to select the most appropriate. The responses vary from highly controlling to highly autonomy supportive, as the examples below illustrate.

Highly controlling: Make him stay after school until the day's assignments are done.

Moderately controlling: Impress upon him the importance of finishing his assignments since he needs to learn this material for his own good.

Moderately autonomy supportive: Let him see how he compares with the other children in terms of his assignments and encourage him to catch up with the others.

Highly autonomy supportive: Let him know that he doesn't have to finish all of his work now and help him work out the cause of the listlessness.

In one study, when preservice teachers were observed teaching, those who gave relatively more controlling responses listened less, gave more directives and commands, gave solutions more often, made fewer comments conveying an understanding of the students' perspective, and were less student-centered in that they gave fewer opportunities for student choice and personal initiative (Reeve, Bolt, & Cai, 1999).

Some teachers fear that increasing student discretion will lead to confusion and chaos rather than constructive student-initiated learning. Their fears are not without cause, for two reasons. First, more skill and planning is required on the teacher's part to maintain order in a classroom in which students are given choices and discretion than in a classroom in which students are always told exactly what to do and how and when to do it. Teachers often lack the skills and the time for such planning. Second, most students are unaccustomed to much freedom, and they do not necessarily use it responsibly.

There are several things teachers can do to minimize the likelihood that their fears of chaos will be borne out and to make sure that students exercise their choice and responsibility effectively. First, teachers should increase student autonomy gradually, giving students an opportunity to show that they can use it responsibly. Second, teachers need to make sure that directions are clear and not too complicated. Written instructions, summarizing the steps of a task, are often helpful and reduce dependency on the teacher for reminding students of next steps. Third, explicit instructions and discussion related to managing time and tasks are helpful. Giving up control can be frightening, but if done carefully and thoughtfully, it can be liberating for the teacher as well as motivating for students.

Knowing Students

Many of the principles of motivation described in this book require a great deal of knowledge about students' skills (e.g., to create optimally challenging tasks), self-confidence, interests, values, and anxieties. Knowing each student well and continually assessing each student's knowledge and interests in order to provide appropriate tasks requires an enormous amount of effort.

Some time can be gained by providing more student autonomy. To the degree that teachers are successful in promoting independence and engaging students more enthusiastically in schoolwork, time spent in management activities and managing students decreases. This gives teachers more time to engage in assessment activities, such as interacting with students individually and in small groups and examining their written work.

Self-Monitoring

Teachers must be aware of their *own* biases, beliefs, expectations, and behavior toward students: Am I smiling more at girls? Sustaining instructional conversations longer with boys? Giving students who are relatively slow to catch on too little time to answer questions? Telling students what to do when they could be making choices?

Monitoring one's own behavior to avoid differential or ineffective behavior toward students is extremely difficult to do while teaching, assessing students, and managing a classroom. It is useful to have an aide, a colleague, or even a trusted parent do observations at first. Students' own perceptions can also be elicited. Self-monitoring gets easier and more automatic with practice and time.

Everything Is Related to Everything Else

Although most instructional practices have been treated independently in this book, all of the practices recommended depend substantially on each other for their effectiveness.

Consider, for example, providing students more choice in tasks. If choice is given in a classroom in which performance outcomes and external evaluation are stressed, students are likely to select easy tasks which will not help them develop new skills. Concerns about performance most likely explain why Clifford (1991) and her colleagues found that, when given a choice, students tended to select tasks that offered very little risk of failure. The older the students in her studies, the less willing they were to take academic risks. Only in a context in which errors and initial failures are considered a natural part of learning, and in which evaluation is based primarily on effort and personal improvement, will students choose tasks that challenge their current skill levels.

Collaborative learning will also work in only some contexts. If implemented in a classroom that is not a "community of learners," in which students do not respect and support each other's learning, attempts can result in more conflict and hurt feelings rather than in collaboration. Collaborative learning will only work effectively if the teacher models—and demands from students—mutual respect, a sense of responsibility for each other's learning, and a value on inclusion and full participation of all students.

Another example of the interconnections among the motivation principles discussed concerns evaluation. A teacher who reduces the emphasis on external evaluation but continues to give boring, too easy, or too difficult tasks will not see increased effort on assignments or the use of effective problem-solving strategies. Indeed, if tasks are repetitive, irrelevant, and boring, none of the principles discussed in the book will improve students' motivation.

Although the links between various practices make the task of increasing student motivation more difficult in some respects, they can also make the task easier because they reinforce each other. For example, giving students choice usually results in students becoming engaged in activities that are more personally interesting, and thus doubly support their intrinsic motivation. Thus, as teachers try to change their classroom practices, they will find that it gets easier and easier.

Beyond the Classroom

No teacher, however good or committed, can meet the challenges described above alone or in a school context that is not supportive of his or her efforts to improve. Teachers can motivate students only if they in turn are motivated. They can make students feel valued and secure only if they feel valued and secure; they can foster enthusiasm for learning in students only if they are enthusiastic about teaching. The school culture can make or break a teacher in the same way that the classroom culture can support or undermine students' efforts to learn. Fortunately, the principles of motivation discussed in previous chapters apply to teachers as well as to students. Below are a few of the important conditions needed for teachers to implement effective teaching strategies.

Resources

The physical conditions of some schools and the lack of resources make it extremely difficult for teachers to model enthusiasm for learning, attend to students' needs, and create open-ended, intrinsically motivating tasks. Teachers who have to run across the school campus to make a phone call to a parent of a student having difficulty, only to find that they are third in line to use the phone, or who have to spend their few minutes of break time taping together textbooks that are falling apart, or photocopying materials because there are not enough for all of the students, or looking for containers they can use to catch the water dripping into their classroom through the roof, cannot easily be upbeat and focused on their students.

Support for Risk Taking

It is not easy for teachers to be self-critical—to examine their own practices and be open to finding them lacking. Teachers need to be confident that they can share the problems they discover in this self-evaluative process with impunity, and that they have the support they need to help them address the problems they find. They need to be able to reveal to administrators and colleagues areas in which they do not believe they are being successful without fearing reprisal or humiliation. The respectful and supportive social context that is required for students to feel comfortable to take risks is just as critical for teachers.

Cooperation and Collaboration

Teachers need access to resources at the school level to help them evaluate and improve their practices. They need to have other adults observe their classrooms, and they need to be able to observe other teachers' classrooms. They need to share problems and receive ideas from other teachers and experts. A school climate that provides opportunities for such teacher collaboration is critical to maximizing student learning. The evidence is clear: students achieve the most in schools where teachers develop a strong professional community, where there is a shared sense of purpose, a collective focus on student learning, collaborative instructional creativity, and reflective professional dialogue (Marks et al., in press).

Time

The kinds of tasks and activities that engage students' interest and enthusiasm and the kind of qualitative evaluative feedback needed to focus their attention on learning and mastery takes a lot more time than assigning pages from a textbook and checking the correctness of students' answers. Considerable time is also required for the teacher collaboration and professional development described.

As schools and instruction are currently organized, teachers simply do not have the time they need to provide effective, motivating instruction. At the elementary level most teachers have no time built into their workday to plan instruction or even to evaluate students' work. Even at the secondary level, the typical one free period a day is not nearly sufficient. Either teacher schedules need to be changed, to include noninstructional time during the day, or the teacher's day or year has to be lengthened (with appropriate compensation) to include time for these activities.

Autonomy

The principle of maximum autonomy applies to teachers as well as to students. Teachers need a free hand to experiment with strategies that are compatible with their skills and personality as well as with their students', and they need to make some of their own choices. To be sure, coherence in a school's curriculum and some articulation across the grades is important. But teachers can be involved in school curriculum decisions, and even after they are made, some flexibility should remain for personalizing instruction.

DeCharms (1976) recognized the importance of the school context in the program he developed to foster feelings of personal causation in students. He argued that if teachers feel like pawns (passive, controlled), their students could not feel like origins (active, responsible agents in their education). In his program teachers were given more responsibility over their school program, and opportunities to set their own goals and make decisions about how to reach those goals, and they were encouraged to do the same for students. The program was unusually successful in improving student achievement. DeCharms (1976, 1984) found that predominantly poor, African American students who had been in the nine experimental "origins" classrooms in sixth and seventh grade made greater achievement gains than students in the control group. The advantage of the origin group persisted through eighth grade, even though neither group of teachers continued training that year. The origin group had a higher high school completion rate than did the control group.

School Policies

Teachers' efforts in individual classrooms can be easily undermined by school policies that are incompatible with teachers' motivational goals. Recognizing this, some motivation researchers have developed interventions to change practices at the school level to support teachers' efforts to change the culture of their class-rooms (Anderman & Maehr, 1994; Midgley, 1994; Maehr & Midgley, 1996; Midgley & Edelin, 1998; Maehr & Anderman, 1993; Urdan, Midgley, & Wood, 1995; Weinstein, Soule, Collins, Cone, Mehlorn, & Stimmonacchi, 1991).

There are a variety of school-level policies that are relevant to the motiva-tional issues discussed in this book. For example, schoolwide decisions about textbooks, curriculum, and even field trips significantly affect the nature of tasks and the real-world relevance of students' educational experiences. Whether teachers are allowed or encouraged to collaborate and whether there is some flex-ibility in class scheduling affect opportunities for multidisciplinary and project learning activities. Maehr and Anderman (1993) point out that even janitorial policies can inhibit project-based learning, which, while messy, can be intrinsi-cally motivating and productive.

What schools recognize publicly through such practices as honor rolls and certificates is important. It is difficult for teachers to focus students' attention on mastery and learning in a school that recognizes only excellence in outcome for high performers. The emphasis on effort or improvement in the classroom needs to be matched at the school level.

Some schools also have grading policies that can affect student motivation. A policy requiring grading on the curve, for example, or even one that limits the number of high grades, promotes a competitive rather than a collaborative con-text. Such a policy can also contradict the message that all students are expected to meet high standards. Grading policies that recognize effort and improvement, or that are based on clearly defined standards, are more likely to promote a posi-tive motivational climate.

Inequitable allocation of resources among students is common—with high-achieving students receiving the most experienced and best-qualified teachers, greater access to college counselors, and additional opportunities (e.g., access to technology and opportunities to work on the school newspaper or yearbook). These differences give a clear message about what (and who) is valued. Such in-equities also affect the quality of instruction and educational experiences that stu-dents receive, which in turn affects their motivation to engage in academic activities.

Ability grouping and tracking is perhaps the most powerful way to empha-size differences in skill levels and to foster an entity concept of ability. The more pervasive and rigid grouping and tracking are, the more they will undermine the motivational goals discussed in this book.

In addition to creating differential opportunities for learning and access to higher education, between-class ability grouping and tracking also often results in a concentration of behavioral and motivation problems. Thus, the student assigned to the "lower" group or track may be disadvantaged by frequent disrup-tions from classmates as well as from a watered-down, unstimulating instruc-tional program delivered by the least experienced teachers. Moreover, children who engage in negative, disruptive behavior have little access to highly moti-vated, achievement-oriented peers (see Eccles & Wigfield, 2000).

Schoolwide testing practices also influence the instructional program and thus student motivation. If teachers are evaluated on the basis of their students' scores on tests of basic, rote skills, it will be difficult for them to emphasize, in their teaching, the kind of problem solving and understanding that engages students' intrinsic interest in school tasks.

The amount of real choice students have in selecting classes and other activities at the school level will influence their sense of self-determination and thus their motivation within classes. In some schools, the most desirable courses and opportunities are not available to the students who are in greatest need of increased motivation.

School Organization

Elementary schools are usually organized to enable teachers to know their students well and to establish trusting, caring relationships. Some schools have even begun to keep the same teacher with a group of students for two to three years (referred to as "looping"). Middle schools and high schools, in contrast, are typically organized in ways that make strong connections between teachers and students difficult.

The organization of middle and junior high schools, with students moving from teacher to teacher throughout the day, is not conducive to positive motivation and, more generally, to positive social–emotional health (Midgley & Edelin, 1998; Wigfield & Eccles, 1994). Many educational experts have proposed alternative organizations that would better meet the needs of young adolescents and promote interest and engagement in academic work. Thus, schools have been urged to experiment with groupings, or "families" of a team of teachers and a relatively small number of students, with the same teacher sometimes teaching more than one subject to reduce the number of teachers each student has contact with during the day. Motivation and middle school experts have also urged more personal and positive teacher-student relationships, more shared authority and control, less emphasis on performance which is based on a competitive standard, and less tracking by ability (Anderman, Maehr, & Midgley, 1999; Carnegie Council, 1989; Eccles & Wigfield, in press; Felner, Kasak, Mulhall, & Flowers, 1997; Lipsitz, Mizell, Jackson, & Austin, 1997; Mac Iver & Plank, 1997; Midgley & Edelin, 1998).

Similarly, smaller learning communities, or schools within schools, are being promoted for the secondary level by many experts. The goal is to provide an environment in which the adults in the school have more opportunities to learn about and develop relationships with students. Studies indicate that such efforts have been very successful in improving adolescents' sense of belonging and feeling of being supported (Felner, Jackson, Kasak, Mulhall, Brand, & Flowers, 1997; Lipsitz, 1997; Midgley & Edelin, 1998). The research reviewed in this book suggests that these kinds of changes should enhance students' motivation to learn, as well as positive social–emotional development and higher academic achievement.

"Press" for Student Learning

As discussed in Chapter 13, one of the most common findings in research on effective schools is that schools that promote high performance have high expectations for student learning (Baker, Terry, Bridger, & Winsor, 1997; Evans, 1997; Lambert & McCombs, 1998; Marks, Doane, & Secada, in press; Newmann, 1992). Along with high expectations for academic success, there is a strong "press" for academic learning in schools that achieve high academic skills. Research comparing Catholic to public schools, for example, suggests that a focus on learning is an important factor in students' typically better performance in Catholic schools (Bryk, Lee, & Holland, 1993). Other studies have found that student effort and performance are higher in schools that press for academic success (Lee, Bryk, & Smith, 1993; Lee & Smith, 1999; Lee, Smith, & Croninger, 1997).

How is a press for learning created? All activities of the school are organized around promoting student learning. Examples of school policies mentioned in Chapter 13, such as calling parents as soon as a student's grades slip, convey the message that all students are expected to meet high expectations. Below are other examples of what one would likely see in a school that focuses on learning:

- The principal is a strong instructional leader and spends a large portion of his or her time in classrooms and working directly with teachers on instruction and assessment.
- Teachers' meetings are focused on topics related to teaching and learning.
- Teachers collaborate regularly on instructional issues and are given opportunities to expand their own teaching skills.
- There are clearly articulated academic standards that are made known to parents and students.
- Students are assessed frequently and those assessments are used to guide instruction.
- Substantive feedback is given on students' work (including homework).
- There are consequences to students for not completing work.
- As soon as students show signs of academic difficulties, there is consultation among staff (e.g., the principal, guidance counselor, school psychologist or social worker, and teacher) and an intervention plan is designed.
- Teachers are available to give some individual assistance to students.
- Parents are consulted and informed about any academic difficulties observed in their child.
- Resources are in place (e.g., tutoring, after school programs, summer programs) to address the needs of children having academic difficulties.
- Children's academic effort and successes (including improvement) are praised and celebrated.

One characteristic of schools that do *not* promote high expectations and a focus on learning is that substantial time is spent on matters that are not directly related to teaching and learning. In these schools principals and teachers are burdened with busywork and must devote time to topics and problems that are only marginally related to student learning. I have seen whole faculty meetings devoted to taking attendance, bulletin boards, and recess schedules. Most of these matters could be handled more efficiently by memos, a small group of teachers, or an administrator. Hoy and Sabo (1998) found in their study of middle schools that achievement gains were much lower in schools in which principals required teachers to spend time on noninstruction-related issues. In contrast, an emphasis on academics and strong collegial connections among teachers was associated with high achievement gains.

A Supportive Context

One caveat about high academic standards deserves attention. If students do not feel secure and supported in their relationships in the school, high academic standards could be very threatening and actually undermine their motivation and learning. In a study by Lee and Smith (1999) of fifth and eighth graders in 304 Chicago city schools, achievement gains were very high (more than a standard deviation above the mean) for students in schools that were high in both academic press *and* social support. But achievement gains for students in schools that were high in academic press and relatively low on social support were *below* average. Shouse (1996) also found that for both poor and middle-class schools, the greatest achievement gains were found when there was a combination of strong community and academic press.

An important point here is that a caring community does not conflict with high standards and a press for learning. To the contrary, students often refer to teachers who pushed them to learn and wouldn't put up with excuses or letting their work slide as evidence that they cared about them.

The importance of social support—creating a caring community for children as well as for adults in a school—is being given increasing attention by school reformers (e.g., Baker, Terry, Bridger, & Winsor, 1997; Sergiovanni, 1994; Wehlage, Rutter, Smith, Lesko, & Fernandez, 1989; Midgley & Edelin, 1998). Studies indicate a profound sense of alienation, disenfranchisement, lack of care, and lack of belonging in some schools, particularly urban high schools. In one study, only 33 percent of the students interviewed claimed that their teachers cared for them, and only 7 percent said they would ask their teachers for advice (Girl Scouts of America, 1991). Adolescents frequently refer to their sense of isolation and lack of meaningful relationships as reasons for dropping out (Institute for Education and Transformation, 1992).

Reformers have promoted the building of positive relationships and social support as a strategy for connecting and motivating students, like Alienated Al, to be engaged in school and academic work. Most schools that have attempted to improve the social climate have implemented collaborative learning arrangements at both the classroom and school level, and usually increase efforts to connect with parents and the broader community. Teachers are available to students to discuss nonacademic issues, as well as to provide individualized academic support. Students are given more voice in school affairs, again at the classroom as well as at the school level. (See, for example, the whole school "caring community" Child Development Project;[4] Battistich, Solomon, Kim, Watson, & Schaps, 1995.)

Beyond the School

Current political stress on accountability makes more difficult some aspects of the recommendations made in this book. Research indicates, for example, that the more teachers are held accountable for student learning the harder it is to for them to share control with students. The effect of accountability on teachers' behavior was demonstrated in a study by Deci, Spiegel, Ryan, Koestner, and Kauffman (1982). They asked psychology students to train another student in an experiment. Student trainers who were told that they were responsible for how well the other student performed talked more, were more critical of the student, gave more commands, and allowed less choice and autonomy than student teachers who were simply instructed to teach the task. In another study, teachers who were told to use a new curriculum to "increase students' performance standards," pressured students more and were less supportive of their autonomy than teachers who were told that the curriculum was designed to enhance students' learning. Their students' performance was also lower than that of the students of teachers who were told to use the curriculum to enhance students' learning. (See also Flink, Boggiano, & Barrett, 1990.)

Indeed, the current emphasis on accountability is accompanied by an emphasis on external control. Recall the media attention to New Jersey principal Joe Clark, holding a baseball bat outside of his high school, claiming that he disciplines his students to learn. Americans were so taken with this image that a movie, *Lean on Me* (1989), depicted him as an effective educator. What was not publicized was the fact that student achievement in his school did not increase and the school's dropout rate doubled (Toch, 1991).

The standards movement is also fostering controlling, teacher-directed instruction that is focused on a narrow range of skills and a narrow range of ways for students to demonstrate what they know. Teachers have confessed to me that they feel they have become so concerned about "covering the curriculum" on which students will be tested that they are unable to risk giving students much discretion. They also find themselves less likely to encourage creative thinking in students, and although they believe multiple choice tests are not appropriate for assessing students' deep understanding, they use them. Teachers use these strategies, which are often counter to their own beliefs about effective instruction and assessment, because they believe that they will enhance performance on the standardized achievement tests. The achievement tests take on this importance

---

[4]Developmental Studies Center, 2000 Embarcadero, Suite 305, Oakland, CA 94606. Telephone: 800-666-7270.

because they are used to judge the school, and in some cases, may even serve as the basis for the schools' resources and for the teachers' own salaries.

The current focus on a traditional, back-to-basics curriculum which emphasizes extrinsic approaches to getting students to work to achieve the higher standards is also short-sighted and misguided. It contradicts everything decades of research have told us about motivation to learn. While short-term gains on narrow assessments of academic skills may be achieved, in the long run such strategies will not achieve the high levels of critical thinking skills that are referred to in the political rhetoric.

Can Progress Be Made?

Most children arrive at school self-confident, eager to learn, and enthusiastic about school tasks. This book was about maintaining this high level of motivation—stemming, sometimes reversing, the common shift toward focusing on extrinsic rewards, being concerned about performance, and losing interest in schoolwork. The task is challenging.

Am I proposing the impossible? I don't think so. I have seen many classrooms—from kindergarten to twelfth grade—in which students are enthusiastically and self-confidently engaged in learning activities. I am convinced that a high level of student motivation and pleasure in learning can be achieved in any classroom.

Each of the many excellent teachers I have observed has a unique approach. Strategies that work effectively for one teacher and group of students can fail in another classroom with another teacher and a different group of students. The principles of effective teaching and the suggestions made in this book, therefore, need to be adapted to each teacher's style and skills and to the specific characteristics of each group of students. Adaptations are also necessary at the school level, depending on state and district policies, the social–political context, the community, and the student population.

Because students need time to adjust, and because teachers need time to experiment and test out new instructional practices, it is important not to be too ambitious, not to try too much too fast. A more effective strategy for teachers, as for students, is to create proximal goals. Initial goals might be as modest as trying to get a particular student to exert some effort or to take a risk, to create tasks that are better linked to students' personal interests and their lives outside of school, or to give more informative evaluative feedback.

As changes are made, their effects need to be observed carefully. Is the student exerting more effort or taking more risks? Do students seem more interested in the tasks? Do they use the substantive evaluative feedback to guide their efforts? There are many examples in this book of specific student behaviors teachers can observe to give them information about their students' beliefs and dispositions related to motivation. Direct, open conversations are also useful. They contribute to a classroom climate of trust, convey teachers' genuine concern for understanding students' views, and provide valuable information on students' perspectives regarding particular instructional practices.

This process of reflection and self-evaluation, making modifications, and observing their effects needs to be repeated over and over. Whether a teacher's purpose is to improve classroom management, increase motivation, or enhance learning, good teachers are continually evaluating, fine-tuning, and reevaluating their practices.

This process of development and reform cannot be done without support. Teachers are at the front lines, but without a broad, societal commitment to making schools places in which teachers and students can thrive, the status quo will prevail. Substantial changes in student motivation and learning require substantial changes in the way schools are organized, for students and for teachers. It will also require community support for innovation and a broad social commitment to making education a top moral and fiscal priority.

APPENDIX 2A

Identifying Motivation Problems

Instructions

1. Observe students for a few days before checking off on the form which behaviors are typically seen. To make some of these judgments you may need to try new teaching practices—e.g., give choices in assignments with different difficulty levels; give some ungraded assignments; provide some time and opportunities to work on unassigned tasks.
2. Select students who appear to have relatively serious motivation problems and rate their behavior in different subject areas or for different types of tasks or learning contexts.
3. If there are two adults in the classroom (e.g., a teacher and an aide), it is instructive for both to fill out the form for the same student. Differences can reveal biases in the teacher's or the aide's perception of a student, or context effects on behavior (because the teacher and aide see the student in different contexts).

Note: The first 12 behaviors are important for performing adequately on basic school tasks. Students who do not demonstrate these behaviors are most likely not mastering the school curriculum as well as they could. The remaining items are highly desirable behaviors that reflect maximum motivation for intellectual pursuits.

Child's Name: _____

1. _____ Pays attention to the teacher
2. _____ Begins work on tasks immediately
3. _____ Follows directions on tasks
4. _____ Maintains attention until tasks are completed
5. _____ Completes work
6. _____ Turns assignments in on time
7. _____ Persists rather than gives up when work appears difficult
8. _____ Works autonomously
9. _____ Volunteers answers in class
10. _____ Test performance reflects skill level demonstrated on assignments
11. _____ Seeks help when it is needed
12. _____ Asks for help that will enable subsequent autonomy (rather than asking for the answer)
13. _____ Is not upset by initial errors or difficulties
14. _____ Enjoys challenging work
15. _____ Works intensely (very focused)
16. _____ Asks questions to expand knowledge beyond immediate lesson
17. _____ Engages in learning activities that are not required
18. _____ Is reluctant to stop working on tasks when highly engaged
19. _____ Engages in learning activities after assignments are completed
20. _____ Appears happy, proud, enthusiastic, and eager
21. _____ Strives to improve skills, even when performing well relative to classmates
22. _____ Initiates challenging learning activities on own
23. _____ Works hard on ungraded tasks

External Reinforcement

Teacher Self Reports

Instructions

This form is designed to help you reflect upon your use of external rewards and punishment. After completing the form examine your responses for inconsistencies between your values and goals and your behaviors.

1. *What reinforcements do you use?*

	never	occasionally	often
▪ social reinforcement (praise)	____	____	____
▪ symbolic rewards (e.g., stickers)	____	____	____
▪ good grades	____	____	____
▪ material rewards (e.g., food, prizes)	____	____	____
▪ public recognition (e.g., paper on bulletin board)	____	____	____
▪ privileges (e.g., play with special materials)	____	____	____
▪ responsibilities (e.g., take roll, errand to the office)	____	____	____
▪ other _____	____	____	____

2. *What punishments do you use?*

	never	occasionally	often
▪ private criticism	____	____	____
▪ public criticism	____	____	____
▪ bad grades	____	____	____
▪ "time out" (social isolation)	____	____	____
▪ loss of privileges (e.g., no recess)	____	____	____
▪ other _____	____	____	____

3. *Upon which behaviors or outcomes is reinforcement contingent?*

	never	occasionally	often
▪ high effort/attention	____	____	____
▪ absolute performance (e.g., few errors)	____	____	____
▪ relative performance (e.g., fewer errors than most other students)	____	____	____

- improved performance ___ ___ ___
- following directions ___ ___ ___
- finishing ___ ___ ___
- creativity ___ ___ ___
- personal initiative ___ ___ ___
- helpfulness ___ ___ ___

4. *Upon which behaviors or outcomes is punishment contingent?*

	never	occasionally	often
■ low effort/inattention	___	___	___
■ absolute performance (e.g., many errors)	___	___	___
■ relative performance (e.g., more errors than most other students)	___	___	___
■ no improvement	___	___	___
■ not following directions	___	___	___
■ not finishing	___	___	___
■ lack of personal initiative	___	___	___
■ dependency (asking for help needlessly)	___	___	___
■ refusal to help	___	___	___
■ misbehavior	___	___	___

5. *Are there any children in your class who are frequently rewarded (e.g., with good grades, praise, or recognition) for good performance that did not require much effort (i.e., was fairly easily achieved)?*

6. *Are there any children in your class who are not rewarded (e.g., with good grades, praise, or recognition) even when they try?*

7. *Are the rewards in your classroom realistically available to all children?*

APPENDIX 3 B

Observations of Teachers' Use of Praise

Instructions

Each time the teacher uses verbal praise, an observer indicates whether the praise was "effective" or "ineffective" according to a set of criteria. Effective praise is described to the left of the slash; ineffective praise is either described on the right of the slash or is the absence of the effective criterion. Put a "+" if the praise was effective according to a particular criterion, a "–" if the praise was ineffective according to the criterion, or nothing if you are not sure or if the criterion is not applicable.

Observers should fill out this form in a variety of situations in which the teacher is likely to praise students (e.g., during reading groups and during whole-class or small-group question-and-answer periods). It is also useful to assess the teacher with different groups of students (e.g., the "high" versus the "low" reading group).

When the form is completed, the teacher should examine criteria for which there are a large number of minuses. These provide specific information regarding ways in which praise might be used more effectively.

Observations of Teachers' Use of Praise*	1	2	3	4	5	6	7	8
(+) contingent on behavior or outcome/ (–) random, unsystematic								
(+) specifies particulars of accomplishment/ (–) global								
(+) spontaneous, credible/ (–) bland, perfunctory								
(+) specifies criteria for praise/ (–)								
(+) provides information about competence/ (–)								
(+) stresses students' own behavior/ (–) social comparison								
(+) focuses on improvement/ (–) focuses on relative performance								
(+) focuses on effort or personal meaning of accomplishment/ (–)								
(+) attributes success to effort and skill/ (–) to ability or external factors								

*Based on Brophy (1981).

Questions for Teachers to Monitor Practices That Affect Achievement-Related Beliefs

Instructions

Reflect on the degree to which you implement each of the principles listed below for maintaining positive achievement-related beliefs.

Tasks/Assignments

1. Are they challenging (i.e., achievable, but require some effort and persistence) for *all* students?
2. Are they organized to provide frequent opportunities for students to observe increases in their skills?

Goals

3. Are goals close enough to be achieved before students get discouraged?
4. Are goals appropriately adjusted to students' individual skill levels?
5. Are students involved in setting their own goals?

Evaluation

6. Do students have diverse opportunities to demonstrate what they know/understand?
7. Have you pointed out what is good, right, or shows improvement?
8. Is feedback clear, specific, and informative?
9. Are rewards based on achieving a clearly-defined standard or set of criteria or on personal improvement?
10. Do students have multiple opportunities to achieve a high grade?
11. Do students celebrate each other's achievements, regardless of their relative level?
12. Are public evaluations minimized?

13. Can students evaluate their own work?
14. Are criteria clear and consistent?

Help-Seeking

15. Do students seek help when they need it?
16. Is assistance limited to what is necessary?
17. Do students seek help from their classmates?

Direct Statements

18. Do you attribute failure to low effort or ineffective strategy?
19. Do you attribute success to effort and competence?

Classroom Structure

20. Are tasks differentiated among students and over time?
21. Do you point out variation in skill levels (within students)?
22. Are all students productively involved in whole-class discussions?
23. Is ability grouping used flexibly and termporarily to address specific skill needs?
24. Do you convey to students the value of many different kinds of skills?
25. Do you give relatively poor-performing students the role of expert?

APPENDIX 11A

Evaluating Tasks

An affirmative answer to the following three questions should be made for all tasks:

1. Do students understand the purpose of the task (what they will learn from it) and exactly what they are expected to do to complete it?

2. Is the task challenging for all students who are expected to complete it? (Will all students be able to complete it with some genuine effort?)

3. Does the task provide students with an opportunity to do substantive intellectual work that will contribute to some learning goal? For example, by engaging them in:
   - higher-order thinking
   - active problem solving
   - thinking about "big ideas"
   - addressing open-ended questions

Tasks should vary from day to day and include one or more of the following characteristics.

They should:

1. be multidimensional
2. be complex, or novel, or contain an element of surprise (e.g., by revealing contradiction in students' thinking)
3. involve active student participation, exploration, or experimentation
4. be personally meaningful
5. allow collaboration

APPENDIX 11B

Evaluating Your Evaluation

1. Do you emphasize learning, mastery, and understanding more than external evaluation?
2. Do you provide substantive feedback that can be used to guide future efforts?
3. Is the information value of evaluation emphasized more than the reward or punishment value?

When grades are given:

1. Are they based on effort, improvement, and achieving a standard, rather than on relative performance?
2. Are grading criteria clear and fair?

APPENDIX 11C

Evaluating Control

1. Are students given the maximum amount of autonomy they can handle, for example by giving them choices in:

   - designing tasks
   - determining how tasks are completed
   - selecting the difficulty level
   - deciding when to do the task

   or by allowing them:

   - to correct their own work
   - to set personal goals

2. Is monitoring done in a way that focuses on students' understanding and skill development rather than on controlling their behavior?

3. Are students given help in a way that facilitates their own accomplishments?

APPENDIX 12A

Strategies for Reducing Anxiety

Preprocessing Problems

- Provide opportunities to reinspect material
- Encourage questions and check for understanding
- Review material frequently
- Give clear, unambiguous instructions
- Provide a fair amount of structure for learning
- Allow variability in pacing of instruction

Processing and Output Problems

- Instruct students in relaxation techniques
- Introduce tasks and tests in a nonthreatening way (e.g., to provide information about which skills need further work)
- Give opportunities to improve written products (e.g., correct errors, rewrite papers, retake tests)
- Provide memory supports during a test (e.g., a sample problem, original text, lecture notes to refer to)
- Eliminate time pressure
- Order questions so that the beginning of a test is easier
- Familiarize students with test format ahead of time

Teacher Efficacy

Instructions

Circle the number that reflects your level of agreement or disagreement with the items below.

1 = strongly disagree
2 = moderately disagree
3 = disagree slightly more than agree

4 = agree slightly more than disagree
5 = moderately agree
6 = strongly agree

1. *The amount a student can learn is primarily related to family background.*   1 2 3 4 5 6

2. If one of my students couldn't do a class assignment, I would be able to accurately assess whether the assignment was at the correct level of difficulty.   1 2 3 4 5 6

3. When I really try, I can get through to the most difficult students.   1 2 3 4 5 6

4. *A teacher is very limited in what he/she can achieve because a student's home environment is a large influence on his/her achievement.*   1 2 3 4 5 6

5. *If parents would do more for their children, I could do more.*   1 2 3 4 5 6

6. If a student did not remember information I gave in a previous lesson, I would know how to increase his/her retention in the next lesson.   1 2 3 4 5 6

7. If a student in my class becomes disruptive and noisy, I feel assured that I know some techniques to redirect him/her quickly.   1 2 3 4 5 6

8. *If students aren't disciplined at home, they aren't likely to accept any discipline.*   1 2 3 4 5 6

9. If I really try hard, I can get through to even the most difficult or unmotivated students.   1 2 3 4 5 6

10. *When it comes right down to it, a teacher really can't do much because most of a student's motivation and performance depends on his or her home environment.*   1 2 3 4 5 6

From Hoy & Woolfolk, 1993, *Elementary School Journal, 93*, pp. 355–372. Reprinted with permission of the University of Chicago Press.

Analysis

1. Subtract from 7 the circled number for each item in italics. (For example, if you circled the "2" for question number 1, the number used in your total score would be $7 - 2 = 5$.)
2. Compute your total score by adding up the 10 item scores and dividing by 10.
3. The higher your total score, the more efficacious you feel as a teacher. If your total score is below 4.0, your feelings that you cannot overcome home effects on students' learning risk undermining your effectiveness as a teacher.

Questions for Teachers to Help Them Monitor Behavior Toward High- and Low-Achievers*

1. Am I as friendly with low-achieving students as I am with high-achieving students?
2. Do I praise or encourage "lows" when they initiate comments?
3. Do I stay with "lows" in failure situations?
4. Do I praise "lows" only for performance that is truly deserving of praise (i.e., that required real effort)?
5. Do I call on "lows" in public situations?
6. How often do "lows" have positive success experiences in public situations?
7. Are "lows" needlessly criticized for wrong answers or failures to respond?
8. Are "lows" placed in a "low group" and treated as group members rather than as individuals?
9. Do I ignore the minor inappropriate behavior of "lows," or do mild violations of classroom rules bring on strong reprimands?
10. Do I make assignments variable, interesting, and challenging for "lows"?
11. How frequently do "lows" have a chance to evaluate their own work and to make important decisions?
12. What are the work preferences of individual students—do they like to work in pairs—and how often are those work preferences honored?
13. Do I intervene with "highs" when they are having difficulty?
14. Do I praise "highs" regardless of their effort or the quality of their performance?

*Adapted from Good and Brophy (1986, p. 501). Copyright © 1986. Adapted by permission of Allyn and Bacon.

REFERENCES

Aboud, F. (1985). The development of a social comparison process in children. *Child Development, 56,* 682–688.

Abramowitz, A., & O'Leary, S. (1991). Behavioral interventions for the classroom: Implications for students with ADHD. *School Psychology Review, 20,* 220–234.

Abu-Hilal, M. (2000). A structural model for predicting mathematics achievement: Its relation with anxiety and self-concept in mathematics. *Psychological Reports, 86,* 835–847.

Ainley, M. (1993). Styles of engagement with learning: Multidimensional assessment of their relationship with strategy use and school achievement. *Journal of Educational Psychology, 85,* 395–405.

Algaze, B. (1995). Cognitive therapy, study counseling, and systematic desensitization in the treatment of test anxiety. In C. Spielberger & P. Vagg (Eds.), *Test anxiety: Theory, assessment, and treatment* (pp. 133–152). Washington, DC: Taylor & Francis.

Alschuler, A. (1968). *How to increase motivation through climate and structure* (Working Paper No. 8-313). Cambridge, MA: Achievement Motivation Development Project, Graduate School of Education, Harvard University.

Alvidrez, J., & Weinstein, R. (1999). Early teacher perceptions and later student academic achievement. *Journal of Educational Psychology, 91,* 731–746.

Amabile, T. (1983). *The social psychology of creativity.* New York: Springer-Verlag.

Amabile, T., DeJong, W., & Lepper, M. (1976). Effects of externally imposed deadlines on subsequent intrinsic motivation. *Journal of Personality and Social Psychology, 34,* 92–98.

Amabile, T., & Hennessey, B. (1992). The motivation for creativity in children. In A. Boggiano & T. Pittman (Eds.), *Achievement and motivation: A social-developmental perspective* (pp. 54–74). Cambridge: Cambridge University Press.

Ames, C. (1981). Competitive versus cooperative reward structure: The influence of individual and group performance factors on achievement attributions and affect. *American Educational Research Journal, 18,* 273–288.

Ames, C. (1984). Competitive, cooperative and individualistic goal structures: A cognitive-motivational analysis. In R. Ames & C. Ames (Eds.), *Research on motivation in education: Vol. 1, Student motivation* (pp. 177–207). New York: Academic Press.

Ames, C. (1986). Conceptions of motivation within competitive and noncompetitive goal structures. In R. Schwarzer (Ed.), *Self-related cognitions in anxiety and motivation* (pp. 229–245). Hillsdale, NJ: Erlbaum.

Ames, C. (1992). Classrooms: Goals, structures, and student motivation. *Journal of Educational Psychology, 84,* 261–271.

Ames, C., & Ames, R. (1981). Competitive versus individualistic goal structures: The salience of past performance information for causal attributions and affect. *Journal of Educational Psychology, 73,* 411–418.

Ames, C., & Ames, R. (1984). Goal structures and motivation. *Elementary School Journal, 85,* 39–52.

Ames, C., & Ames, R. (1990). Motivation and effective teaching. In L. Friedman (Ed.), *Good instruction: What teachers can do in the classroom.* North Central Regional Education Laboratory.

Ames, C., & Archer, J. (1988). Achievement goals in the classroom: Students' learning strategies and motivation processes. *Journal of Educational Psychology, 80,* 260–267.

Ames, C., & Felker, D. (1979). An examination of children's attribution and achievement-related evaluations in competitive, cooperative, and individualistic reward structures. *Journal of Educational Psychology, 71,* 413–420.

Anderman, E., & Maehr, M. (1994). Motivation and schooling in the middle grades. *Review of Educational Research, 65,* 287–309.

Anderman, E., Maehr, M., & Midgley, C. (1999). Declining motivation after the transition to middle school: Schools can make a difference. *Journal of Research and Development in Education, 32,* 131–147.

Anderson, L. (1981). Short-term students' responses to classroom instruction. *Elementary School Journal, 82,* 97–108.

Anderson, L. (1984). The environment of instruction: The function of seatwork in a commercially developed curriculum. In G. Duffy, L. Roehler, & J. Mason (Eds.), *Comprehensive instruction: Perspectives and suggestions* (pp. 93–103). New York: Longmans.

Anderson, L., & Burns, R. (1987). Values, evidence, and mastery learning. *Review of Educational Research, 57,* 215–223.

Anderson, L., Evertson, C., & Brophy, J. (1979). An experimental study of effective teaching in first-grade reading groups. *Elementary School Journal, 79,* 193–223.

Anderson, R. (1982). Allocation of attention during reading. In A. Flammer & W. Kintsch (Eds.), *Discourse processing* (pp. 292–305). New York: North-Holland.

Anderson, R., Shirey, L., Wilson, P., & Fielding, L.

(1987). Interestingness of children's reading material. In R. Snow & M. Farr (Eds.), *Aptitude, learning, and instruction, Volume III: Cognitive and affective process analyses* (pp. 287–299). Hillsdale, NJ: Erlbaum.

Anderson, S., & Sauser, W. (1995). Measurement of test anxiety: An overview. In C. Spielberger & P. Vagg (Eds.), *Test anxiety: Theory, assessment, and treatment* (pp. 15–33). Washington, DC: Taylor & Francis.

Anton, W., & Klisch, M. (1995). Perspectives on mathematics anxiety and test anxiety. In C. Spielberger & P. Vagg (Eds.), *Test anxiety: Theory, assessment, and treatment* (pp. 93–106). Washington, DC: Taylor & Francis.

Anton, W., & Lillibridge, E. M. (1995). Case studies of test-anxious students. In C. Spielberger & P. Vagg (Eds.), *Test anxiety: Theory, assessment, and treatment* (pp. 61–78). Washington, DC: Taylor & Francis.

Apple, M., & King, N. (1978). What do schools teach? In G. Willis (Ed.), *Qualitative evaluation: Concepts and cases in curriculum criticism* (pp. 444–465). Berkeley, CA: McCutchan.

Arbreton, A. (1998). Student goal orientation and help-seeking strategy use. In S. Karabenick (Ed.), *Strategic help seeking: Implications for learning and teaching* (pp. 95–116). Mahwah, NJ: Erlbaum.

Aronfreed, J. (1969). The concept of internalization. In D. Goslin (Ed.), *Handbook of socialization theory and research* (pp. 263–323). New York: Rand-McNally.

Aronson, E., Stephan, C., Sikes, J., Blaney, N., & Snapp, M. (1978). *The jigsaw classroom.* Beverly Hills, CA: Sage Publications.

Ashton, P., & Webb, R. (1986). *Making a difference: Teachers' sense of efficacy and student achievement.* New York: Longman.

Atkinson, J. (1964). *An introduction to motivation.* Princeton, NJ: Van Nostrand.

Babad, E. (1990). Measuring and changing teachers' differential behavior as perceived by students and teachers. *Journal of Educational Psychology, 82,* 683–690.

Babad, E. (1992). Teacher expectancies and nonverbal behavior. In R. Feldman (Ed.), *Applications of nonverbal behavioral theories and research* (pp. 167–190). Hillsdale, NJ: Erlbaum Associates.

Baker, J. (1998). The social context of school satisfaction among urban, low-income African-American students. *School Psychology Quarterly, 13,* 25–44.

Baker, J. (1999). Teacher-student interaction in urban at-risk classrooms: Differential behavior, relationship quality, and student satisfaction with school. *The Elementary School Journal, 100,* 57–70.

Baker, J., Terry, T., Bridger, R., & Winsor, A. (1997). Schools as caring communities: A relational approach to school reform. *School Psychology Review, 26,* 586–602.

Baker, L., & Wigfield, A. (1999). Dimensions of children's motivation for reading and their relations to reading activity and reading achievement. *Reading Research Quarterly, 34,* 452–477.

Ball, D. (1993). With an eye on the mathematical horizon: Dilemmas of teaching elementary school mathematics. *The Elementary School Journal, 93,* 373–397.

Ball, S. (1995). Anxiety and test performance. In C. Spielberger & P. Vagg (Eds.), *Test anxiety: Theory, assessment, and treatment* (pp. 107–113). Washington, DC: Taylor & Francis.

Bandalos, D., Yates, K., & Thorndike-Christ, T. (1995). Effects of math self-concept, perceived self-efficacy, and attributions for failure and success on test anxiety. *Journal of Educational Psychology, 87,* 611–623.

Bandura, A. (1965). Influence of models' reinforcement contingencies on the acquisition of imitative responses. *Journal of Personality and Social Psychology, 1,* 589–595.

Bandura, A. (1977). *Social learning theory.* Englewood Cliffs, NJ: Prentice Hall.

Bandura, A. (1982). Self-efficacy mechanism in human agency. *American Psychologist, 37,* 122–147.

Bandura, A. (1986). *Social foundations of thought and action: Social cognitive theory.* Englewood Cliffs, NJ: Prentice Hall.

Bandura, A. (1988). Self efficacy conception of anxiety. *Anxiety Research: An International Journal, 1,* 77–98.

Bandura, A. (1991). Self-regulation of motivation through anticipatory and self-regulatory mechanisms. In R. Dienstbier (Ed.), *Perspectives on motivation: Nebraska Symposium on Motivation, Vol. 38* (pp. 237–288). Lincoln: University of Nebraska Press.

Bandura, A. (1992a). Exercise of personal agency through the self-efficacy mechanism. In R. Schwarzer (Ed.), *Self-efficacy: Thought control of action* (pp. 3–64). Washington: Hemisphere Publishing.

Bandura, A. (1992b). Social cognitive theory of social referencing. In S. Feinman (Ed.), *Social referencing and the social construction of reality in infancy* (pp. 175–208). New York: Plenum Press.

Bandura, A. (1993). Perceived self-efficacy in cognitive development and functioning. *Educational Psychologist, 28,* 117–148.

Bandura, A. (1995). Exercise of personal and collective efficacy in changing societies. In A. Bandura (Ed.), *Self-efficacy in changing societies* (pp. 1–45). New York: Cambridge University Press.

Bandura, A. (1997). *Self-efficacy: The exercise of control.* New York: Freeman.

Bandura, A., Barbaranelli, C., Caprara, G., & Pastorelli, C. (1996). Multifaceted impact of self-efficacy beliefs on academic functioning. *Child Development, 67,* 1206–1222.

Bandura, A., & Schunk, D. (1981). Cultivating competence, self-efficacy, and intrinsic interests through proximal self-motivation. *Journal of Personality and Social Psychology, 41,* 586–598.

Bandura, A., & Walters, R. (1963). *Social learning and personality development*. New York: Holt, Rinehart, & Winston.

Barker, G., & Graham, S. (1987). Developmental study of praise and blame as attributional cues. *Journal of Educational Psychology, 79*, 62–66.

Baron, R., Tom, D., & Cooper, H. (1985). Social class, race, and teacher expectations. In J. Dusek (Ed.), *Teacher Expectations* (pp. 251–269). Hillsdale, NJ: Erlbaum.

Barwick, N. (1995). Pandora's box: An investigation of essay anxiety in adolescents. *Psychodynamic Counselling, 1*, 560–575.

Basile, D. (1982). Do attitudes about writing change as composition skills improve? *Community College Review, 9*, 22–27.

Battistich, V., Solomon, D., Kim, D., Watson, M., & Schaps, E. (1995). Schools as communities, poverty levels of student populations, and students' attitudes, motives, and performance: A multilevel analysis. *American Educational Research Journal, 32*, 627–658.

Baumert, J., Evans, R., & Geiser, H. (1998). Technical problem solving among 10-year-old students as related to science achievement, out-of-school experience, domain specific control beliefs, and attribution patterns. *Journal of Research in Science Teaching, 35*, 987–1013.

Becker, J. (1981). Differential treatment of females and males in mathematics classes. *Journal for Research in Mathematics Education, 12*, 40–53.

Bedell, J., & Marlowe, H. (1995). An evaluation of test anxiety scales: Convergent, divergent, and predictive validity. In C. Spielberger & P. Vagg (Eds.), *Test anxiety: Theory, assessment, and treatment* (pp. 35–45). Washington, DC: Taylor & Francis.

Benjamin, M., McKeachie, W., & Lin, Y-G. (1987). Two types of test anxious students: Support for an information processing model. *Journal of Educational Psychology, 59*, 128–132.

Benjamin, M., McKeachie, W., Lin, Y-G., & Holinger, D. (1981). Test anxiety: Deficits in information processing. *Journal of Educational Psychology, 73*, 816–824.

Bennett, T., & Flores, M. (1998). Help giving in achievement contexts: A developmental and cultural analysis of the effects of children's attributions and affects on their willingness to help. *Journal of Educational Psychology, 90*, 659–669.

Benware, C., & Deci, E. (1984). Quality of learning with an active versus passive motivational set. *American Educational Research Journal, 21*, 755–765.

Bergin, D. (1999). Influences on classroom interest. *Educational Psychologist, 34*, 87–98.

Berlyne, D. (1966). Curiosity and exploration. *Science, 153*, 25–33.

Berry, J., & West, R. (1993). Cognitive self-efficacy in relation to personal mastery and goal setting across the life-span. *International Journal of Behavioral Development, 16*, 351–379.

Betz, N. (1978). Prevalence, distribution, and correlates of math anxiety in college students. *Journal of Counseling Psychology, 25*, 441–448.

Black, A., & Deci, E. (2000). The effects of instructors' autonomy support and students' autonomous motivation on learning organic chemistry: A self-determination theory perspective. *Science Education, 84*, 740–756.

Block, J. (Ed.). (1974). *Schools, society, and mastery learning*. New York: Holt, Rinehart & Winston.

Block J. (1979). Mastery learning: The current state of the craft. *Educational Leadership, 37*, 114–117.

Block, J., Efthim, H., & Burns, R. (1989). *Building effective mastery learning schools*. New York: Longman.

Bloom, B. (1981). *All our children learning*. New York: McGraw-Hill.

Blumenfeld, P. (1992). Classroom learning and motivation: Clarifying and expanding goal theory. *Journal of Educational Psychology, 84*, 272–281.

Blumenfeld, P., Hamilton, V., Bossert, S., Wessels, K., & Meece, J. (1983). Teacher talk and student thought: Socialization into the student role. In J. M. Levine & M. C. Wang (Eds.), *Teacher and student perceptions: Implications for learning* (pp. 143–192). Hillsdale, NJ: Erlbaum.

Blumenfeld, P., Pintrich, P., & Hamilton, V. (1986). Children's concepts of ability, effort, and conduct. *American Educational Research Journal, 23*, 95–104.

Blumenfeld, P., Pintrich, P., Meece, J., & Wessels, K. (1982). The formation and role of self-perceptions of ability in elementary classrooms. *Elementary School Journal, 82*, 401–420.

Blumenfeld, P., Puro, P., & Mergendoller, J. (1992). Translating motivation into thoughtfulness. In H. Marshall (Ed.), *Redefining student learning: Roots of educational change* (pp. 207–239). Norwood, NJ: Ablex.

Blumenfeld, P., Soloway, E., Marx, R., Krajcik, J., Guzdial, M., & Palincsar, A. (1991). Motivation project-based learning: Sustaining the doing, supporting the learning. *Educational Psychologist, 26*, 369–398.

Boggiano, A., Pittman, T., & Ruble, D. (1982). The mastery hypothesis and the over-justification effect. *Social Cognition, 1*, 38–49.

Boggiano, A., & Ruble, D. (1979). Competence and the overjustification effect: A developmental study. *Journal of Personality and Social Psychology, 37*, 1462–1468.

Bong, M. (1997). Generality of academic self-efficacy judgments: Evidence of hierarchical relations. *Journal of Educational Psychology, 89*, 696–709.

Borko, H., & Eisenhart, M. (1986). Students' conceptions of reading and their experiences in school. *Elementary School Journal, 86*, 589–611.

Borkowski, J., Weyhing, R., & Carr, M. (1988). Effects of attributional retraining on strategy-based reading comprehension in learning-disabled students. *Journal of Educational Psychology. 80*, 46–53.

Bornstein, P., & Quevillon, R. (1976). The effects of a self-instructional package on overactive preschool boys. *Journal of Applied Behavior Analysis, 9*, 179–188.

Bossert, S. (1979). *Tasks and social relationships in classrooms.* (The Arnold and Caroline Rose Monograph Series of the American Sociological Association.) Cambridge: Cambridge University Press.

Bouffard-Bouchard, T. (1990). Influence of self-efficacy on performance in a cognitive task. *Journal of Social Psychology, 139*, 353–363.

Brattesani, K., Weinstein, R., & Marshall, H. (1984). Student perceptions of differential teacher treatment as moderators of teacher expectation effects. *Journal of Educational Psychology, 76*, 236–247.

Brockner, J. (1979). Self-esteem, self-consciousness, and task performance: Replications, extensions, and possible explanations. *Journal of Personality and Social Psychology, 37*, 447–461.

Brophy, J. (1981). Teacher praise: A functional analysis. *Review of Educational Research, 51*, 5–32.

Brophy, J. (1983a). Fostering student learning and motivation in the elementary school classroom. In S. Paris, G. Olson, & H. Stevenson (Eds.), *Learning and motivation in the classroom* (pp. 283–305). Hillsdale, NJ: Erlbaum.

Brophy, J. (1983b). Research on the self-fulfilling prophecy and teacher expectations. *Journal of Educational Psychology, 75*, 631–661.

Brophy, J. (1985). Interactions of male and female students with male and female teachers. In L. Wilkinson & C. Marrett (Eds.), *Gender influences in classroom interaction* (pp. 115–142). Hillsdale, NJ: Erlbaum Associates.

Brophy, J. (1986). *Socializing student motivation to learn.* (Institute for Research Teaching Research Series No. 169.) East Lansing, Michigan: Michigan State University.

Brophy, J. (1987). On motivating students. In D. Berliner & B. Rosenshine (Eds.), *Talks to teachers* (pp. 201–245). New York: Random House.

Brophy, J., & Alleman, J. (1991). A caveat: Curriculum integration isn't always a good idea. *Educational Leadership, 49*, 66.

Brophy, J., & Evertson, C. (1978). Context variables in teaching. *Educational Psychologist, 12*, 310–316.

Brophy, J., Evertson, C., Anderson, L., Baum, M., & Crawford, J. (1976). *Student personality and teaching: Final report of the Student Attribute Study.* Educational Resources Information Center, (ERIC Document Reproduction Service No. ED 121 799).

Brophy, J., & Rohrkemper, M. (1981). The influence of problem ownership on teachers' perceptions of and strategies for coping with problem students. *Journal of Educational Psychology, 73*, 295–311.

Brophy, J., Rohrkemper, M., Rashid, H., & Goldberger, M. (1983). Relationships between teachers' presentations of classroom tasks and students' engagements in those tasks. *Journal of Educational Psychology, 75*, 544–552.

Brouwers, A., & Welko, T. (2000). A longitudinal study of teacher burnout and perceived self-efficacy in classroom management. *Teaching and Teacher Education, 16*, 239–253.

Bruch, M., Juster, H., & Kaflowitz, N. (1983). Relationships of cognitive components of test anxiety to test performance: Implications for assessment and treatment. *Journal of Counseling Psychology, 30*, 527–536.

Bruner, J. (1966). *Toward a theory of instruction.* Cambridge, MA: Harvard University Press.

Bryk, A., Lee, V., & Holland, P. (1993). *Catholic schools and the common good.* Cambridge, MA: Harvard University Press.

Burhans, K., & Dweck, C. (1995). Helplessness in early childhood: The role of contingent worth. *Child Development, 66*, 1719–1738.

Burns, M. (1987). *A collection of math lessons: From grades 3 through 6.* New York: Cuisennaire.

Butler, D. (1998a). The strategic content learning approach to promoting self-regulated learning. In B. Zimmerman & D. Schunk (Eds.), *Developing self-regulated learning: From teaching to self-reflective practice* (pp. 160–183). New York: Guilford Press.

Butler, D. (1998b). The strategic content learning approach to promoting self-regulated learning: A report of three studies. *Journal of Educational Psychology, 90*, 682–697.

Butler, R. (1987). Task-involving and ego-involving properties of evaluation: Effects of different feedback conditions on motivational perceptions, interest, and performance. *Journal of Educational Psychology, 79*, 474–482.

Butler, R. (1988). Enhancing and undermining intrinsic motivation: The effects of task-involving and ego-involving evaluation on interest and performance. *British Journal of Educational Psychology, 58*, 1–14.

Butler, R. (1989). Mastery versus ability appraisal: A developmental study of children's observations of peers' work. *Child Development, 60*, 1350–1361.

Butler, R. (1992). What young people want to know when: Effects of mastery and ability goals on interest in different kinds of social comparisons, *Journal of Personality and Social Psychology, 62*, 934–943.

Butler, R. (1994). Teacher communications and student interpretations: Effects of teacher responses to failing students on attributional inferences in two age groups. *British Journal of Educational Psychology, 64*, 277–294.

Butler, R. (1995). Motivational and informational functions and consequences of children's attention to peers' work. *Journal of Educational Psychology, 87*, 347–360.

Butler, R. (1998). Determinants of help seeking: Relations between perceived reasons for classroom help-avoidance and help seeking behaviors in an experimental context. *Journal of Educational Psychology, 90*, 630–643.

Butler, R. (1999). Information seeking and achievement motivation in middle childhood and adolescence: The role of conceptions of ability. *Developmental Psychology, 35,* 146–163.

Butler, R., & Nisan, M. (1986). Effects of no feedback, task-related comments, and grades on intrinsic motivation and performance. *Journal of Educational Psychology, 78,* 210–216.

Butler, R., & Neuman, O. (1995). Effects of task and ego achievement goals on help-seeking behaviors and attitudes. *Journal of Educational Psychology, 87,* 261–171.

Butler, R., & Ruzany, N. (1993). Age and socialization effects on the development of social comparison motives and normative ability assessment in kibbutz and urban children. *Child Development, 64,* 532–543.

Byrne, B. (1996). Academic self-concept: Its structure, measurement, and relation to academic achievement. In B. Bracken (Ed.), *Handbook of self-concept: Developmental, social, & clinical considerations* (pp. 287–316). New York: John Wiley & Sons.

Byrne, B., & Gavin, D. (1996). The Shavelson model revisited: Testing for the structure of academic self-concept across pre-, early, and late adolescents. *Journal of Educational Psychology, 88,* 215–228.

Cain, K., & Dweck, C. (1989). The development of children's conceptions of intelligence: A theoretical framework. In R. Sternberg (Ed.), *Advances in the psychology of human intelligence, Vol. 5* (pp. 47–82). Hillsdale, NJ: Erlbaum.

Cameron, J., & Pierce, W. (1994). Reinforcement, reward, and intrinsic motivation: A meta-analysis. *Review of Educational Research, 64,* 363–423.

Carnegie Council on Adolescent Development (1989). *Turning points: Preparing American youth for the 21st century.* New York: Carnegie Corporation.

Carpenter, T., Corbitt, M., Kepner, H., Lindquist, M., & Reys, R. (1981). *Results from the second mathematics assessment of the National Assessment of Educational Progress.* Reston, VA: National Council of Teachers of Mathematics.

Casady, M. (1975). The tricky business of giving rewards. *Psychology Today, 8,* 52.

Chen, C., & Stevenson, H. (1995). Motivation and mathematics achievement: A comparative study of Asian-American, Caucasian-American, and east Asian high school students. *Child Development, 66,* 1215–1234.

Chester, M., & Beaudin, B. (1996). Efficacy beliefs of newly hired teachers in urban schools. *American Educational Research Journal, 33,* 233–257.

Clark, M. (1997). Teacher response to learning disability: A test of attributional principles. *Journal of Learning Disabilities, 30,* 69–79.

Clifford, M. (1988). Failure tolerance and academic risk-taking in ten- to twelve-year-old students. *British Journal of Educational Psychology, 58,* 15–27.

Clifford, M. (1991). Risk taking: Theoretical, empirical, and educational considerations. *Educational Psychologist, 26,* 263–297.

Cochran, L., Feng, H., Cartledge, G., & Hamilton, S. (1993). The effects of cross-age tutoring on the academic achievement, social behaviors, and self-perceptions of low-achieving African males with behavioral disorders. *Behavioral Disorders, 18,* 292–302.

Cohen, E. (1994). *Designing groupwork: Strategies for heterogeneous classrooms* (2nd ed.). New York: Teachers College Press.

Cohen, E., Bianchini, J., Cossey, R, Holthuis, N., Morphew, C., & Whitcomb, J. (1997). What did students learn?: 1982–1994. In E. Cohen & R. Lotan (1997). *Working for equity in heterogeneous classrooms* (pp. 137–165). New York: Teachers College Press.

Cohen, E., & Lotan, R. (1995). Producing equal-status interaction in the heterogeneous classroom. *American Educational Research Journal, 32,* 99–120.

Cohen, E., & Lotan, R. (1997). *Working for equity in heterogeneous classrooms.* New York: Teachers College Press.

Cohen, H. (1973). Behavior modification in socially deviant youth. In C. Thoresen (Ed.), *Behavior modification in education: Seventy-second yearbook of the National Society for the Study of Education, 72, Part I* (pp. 291–314). Chicago: University of Chicago Press.

Coladarci, T., & Breton, W. (1997). Teacher efficacy, supervision, and the special education resource-room teacher. *Journal of Educational Research, 90,* 230–239.

Cole, D., Martin, J., Peeke, L., Seroczynski, A., & Fier, J. (1999). Children's over- and underestimation of academic competence: A longitudinal study of gender differences, depression, and anxiety. *Child Development, 70,* 459–473.

Collins, J. (1982, March). *Self-efficacy and ability in achievement behavior.* Paper presented at the annual meeting of the American Educational Research Association, New York.

Comer, J. (1993). *School power: Implications of an intervention project.* New York: Free Press.

Connell, J. (1985). A new multidimensional measure of children's perceptions of control. *Child Development, 56,* 1018–1041.

Connell, J. (1991). Context, self, and action: A motivational analysis of self-system processes across the life span. In D. Cicchetti & M. Beeghly (Eds.), *The self in transition: Infancy to childhood* (pp. 61–97). Chicago: University of Chicago Press.

Connell, J., & Ryan, R. (1984). A developmental theory of motivation in the classroom. *Teacher Education Quarterly, 11,* 64–77.

Connell, J., Spencer, M., & Aber, L. (1994). Educational risk and resilience in African-American youth: Context, self, action, and outcomes in school. *Child Development, 65,* 493–506.

Connell, J., & Wellborn, J. (1991). Competence, autonomy, and relatedness: A motivational analysis of self-system processes. In M. Gunnar & L. Sroufe (Eds.), *Self processes in development: Minnesota Symposium on Child Psychology, Vol. 23* (pp. 43–77). Hillsdale, NJ: Erlbaum.

Cooper, H., & Tom, D. (1984). Teacher expectations research: A review with implications for classroom instruction. *Elementary School Journal, 85,* 77–89.

Cordova, D., & Lepper, M. (1996). Intrinsic motivation and the process of learning: Beneficial effects of contextualization, personalization, and choice. *Journal of Educational Psychology, 88,* 715–730.

Corno, L. (1989). Self-regulated learning: A volitional analysis. In B. Zimmerman & D. Schunk (Eds.), *Self-regulated learning and academic achievement: Theory, research, and practice* (pp. 111–141). New York: Springer-Verlag.

Corno, L., & Randi, J. (1999). A design theory for classroom instruction in self-regulated learning. In C. Reigeluth (Ed.), *Instructional-design theories and models: A new paradigm of instructional theory, Vol. 2* (pp. 293–318). Mahwah, NJ: Erlbaum.

Corno, L., & Rohrkemper, M. (1985). The intrinsic motivation to learn in classrooms. In C. Ames & R. Ames (Eds.), *Research on motivation in education, Vol. 2: The classroom milieu* (pp. 53–90). Orlando, FL: Academic Press.

Cosden, M., & Haring, T. (1992). Cooperative learning in the classroom: Contingencies, group interactions, and students with special needs. *Journal of Behavioral Education, 2,* 53–71.

Covington, M. (1984). The self-worth theory of achievement motivation: Findings and implications. *The Elementary School Journal, 85,* 5–20.

Covington, M. (1992). *Making the grade: A self-worth perspective on motivation and school reform.* Cambridge: Cambridge University Press.

Covington, M. (1998). *The will to learn: A guide for motivating young people.* New York, NY: Cambridge University Press.

Covington, M. (1999). Caring about learning: The nature and nurturing of subject-matter appreciation. *Educational Psychologist, 34,* 127–136.

Covington, M., & Beery, R. (1976). *Self-worth and school learning.* New York: Holt, Rinehart and Winston.

Covington, M., & Omelich, C. (1979a). Effort: The double-edged sword in school achievement. *Journal of Educational Psychology, 71,* 169–182.

Covington, M., & Omelich, C. (1979b). It's best to be able and virtuous too: Student and teacher evaluative responses to successful effort. *Journal of Educational Psychology, 71,* 688–700.

Covington, M., & Omelich, C. (1981). As failures mount: Affective and cognitive consequences of ability demotion in the classroom. *Journal of Educational Psychology, 73,* 796–808.

Covington, M., & Omelich, C. (1984a). An empirical examination of Weiner's critique of attribution research. *Journal of Educational Psychology, 76,* 1214–1225.

Covington, M., & Omelich, C. (1984b). Task-oriented versus competitive learning structures: Motivational and performance consequences. *Journal of Educational Psychology, 7,* 1038–1050.

Covington, M., & Omelich, C. (1988). Achievement dynamics: The interaction of motives, cognitions, and emotions over time. *Anxiety Research, 1,* 165–183.

Covington, M., Spratt, M., & Omelich, C. (1980). Is effort enough or does diligence count too? Student and teacher reactions to effort stability in failure. *Journal of Educational Psychology, 72,* 717–729.

Cramer, J., & Oshima, T. (1992). Do gifted females attribute their math performance differently than other students? *Journal for the Education of the Gifted, 16,* 18–35.

Crandall, V. C. (1967). Achievement behavior in young children. In W. W. Hartup & N. L. Smothergill (Eds.), *The young child: Reviews of Research* (pp. 165–185). Washington, DC: National Association for the Education of Young Children.

Crandall, V. J. (1963). Achievement. In H. Stevenson (Ed.), *Child psychology: Sixty-second yearbook of the National Society for the Study of Education* (pp. 416–459). Chicago: University of Chicago Press.

Crandall, V., Katkovsky, W., & Crandall, V. (1965). Children's beliefs in their own control of reinforcement in intellectual-academic achievement situations. *Child Development, 36,* 91–109.

Crockenberg, S., & Bryant, B. (1978). Socialization: The "implicit curriculum" of learning environments. *Journal of Research Development in Education, 12,* 69–78.

Csikszentmihalyi, M. (1975). *Beyond boredom and anxiety.* San Francisco: Jossey Bass.

Csikszentmihalyi, M. (1988). The flow experience and its significance for human psychology. In M. Csikszentmihalyi & I. Csikszentmi-halyi (Eds.), *Optimal experience* (pp. 15–35). Cambridge, MA: Cambridge University Press.

Daly, J. (1985). Writing apprehension. In M. Rose (Ed.), *When a writer can't write* (pp. 43–82). New York: Guilford Press.

Daly, J., & Miller, M. (1975a). The empirical development of an instrument to measure writing apprehension. *Research in the teaching of English, 9,* 242–249.

Daly, J., & Miller, M. (1975b). Further studies in writing apprehension: SAT scores, success expectations, willingness to take advanced courses, and sex differences. *Research in the teaching of English, 9,* 250–256.

Daly, J., Vangelisti, A., & Witte, S. (1988). Writing apprehension in the classroom context. In B. Rafoth & D. Rubin (Eds.), *The social construction of written communication* (pp. 147–171). Norwood, NJ: Ablex Publishing.

Damon, W. (1995). *Greater expectations: Overcoming the culture of indulgence in America's homes and schools.* New York: Free Press.

Danner, F., & Lonky, E. (1981). A cognitive-developmental approach to the effects of rewards on intrinsic motivation. *Child Development, 52,* 1043–1052.

Deaux, K. (1976). Sex: A perspective on the attributional process. In J. Harvey, W. Ickes, & R. Kidd (Eds.), *New directions in attribution research: Vol. 1* (pp. 335–352). Hillsdale, NJ: Erlbaum.

deCharms, R. (1976). *Enhancing motivation change in the classroom.* New York: Irvington Publishers.

deCharms, R. (1983). Intrinsic motivation, peer tutoring, and cooperative learning: Practical maxims. In J. Levine & M. Wang (Eds.), *Teacher and student perceptions: Implications for learning* (pp. 391–398). Hillsdale, NJ: Erlbaum.

deCharms, R. (1984). Motivating enhancement in educational settings. In R. Ames & C. Ames (Eds.), *Research on motivation in education, Vol. 1: Student motivation* (pp. 275–310). New York: Academic Press.

Deci, E. (1971). The effects of externally mediated rewards on intrinsic motivation. *Journal of Personality and Social Psychology, 18,* 105–115.

Deci, E. (1975). *Intrinsic Motivation.* New York: Plenum.

Deci, E. (1992). The relation of interest to the motivation of behavior: A self-determination theory perspective. In K. Renninger, S. Hidi, & A. Krapp (Eds.), *The role of interest in learning and development* (pp. 43–70). Hillsdale, NJ: Erlbaum.

Deci, E., Koestner, R., & Ryan, R. (1999). A meta-analytic review of experiments examining the effects of extrinsic rewards on intrinsic motivation. *Psychological Bulletin, 125,* 627–668.

Deci, E., Nezlek, J., & Sheinman, L. (1981). Characteristics of the rewarder and intrinsic motivation of the rewardee. *Journal of Personality and Social Psychology, 40,* 1–10.

Deci, E., & Ryan, R. (1985). *Intrinsic motivation and self-determination in human behavior.* New York: Plenum Press.

Deci, E., & Ryan, R. (1987). The support of autonomy and the control of behavior. *Journal of Personality and Social Psychology, 53,* 1024–1037.

Deci, E., & Ryan, R. (1991). A motivational approach to self: Integration in personality. In R. Dienstbier (Ed.), *Nebraska Symposium on motivation, 1990: Perspectives on motivation. Current theory and research in motivation,* Vol. 38. Lincoln, NE: University of Nebraska Press.

Deci, E., & Ryan, R. (1992). The initiation and regulation of intrinsically motivated learning and achievement. In A. Boggiano & T. Pittman (Eds.), *Achievement and motivation: A social-developmental perspective* (pp. 9–36). Cambridge: Cambridge University Press.

Deci, E., Schwartz, A., Sheinman, L., & Ryan, R. (1981). An instrument to assess adults' orientations toward control versus autonomy with children: Reflections on intrinsic motivation and perceived competence. *Journal of Educational Psychology, 73,* 642–650.

Deci, E., Spiegel, N., Ryan, R., Koestner, R., & Kauffman, M. (1982). Effects of performance standards on teaching styles: Behavior of controlling teachers. *Journal of Educational Psychology, 74,* 852–859.

Deci, E., Vallerand, R., Pelletier, L., & Ryan, R. (1991). Motivation and education: The self-determination perspective. *The Educational Psychologist, 26,* 325–346.

Delgado-Gaitan, C. (1993). Parenting in two generations of Mexican American families. *International Journal of Behavior Development, 16,* 409–427.

De Martini-Scully, D., Bray, M., & Kehle, T. (2000). Strategies for behavioral change: A packaged intervention to reduce disruptive behaviors in general education students. *Psychology in the Schools, 37,* 149–156.

Dembo, M., & Eaton, M. (2000). Self-regulation of academic learning in middle-level schools. *The Elementary School Journal, 100,* 473–490.

Demster, F., & Corkill, A. (1999). Interference and inhibition in cognition and behavior: Unifying themes for educational psychology. *Educational Psychology Review, 11,* 1–88.

Dendato, K., & Diener, D. (1986). Effectiveness of cognitive/relaxation therapy and study-skills training in reducing self-reported anxiety and improving the academic performance of test-anxious students. *Journal of Counseling Psychology, 33,* 131–135.

Dev, P. (1998). Intrinsic motivation and the student with learning disabilities. *Journal of Research and Development in Education, 31,* 98–108.

Diaz, R., & Berk, L. (1999). A Vygotskian critique of self-instructional training. In P. Lloyd & C. Fernyhough (Eds.), *Lev Vygotsky: Critical assessments: Future directions, Vol. IV* (pp. 221–252). New York, NY: Routledge.

Diener, C., & Dweck, C. (1978). An analysis of learned helplessness: Continuous changes in performance, strategy, and achievement cognitions following failure. *Journal of Personality and Social Psychology, 36,* 451–462.

Diener, C., & Dweck, C. (1980). An analysis of learned helplessness, Vol. II. The processing of success. *Journal of Personality and Social Psychology, 39,* 940–952.

Dulany, D. (1968). Awareness, rules, and propositional control: A confrontation with S-R behavior theory. In T. Dixon & D. Horton (Eds.), *Verbal behavior and general behavior theory* (pp. 340–387), Englewood Cliffs, NJ: Prentice Hall.

Dunn, P., & Shapiro, S. (1999). Gender differences in the achievement goal orientations of ADHD children. *Cognitive Therapy and Research, 23,* 327–344.

Dusek, J. (1975). Do teachers bias children's learning? *Review of Educational Research, 45,* 661–684.

Dusek, J. (Ed.) (1985). *Teacher expectancies.* Hillsdale, NJ: Erlbaum.

Dusek, J., & Joseph, G. (1983). The bases of teacher

expectancies: A meta-analysis. *Journal of Educational Psychology, 75,* 327–346.

Dusek, J., Kermis, M., & Mergler, N. (1975). Information processing in low- and high-test-anxious children as a function of grade level and verbal labeling. *Developmental Psychology, 11,* 651–652.

Dusek, J., Mergler, N., & Kermis, M. (1976). Attention, encoding, and information processing in low- and high-test-anxious children. *Child Development, 47,* 201–207.

Dweck, C. (1975). The role of expectations and attributions in the alleviation of learned helplessness. *Journal of Personality and Social Psychology, 31,* 674–685.

Dweck, C. (1986). Motivational processes affecting learning. *American Psychologist, 41,* 1040–1048.

Dweck, C. (2000). *Self-theories: Their role in motivation, personality, and development.* Philadelphia, PA: Psychology Press.

Dweck, C. (in press). The development of ability conceptions. In A. Wigfield & J. Eccles (Eds.), *The Development of Achievement Motivation.* San Diego: Academic Press.

Dweck, C., & Bempechat, J. (1983). Children's theories of intelligence: Consequences for learning. In S. Paris, G. Olson, & H. Stevenson (Eds.), *Learning and motivation in the classroom* (pp. 239–255). Hillsdale, NJ: Erlbaum.

Dweck, C., & Elliott, E. (1983). Achievement motivation. In P. Mussen (Ed.), *Handbook of child psychology, Vol. IV: Socialization, personality, and social development* (pp. 643–691). New York: Wiley.

Dweck, C., & Goetz, T. (1978). Attributions and learned helplessness. In W. Harvey & R. Kidd (Eds.), *New directions in attribution research, Vol. 2* (pp. 157–179). Hillsdale, NJ: Erlbaum.

Dweck, C., & Leggett, E. (1988). A social-cognitive approach to motivation and personality. *Psychological Review, 95,* 256–273.

Dweck, C., & Reppucci, N. (1973). Learned helplessness and reinforcement responsibility in children. *Journal of Personality and Social Psychology, 25,* 109–116.

Dweck, C., & Sorich, L. (1999). Mastery-oriented thinking. In C.R. Snyder (Ed.), *Coping: The psychology of what works* (pp. 232–251). New York: Oxford University Press.

Eccles, J. (1980). Self-perceptions, task perceptions, and academic choice: Origins and change. Final Report to National Institute of Education. Washington, DC.

Eccles, J. (1984). Sex differences in achievement patterns. In T. Sonderegger (Ed.), *Nebraska Symposium on Motivation, Vol. 32* (pp. 97–132). Lincoln, NE: University of Nebraska Press.

Eccles, J. (1993). School and family effects on the ontogeny of children's interests, self-perceptions, and activity choice. In J. Jacobs (Ed.), *Nebraska Symposium on Motivation, 1992: Developmental*

perspectives on motivation (pp. 145–208). Lincoln, NE: University of Nebraska Press.

Eccles, J. (1994). Understanding women's educational and occupational choices: Applying the Ecccles et al. model of achievement-related choices. *Psychology of Women Quarterly, 18,* 585–609.

Eccles, J., Adler, T., Futterman, R., Goff, S., Kaczala, C., Meece, J., & Midgley, C. (1983). Expectancies, values, and academic behavior. In J. T. Spence (Ed.), *Achievement and achievement motives: Psychological and sociological approaches* (pp. 75–146). San Francisco: Freeman.

Eccles, J., Barber, B., & Jozefowicz, D. (1998). Linking gender to educational, occupational, and recreational choices: Applying the Eccles et al. model of achievement-related choices. In W. Swann, J. Langlois, & L. Gilbert (Eds.), *Sexism and stereotypes in modern society: The gender science of Janet Taylor Spence* (pp. 153–192). Washington, DC: APA Press.

Eccles, J., Barber, B., Jozefowicz, D., Malenchuk, O., & Vida, M. (2000). Self-evaluations of competence, task values, and self-esteem. In N. Johnson, M. Roberts, & J. Worrell (Eds.), *Girls and adolescence* (pp. 53–84). Washington, DC: APA Press.

Eccles, J., & Blumenfeld, P. (1985). Classroom experiences and student gender: Are there differences and do they matter? In L. Wilkinson & C. Marrett (Eds.), *Gender influences in classroom interaction* (pp. 79–114). Hillsdale, NJ: Erlbaum Associates.

Eccles, J., Early, D., Fraser, K., Belansky, E., & McCarthy, K. (1997). The relation of connection, regulation, and support for autonomy to adolescents' functioning. *Journal of Adolescent Research, 12,* 263–286.

Eccles, J., & Midgley, C. (1989). Stage environment fit: Developmentally appropriate classrooms for early adolescents. In R. Ames & C. Ames (Eds.), *Research on motivation in education, Vol. 3: Goals and cognitions* (pp. 139–186). New York: Academic Press.

Eccles, J., & Roeser, R. (1999). School and community influence on human development. In M. Bornstein & M. Lamb (Eds.), *Developmental psychology: An advanced textbook* (pp. 503–554). Mahwah, NY: Erlbaum.

Eccles, J., Roeser, R., Wigfield, A., & Freedman-Doan, C. (1999). Academic and motivational pathways through middle childhood. In L. Balter & C. Tamis-LeMonda (Eds.), *Child Psychology: A handbook of contemporary issues* (pp. 287–317). Philadelphia, PA: Psychology Press.

Eccles, J., & Wigfield, A. (1995). In the mind of the actor: The structure of adolescents' achievement task values and expectancy-related beliefs. *Personality and Social Psychology Bulletin, 21,* 215–225.

Eccles, J., & Wigfield, A. (2000). Schooling's influences on motivation and achievement. In S. Danzinger & J. Waldfogel (Eds.), *Securing the future: Investing in children from birth to college* (pp. 153–181). New York: Russell Sage Foundation.

Eccles, J., & Wigfield, A. (in press). Students' motivation during the middle school years. In J. Aronson & D. Cordova (Eds.), *Improving academic achievement: Contributions of social psychology.* Orlando, FL: Academic Press.

Eccles, J., Wigfield, A., Harold, R., & Blumenfeld, P. (1993). Age and gender differences in children's self- and task perceptions during elementary school. *Child Development, 64,* 830–847.

Eccles, J., Wigfield, A., Midgley, C., Reuman, D., Mac Iver, D., & Feldlaufer, H. (1993). Negative effects of traditional middle schools on students' motivation. *The Elementary School Journal, 93,* 553–574.

Eccles, J., Wigfield, A., & Schiefele, U. (1997). Motivation to succeed. In B. Damon (Ed.), *Handbook of child psychology* (5th ed.): Vol. 3, *Social, emotional, and personality development* (pp. 1017–1095). New York: Wiley.

Eckert, P. (1989). *Jocks and burnouts: Social categories and identity in the high school.* New York: Teachers College Press.

Edelstein, W., Grundmann, M., & Mies, A. (2000). The development of internal versus external control beliefs in developmentally relevant contexts of children's and adolescents' lifeworlds. In W. Perrig & A. Grob (Eds), *Control of human behavior, mental processes, and consciousness: Essays in honor of the 60th birthday of August Flammer* (pp. 377–390). Mahway, NJ: Lawrence Erlbaum.

Eder, D. (1983). Ability grouping and students' academic self-concepts: A case study. *The Elementary School Journal, 84,* 149–161.

Eisenberger, R. (1992). Learned industriousness. *Psychological Review, 99,* 248–267.

Eisenberger, R. (1997). Can salient reward increase creative performance without reducing intrinsic creative interest? *Journal of Personality & Social Psychology, 72,* 652–663.

Elbaum, B., Schumm, J., & Vaughn, S. (1997). Urban middle-elementary students' perceptions of grouping formats for reading instruction. *The Elementary School Journal, 97,* 475–500.

Elliot, A. (1999). Approach and avoidance motivation and achievement goals. *Educational Psychologist, 34,* 169–191.

Elliot, A., & Harackiewicz, J. (1996). Approach and avoidance achievement goals and intrinsic motivation: A mediational analysis. *Journal of Personality and Social Psychology, 70,* 461–475.

Elliot, A., McGregor, H., & Gable, S. (1999). Achievement goals, study strategies, and exam performance: A mediational analysis. *Journal of Educational Psychology, 91,* 549–563.

Elliott, E., & Dweck, C. (1988). Goals: An approach to motivation and achievement. *Journal of Personality and Social Psychology, 54,* 5–12.

Entwisle, D., & Hayduk, L. (1978). *Too great expectations: The academic outlook of young children.* Baltimore, MD: Johns Hopkins University Press.

Estes, W. (1972). Reinforcement in human behavior. *American Scientist, 60,* 723–729.

Evans, K., & King, J. (1994). Research on ODE. What we know and don't know. *Educational Leadership, 51* (6), 1217.

Evans, L. (1997). Understanding teacher morale and job satisfaction. *Teaching and Teacher Education, 13,* 831–845.

Everson, H., Millsap, R., & Rodriguez, C. (1991). Isolating gender differences in test anxiety: A confirmatory factor analysis of the Test Anxiety Inventory. *Educational & Psychological Measurement, 51,* 243–251.

Everson, H., Smodlaka, I., & Tobias, S. (1994). Exploring the relationship of test anxiety and metacognition on reading test performance: A cognitive analysis. *Anxiety, Stress & Coping: An International Journal, 7,* 85–96.

Everson, H., Tobias, S., Hartman, H., & Gourgey, A. (1993). Test anxiety and the curriculum: The subject matters. *Anxiety, Stress & Coping: An International Journal, 6,* 1–8.

Eysenck, M. (1991). Anxiety and attention. In R. Schwarzer & R. A.Wicklund (Eds.), *Anxiety and self-focused attention* (pp. 125–131). New York: Harwood Academic.

Fagot, B. (1973). Influence of teacher behavior in the preschool. *Developmental Psychology, 9,* 196–206.

Fantuzzo, J., McDermott, P., Manz, P., Hampton, V., & Burdick, N. (1996). The pictorial scale of perceived competence and social acceptance: Does it work with low-income urban children? *Child Development, 67,* 1071–1084.

Fantuzzo, J., & Polite, K. (1990). School-based, behavioral self-management: A review and analysis. *School Psychology Quarterly, 5,* 180–198.

Farnham-Diggory, S., & Ramsey, B. (1971). Play persistence: Some effects of interruptions, social reinforcement, and defective toys. *Developmental Psychology, 4,* 297–298.

Feld, S., & Lewis, J. (1969). The assessment of achievement anxieties in children. In C. P. Smith (Ed.), *Achievement-related motives in children* (pp. 151–199). New York: Russell Sage Foundation.

Feldlaufer, H., Midgley, C., & Eccles, J. S. (1988). Student, teacher, and observer perceptions of the classroom environment before and after the transition to junior high school. *Journal of Early Adolescence, 8,* 133–156.

Felner, R., Jackson, A., Kasak, D., Mulhall, P., Brand, S., & Flowers, N. (1997). The impact of schol reform for the middle years: Longitudinal study of a network engaged in Turnin Points-based comprehensive school transformation. *Phi Delta Kappan, 78,* 528–532, 541–550.

Felson, R., & Reed, M. (1986). Reference groups and self-appraisals of academic ability and performance. *Social Psychology Quarterly, 49,* 103–109.

Fincham, F., Hokoda, A., & Sanders, R. (1989). Learned helplessness, test anxiety, and academic achievement: A longitudinal analysis. *Child Development, 60,* 138–145.

Fletcher, T., & Spielberger, C. (1995). Comparison of cognitive therapy and rational-emotive therapy in the treatment of test anxiety. In C. Spielberger & P. Vagg (Eds.), *Test anxiety: Theory, assessment, and treatment* (pp. 153–169). Washington, DC: Taylor & Francis.

Flink, C., Boggiano, A., & Barrett, M. (1990). Controlling teaching strategies: Undermining children's self-determination and performance. *Journal of Personality and Social Psychology, 59,* 916–924.

Flink, C., Boggiano, A., Main, D., Barrett, M., & Katz, P. (1992). Children's achievement-related behaviors: The role of extrinsic motivational orientations. In A. Boggiano & T. Pittman (Eds.), *Achievement and motivation: A social-developmental perspective* (pp. 189–214). Cambridge: Cambridge University Press.

Fogg, B., & Nass, C. (1997). Silicon sycophants: The effects of computers that flatter. *International Journal of Human-Computer Studies, 46,* 551–561.

Forsterling, F. (1985). Attributional retraining: A review. *Psychological Bulletin, 98,* 495–512.

Fox, K. (1980). Treatment of writing apprehension and its effects on composition. *Research in the Teaching of English, 14,* 39–49.

Freedman, J., Cunningham, J., & Krismer, K. (1992). Inferred values and the reverse-incentive effect in induced compliance. *Journal of Personality and Social Psychology, 62,* 357–368.

Freedman-Doan, C., Wigfield, A., Eccles, J., Blumenfeld, P., Arbreton, A., & Harold, R. (2000). What am I best at? Grade and gender differences in children's beliefs about ability improvement. *Journal of Applied Developmental Psychology, 21,* 379–402.

Frieze, I. (1975). Women's expectations for and causal attributions of success and failure. In M. Mednick, S. Tangri, & L. Hoffman (Eds.), *Women and achievement* (pp. 158–171). New York: Wiley.

Fuchs, L., Fuchs, D., Karns, K., Hamlett, C., Katzaroff, M., & Dutka, S. (1997). Effects of task-focused goals on low-achieving students with and without learning disabilities. *American Educational Research Journal, 34,* 513–543.

Fuligni, A., Eccles, J., & Barbar, B. (1995). The long-term effects of seventh-grade ability grouping in mathematics. *Journal of Early Adolescence, 15,* 58–89.

Gaa, J. (1973). Effects of individual goal-setting conferences on achievement, attitudes, and goal-setting behavior. *Journal of Experimental Education, 42,* 22–28.

Garbarino, J. (1975). The impact of anticipated rewards on cross-age tutoring. *Journal of Personality and Social Psychology, 32,* 421–428.

Garibaldi, A. (1993). Creating prescriptions for success in urban schools: Turning the corner on pathological explanations for academic failure. In T. Tomlinson (Ed.), *Motivating students to learn: Overcoming barriers to high achievement* (pp. 125–138). Berkeley: McCutchan.

Garner, R., Alexander, P., Gillingham, M., Kulikowich, J., & Brown, R. (1991). Interest and learning from text. *American Educational Research Journal, 28,* 643–659.

Garnier, H., Stein, J., & Jacobs, J. (1997). The process of dropping out of high school: A 19-year perspective. *American Educational Research Journal, 34,* 395–419.

Georgiou, S. (1999). Achievement attributions of sixth grade children and their parents. *Educational Psychology, 19,* 399–412.

Gibbs, J., & Allen, A. (1978). *Tribes: A process for peer involvement.* Oakland, CA: Center-Source Publications.

Gibson, S., & Dembo, M. (1984). Teacher efficacy: A construct validation. *Journal of Educational Psychology, 76,* 569–582.

Gillies, R., & Ashman, A. (2000). The effects of cooperative learning on students with learning difficulties in the lower elementary school. *Journal of Special Education, 34,* 19–27.

Girl Scouts of America (1991). *Girl Scouts survey on the beliefs and moral values of America's children.* New York: Author.

Goddard, R., Hoy, W., & Hoy, A. (2000). Collective teacher efficacy: Its meaning, measure, and impact on student achievement. *American Education Research Journal, 37,* 479–507.

Goldberg, M., Passow, A., & Justman, J. (1966). *The effects of ability grouping.* New York: Teachers College Press.

Goldenberg, C. (1989). Making success a more common occurrence for children at risk for failure: Lessons from Hispanic first-graders learning to read. In J. Allen & J. Mason (Eds.), *Risk makers, risk takers, risk breakers: Reducing the risk for young literacy learners* (pp. 48–78). Portsmouth, NJ: Heinemann.

Goldenberg, C. (1992). The limits of expectations: A case for case knowledge about teacher expectancy effects. *American Educational Research Journal, 29,* 517–544.

Gonzalez, H. (1995). Systematic desensitization, study skills counseling, and anxiety-coping training in the treatment of test anxiety. In C. Spielberger & P. Vagg (Eds.), *Test anxiety: Theory, assessment, and treatment* (pp. 117–132). Washington, DC: Taylor & Francis.

Good, T. (1987). Teacher expectations. In D. Berliner & B. Rosenshine (Eds.), *Talks to teachers* (pp. 159–200). New York: Random House.

Good, T., & Brophy, J. (1978). *Looking in classrooms* (2nd ed.). New York: Harper & Row.

Good, T., & Brophy, J. (1986). *Educational psychology* (3rd ed.). White Plains, NY: Longman.

Good, T., Slavings, R., Harel, K., & Emerson, H. (1987). Student passivity: A study of question asking in

K–12 classrooms. *Sociology of Education, 60*, 181–199.

Goodenow, C. (1993). Classroom belonging among early adolescent students: Relationships to motivation and achievement. *Journal of Early Adolescence, 13*, 21–43.

Goodlad, J. (1984). *A place called school.* New York: McGraw-Hill.

Gottfried, A. (1985). Academic intrinsic motivation in elementary and junior high school students. *Journal of Educational Psychology, 77*, 631–645.

Gottfried, A. (1990). Academic intrinsic motivation in young elementary school children. *Journal of Educational Psychology, 82*, 525–538.

Graham, L., & Wong, B. (1993). Comparing two modes of teaching a question-answering strategy for enhancing reading comprehension: Didactic and self-instructional training. *Journal of Learning Disabilities, 26*, 270–279.

Graham, S. (1984a). Communicating sympathy and anger to Black and White children: The cognitive (attributional) consequences of affective cues. *The Journal of Personality and Social Psychology, 47*, 14–28.

Graham, S. (1984b). Teacher feelings and student thoughts: An attributional approach to affect in the classroom. *Elementary School Journal, 85*, 91–104.

Graham, S. (1990). Communicating low ability in the classroom: Bad things good teachers sometimes do. In S. Graham & V. Folkes (Eds.), *Attribution theory: Applications to achievement, mental health, and interpersonal conflict* (pp. 17–36). Hillsdale, NJ: Erlbaum.

Graham, S. (1991). A review of attribution theory in achievement contexts. *Educational Psychology Review, 3*, 5–39.

Graham, S. (1994). Classroom motivation from an attributional perspective. In H. Drillings & M. Drillings (Eds.), *Motivation: Theory and research* (pp. 31–48). Hillsdale, NJ: Erlbaum.

Graham, S. (1997). Using attribution theory to understand social and academic motivation in African American youth. *Educational Psychologist, 32*, 21–34.

Graham, S., & Barker, G. (1990). The downside of help: An attributional-developmental analysis of helping behavior as a low ability cue. *Journal of Educational Psychology, 82*, 7–14.

Graham, S., Doubleday, C., & Guarino, P. (1984). The development of relations between perceived controllability and the emotions of pity, anger, and guilt. *Child Development, 55*, 561–565.

Graham, S., & Golan, S. (1991). Motivational influences on cognition: Task involvement, ego involvement, and depth of information processing. *Journal of Educational Psychology, 83*, 187–194.

Graham, S., Taylor, A., & Hudley, C. (1998). Exploring achievement values among ethnic minority early adolescents. *Journal of Educational Psychology, 90*, 606–620.

Graham, S., & Weiner, B. (1993). Attributional applications in the classroom. In T. Tomlinson (Ed.), *Motivating students to learn: Overcoming barriers to high achievement* (pp. 179–195). Berkeley: McCutchan.

Graham, S., & Weiner, B. (1996). Theories and principles of motivation. In D. Berliner & R. Calfee (Eds.), *Handbook of educational psychology* (pp. 63–84). New York: Macmillan.

Grant, L. (1985). Race-Gender status, classroom interaction, and children's socialization in elementary school. In L. Wilkinson & C. Marrett (Eds.), *Gender influences in classroom interaction* (pp. 57–78). Orlando, FL: Academic Press.

Gross, T., & Mastenbrook, M. (1980). Examination of the effects of state anxiety on problem-solving efficiency under high and low memory conditions. *Journal of Educational Psychology, 72*, 605–609.

Grundy, D. (1993). Parricide postponed: A discussion of some writing problems. *Contemporary Psychoanalysis, 29*, 693–710.

Gullickson, A. (1985). Student evaluation techniques and their relationship to grade and curriculum. *Journal of Educational Research, 79*, 96–100.

Guskey, T. (1985). *Implementing mastery learning.* Belmont, CA: Wadsworth.

Guskey, T. (1997). *Implementing mastery learning* (2nd ed.). Belmont, CA: Wadsworth.

Guskey, T. (1990). Cooperative mastery learning strategies, *The Elementary School Journal, 91*, 33–42.

Guskey, T., & Passaro, P. (1994). Teacher efficacy: A study of construct dimensions. *American Educational Research Journal, 31*, 627–643.

Guskey, T., & Pigott, T. (1988). Research on group-based mastery learning programs: A meta-analysis. *Journal of Educational Research, 8*, 197–216.

Guthrie J., & Alao, S. (1997). Designing contexts to increase motivation for reading. *Educational Psychologist, 32*, 95–107.

Guthrie, J., Van Meter, P., Hancock, G., Alao, S., Anderson, E., & McCann, A. (1998). Does concept-oriented reading instruction increase strategy use and conceptual learning from text? *Journal of Educational Psychology, 90*, 261–278.

Guthrie, J., Wigfield, A., & VonSecker, C. (2000). Effects of integrated instruction on motivation and strategy use in reading. *Journal of Educational Psychology, 92*, 331–341.

Gutman, L., & Sulzby, E. (2000). The role of autonomy-support versus control in the emergent writing behaviors of African-American kindergarten children. *Reading Research & Instruction, 39*, 170–183.

Hackett, G. (1995). Self-efficacy in career choice and development. In A. Bandura (Ed.), *Self-efficacy in changing societies* (pp. 232–258). New York: Cambridge University Press.

Hackett, G., & Betz, N. (1992). Self-efficacy perceptions and the career-related choices of college students. In D. Schunk & J. Meece (Eds.), *Student perceptions in the classroom* (pp. 229–246). Hillsdale, NJ: Erlbaum Associates.

Hallahan, D., & Sapona, R. (1983). Self-monitoring of attention with learning-disabled children: Past research and current issues. *Journal of Learning Disabilities, 16,* 616–620.

Hallinan, M., & Sorensen, A. (1983). The formation and stability of instructional groups. *American Sociological Review, 48,* 838–851.

Hamilton, H., & Gordon, D. (1978). Teacher-child interactions in preschool and task persistence. *American Educational Research Journal, 15,* 459–466.

Hancock, D. (2000). Impact of verbal praise on college students on homework. *Journal of Educational Research, 93,* 384–389.

Harackiewicz, J., Abrahams, S., & Wageman, R. (1987). Performance evaluation and intrinsic motivation: The effects of evaluative focus, rewards, and achievement orientation. *Journal of Personality and Social Psychology, 53,* 1015–1023.

Harackiewicz, J., Barron, K., & Elliot, A. (1998). Rethinking achievement goals: When are they adaptive for college students and why? *Educational Psychologist, 33,* 1–21.

Harackiewicz, J., Barron, K., Tauer, J., Carter, S., & Elliot, A. (2000). Short-term and long-term consequences of achievement goals: Predicting interest and performance over time. *Journal of Educational Psychology, 92,* 316–330.

Harackiewicz, J., & Elliot, A. (1993). Achievement goals and intrinsic motivation. *Journal of Personality and Social Psychology, 65,* 904–915.

Harackiewicz, J., Manderlink, G., & Sansone, C. (1992). Competence processes and achievement motivation: Implications for intrinsic motivation. In A. Boggiano & T. Pittman (Eds.), *Achievement and motivation: A social-developmental perspective* (pp. 115–137). Cambridge: Cambridge University Press.

Harnisch, D., Hill, K., & Fyans, L. (1980, April). *Development of a shorter, more reliable, and more valid measure of test motivation.* Paper presented at the annual meeting of the National Council on Measurement in Education, Boston.

Harter, S. (1974). Pleasure derived from cognitive challenge and mastery. *Child Development, 45,* 661–669.

Harter, S. (1978a). Effectance motivation reconsidered: Toward a developmental model. *Human Development, 21,* 34–64.

Harter, S. (1978b). Pleasure derived from challenge and the effects of receiving grades on children's difficulty level choices. *Child Development, 49,* 788–799.

Harter, S. (1981). A new self-report scale of intrinsic versus extrinsic orientation in the classroom: Motivational and informational components. *Developmental Psychology, 17,* 300–312.

Harter, S. (1982). The perceived competence scale for children. *Child Development, 53,* 87–97.

Harter, S. (1987). The determinants and mediational role of global self-worth in children. In N. Eisenberg (Ed.), *Contemporary topics in developmental psychology* (pp. 219–241). New York: Wiley & Sons.

Harter, S. (1992). The relationship between perceived competence, affect, and motivational orientation within the classroom: Process and patterns of change. In A. Boggiano & T. Pittman (Eds.), *Achievement and motivation: A social-developmental perspective* (pp. 77–114). Cambridge: Cambridge University Press.

Harter, S. (1999). *The construction of the self: A developmental perspective.* New York: Guilford Press.

Harter, S. (2000). The development of self-representations. In W. Damon (Series Ed.) & N. Eisenberg (Volume Ed.), *Handbook of child psychology, Vol. 3: Social, emotional, and personality development* (5th ed.). New York: Wiley.

Harter, S., & Pike, R. (1984). The pictorial scale of perceived competence and social acceptance for young children. *Child Development, 55,* 1969–1982.

Harter, S., Waters, P., & Whitesell, N. (1998). Relational self-worth: Differences in perceived worth as a person across interpersonal contexts among adolescents. *Child Development, 69,* 756–766.

Harter, S., Waters, P., Whitesell, N., & Kastelic, D. (1998). Level of voice among female and male high school students: Relational context, support, and gender orientation. *Developmental Psychology, 34,* 892–901.

Harter, S., Whitesell, N., & Kowalski, P. (1992). Individual differences in the effects of educational transitions on young adolescent's perceptions of competence and motivational orientation. *American Educational Research Journal, 29,* 777–807.

Harter, S., Whitesell, N., & Junkin, L. (1998). Similarities and differences in domain-specific and global self-evaluations of learning-disabled, behaviorally disordered, and normally achieving adolescents. *American Educational Research Journal, 35,* 653–680.

Hattie, J., Biggs, J., & Purdie, N. (1996). Effects of learning skills interventions on student learning: A meta-analysis. *Review of Educational Research, 66,* 99–136.

Hayes, S., Rosenfarb, I., Wolfert, E., Munt, E., Korn, Z., & Zettle, R. (1985). Self-reinforcement effects: An artifact of social standing setting? *Journal of Applied Behavior Analysis, 18,* 201–204.

Heckhausen, H. (1984). Emergent achievement behavior: Some early developments. In J. Nicholls (Ed.), *Advances in motivation and achievement, Vol. 3: The development of achievement motivation* (pp. 1–32). Greenwich, CT: JAI.

Helmke, A. (1988). The role of classroom context factors for the achievement-impairing effect of test anxiety. *Anxiety Research, 1,* 37–52.

Hembree, R. (1988). Correlates, causes, effects, and treatment of test anxiety. *Review of Educational Research, 58,* 47–77.

Hembree, R. (1990). The nature, effects, and relief of

mathematics anxiety. *Journal for Research in Mathematics Education, 21,* 33–46.

Henk, W., & Melnick, S. (1998). Upper elementary-aged children's reported perceptions about good readers: A self-efficacy influenced update in transitional literacy contexts. *Reading Research and Instruction, 38,* 57–80.

Hennessey, B. (2000). Rewards and creativity. In C. Sansone & J. Harackiewicz (Eds.), *Intrinsic and extrinsic motivation: The search for optimal motivation and performance* (pp. 55–77). San Diego: Academic Press.

Hidi, S. (2000). An interest researcher's perspective: The effects of extrinsic and intrinsic factors on motivation. In C. Sansone & J. Harackiewicz (Eds.), *Intrinsic and extrinsic motivation: The search for optimal motivation and performance* (pp. 309–339). San Diego: Academic Press.

Hidi, S., & Anderson, V. (1992). Situation interest and its impact on reading and expository writing. In K. Renninger, S. Hidi, & A. Krapp (Eds.), *The role of interest in learning and development* (pp. 215–238). Hillsdale, NJ: Erlbaum Associates.

Hidi, S., & Harackiewicz, J. (2000). Motivating the academically unmotivated: A critical issue for the 21st century. *Review of Educational Research, 70,* 151–179.

Higgins, E., & Parsons, J. (1983). Social cognition and the social life of the child: Stages as subcultures. In E. T. Higgins, D. N. Ruble, & W. W. Hartup (Eds.), *Social cognition and social development: A sociocultural perspective* (pp. 15–62). New York: Cambridge University Press.

Hill, K. (1980). Motivation, evaluation, and educational testing policy. In L. J. Fyans (Ed.), *Achievement motivation: Recent trends in theory and research* (pp. 34–95). New York: Plenum.

Hill, K. (1984). Debilitating motivation and testing: A major educational problem, possible solutions, and policy applications. In R. Ames & C. Ames (Eds.), *Research on motivation in education, Vol. 1: Student motivation* (pp. 245–272). New York: Academic Press.

Hill, K., & Eaton, W. (1977). The interaction of test anxiety and success/failure experiences in determining children's arithmetic performance. *Developmental Psychology, 13,* 205–211.

Hill, K., & Sarason, S. (1966). The relation of test anxiety and defensiveness to test and school performance over the elementary-school years: A further longitudinal study. *Monographs of the Society for Research in Child Development, 104,* 31 (Whole No. 2).

Hill, K., & Wigfield, A. (1984). Test anxiety: A major educational problem and what can be done about it. *The Elementary School Journal, 85,* 105–126.

Hofer, B., Yu, S., & Pintrich, P. (1998). Teaching college students to be self-regulated learners. In D.H. Schunk & B.J. Zimmerman (Eds.), *Self-regulated learning: From teaching to self-reflective practice* (pp. 57–85). New York: Guilford Press.

Hoge, R., & Renzulli, J. (1993). Exploring the link between giftedness and self-concept. *Review of Educational Research, 63,* 449–465.

Holroyd, K., & Appel, M. (1980). Test anxiety and physiological responding. In I. Sarason (Ed.), *Test anxiety: Theory research, and applications* (pp. 129–151). Hillsdale, NJ: Erlbaum.

Hom, H., & Murphy, M. (1985). Low need achievers' performance: The positive impact of a self-determined goal. *Personality and Social Psychology Bulletin, 11,* 275–285.

Howes, C., Phillipsen, L., & Peisner-Feinberg, E. (2000). The consistency of perceived teacher-child relationships between preschool and kindergarten. *Journal of School Psychology, 38,* 113–132.

Hoy, W., & Sabo, D. (1998). *Quality middle schools: Open and healthy.* Thousand Oaks, CA: Corwin Press.

Hoy, W., & Woolfolk, A. (1993). Teachers' sense of efficacy and the organizational health of schools. *The Elementary School Journal, 93,* 355–372.

Hughes, B., Sullivan, H., & Mosley, M. (1985). External evaluation, task difficulty, and continuing motivation. *Journal of Educational Research, 78,* 210–215.

Hull, C. (1943). *Principles of behavior.* New York: Appleton-Century-Crofts.

Hull, C. (1951). *Essentials of behavior.* New Haven: Yale University Press.

Hulton, R., & DeVries, D. (1976). *Team competition and group practice: Effects on student achievement and attitudes* (Report No. 212). Baltimore, MD: Johns Hopkins University, Center for Social Organization of Schools.

Humphrey, L., Karoly, P., & Kirschenbaum, D. (1978). Self-management in the classroom: Self-imposed response cost versus self-reward. *Behavior Therapy, 9,* 592–601.

Hunt, J. McV. (1965). Intrinsic motivation and its role in psychological development. In D. Levine (Ed.), *Nebraska symposium on motivation, Vol. 13* (pp. 189–282). Lincoln: University of Nebraska Press.

Hunter, M., Ames, D., & Koopman, R. (1983). Effects of stimulus complexity and familiarization time on infant preferences for novel and familiar stimuli. *Developmental Psychology, 19,* 338–352.

Husman, J., & Lens, W. (1999). The role of the future in student motivation. *Educational Psychologist, 34,* 113–125.

Institute for Education and Transformation (1992). *Voices from the inside: A report on schooling from inside the classroom—Part I: Naming the problem.* Claremont, CA: Claremont Graduate School.

Irvine, J. (1990). *Black students and school failure.* Westport, CT: Greenwood Press.

Iyengar, S., & Lepper, M. (1999). Rethinking the value of choice: A cultural perspective on intrinsic motivation. *Journal of Personality & Social Psychology, 76,* 349–366.

Jackson, P. (1968). *Life in classrooms.* New York: Holt.

Jacob, R., & Pelham, W. (2000). In B. Sadock & V. Sadock (Eds.), *Kaplan & Sadock's Comprehensive*

Textbook of Psychiatry, Vol. 2 (7th edition, pp. 2081–2128). Philadelphia: Lippincott Williams & Wilkins Publishers.

Jacobs, J., & Eccles, J. (1992). The impact of mothers' gender-role stereotypic beliefs on mothers' and children's ability perceptions. *Journal of Personality and Social Psychology, 63,* 932–944.

Jacobs, J., & Eccles, J. (2000). Parents, task values, and real-life achievement-related choices. In C. Sansone & J. Harackiewicz (Eds.), *Intrinsic and extrinsic motivation: The search for optimal motivation and performance* (pp. 405–439). San Diego: Academic Press.

Jagacinski, C. (1992). The effects of task involvement and ego involvement on achievement-related cognitions and behaviors. In D. Schunk & J. Meece (Eds.), *Student perceptions in the classroom* (pp. 307–326). Hillsdale, NJ: Erlbaum.

Jagacinski, C., & Nicholls, J. (1984). Conceptions of ability and related affects in task involvement and ego involvement. *Journal of Educational Psychology, 76,* 909–919.

Jagacinski, C., & Nicholls, J. (1990). Reducing effort to protect perceived ability: "They'd do it but I wouldn't." *Journal of Educational Psychology, 82,* 15–21.

Johnson, D., & Johnson, R. (1985a). The internal dynamics of cooperative learning groups. In R. Slavin, S. Sharan, S. Kagan, R. Hertz, R. Lazarowitz, N. Webb, & R. Schmuck (Eds.), *Learning to cooperate, cooperating to learn* (pp. 103–124). New York: Plenum Press.

Johnson, D., & Johnson, R. (1985b). Motivational processes in cooperative, competitive, and individualistic learning situations. In C. Ames & R. Ames (Eds.), *Research on motivation in education, Vol. 2: The classroom milieu* (pp. 249–286). Orlando FL: Academic Press.

Johnson, D., & Johnson, R. (1989). Toward a cooperative effort. *Educational Leadership, 46,* 80–81.

Johnson, D., Johnson, R., Holubec, E., & Roy, P. (1984). *Circles of learning: Cooperation in the classroom.* Alexandria, VA: Association for Supervision and Curriculum Development.

Jones, G., & Wheatley, J. (1990). Gender differences in teacher-student interactions in science classrooms. *Journal of Research in Science Teaching, 27,* 861–874.

Jussim, L. (1991). Social perception and social reality: A reflection-construction model. *Psychological Review, 98,* 54–73.

Jussim, L., & Eccles, J. (1992). Teacher expectations II: Construction and reflection of student achievement. *Journal of Personality and Social Psychology, 63,* 947–961.

Jussim, L., & Eccles, J. (1995). Naturally occurring interpersonal expectancies. In N. Eisenberg (Ed.), *Social Development: Review of Personality and Social Psychology, 15* (pp. 74–108). Thousand Oaks, CA: Sage Publications.

Jussim, L., Eccles, J., & Madon, S. (1996). Social perception, social stereotypes, and teacher expectations: Accuracy and the quest for the powerful self-fulfilling prophecy. In M. Zanna (Ed.), *Advances in Experimental Social Psychology, Vol. 28* (pp. 281–388). New York: Academic Press.

Jussim, L., Madon, S., & Chatman, C. (1994). Teacher expectations and student achievement: Self-fulfilling prophecies, biases, and accuracy. In L. Heath, R. Tindale, J. Edwards, E. Posavac, F. Bryant, E. Henderson-King, Y. Suarez-Balcazar, & J. Myers (Eds.), *Applications of heuristics and biases to social issues* (pp. 303–334). New York: Plenum Press.

Juvonen, J. (2000). The social functions of attributional face-saving tactics among early adolescents. *Educational Psychological Review, 12,* 15–32.

Kagan, J. (1972). Motives and development. *Journal of Personality and Social Psychology, 22,* 51–66.

Kahle, J. (1990). Real students take chemistry and physics: Gender issues. In K. Tobin, J. Kahle, & B. Fraser (Eds.), *Windows into science classrooms: Problems associated with higher-level cognitive learning* (pp. 92–134). New York: Falmer.

Kahle, J. (1996a). Equitable science education: A discrepancy model. In L. Parker, L. Rennie, & B. Fraser (Eds.), *Gender, science and mathematics* (pp. 129–139). Dordrecht, Netherlands: Kluwer Academic Publishers.

Kahle, J. (1996b). Opportunities and obstacles: Science education in the schools. In C. Davis, A. Ginorio, C. Hollenshead, B. Lazarus, & P. Rayman (Eds.), *The equity equation: Fostering the advancement of women in the sciences, mathematics, and engineering* (pp. 57–95). San Francisco: Jossey-Bass Publishers.

Kahle, J., & Damnjanovic, A. (1994). The effect of inquiry activities on elementary students' enjoyment, ease, and confidence in doing science: An analysis by sex and race. *Journal of Women and Minorities in Science and Engineering, 1,* 17–28.

Kahle, J., & Meece, J. (1993). Research on gender issues in the classroom. In D. Gabel (Ed.), *Handbook of research on science teaching and learning.* New York: Macmillan Publishing Company.

Kamann, M., & Wong, B. (1993). Inducing adaptive coping self-statements in children with learning disabilities through self-instruction training. *Journal of Learning Disabilities, 26,* 630–638.

Kamii, C. (1984). Viewpoint: Obedience is not enough. *Young Children, 39,* 11–14.

Kamins, M., & Dweck, C. (1999). Person versus process praise and criticism: Implications for contingent self-worth and coping. *Developmental Psychology, 35,* 835–847.

Kaplan, A., & Maehr, M. (1999). Achievement goals and student well-being. *Contemporary Educational Psychology, 24,* 330–358.

Kaplan, A., & Midgley, C. (2000). The relationship between perceptions of the classroom goals structure and early adolescents' affect in school: The mediating role of coping strategies. *Learning and Individual Differences, 11,* 187–202.

Karabenick, S., & Youssef, Z. (1968). Performance as a

function of achievement motive level and perceived difficulty. *Journal of Personality and Social Psychology, 10*, 414–419.

Kazdin, A. (1974). Self-monitoring and behavior change. In M. Mahoney & C. Thoresen (Eds.), *Self-control: Power to the person* (pp. 218–246). Monterey, CA: Brooks-Cole.

Kazdin, A. (1988). The token economy: A decade later. In G. Davey & C. Cullen (Eds.), *Human operant conditioning and behavior modification* (pp. 119–137). New York: Wiley.

Kazdin, A., & Bootzin, R. (1972). The token economy: An evaluative review. *Journal of Applied Behavior Analysis, 5*, 343–372.

Keith, L., & Bracken, B. (1996). Self-concept instrumentation: A historical and evaluative review. In B. Bracken (Ed.), *Handbook of self-concept: Developmental, social, & clinical considerations* (pp. 91–170). New York: John Wiley & Sons.

Keller, F. (1968). Goodbye, teacher. . . . *Journal of Applied Behavior Analysis, 1*, 79–89.

Kelly, H. (1967). Attribution theory in social psychology. In D. Levine (Ed.), *Nebraska symposium on motivation* (pp. 192–238). Lincoln: University of Nebraska Press.

Kern, L., Dunlap, G., Childs, K., & Clarke, S. (1994). Use of a classwide self-management program to improve the behavior of students with emotional and behavioral disorders. *Education and Treatment of Children, 17*, 445–458.

Kimball, M. (1989). A new perspective on women's math achievement. *Psychological Bulletin, 105*, 198–214.

Kirby, K., Fowler, S., & Baer, D. (1991). Reactivity in self-recording: Obtrusiveness of recording procedure and peer comments. *Journal of Applied Behavior Analysis, 24*, 487–498.

Kohn, A. (1993). *Punished by rewards: The trouble with gold stars, incentive plans, A's, praise, and other bribes.* New York: Houghton Mifflin.

Kolb, K., & Jussim, L. (1994). Teacher expectations and underachieving gifted children. *Roeper Review, 17*, 26–30.

Krapp, A. (1999). Interest, motivation and learning: An educational psychological perspective. *European Journal of Psychology of Education, 14*, 23–40.

Krohne, H. (1992). Developmental conditions of anxiety and coping: A two-process model of child-rearing effects. In K. Hagtvet & T. Johnsen (Eds.), *Advances in test anxiety research, Vol. 7* (pp. 143–155). Amsterdam: Swets & Zeitlinger.

Kulik, C-L., Kulik, J., & Bangert-Drowns, R. (1990a). Effectiveness of mastery learning programs: A meta-analysis. *Review of Educational Research, 60*, 265–299.

Kulik, J., Kulik, C-L., & Bangert-Drowns, R. (1990b). Is there better evidence on mastery learning? A response to Slavin. *Review of Educational Research, 60*, 303–307.

Lambert, N., & McCombs, B. (Eds.) (1998). *How students learn: Reforming schools through learner-centered education.* Washington, DC: American Psychological Association.

Laosa, L. (1982). School, occupation, culture and family: The impact of parental schooling on the parent-child relationship. *Journal of Educational Psychology, 74*, 791–827.

Lazarus, M. (1975, June 28). Rx for mathophobia. *Saturday Review, 2*, 46–48.

Lee, S., Ichikawa, V., & Stevenson, H. W. (1987). Beliefs and achievement in mathematics and reading: A cross-national study of Chinese, Japanese, and American children and their mothers. In M. Maehr & D. Kleiber (Eds.), *Advances in motivation and achievement, Vol. 5: Enhancing motivation* (pp. 149–179). Greenwich, CT: JAI Press.

Lee, V., Bryk, A., & Smith, J. (1993). The organization of effective secondary schools. In L. Darling-Hammond (Ed.), *Review of Research in Education, 19*, 171–268.

Lee, V., Dedick, R., & Smith, J. (1991). The effect of the social organization of schools on teachers' efficacy and satisfaction. *Sociology of Education, 64*, 190–208.

Lee, V., & Smith, J. (1999). Social support and achievement for young adolescents in Chicago: The role of school academic press. *American Educational Research Journal, 36*, 907–945.

Lee, V., Smith, J., & Croninger, R. (1997). How high school organization influences the equitable distribution of learning in mathematics and science. *Sociology of Education, 70*, 128–150.

Lefcourt, H. (1976). *Locus of control: Current trends in theory and research.* Hillsdale, NJ: Erlbaum.

Lefcourt, H. (1992). Durability and impact of the locus of control construct. *Psychological Bulletin, 112*, 411–414.

Leinhardt, G., Seewald, A., & Engel, M. (1979). Learning what's taught: Sex differences in instruction. *Journal of Educational Psychology, 71*, 432–439.

Lenz, R. (1992). Self-managed learning strategy systems for children and youth. *School Psychology Review, 21*, 211–228.

Leonard, J., Reyes, O., Danner, K., & de la Torre, G. (1994). Academic achievement as a buffer to peer rejection for transfer children. *Journal of Instructional Psychology, 21*, 351–352.

Lepper, M. (1973). Dissonance, self-perception, and honesty in children. *Journal of Personality and Social Psychology, 25*, 65–74.

Lepper, M. (1981). Intrinsic and extrinsic motivation in children: Detrimental effects of superfluous social controls. In A. Collins (Ed.), *Aspects of the development of competence: The Minnesota Symposia on Child Psychology, Vol. 14* (pp. 155–214). Hillsdale, NJ: Erlbaum.

Lepper, M. (1988). Motivational considerations in the study of instruction. *Cognition and Instruction, 5*, 289–309.

Lepper, M., Aspinwall, L., Mumme, D., & Chabay, R. (1990). Self-perception and social-perception processes in tutoring: Subtle social control strategies of expert tutors. In J. Olson & M. Zanna (Eds.), *Self-inference processes: The Ontario Symposium, Vol. 6* (pp. 217–237). Hillsdale, NJ: Erlbaum.

Lepper, M., & Cordova, D. (1992). A desire to be taught: Instructional consequences of intrinsic motivation. *Motivation and Emotion, 3,* 187–209.

Lepper, M., Greene, D., & Nisbett, R. (1973). Undermining children's intrinsic interest with intrinsic rewards: A test of the over-justification hypothesis. *Journal of Personality and Social Psychology, 28,* 129–137.

Lepper, M., & Henderlong, J. (2000). Turning "play" into "work" and "work" into "play": 25 years of research on intrinsic versus extrinsic motivation. In C. Sansone & J. Harackiewicz (Eds.), *Intrinsic and extrinsic motivation: The search for optimal motivation and performance* (pp. 257–307). San Diego: Academic Press.

Lepper, M., Keavney, M., & Drake, M. (1996). Intrinsic motivation and extrinsic rewards: A commentary on Cameron and Pierce's meta-analysis. *Review of Educational Research, 66,* 5–32.

Lepper, M., & Malone, T. (1987). Intrinsic motivation and instructional effectiveness in computer-based education. In R. Snow & M. Farr (Eds.), *Aptitude, learning, and instruction, Vol. III: Cognitive and affective process analysis* (pp. 255–286). Hillsdale, NJ: Erlbaum.

Lepper, M., Sethi, S., Dialdin, D., & Drake, M. (1997). Intrinsic and extrinsic motivation: A developmental perspective. In S. Luthar, J. Barack, D. Cicchetti, & J. Weisz (Eds.), *Developmental psychopathology: Perspectives on adjustment, risk and disorder* (pp. 21–50). Cambridge: Cambridge University Press.

Levine, J. (1983). Social comparison and education. In J. Levine & M. Wang (Eds.), *Teacher and student perceptions: Implications for learning* (pp. 29–55). Hillsdale, NJ: Erlbaum.

Lewin, K., Lippitt R., & White, R. (1939). Pattern of aggressive behavior in experimentally created "social climates." *Journal of Social Psychology, 10,* 271–299.

Lewis, M., Alessandri, S., & Sullivan, M. (1992). Differences in shame and pride as a function of children's gender and task difficulty. *Child Development, 63 (2),* 630–638.

Licht, B. (1992). The achievement-related perceptions of children with learning problems. In D. Schunk & J. Meece (Eds.), *Student perceptions in the classroom* (pp. 247–264). Hillsdale, NJ: Erlbaum.

Licht, B. (1993). Learning disabled children's achievement related beliefs: Impact on their motivation and strategic learning. In L. Meltzer (Ed.), *Strategy assessment and instruction for students with learning disabilities: From theory to practice* (pp. 195–220). Austin, TX: ProEd.

Licht, B., & Dweck, C. (1984). Determinants of academic achievement: The interaction of children's achievement orientations with skill area. *Developmental Psychology, 20,* 628–636.

Linnenbrink, E., & Pintrich, P. (2000). Multiple pathways to learning and achievement: The role of goal orientation in fostering adaptive motivation, affect, and cognition. In C. Sansone & J. Harackiewicz (Eds.), *Intrinsic and extrinsic motivation: The search for optimal motivation and performance* (pp. 195–227). San Diego: Academic Press.

Lipinski, D., Black, J., Nelson, R., & Ciminero, A. (1974). Influence of motivational variables on the reactivity and reliability of self-recording. *Journal of Consulting and Clinical Psychology, 42,* 118–123.

Lipsitz, J. (1997). Middle Grades Improvement Program. *Phi Delta Kappan, 78,* 533–540.

Lipsitz, J., Mizell, M., Jackson, A., & Austin, L. (1997). Speaking with one voice: A manifesto for middle-grades reform. *Phi Delta Kappan,* 533–540.

Litrownik, A., & Freitas, J. (1980). Self-monitoring in moderately retarded adolescents: Reactivity and accuracy as a function of valence. *Behavior Therapy, 11,* 245–255.

Little, T., Oettingen, G., Stetsenko, A., & Baltes, P. (1995). Children's action-control beliefs about school performance: How do American children compare with German and Russian children? *Journal of Personality and Social Psychology, 69,* 686–700.

Locke, E., Shaw, K., Saari, L., & Latham, G. (1981). Goal setting and task performance: 1969–1980. *Psychological Bulletin, 90,* 125–152.

Luria, A. (1961). *The role of speech in the regulation of normal and abnormal behaviors.* New York: Liveright.

Luster, T., & McAdoo, H. (1996). Family and child influences on educational attainment: A secondary analysis of the High/Scope Perry Preschool Data. *Developmental Psychology, 32,* 26–39.

Luthar, S. (1995). Social competence in the school setting: Prospective cross-domain associations among inner-city teens. *Child Development, 66,* 416–429.

Lynch, M., & Cicchetti, M. (1997). Children's relationships with adults and peers: An examination of elementary and junior high school students. *Journal of School Psychology, 35,* 81–99.

Maag, J., Rutherford, R., & DiGangi, S. (1992). Effects of self-monitoring and contingent reinforcement on on-task behavior and academic productivity of learning-disabled students: A social validation study. *Psychology in the Schools, 29,* 157–172.

Mace, F., & Kratochwill, T. (1988). Self-monitoring. In J. Will, S. Elliott, & F. Gresham (Eds.), *Handbook of behavior therapy in education* (pp. 489–522). New York: Plenum Press.

Mac Iver, D. (1990). *A national description of report card entries in the middle grades* (Rep. No. 9). Baltimore,

MD: Johns Hopkins University, Center for Research on Effective Schooling for Disadvantaged Students.

Mac Iver, D., & Plank, J. (1997). Improving urban schools: Developing the talents of students placed at risk. In J. Irvin (Ed.), *What current research says to the middle level practitioner* (pp. 243–256). Columbus, OH: National Middle School Association.

Mac Iver, D., Stipek, D., & Daniels, D. (1991). Explaining within-semester changes in student effort in junior high school and senior high school courses. *Journal of Educational Psychology, 83,* 201–211.

Maehr, M. (1984). Meaning and motivation: Toward a theory of personal investment. In R. Ames & C. Ames (Eds.), *Research on motivation in education, Vol. 1: Student motivation* (pp. 115–144). Orlando, FL: Academic Press.

Maehr, M., & Anderman, E. (1993). Reinventing schools for early adolescents: Emphasizing task goals. *Elementary School Journal, 93,* 593–610.

Maehr, M., & Midgley, C. (1996). *Transforming school cultures.* Boulder CO: Westview Press.

Mahn, C. S., & Greenwood, G. E. (1990). Cognitive behavior modification: Use of self-instruction strategies by first-graders on academic tasks. *Journal of Educational Research, 83,* 158–161.

Major, B., Spencer, S., Schmader, T., Wolfe, C., & Crocker, J. (1998). Coping with negative stereotypes about intellectual performance: The role of psychological disengagement. *Personality and Social Psychology Bulletin, 24,* 34–50.

Manderlink, G., & Harackiewicz, J. (1984). Proximal vs. distal goal setting and intrinsic motivation. *Journal of Personality and Social Psychology, 47,* 918–928.

Marks, H., Doane, K., & Secada, W. (in press). Support for student achievement. In F. Newmann and Associates, *Restructuring for student achievement: The impact of structure and culture in 24 schools.* San Francisco: Jossey-Bass.

Marsh, H. (1984). Relations among dimensions of self-attribution, dimensions of self-concept, and academic achievement. *Journal of Educational Psychology, 76,* 3–32.

Marsh, H. (1987). The big-fish-little-pond effect on academic self-concept. *Journal of Educational Psychology, 79,* 280–295.

Marsh, H. (1993). Physical fitness self-concept: Relations of physical fitness to field and technical indicators for boys and girls aged 9–15. *Journal of Sport and Exercise Psychology, 15,* 184–206.

Marsh, H., Barnes, J., Cairns, L., & Tidman, M. (1984). Self-description questionnaire: Age and sex effects in the structure and level of self-concept for preadolescent children. *Journal of Educational Psychology, 76,* 940–956.

Marsh, H., Byrne, B., & Yeung, A. (1999). Causal ordering of academic self-concept and achieve-ment: Reanalysis of a pioneering study and revised recommendations. *Educational Psychologist, 34,* 154–157.

Marsh, H., Cairns, L., Relich, J., Barnes, J., & Debus, R. (1984). The relationship between dimensions of self-attribution and dimensions of self-concept. *Journal of Educational Psychology, 76,* 3–32.

Marsh, H., Chessor, D., Craven, R., & Roche, L. (1995). The effects of gifted and talented programs on academic self-concept: The big fish strikes again. *American Educational Research Journal, 32,* 285–319.

Marsh, H., Craven, R., & Debus, R. (1998). Structure, stability, and development of young children's self-concepts: A multicohort-multioccasion study. *Child Development, 69,* 1030–1053.

Marsh, H., & Gouvernet, P. (1989). Multidimensional self-concepts and perceptions of control: Construct validation of responses by children. *Journal of Educational Psychology, 81,* 57–69.

Marsh, H., & Hattie, J. (1996). Theoretical perspectives on the structure of self-concept. In B. Bracken (Ed.), *Handbook of self-concept: Developmental, social, and clinical considerations* (pp. 38–90). New York: John Wiley & Sons.

Marsh, H., & Holmes, I. (1990). Multidimensional self-concepts: Construct validation of responses by children. *American Educational Research Journal, 27,* 89–117.

Marsh, H., Kong, C., & Hau, K. (2000). Longitudinal, multilevel models of the big-fish-little-pond effect on academic self-concept: Counterbalancing contrast and reflected-glory effects in Hong Kong schools. *Journal of Personality & Social Psychology, 78,* 337–349.

Marsh, H., Smith, I., & Barnes, J. (1983). Multitrait-multimethod analyses of the self-description questionnaire: Student-teacher agreement on multidimensional ratings of student self-concept. *American Educational Research Journal, 26,* 333–357.

Marsh, H., & Yeung, A. (1997a). Causal effects of academic self-concept on academic achievement: Structural equation models of longitudinal data. *Journal of Educational Psychology, 89,* 41–54.

Marsh, H., & Yeung, A. (1997b). Coursework selection: The effects of academic self-concept and achievement. *American Educational Research Journal, 34,* 691–720.

Marsh, H., & Yeung, A. (1998). Longitudinal structural equation models of academic self-concept and achievement: Gender differences in the development of math and English constructs. *American Educational Research Journal, 35,* 705–738.

Marshall, H., & Weinstein, R. (1984). Classroom factors affecting students' self-evaluation: An interactional model. *Review of Educational Research, 54,* 301–325.

Marshall, H., & Weinstein, R. (1986). Classroom context of student-perceived differential teacher treatment. *Journal of Educational Psychology, 78,* 441–453.

Marzano, R. (1994). Lessons from the field about outcome-based performance assessments. *Educational Leadership, 51* (6), 44–50.

Matheny, K., & Edwards, C. (1974). Academic improvement through an experimental classroom management system. *Journal of School Psychology, 12,* 222–232.

McAllister, H. (1996). Self-serving bias in the classroom: Who shows it? Who knows it? *Journal of Educational Psychology, 88,* 123–131.

McClelland, D. (1961). *The achieving society.* New York: The Free Press.

McClelland, D. (1971). *Motivational trends in society.* New York: General Learning Press.

McCombs, B. (1994). Strategies for assessing and enhancing motivation: Keys to promoting self-regulated learning and performance. In H. O'Neil & M. Drillings (1994), *Motivation: Theory and Research* (pp. 49–69). Hillsdale, NJ: Erlbaum.

McDermott, R. (1987). The explanation of minority school failure, again. *Anthropology and Education Quarterly, 18,* 361–364.

McFarland, D. (2000). Classroom situations and multivocal success: Using interaction frameworks and role-distance to characterize classroom behavior. Paper presented at the American Sociological Association Conference, Washington, DC.

McGinnis, J., Friman, P., & Carlyon, W. (1999). The effect of token rewards on "intrinsic" motivation for doing math. *Journal of Applied Behavior Analysis, 32,* 375–379.

McGraw, K., & McCullers, J. (1979). Evidence of a detrimental effect of extrinsic incentives on breaking a mental set. *Journal of Experimental Social Psychology, 15,* 285–294.

McInerney, V., McInerney, D., & Marsh, H. (1997). Effects of metacognitive strategy training within a cooperative group learning context on computer achievement and anxiety: An aptitude-treatment interaction study. *Journal of Educational Psychology, 89,* 686–695.

McMullin, D., & Steffen, J. (1982). Intrinsic motivation and performance standards. *Social Behavior and Personality, 10,* 47–56.

Meece, J. (1991). The classroom context and students' motivational goals. In M. Maehr & P. Pintrich (Eds.), *Advances in motivation and achievement, Vol. 7* (pp. 261–285). Greenwich, CT: JAI Press.

Meece, J. (1994). The role of motivation in self-regulated learning. In D. Schunk & B. Zimmerman (Eds.), *Self-regulation of learning and performance* (pp. 25–44). Hillsdale, NJ: Erlbaum.

Meece, J., Blumenfeld, P., & Hoyle, R. (1988). Students' goal orientations and cognitive engagement in classroom activities. *Journal of Educational Psychology, 80,* 514–523.

Meece, J., Blumenfeld, P., & Puro, P. (1989). A motivational analysis of elementary science learning environments. In M. Matyas, K. Tobin, & B. Fraser (Eds.), *Looking into windows: Qualitative research in science education* (pp. 13–23). Washington, DC: American Association for the Advancement of Science.

Meece, J., & Courtney, D. (1992). Gender differences in students' perceptions: Consequences for achievement-related choices. In D. Schunk & J. Meece (Eds.), *Student perceptions in the classroom* (pp. 209–228). Hillsdale, NJ: Erlbaum.

Meece, J., & Holt, K. (1993). A pattern analysis of students' achievement goals. *Journal of Educational Psychology, 85,* 582–590.

Meece, J., Wigfield, A., & Eccles, J. (1990). Predictors of math anxiety and its influence on young adolescents' course enrollment intentions and performance in mathematics. *Journal of Educational Psychology, 82,* 60–70.

Meichenbaum, D. (1977). *Cognitive behavior modification.* New York: Plenum Press.

Meichenbaum, D., & Asarnow, J. (1979). Cognitive-behavioral modification and metacognitive development: Implications for the classroom. In P. Kendall & S. Hollon (Eds.), *Cognitive-behavioral interventions and procedures* (pp. 11–35). New York: Academic Press.

Meid, E. (1971). *The effects of two types of success and failure on children's discrimination learning and evaluation of performance.* Doctoral dissertation, Yale University.

Meyer, D., Turner, J., & Spencer, C. (1997). Challenge in a mathematics classroom: Students' motivation and strategies in project-based learning. *The Elementary School Journal, 97,* 501–521.

Meyer, W. (1982). Indirect communications about perceived ability estimates. *Journal of Educational Psychology, 74,* 888–897.

Meyer, W. (1992). Paradoxical effects of praise and criticism on perceived ability. In W. Stroebe & M. Hewstone (Eds.), *European review of social psychology, Vol. 3* (pp. 259–283). Chichester, England: John Wiley & Sons.

Mickelson, R. (1990). The attitude-achievement paradox among black adolescents. *Sociology of Education, 63,* 44–61.

Middleton, M., & Midgley, C. (1997). Avoiding the demonstration of lack of ability: An under explored aspect of goal theory. *Journal of Educational Psychology, 89,* 710–718.

Midgley, C. (1994). Motivation and middle level schools. In P. Pintrich & M. Maehr (Eds.), *Advances in motivation and achievement, Vol. 8: Motivation and adolescent development* (pp. 219–276). Greenwich, CT: JAI.

Midgley, C., Anderman, E., & Hicks, L. (1995). Differences between elementary and middle school teachers and students: A goal theory approach. *Journal of Early Adolescence, 15,* 90–113.

Midgley, C., Arunkumar, R., & Urdan, T. (1996). "If I don't do well tomorrow, there's a reason": Predictors of adolescents' use of academic self-handicapping strategies. *Journal of Educational Psychology, 88*, 423–434.

Midgley, C., & Edelin, K. (1998). Middle school reform and early adolescent well-being: The good news and the bad. *Educational Psychologist, 33*, 195–206.

Midgley, C., Feldlaufer, H., & Eccles, J. (1988). The transition to junior high school: Beliefs of pre- and posttransition teachers. *Journal of Youth and Adolescence, 17*, 543–562.

Midgley, C., Feldlaufer, H., & Eccles, J. (1989). Student/teacher relations and attitudes toward mathematics before and after the transition to junior high school. *Child Development, 60*, 981–992.

Midgley, C., Kaplan, A., Middleton, M., Maehr, M., Urdan, T., Anderman, L., Anderman, E., & Roeser, R. (1998). The development and validation of scales assessing students' achievement goal orientations. *Contemporary Educational Psychology, 23*, 113–131.

Midgley, C., & Urdan, T. (1995). Predictors of middle school students' use of self-handicapping strategies. *Journal of Early Adolescence, 15*, 389–411.

Miller, A. (1985). A developmental study of the cognitive basis of performance impairment after failure. *Journal of Personality and Social Psychology, 49*, 529–538.

Miller, A. (1986). Performance impairment after failure: Mechanism and sex differences. *Journal of Educational Psychology, 78*, 486–491.

Miller, D., & Hom, H. (1990). Influence of extrinsic and ego incentive value on persistence after failure and continuing motivation. *Journal of Educational Psychology, 82*, 539–545.

Miller, D., & Hom, H. (1997). Conceptions of ability and the interpretation of praise, blame, and material rewards. *The Journal of Experimental Education, 65*, 163–177.

Miller, D., & Ross, M. (1975). Self-serving bias in the attribution of causality: Fact or fiction? *Psychological Bulletin, 82*, 213–235.

Miserandino, M. (1996). Children who do well in school: Individual differences in perceived competence and autonomy in above-average children. *Journal of Educational Psychology, 88*, 203–214.

Mitchell, C., & Collins, L. (1991). *Math anxiety*. Dubuque, IA: Kendall/Hunt Publishing.

Mitchell, M. (1993). Situational interest: Its multifaceted structure in the secondary school mathematics classroom. *Journal of Educational Psychology, 85*, 424–436.

Moeller, J., & Koeller, O. (1999). Spontaneous cognitions following academic test results. *Journal of Experimental Education, 67*, 150–164.

Molden, D., & Dweck, C. (2000). Meaning and motivation. In C. Sansone & J. Harackiewicz (Eds.), *Intrinsic and extrinsic motivation: The search for optimal motivation and performance* (pp. 131–159). San Diego: Academic Press.

Mone, M., & Baker, D. (1992). A social-cognitive, attributional model of personal goals: An empirical evaluation. *Motivation & Emotions, 16*, 297–321.

Moneta, G., & Csikszentmihalyi, M. (1996). The effect of perceived challenges and skills on the quality of subjective experience. *Journal of Personality, 64* (2), 275–310.

Morris, W., & Nemcek, D. (1982). The development of social comparison motivation among preschoolers: Evidence of a stepwise progression. *Merrill-Palmer Quarterly, 28*, 413–425.

Morse, L., & Handley, H. (1985). Listening to adolescents: Gender differences in science classroom interaction. In L. Wilkinson & C. Marrett (Eds.), *Gender influences in classroom interaction* (pp. 37–56). Orlando, FL: Academic Press.

Mosatche, H., & Bragonier, P. (1981). An observational study of social comparison in preschoolers. *Child Development, 52*, 376–378.

Mosteller, F., Light, R., & Sachs, J. (1996). Sustained inquiry in education: Lessons from skill grouping and class size. *Harvard Educational Review, 66*, 797–842.

Mueller, C., & Dweck, C. (1998). Intelligence praise can undermine motivation and performance. *Journal of Personality and Social Psychology, 75*, 33–52.

Muijs, R. (1997). Predictors of academic achievement and academic self-concept: A longitudinal perspective. *British Journal of Educational Psychology, 67*, 263–277.

Munk, D., & Repp, A. (1994). The relationship between instructional variables and problem behavior: A review. *Exceptional Children, 60*, 390–401.

Murdock, T. (1999). The social context of risk: Status and motivational predictors of alienation in middle school. *Journal of Educational Psychology, 91*, 62–75.

Mussen, P., & Eisenberg, N. (2000). Child-rearing and pro-social behavior. In D. Stipek & A. Bohart (Eds.), *Constructive and destructive behavior: Implications for family, school, and society*. Washington, DC: American Psychological Association.

Nadler, A. (1998). Relationship, esteem, and achievement perspectives on autonomous and dependent help seeking. In S. Karabenick (Ed.), *Strategic help seeking: Implications for learning and teaching* (pp. 61–93). Mahwah, NJ: Erlbaum.

National Council of Teachers of Mathematics (2000). *Principles and standards for school mathematics*. Reston, VA: Author.

Naveh-Benjamin, M. (1991). A comparison of training programs intended for different types of test-anxious students: Further support for an information processing model. *Journal of Educational Psychology, 83*, 134–139.

Naveh-Benjamin, M., McKeachie, W., & Lin, Y-G. (1987). Two types of test-anxious students: Support for an information processing model. *Journal of Educational Psychology, 79*, 131–136.

Nelson-Le Gall, S. (1981). Help-seeking: An understudied problem-solving skill in children. *Developmental Review, 1,* 224–246.

Nelson-Le Gall, S. (1990). Classroom help-seeking behavior of African-American children. *Education and urban society, 24,* 27–40.

Nelson-Le Gall, S. (1992). Children's instrumental help seeking: Its role in the social acquisition of knowledge and skill. In R. Hertz-Lazarowitz & N. Miller (Eds.), *Interaction in cooperative groups: The theoretical anatomy of group learning* (pp. 49–68). New York: Cambridge University Press.

Nelson-Le Gall, S. (1993). Perceiving and displaying effort in achievement settings. In T. Tomlinson (Ed.), *Motivating students to learn: Overcoming barriers to high achievement* (pp. 225–244). Berkeley, CA: McCutchan Publishing.

Nelson-Le Gall, S., & Resnick, L. (1998). Help seeking, achievement motivation, and the social practice of intelligence in school. In S. Karabenick (Ed.), *Strategic help seeking: Implications for learning and teaching* (pp. 39–60). Mahwah, NJ: Erlbaum.

Newman, R. (1998a). Adaptive help seeking: A role of social interaction in self-regulated learning. In S. Karabhenick (Ed.), *Strategic help seeking: Implications for learning and teaching* (pp. 13–37). Mahwah, NJ: Erlbaum.

Newman, R. (1998b). Students' help seeking during problem solving: Influences of personal and contextual achievement goals. *Journal of Educational Psychology, 90,* 644–658.

Newman, R. (2000). Social influences on the development of children's adaptive help seeking: The role of parents, teachers, and peers. *Developmental Review, 20,* 350–404.

Newman, R., & Goldin, L. (1990). Children's reluctance to seek help with schoolwork. *Journal of Educational Psychology, 82,* 92–100.

Newman, R., & Schwager, M. (1992). Student perceptions and academic help-seeking. In D. Schunk & J. Meece (Eds.), *Student perceptions in the classroom* (pp. 123–146). Hillsdale, NJ: Erlbaum.

Newmann, F. (Ed.) (1992). *Student engagement and achievement in American secondary schools.* New York: Teachers College Press.

Nicholls, J. (1978). The development of the concepts of effort and ability, perception of own attainment, and the understanding that difficult tasks require more ability. *Child Development, 49,* 800–814.

Nicholls, J. (1979a). Development of perception of own attainment and causal attributions for success and failure in reading. *Journal of Educational Psychology, 71,* 94–99.

Nicholls, J. (1979b). Quality and equality in intel-lectual development: The role of motivation in education. *American Psychologist, 34,* 1071–1083.

Nicholls, J. (1980). A re-examination of boys' and girls' causal attributions for success and failure based on New Zealand data. In L. Fyans (Ed.), *Achievement motivation: Recent trends in theory and research* (pp. 266–288). New York: Plenum Press.

Nicholls, J. (1983). Conception of ability and achievement motivation: A theory and its implications for education. In S. Paris, G. Olson, & H. Stevenson (Eds.), *Learning and motivation in the classroom* (pp. 211–237). Hillsdale, NJ: Erlbaum.

Nicholls, J. (1984). Achievement motivation: Conceptions of ability, subjective experience, task choice, and performance. *Psychological Review, 91,* 328–346.

Nicholls, J. (1990). What is ability and why are we mindful of it? A developmental perspective. In R. Sternberg & J. Kolligian, Jr. (Eds.), *Competence considered* (pp. 11–40). New Haven: Yale University Press.

Nicholls, J. (1992). Students as educational theorists. In D. Schunk & J. Meece (Eds.), *Student perceptions in the classroom* (pp. 267–286). Hillsdale NJ: Erlbaum.

Nicholls, J., Cobb, P., Wood, T., Yackel, E., & Patashnick, M. (1990). Assessing students' theories of success in mathematics: Individual and classroom differences. *Journal for Research in Mathematics Education, 21,* 109–122.

Nicholls, J., Cobb, P., Yackel, E., Wood, T., & Wheatley, G. (1990). Students' theories about mathematics and their mathematical knowledge: Multiple dimensions of assessment. In G. Kulm (Ed.), *Assessing higher order thinking in mathematics* (pp. 137–154). Washington, DC: American Association for the Advancement of Science.

Nicholls, J., Jagacinski, C., & Miller, A. (1986). Conceptions of ability in children and adults. In R. Schwarzer (Ed.), *Self-related cognitions in anxiety and motivation* (pp. 265–284). Hillsdale, NJ: Erlbaum.

Nicholls, J., & Miller, A. (1984a). Conceptions of ability and achievement motivation. In R. Ames & C. Ames (Eds.), *Research on motivation in education, Vol. 1: Student motivation* (pp. 39–73). New York: Academic Press.

Nicholls, J., & Miller, A. (1984b). Development and its discontents: The differentiation of the concept of ability. In J. Nicholls (Ed.), *Advances in motivation and achievement, Vol. 3: The development of achievement motivation* (pp. 185–218). Greenwich, CT: JAI Press.

Niedenthal, P., Tangney, J., & Gavanski, I. (1994). "If only I weren't" versus "If only I hadn't": Distinguishing shame and guilt in counterfactual thinking. *Journal of Personality and Social Psychology, 67,* 585–595.

Nolen, S. (1988). Reasons for studying: Motivational orientations and study strategies. *Cognition and Instruction, 5,* 269–287.

Nottelmann, E., & Hill, K. (1977). Test anxiety and off-task behavior in evaluative situations. *Child Development, 48,* 225–231.

Oakes, J. (1990). *Multiplying inequalities: The effects of race, social class, and tracking on opportunities to learn math and science.* Santa Monica, CA: Rand.

Oakes, J., & Goodlad, J. (1985). *Keeping track: How schools structure inequality*. New Haven, CT: Yale University Press.

Ogbu, J. (1992). Understanding cultural diversity and learning. *Educational Researcher, 21*, 5–14.

Ogbu, J. (1997). Understanding the school performance of urban blacks: Some essential background knowledge. In H. Walberg, R. Reyes, & R. Weissberg (Eds.), *Children and youth: Interdisciplinary perspectives*. Thousand Oaks, CA: Sage.

O'Leary, S., & Dubey, D. (1979). Applications of self-control procedures by children: A review. *Journal of Applied Behavior Analysis, 12*, 449–465.

Osborne, J. (1997). Race and academic disidentification. *Journal of Educational Psychology, 89*, 728–735.

Pajares, F. (1996). Self-efficacy beliefs in academic settings. *Review of Educational Research, 66*, 543–578.

Pajares, F. (1997). Current directions in self-efficacy research. In M. Maehr & P. Pintrich (Eds.), *Advances in motivation and achievement, Vol. 10* (pp. 1–49). Greenwich, CT: JAI Press.

Pajares, F., & Miller, M. (1994). Role of self-efficacy and self-concept beliefs in mathematical problem solving: A path analysis. *Journal of Educational Psychology, 86*, 193–203.

Pajares, F., Miller, M., & Johnson, M. (1999). Gender differences in writing self-beliefs of elementary school students. *Journal of Educational Psychology, 91*, 50–61.

Pajares, F., & Urdan, T. (1996). Exploratory factor analysis of the Mathematics Anxiety Scales. *Measurement & Evaluation in Counseling & Development, 1*, 35–47.

Pajares, F., & Valiante, G. (1997). Influence of self-efficacy on elementary students' writing. *Journal of Educational Research, 90*, 353–360.

Palardy, J. (1969). What teachers believe—what children achieve. *Elementary School Journal, 69*, 370–374.

Palincsar, A., & Brown, A. (1984). Reciprocal teaching of comprehension-fostering and comprehension-monitoring activities. *Cognition and Instruction, 1*, 117–175.

Palincsar, A., & Brown, A. (1987). Advances in improving the cognitive performance of handicapped students. In M. Wang, M. Reynolds, & H. Walberg (Eds.), *Handbook of special education: Research and practice, Vol. 1: Learner characteristics and adaptive education* (pp. 93–112). Oxford: Pergamo.

Pallas, A., Entwisle, D., Alexander, K., & Stluka, M. (1994). Ability-group effects: Instructional, social, or institutional? *Sociology of Education, 67*, 27–46.

Paris, S., Cross, D., & Lipson, M. (1984). Informed strategies for learning: A program to improve children's reading awareness and comprehension. *Journal of Educational Psychology, 76*, 1239–1252.

Parker, L., & Lepper, M. (1992). The effects of fantasy contexts on children's learning and motivation: Making learning more fun. *Journal of Personality and Social Psychology, 62*, 625–633.

Parsons, J., Adler, T., & Kaczala, C. (1982). Socialization of achievement attitudes and beliefs: Parental influences. *Child Development, 53*, 310–339.

Parsons, J., Meece, J., Adler, T., & Kaczala, C. (1982). Sex differences in attributions and learned helplessness. *Sex Roles, 8*, 431–432.

Patrick, B., Skinner, E., & Connell, J. (1993). What motivates children's behavior and emotion? Joint effects of perceived control and autonomy in the academic domain. *Journal of Personality and Social Psychology, 65*, 781–791.

Pearlman, C. (1984). The effects of level of effectance motivation, IQ, and a penalty/reward contingency on the choice of problem difficulty. *Child Development, 55*, 537–542.

Pelletier, L., & Vallerand, R. (1996). Supervisors' beliefs and subordinates' intrinsic motivation: A behavioral confirmation analysis. *Journal of Personality and Social Psychology, 71*, 331–340.

Pepitone, E. (1972). Comparison behavior in elementary school children. *American Educational Research Journal, 9*, 43–63.

Perry, N. (1998). Young children's self-regulated learning and contexts that support it. *Journal of Educational Psychology, 90*, 715–729.

Peterson, P., & Swing, S. (1982). Beyond time on task: Students' reports of their thought processes during classroom instruction. *The Elementary School Journal, 21*, 487–515.

Phillips B., Pitcher, G., Worsham, M., & Miller, S. (1980). Test anxiety and the school environment. In I. Sarason (Ed.), *Test anxiety: Theory, research, and applications* (pp. 327–346). Hillsdale, NJ: Erlbaum.

Phillips, D. (1984). The illusion of incompetence among academically competent children. *Child Development, 55*, 2000–2016.

Phillips, D., & Zimmerman, M. (1990). The developmental course of perceived competence and incompetence among competent children. In J. Kolligian & R. Sternberg (Eds.), *Competence considered* (pp. 41–66). New Haven, CT: Yale University Press.

Piaget, J. (1952). *The origins of intelligence in children*. New York: W. W. Norton.

Pianta, R. (1994). Patterns of relationships between children and kindergarten teachers. *Journal of School Psychology, 32*, 15–31.

Pianta, R. (1999). *Enhancing relationships between children and teachers*. Washington, DC: American Psychological Association.

Pianta, R., & Nimetz, S. (1991). Relationships between children and teachers: Associations with classroom and home behavior. *Journal of Applied Developmental Psychology, 12*, 379–393.

Pianta, R., & Steinberg, M. (1992). Teacher-child relationships and the process of adjusting to school. In R. Pianta (Ed.), *Beyond the parent: The role of other adults in children's lives* (pp. 61–80). San Francisco: Jossey-Bass.

Pianta, R., Steinberg, M., & Rollins, K. (1995). The first two years of school: Teacher-child relationships and deflections in children's classroom adjustment. *Development and Psychopathology, 7,* 295–312.

Pigott, R., & Cowen, E. (2000). Teacher race, child race, racial conguence, and teacher ratings of children's school adjustment. *Journal of School Psychology, 38,* 177–196.

Pintrich, P. (1999). The role of goal orientation in self-regulated learning. In M. Boekaerts (Ed.), *Handbook of self-regulation.* San Diego, CA: Academic Press.

Pintrich, P. (2000). Multiple goals, multiple pathways: The role of goal orientation in learning and achievement. *Journal of Educational Psychology, 92,* 544–555.

Pintrich, P., & Blumenfeld, P. (1985). Classroom experience and children's self-perceptions of ability, effort, and conduct. *Journal of Educational Psychology, 77,* 646–657.

Pintrich, P., & De Groot, E. (1990). Motivational and self-regulated learning components of classroom academic performance. *Journal of Educational Psychology, 82,* 33–40.

Pintrich, P., Roeser, R., & De Groot, E. (1994). Classroom and individual differences in early adolescents' motivation and self-regulated learning. *Journal of Early Adolescence, 14,* 139–161.

Pintrich, P., & Schrauben, B. (1992). Students' motivational beliefs and their cognitive engagement in classroom academic tasks. In D. Schunk & J. Meece (Eds.), *Student perceptions in the classroom: Causes and consequences* (pp. 149–183). Hillsdale, NJ: Erlbaum.

Pittman, T., Davey, M., Alafat, K., Wetherill, K., & Kramer, N. (1980). Informational versus controlling verbal rewards. *Personality and Social Psychology Bulletin, 6,* 228–233.

Pittman, T., Emery, J., & Boggiano, A. (1982). Intrinsic and extrinsic motivational orientations: Reward-induced changes in preference for complexity. *Journal of Personality and Social Psychology, 42,* 789–797.

Plaks, J., Stroessner, S., Dweck, C., & Sherman, J. (2001). Person theories and attention allocation: Preferences for stereotypic versus counterstereotypic information. *Journal of Personality and Social Psychology, 80,* 876–893.

Plant, R., & Ryan, R. (1985). Intrinsic motivation and the effects of self-consciousness, self-awareness, and ego-involvement: An investigation of internally-controlling styles. *Journal of Personality, 53,* 435–449.

Plass, J., & Hill, K. (1986). Children's achievement strategies and test performance: The role of time pressure, evaluation anxiety, and sex. *Developmental Psychology, 22,* 31–36.

Poon, W-T., & Lau, S. (1999). Coping with failure: Relationship with self-concept discrepancy and attributional style. *The Journal of Social Psychology, 139,* 639–653.

Pressley, M., El-Dinary, P., Marks, M., Brown, R., & Stein, S. (1992). Good strategy instruction is motivating and interesting. In K. Renninger, S. Hidi, & A. Krapp (Eds.), *The role of interest in learning and development* (pp. 333–358). Hillsdale, NJ: Erlbaum.

Putnam, J., Markovchick, K., Johnson, D., & Johnson, R. (1996). Cooperative learning and peer acceptance of students with learning disabilities. *Journal of Social Psychology, 136,* 741–752.

Ramey, S., Lanzi, R., Phillips, M., & Ramey, C. (1998). Perspectives of former head start children and their parents on the transition to school. *Elementary School Journal, 98,* 311–327.

Randhawa, B. (1994). Self-efficacy in mathematics, attitudes, and achievement of boys and girls from restricted samples in two countries. *Perceptual & Motor Skills, 79,* 1011–1018.

Randhawa, B., Beamer, J., & Lundberg, I. (1993). Role of mathematics self-efficacy in the structural model of mathematics achievement. *Journal of Educational Psychology, 85,* 41–48.

Raudenbush, S., Rowen, B., & Cheong, Y. (1992). Contextual effects on the self-perceived efficacy of high school teachers. *Sociology of Education, 65,* 150–167.

Reeve, J., Bolt, E., & Cai, Y. (1999). Autonomy-supportive teachers: How they teach and motivate students. *Journal of Educational Psychology, 91,* 537–548.

Renick, J., & Harter, S. (1989). Impact of social comparisons on the developing self-perceptions of learning disabled students. *Journal of Educational Psychology, 81,* 631–638.

Rennie, L., Parker, L., & Kahle, J. (1996). Informing teaching and research in science education through gender equity initiatives. In L. Parker, L. Rennie, & B. Fraser (Eds.), *Gender, science and mathematics* (pp. 203–221). Dordrecht, Netherlands: Kluwer Academic Publishers.

Renninger, K. (2000). Individual interest and its implications for understanding intrinsic motivation. In C. Sansone & J. Harackiewicz (Eds.), *Intrinsic and extrinsic motivation: The search for optimal motivation and performance* (pp. 373–404). San Diego: Academic Press.

Renninger, K., Hidi, S., & Krapp, A. (Eds.) (1992). *The role of interest in learning and development.* Hillsdale, NJ: Erlbaum.

Reuman, D. (1989). How social comparison mediates the relation between ability-grouping practices and students' achievement expectancies in mathematics. *Journal of Educational Psychology, 81,* 178–189.

Reyna, C., & Weiner, B. (in press). Justice and utility in the classroom: An attributional analysis of the goals of teachers' punishment and intervention strategies. *Journal of Educational Psychology.*

Rheinberg, F. (1983). Achievement evaluation: A fundamental difference and its motivational consequences. *Studies in Educational Evaluation, 9,* 185–194.

Richmond, V., & Dickson-Markman, F. (1985). Validity of the writing apprehension test: Two studies. *Psychological Reports, 56,* 255–259.

Riggs, J. (1992). Self-handicapping and achievement. In A. Boggiano & T. Pittman (Eds.), *Achievement and motivation: A social-developmental perspective* (pp. 244–267). Cambridge: Cambridge University Press.

Ritts, V., Patterson, M., & Tubbs, M. (1992). Expectations, impressions, and judgments of physically attractive students: A review. *Review of Educational Research, 62,* 413–426.

Robertson, D., & Keely, S. (1974). *Evaluation of a mediational training program for impulsive children by a multiple case study design.* Paper presented at the annual meeting of the American Psychological Association.

Robertson, J. (2000). Is attributional training a worthwhile classroom intervention for K–12 students with learning difficulties? *Educational Psychology Review, 12,* 111–134.

Robinson, T., Smith, S., Miller, D., & Brownell, M. (1999). Cognitive behavior modification of hyperactivity-impulsivity and aggression: A meta-analysis of school-based studies. *Journal of Educational Psychology, 91,* 195–203.

Roeser, R., Eccles, J., & Sameroff, A. (1998). Academic and emotional functioning in early adolescence: Longitudinal relations, patterns, and predictions by experience in middle school. *Development and Psychopathology, 10,* 321–352.

Roeser, R., Eccles, J., & Sameroff, A. (2000). School as a context of early adolescents' academic and social-emotional development: A summary of research findings. *The Elementary School Journal, 100,* 443–471.

Roeser, R., Midgley, C., & Urdan, T. (1996). Perceptions of the school psychological environment and early adolescents' psychological and behavioral functioning in school: The mediating role of goals and belonging. *Journal of Educational Psychology, 90,* 408–422.

Rogers, C. (1951). *Client centered therapy.* New York: Houghton-Mifflin.

Rose, M. (Ed.) (1985). *When a writer can't write: Studies in writer's block and other composing process problems.* New York: Guilford.

Rosen, B., & D'Andrade, R. C. (1959). The psychosocial origins of achievement motivation. *Sociometry, 22,* 185–218.

Rosenbaum, J. (1980). Social implications of educational grouping. In D. Berliner (Ed.), *Review of research in education, Vol. 8* (pp. 361–401). Washington, DC: American Educational Research Association.

Rosenbaum, M., & Drabman, R. (1979). Self-control training in the classroom: A review and critique. *Journal of Applied Behavior Analysis, 12,* 467–485.

Rosenholtz, S., & Rosenholtz, S. (1981). Classroom organization and the perception of ability. *Sociology of Education, 54,* 132–140.

Rosenholtz, S., & Simpson, C. (1984a). Classroom organization and student stratification. *Elementary School Journal, 85,* 21–38.

Rosenholtz, S., & Simpson, C. (1984b). The formation of ability conceptions: Developmental trend or social construction? *Review of Educational Research, 54,* 31–63.

Rosenthal, R. (1974). *On the social psychology of the self-fulfilling prophecy: Further evidence for Pygmalion effects and their mediating mechanisms.* New York: MSS Modular Publications.

Rosenthal, R., & Jacobson, L. (1968). *Pygmalion in the classroom: Teacher expectation and pupils' intellectual development.* New York: Holt, Rinehart, & Winston.

Ross, J. (1995). Effects of feedback on student behavior in cooperative learning. *Elementary School Journal, 96,* 125–143.

Ross, J., Cousins, J., & Gadalla, T. (1996). Within-teacher predictors of teacher efficacy. *Teaching and Teacher Education, 12,* 385–400.

Ross, L., & Nisbett, R. (1991). *The person and the situation: Perspectives of social psychology.* New York: McGraw-Hill Book Company.

Rotter, J. (1966). Generalized expectancies for internal versus external control of reinforcement. *Psychological Monographs, 1* (Whole No. 609).

Rotter, J. (1975). Some problems and misconceptions related to the construct of internal versus external control of reinforcement. *Journal of Consulting and Clinical Psychology, 43,* 56–67.

Rotter, J. (1990). Internal versus external control of reinforcement: A case history of a variable. *American Psychologist, 45,* 489–493.

Ruble, D. (1983). The development of social comparison processes and their role in achievement-related self-socialization. In E. T. Higgins, D. N. Ruble, & W. W. Hartup (Eds.), *Social cognition and social development: A socio-cultural perspective* (pp. 134–157). New York: Cambridge University Press.

Ruble, D., & Frey, K. (1991). Changing patterns of comparative behavior as skills are acquired: A functional model of self-evaluation. In J. Suls & T. Wills (Eds.), *Social comparison: Contemporary theory and research* (pp. 79–113). Hillsdale, NJ: Erlbaum.

Ruble, D., Grosovsky, E., Frey, K., & Cohen, R. (1992). Developmental changes in competence assessment. In A. Boggiano & T. Pittman (Eds.), *Achievement and motivation: A social–developmental perspective* (pp. 138–164). Cambridge: Cambridge University Press.

Rueda, R., & Moll, L. (1994). A sociocultural perspective on motivation. In H. O'Neil Jr. & M. Drillings (Eds.), *Motivation: Theory and research* (pp. 117–137). Hillsdale, NJ: Erlbaum.

Ryan, A., Gheen, M., & Midgley, C. (1998). Why do

some students avoid asking for help? An examination of the interplay among students' academic efficacy, teachers' social-emotional role, and the classroom goal structure. *Journal of Educational Psychology, 90,* 528–535.

Ryan, A., Hicks, L., & Midgley, C. (1997). Social goals, academic goals, and avoiding seeking help in the classroom. *Journal of Early Adolescence, 17,* 152–171.

Ryan, A., & Pintrich, P. (1997). "Should I ask for help?" The role of motivation and attitudes in adolescents' help seeking in math class. *Journal of Educational Psychology, 89,* 329–341.

Ryan, A., & Pintrich, P. (1998). Achievement and social motivational influences on help seeking in the classroom. In S. Karabenick (Ed.), *Strategic help-seeking: Implications for learning and teaching* (pp. 117–139). Mahwah, NJ: Erlbaum.

Ryan, R. (1982). Control and information in the intrapersonal sphere: An extension of cognitive evaluation theory. *Journal of Personality and Social Psychology, 43,* 450–461.

Ryan, R., & Connell, J. (1989). Perceived locus of causality and internalization: Examining reasons for acting in two domains. *Journal of Personality and Social Psychology, 57,* 749–761.

Ryan, R., Connell, J., & Grolnick, W. (1992). When achievement is *not* intrinsically motivated: A theory of internalization and self-regulation in school. In A. Boggiano & T. Pittman (Eds.), *Achievement and motivation: A social-developmental perspective* (pp. 167–188). Cambridge: Cambridge University Press.

Ryan, R., Connell, J., & Plant, R. (1990). Emotions in nondirected text learning. *Learning and Individual Differences, 2,* 1–17.

Ryan, R., & Deci, E. (2000a). Self-determination theory and the facilitation of intrinsic motivation, social development, and well being. *American Psychologist, 55,* 68–78.

Ryan, R., & Deci, E. (2000b). When rewards compete with nature: The undermining of intrinsic motivation and self-regulation. In C. Sansone & J. Harackiewicz (Eds.), *Intrinsic and extrinsic motivation: The search for optimal motivation and performance* (pp. 13–54). San Diego: Academic Press.

Ryan, R., & Grolnick, W. (1986). Origins and pawns in the classroom: Self-report and projective assessments of individual differences in children's perceptions. *Journal of Personality and Social Psychology, 50,* 350–358.

Ryan, R., & La Guardia, J. (in press). Achievement motivation within a pressured society: Intrinsic and extrinsic motivations to learn and the politics of school reform. In T. Urdan (Ed.), *Advances in motivation and achievement, Vol. II* (pp. 45–85). Greenwich, CT: JAI Press.

Ryan, R., & Stiller, J. (1991). The social contexts of internalization: Parent and teacher influences on autonomy, motivation, and learning. In P. Pintrich & M. Maehr (Eds.), *Advances in motivation*

and achievement, Vol. 7 (pp. 115–149). Greenwich, CT: JAI Press.

Sapp, M. (1999). *Test anxiety: Applied research, assessment, and treatment interventions* (2nd edition). New York: University Press of America.

Sapp, M., Farrell, W., & Durand, H. (1995). The effects of mathematics, reading, and writing tests in producing worry and emotionality: Test anxiety with economically and educationally disadvantaged college students. *College Student Journal, 29,* 122–125.

Sarason, I. (1958). The effects of anxiety, reassurance, and meaningfulness of material to be learned, on verbal learning. *Journal of Experimental Psychology, 56,* 472–477.

Sarason, I. (1961). A note on anxiety, instructions, and word association performance. *Journal of Abnormal and Social Psychology, 62,* 153–154.

Sarason, I. (1973). Test anxiety and cognitive modeling. *Journal of Personality and Social Psychology, 28,* 58–61.

Sarason, I. (1975). Test anxiety, attention and the general problem of anxiety. In I. Sarason & C. Spielberger (Eds.), *Stress and anxiety, Vol. 1* (pp. 165–187). Washington, DC: Hemisphere.

Sarason, I. (1978). The Test Anxiety Scale: Concept and research. In C. Spielberger & I. Sarason (Eds.), *Stress and anxiety, Vol. 5* (pp. 193–216). Washington, DC: Hemisphere.

Sarason, I. (1984). Stress, anxiety, and cognitive interference: Reactions to tests. *Journal of Personality and Social Psychology, 46,* 929–938.

Sarason, I. G., & Sarason, B. R. (1990). Test anxiety. In H. Leitenberg (Ed.), *Handbook of social and evaluation anxiety* (pp. 475–495). New York: Plenum.

Sarason, S. (1993). *The case for change: Rethinking the preparation of educators.* San Francisco, CA: Jossey-Bass, Inc.

Sarason, S., Davidson, K., Lighthall, F., Waite, R., & Ruebush, B. (1960). *Anxiety in elementary school children.* New York: Wiley.

Schank, R. (1979). Interestingness: Controlling inferences. *Artificial Intelligence, 12,* 273–297.

Schiefele, U. (1996). Topic interest, text representation, and quality of experience. *Contemporary Educational Psychology, 21,* 3–18.

Schiefele U., & Krapp, A. (1996) Topic interest and free recall of expository test. *Learning and Individual Differences, 8,* 141–160.

Schmitz, B., & Skinner, E. (1993). Perceived control, effort, and academic performance: Inter-individual, intraindividual, and multivariate time-series analyses. *Journal of Personality and Social Psychology, 64,* 1010–1028.

Schunk, D. (1982). Effects of effort and attributional feedback on children's perceived self-efficacy and achievement. *Journal of Educational Psychology, 74,* 548–556.

Schunk, D. (1983). Ability versus effort attributional feedback: Differential effects on self-efficacy and achievement. *Journal of Educational Psychology, 75,* 848–856.

Schunk, D. (1984a). Self-efficacy perspective on achievement behavior. *Educational Psychologist, 19,* 48–58.

Schunk, D. (1984b). Sequential attributional feedback and children's achievement behaviors. *Journal of Educational Psychology, 76,* 1159–1169.

Schunk, D. (1985a). Participation in goal setting: Effects on self-efficacy and skills of learning disabled children. *Journal of Special Education, 19,* 307–317.

Schunk, D. (1985b). Self-efficacy and school learning. *Psychology in the Schools, 22,* 209–223.

Schunk, D. (1989). Self-efficacy and cognitive achievement: Implications for students with learning problems. *Journal of Learning Disabilities, 22,* 14–22.

Schunk, D. (1990). Goal setting and self-efficacy during self-regulated learning. *Educational Psychologist, 25,* 71–86.

Schunk, D. (1991). Goal setting and self-evaluation: A social cognitive perspective on self-regulation. In M. Maehr & P. Pintrich (Eds.), *Advances in motivation and achievement: Vol. 7* (pp. 85–113). Greenwich, CT: JAI Press.

Schunk, D. (1995). Self-efficacy and education and instruction. In J. Maddux (Ed.), *Self-efficacy, adaptation, and adjustment: Theory, research, and application* (pp. 281–303). New York: Plenum Press.

Schunk, D. (1996). Goal and self-evaluative influences during children's cognitive skill learning. *American Educational Research Journal, 33,* 359–382.

Schunk, D., & Hanson, A. (1985). Peer models: Influence on children's self-efficacy and achievement. *Journal of Educational Psychology, 77,* 313–322.

Schuster, B., Ruble, D., & Weinert, F. (1998). Causal inferences and the positivity bias in children: The role of the covariation principle. *Child Development, 69,* 1577–1596.

Schwartz, S. (1996). Hidden messages in teacher talk: Praise and empowerment. *Teaching Children Mathematics,* March, 396–401.

Schwarzer, R., & Jerusalem, M. (1992). Advances in anxiety theory: A cognitive process approach. In K. Hagtvet & T. Johnsen (Eds.), *Advances in test anxiety research, Vol. 7* (pp. 2–17). Amsterdam: Swets & Zeitlinger.

Schweiker-Marra, K., & Marra, W. (2000). Investigating the effects of prewriting activities on writing performance and anxiety of at-risk students. *Reading Psychology, 2,* 99–114.

Sears, P. (1940). Level of aspiration in academically successful and unsuccessful children. *Journal of Abnormal and Social Psychology, 35,* 498–536.

Sedek, G., & McIntosh, D. (1998). Intellectual helplessness: Domain specificity, teaching styles, and school achievement. In M. Kofta, G. Weary, & G. Sedek (Eds.), *Personal control in action: Cognitive and motivational mechanisms* (pp. 419–443). New York: Plenum Press.

Selfe, C. (1985). An apprehensive writer composes. In M. Rose (Ed.), *When a writer can't write: Studies in writer's block and other composing process problems* (pp. 83–95). New York: Guilford.

Seligman, M., & Maier, S. (1967). Failure to escape traumatic shock. *Journal of Experimental Psychology, 74,* 1–9.

Sergiovanni, T. (1994). *Building community in schools.* San Francisco: Jossey-Bass.

Sexton, M., Harris, K., & Graham, S. (1998). Self-regulated strategy development and the writing process: Effects on essay writing and attributions. *Exceptional Children, 64,* 295–311.

Sexton, T., & Tuckman, B. (1991). Self-beliefs and behavior: The role of self-efficacy and outcome expectation over time. *Personality and Individual Differences, 12,* 725–736.

Sgoutas-Emch, S., & Johnson, C. (1998). Is journal writing an effective method of reducing anxiety towards statistics? *Journal of Instructional Psychology, 25,* 49–57.

Shapira, Z. (1976). Expectancy determinants of intrinsically motivated behavior. *Journal of Personality and Social Psychology, 34,* 1235–1244.

Shapiro, E. (1984). Self-monitoring procedures. In T. Ollendick & M. Hersen (Eds.), *Child behavioral assessment: Principles and procedures* (pp. 148–165). New York: Pergamon Press.

Shapiro, E., & Bradley, K. (1996). Treatment of academic problems. In M. Reinecke, F. Dattilio, & A. Freeman (Eds.), *Cognitive therapy with children and adolescents: A casebook for clinical practice* (pp. 344–366). New York: Guilford.

Shapiro, E., & Cole, C. (1994). *Behavior change in the classroom: Self-management interventions.* New York: Guilford.

Sharan, S. (1980). Cooperative learning in small groups: Recent methods and effects on achievement, attitudes, and ethnic relations. *Review of Educational Research, 50,* 241–271.

Sh???sher, P., & Dembo, M. (1996). The effects of efficacy-building instruction on the use of learning strategies. ERIC, ED395301.

Sheldon, K., & Elliot, A. (1998). Not all personal goals are personal: Comparing autonomous and controlled reasons as predictors of effort and attainment. *Personality and Social Psychology Bulletin, 24,* 546.

Sheldon, K., & Kasser, T. (1998). Pursuing personal goals: Skills enable progress but not all progress is beneficial. *Personality and Social Psychology Bulletin, 24,* 1319–1331.

Shell, D., Colvin, C., & Bruning, R. (1995). Self-efficacy, attribution, and outcome expectancy mechanisms in reading and writing achievement: Grade-level and achievement-level differences. *Journal of Educational Psychology, 87,* 386–398.

Sherman, J. (1979). Predicting mathematics performance in high school girls and boys. *Journal of Educational Psychology, 71,* 242–249.

Sherman, J. (1992). Reflections on PSI: Good news and

bad. *Journal of Behavioral Analysis*, 25, 59–64.

Shirey, L. (1992). Importance, interest, and selective attention. In K. Renninger, S. Hidi, & A. Krapp (Eds.), *The role of interest in learning and development* (pp. 281–296). Hillsdale, NJ: Erlbaum.

Shouse, R. (1996). Academic press and sense of community: Conflict and congruence in American high schools. *Research in Sociology of Education and Socialization*, 11, 173–202.

Shultz, T., & Zigler, E. (1970). Emotional concomitants of visual mastery in infants: The effects of stimulus movement on smiling and vocalizing. *Journal of Experimental Child Psychology*, 10, 390–402.

Sieber, J., O'Neil, H., & Tobias, S. (1977). *Anxiety, learning, and instruction*. Hillsdale, NJ: Erlbaum.

Siegel, J., & Shaughnessy, M. (1996). An interview with Bernard Weiner. *Educational Psychology Review*, 8, 165–174.

Simpson, C., & Rosenholtz, S. (1986). Classroom structure and the social construction of ability. In J. Richardson (Ed.), *Handbook of theory and research for the sociology of education* (pp. 113–138). New York: Greenwood Press.

Simpson, S., Licht, B., Wagner, R., & Stader, S. (1996). Organization of children's academic ability-related self-perceptions. *Journal of Educational Psychology*, 88, 387–396.

Skaalvik, E. (1997a). Issues in research on self-concept. In M. Maehr & P. Pintrich (Eds.), *Advances in motivation and achievement, Vol. 10* (pp. 51–98). Greenwich, CN: JAI Press.

Skaalvik, E. (1997b). Self-enhancing and self-defeating ego orientation: Relations with task and avoidance orientation, achievement, self-perceptions, and anxiety. *Journal of Educational Psychology*, 89, 71–81.

Skaalvik, E., & Rankin, R. (1990). Math, verbal, and general academic self-concept: The internal/external frame of reference model and gender differences in self-concept structure. *Journal of Educational Psychology*, 82, 546–554.

Skaalvik, E., & Rankin, R. (1995). A test of the internal/external frame of reference model at different levels of math and verbal self-perception. *American Educational Research Journal*, 32, 161–184.

Skinner, B. (1974). *About behaviorism*. New York: Knopf.

Skinner, E. (1990). Age differences in the dimensions of perceived control during middle childhood: Implications for developmental conceptualizations and research. *Child Development*, 61, 1882–1890.

Skinner, E. (1995). *Perceived control, motivation, & coping*. Thousand Oaks, CA: Sage Publications.

Skinner, E., & Belmont, M. (1993). Motivation in the classroom: Reciprocal effects of teacher behavior and student engagement across the school year. *Journal of Educational Psychology*, 85, 571–581.

Skinner, E., Chapman, M., & Baltes, P. (1988). Control, means-ends, and agency beliefs: A new conceptualization and its measurement during childhood. *Journal of Personality and Social Psychology*, 54, 117–133.

Skinner, E., & Wellborn, J. (1994). Coping during childhood and adolescence: A motivational perspective. In R. Lerner & M. Perlmutter (Eds.), *Life-span development and behavior, Vol. 12* (pp. 91–133).

Skinner, E., Wellborn, J., & Connell, J. (1990). What it takes to do well in school and whether I've got it: The role of perceived control in children's engagement and school achievement. *Journal of Educational Psychology*, 82, 22–32.

Skinner, E., Zimmer-Gembeck, M., & Connell, J. (1998). Individual differences and the development of perceived control. *Monographs of the Society in Child Development*, 63 (2-3), 1–220.

Slavin, R. (1980). *Using student team learning* (Rev. ed.). Baltimore, MD: Johns Hopkins University, Center for Social Organization of Schools.

Slavin, R. (1984). Students motivating students to excel: Cooperative incentives, cooperative tasks, and student achievement. *Elementary School Journal*, 84, 53–63.

Slavin, R. (1987). Developmental and motivational perspectives on cooperative learning: A reconciliation. *Child Development*, 58, 1161–1167.

Slavin, R. (1990). *Cooperative learning: Theory, research and practice*. Englewood Cliffs, NJ: Prentice Hall.

Slavin, R. (1993). Ability grouping in the middle grades: Achievement effects and alternatives. *Elementary School Journal*, 93, 535–552.

Slavin, R. (1997). When does cooperative learning increase student achievement? In E. Dubinsky and D. Mathews (Eds.), *Readings in cooperative learning for undergraduate mathematics* (pp. 71–84). Washington, DC: The Mathematical Association of America.

Slavin, R., Sharan, S., Kagan, S., Hertz-Lazarowitz, N., Webb, N., & Schmuck, R. (1985). *Learning to cooperate, cooperating to learn*. New York: Plenum Press.

Smiley, P., & Dweck, C. (1994). Individual differences in achievement goals among young children. *Child Development*, 65, 1723–1743.

Smith, M. (1980). Meta-analysis of research on teacher expectations. *Evaluation in Education*, 4, 53–55.

Sohn, D. (1982). Sex differences in achievement self-attributions: An effect-size analysis. *Sex Roles*, 8, 345–357.

Spear, P., & Armstrong, S. (1978). Effects of performance expectancies created by peer comparison as related to social reinforcement, task difficulty, and age of child. *Journal of Experimental and Child Psychology*, 25, 254–266.

Speidel, G., & Tharp, R. (1980). What does self-reinforcement reinforce? An empirical analysis of the contingencies in self-determined reinforcement. *Child Behavior Therapy*, 2, 1–22.

Spielberger, C., & Starr, L. (1994). Curiosity and

exploratory behavior. In H. O'Neil & M. Drillings (Eds.), *Motivation: Theory and research* (pp. 221–243). Hillsdale, NJ: Erlbaum.

Spielberger, C., & Vagg, P. (1995). Test anxiety: A transactional process model. In C. Spielberger & P. Vagg (Eds.), *Test anxiety: Theory, assessment, and treatment* (pp. 3–14). Washington, DC: Taylor & Francis.

Stallings, J. (1985). School, classroom, and home influences on women's decisions to enroll in advanced mathematics courses. In S. Chipman, L. Brush, & D. Wilson (Eds.), *Women and mathematics: Balancing the equation* (pp. 199–223). Hillsdale, NJ: Erlbaum.

Steele, C. (1997). A threat in the air: How stereotypes shape intellectual identify and performance. *American Psychologist, 52,* 613–629.

Steele, C. (1999). Thin ice: "Stereotype threat" and Black college students. *The Atlantic Monthly, 284* (2), 44–54.

Stein, M., Grover, B., & Henningsen, M. (1996). Building student capacity for mathematical thinking and reasoning: An analysis of mathematical tasks used in reform classrooms. *American Educational Research Journal, 33,* 455–488.

Stevenson, H., Lee, S., & Stigler, J. (1986). Mathematics achievement of Chinese, Japanese, and American children. *Science, 231,* 693–699.

Stevenson, H., & Stigler, J. (1992). *The Learning Gap.* New York: Summit Books.

Stigler, J., & Stevenson, H. (1991). How Asian teachers polish each lesson to perfection. *American Educator, 15,* 12–20.

Stipek, D. (1984a). Developmental aspects of motivation in children. In R. Ames & C. Ames (Eds.), *Research on motivation in education, Vol. 1: Student motivation* (pp. 145–174). New York: Academic Press.

Stipek, D. (1984b). Young children's performance expectations: Logical analysis or wishful thinking? In J. Nicholls (Ed.), *The development of achievement motivation* (pp. 33–56). Greenwich, CT: JAI Press.

Stipek, D. (1984c). Sex differences in children's attributions for success and failure on math and spelling tests. *Sex Roles, 11,* 969–981.

Stipek, D. (1997). Success in school—for a Head Start in life. In S. Luthar, J. Burack, D. Cicchetti, & J. Weisz (Eds.), *Developmental psychopathology: Perspectives on risk and disorder* (pp. 75–92). New York: Cambridge University Press.

Stipek, D. (2001). Pathways to constructive behavior: Importance of academic achievement in the early elementary grades. In A. Bohart & D. Stipek (Eds.), *Constructive and destructive behavior: Implications for family, school, and society* (pp. 291–315). Washington, DC: American Psychological Association.

Stipek, D., & Daniels, D. (1990). Children's use of dispositional attributions in predicting the performance and behavior of classmates. *Journal of Applied Developmental Psychology, 11,* 13–28.

Stipek, D., de la Sota, A., & Weishaupt, L. (1999). Life lessons: An embedded classroom approach to preventing high risk behaviors among preadolescents. *The Elementary School Journal, 99,* 433–452.

Stipek, D., & Gralinski, H. (1991). Gender differences in children's achievement-related beliefs and emotional responses to success and failure in math. *Journal of Educational Psychology, 83,* 361–371.

Stipek, D., & Gralinski, H. (1996). Children's theories of intelligence and school performance. *Journal of Educational Psychology, 88,* 397–407.

Stipek, D., & Greene, J. (2001). Achievement motivation in early childhood: Cause for concern or celebration? In S. Golbeck (Ed.), *Psychological perspectives on early childhood education: Reframing dilemmas in research and practice* (pp. 64–91). Mahwah, NJ: Erlbaum.

Stipek, D., & Kowalski, P. (1989). Learned helplessness in task-orienting versus performance-orienting testing conditions. *Journal of Educational Psychology, 81,* 384–391.

Stipek, D., & Mac Iver, D. (1989). Developmental change in children's assessment of intellectual competence. *Child Development, 60,* 521–538.

Stipek, D., & Seal, K. (2001). *Motivated minds: Raising children to love learning.* New York: Henry Holt.

Stipek, D., & Tannatt, L. (1984). Children's judgments of their own and their peers' academic competence. *Journal of Educational Psychology, 76,* 75–84.

Stodolsky, S. (1985). Telling math: Origins of math aversion and anxiety. *Educational Psychologist, 20,* 125–133.

Stodolsky, S., & Grossman, P. (1995). The impact of subject matter on curricular activity: An analysis of five academic subjects. *American Educational Research Journal, 32,* 227–249.

Strein, W. (1993). Advances in research on academic self-concept: Implications for school psychology. *School Psychology Review, 22,* 273–284.

Sulzer-Azaroff, B., & Mayer, G. (1986). *Achieving educational excellence.* New York: Holt, Rinehart, & Winston.

Sutherland, K., Wehby, J., & Copeland, S. (2000). Effect of rates of varying behavior-specific praise on the on-task behavior on students with EBD. *Journal of Emotional & Behavioral Disorders, 8,* 2–8, 26.

Swanson, H., & Scarpati, S. (1985). Self-instruction training to increase academic performance of educationally handicapped children. *Child and Family Behavior Therapy, 6,* 23–39.

Tang, S., & Hall, V. (1995). The overjustification effect: A meta-analysis. *Applied Cognitive Psychology, 9,* 365–404.

Taylor, R., Casten, R., Flickinger, S., Roberts, D., &

Fulmore, C. (1994). Explaining the school performance of African-American adolescents. *Journal of Research on Adolescence, 4*, 21–44.

Thorkildsen, T., & Nicholls, J. (1998). Fifth-graders' achievement orientations and beliefs: Individual and classroom differences. *Journal of Educational Psychology, 90*, 179–201.

Thorndike, E. (1898). Animal intelligence: An experimental study of the associative processes in animals. *Psychological Review Monograph Supplements, 2* (No. 4).

Thurlow, M., Christensen, S., & Ysseldyke, J. (1983). *Referral research. An integrative summary of findings.* Minneapolis: University of Minnesota.

Tobias, S. (1992). The impact of test anxiety cognition in school learning. In K. A. Hagtvet & T. B. Johnsen (Eds.), *Advances in test anxiety research, Vol. 7* (pp. 18–31). Amsterdam: Swets & Zeitlinger.

Tobias, S. (1994). Interest, prior knowledge, and learning. *Review of Educational Research, 64*, 37–54.

Tobias, S., & Weissbrod, C. (1980). Anxiety and mathematics: An update. *Harvard Educational Review, 50*, 63–70.

Tobin K., Kahle, J., & Fraser, B. (Eds.) (1990). *Windows into science classrooms: Problems associated with higher-level cognitive learning in science.* London: Falmer Press.

Toch, T. (1991). *In the name of excellence: The struggle to reform the nations' schools, why it's failing, and what should be done.* New York: Oxford University Press.

Tollefson, N., Tracy, D., Johnsen, E., Farmer, A., & Buenning, M. (1984). Goal setting and personal responsibility training for LD adolescents. *Psychology in the Schools, 21*, 224–233.

Topman, R., Kleijn, W., van der Ploeg, H., & Masset, E. (1992). Test anxiety, cognitions, study habits and academic performance: A prospective study. In K. Hagtvet & T. Johnsen (Eds.), *Advances in test anxiety research, Vol. 7* (pp. 239–259). Amsterdam: Swets & Zeitlinger.

Trudewind, C. (1982). The development of achievement motivation and individual differences: Ecological determinants. In W. Hartup (Ed.), *Review of Child Development Research, Vol. 6* (pp. 669–703). Chicago: University of Chicago Press.

Tschannen-Moran, M., Woolfolk Hoy, A., & Hoy, W. (1998). Teacher efficacy: Its meaning and measure. *Review of Educational Research, 68*, 202–248.

Turner, J. (1995). The influence of classroom contexts on young children's motivation for literacy. *Reading Research Quarterly, 30*, 410–441.

Turner, J., Meyer, D., Cox, K., Logan, C., DiCintio, M., & Thomas, C. (1998). Creating contexts for involvement in mathematics. *Journal of Educational Psychology, 90*, 730–745.

Turner, J., Thorpe, P., & Meyer, D. (1998). Students' reports of motivation and negative affect: A theoretical and empirical analysis. *Journal of Educational Psychology, 90*, 758–771.

Tuss, P., Zimmer, J., & Ho, H. (1995). Causal attributions of underachieving fourth grade students in China, Japan, and the United States. *Journal of Cross-Cultural Psychology, 26*, 408–425.

Urdan, T., & Maehr, M. (1995). Beyond a two-goal theory of motivation and achievement: A case for social goals. *Review of Educational Research, 65*, 213–243.

Urdan, T., Midgley, C., & Anderman, E. (1998). The role of classroom goal handicapping strategies. *American Educational Research Journal, 35*, 101–122.

Urdan, T., Midgley, C., & Wood, S. (1995). Special issues in reforming middle level schools. *Journal of Early Adolescence, 15*, 9–37.

Utman, C. (1997). Performance effects of motivational state: A meta-analysis. *Personality and Social Psychology Review, 1*, 170–182.

Vagg, P., & Spielberger, C. (1995). Treatment of test anxiety: Application of the transactional process model. In C. Spielberger & P. Vagg (Eds.), *Test anxiety: Theory, assessment, and treatment* (pp. 197–215). Washington, DC: Taylor & Francis.

Valeski, T., & Stipek, D. (2001). Young children's attitudes toward school: Causes and consequences. *Child Development.*

Vallerand, R., Fortier, M., & Guay, F. (1997). Self-determination and persistence in a real-life setting: Toward a motivational model of high school dropout. *Journal of Personality and Social Psychology, 72*, 1161–1176.

Vallerand, R., Gauvin, L., & Halliwell, W. (1986). Negative effects of competition on children's intrinsic motivation. *Journal of Social Psychology, 126*, 649–657.

Vanfossen, B., Jones, J., & Spade, J. (1987). Curriculum tracking and status maintenance. *Sociology of Education, 60*, 104–122.

Van Laar, C. (2000). The paradox of low academic achievement but high self-esteem in African American students: An attributional account. *Educational Psychology Review, 12*, 33–61.

Van Overwalle, F., Mervielde, I., & De Schuyter, J. (1995). Structural modeling of the relationships between attributional dimensions, emotions, and performance of college freshmen. *Cognition and Emotion, 9*, 59–85.

Varnon, C., & King, R. (1993). A tidal wave of change—OBE in the USA. *Outcomes, 12*, 16–19.

Vaughn, S., Schumm, J., Klingner, J., & Samuell, L. (1995). Students' views of instructional practices: Implications for inclusion. *Learning Disabilities Quarterly, 18*, 236–248.

Vauras, M., Kinnunen, R., & Rauhanummi, T. (1999). The role of metacognition in the cointegrated strategy intervention. *European Journal of Psychology of Education, 14*, 555–569.

Vermeer, H., Boekaerts, M., & Seegers, G. (2000). Motivational and gender differences: Sixth-grade students' mathematical problem-solving behavior. *Journal of Educational Psychology, 92*, 308–315.

Vlahovic-Stetic, V., Vidovic, V., & Arambasic, L. (1999).

Motivational characteristics in mathematical achievement: A study of gifted high-achieving, gifted underachieving, and non-gifted pupils. *High Ability Studies, 10*, 37–49.

Vygotsky, L. (1962). *Thought and language*. Cambridge, MA: MIT Press.

Vygotsky, L. (1978). *Mind in society: The development of higher psychological processes*. Cambridge, MA: Harvard University Press.

Wade, S. (1992). How interest affects learning from text. In K. Renninger, S. Hidi, & A. Krapp (Eds.), *The role of interest in learning and development* (pp. 255–277). Hillsdale, NJ: Erlbaum.

Wahlberg, T. (1998). Cognitive-behavioral modification for children and young adolescents with special problems. In A. Rotatori, J. Schwenn, & S. Burkhardt (Eds.), *Advances in special education, Vol. 11: Issues, practices and concerns in special education* (pp. 223–253). Greenwich, CT: JAI Press.

Walker, D., Greenwood, C., & Terry, B. (1994). Management of classroom disruptive behavior and academic performance problems. In L.W. Craighead, W.E. Craighead, A. Kazdin, & M. Mahoney (Eds.), *Cognitive and behavioral interventions: An empirical approach to mental health problems* (pp. 215–234). Boston: Allyn & Bacon.

Walker, I., & Crogan, M. (1998). Academic performance, prejudice, and the jigsaw classroom: New pieces to the puzzle. *Journal of Community & Applied Social Psychology, 8*, 381–393.

Wall, S. (1983). Children's self-determination of standards in reinforcement contingencies: A re-examination. *Journal of School Psychology, 21*, 123–131.

Wang, M., & Palincsar, A. (1989). Teaching students to assume an active role in their learning. In M. Reynolds (Ed.), *Knowledge base for the beginning teacher* (pp. 71–84). New York: Pergamon Press.

Webb, F., Covington, M., & Guthrie, J. (1993). Carrots and sticks: Can school policy influence student motivation? In T. Tomlinson (Ed.), *Motivating students to learn: On overcoming barriers to high achievement* (pp. 99–124). Berkeley, CA: McCutchan Publishing.

Webb, N. (1984). Student interaction and learning in small-group and whole-class settings. In P. Peterson, L. Wilkinson, & M. Hallinan (Eds.), *The social context of instruction: Group organization and group processes* (pp. 153–170). Orlando, FL: Academic Press.

Webb, N. (1985). Student interaction and learning in small groups: A research summary. In R. Slavin, S. Sharan, S. Kagan, R. Hertz-Lazarowitz, C. Webb, & R. Schmuck (Eds.), *Learning to cooperate, cooperating to learn* (pp. 147–172). New York: Plenum.

Wehlage, G., Rutter, R., Smith, G., Lesko, N., & Fernandez, R. (1989). *Reducing the risk: Schools as communities of support*. New York: The Falmer Press.

Weiner, B. (1980). *Human motivation*. New York: Holt, Rinehart, & Winston.

Weiner, B. (1983). Some methodological pitfalls in attributional research. *Journal of Educational Psychology, 75*, 530–543.

Weiner, B. (1986). *An attributional theory of motivation and emotion*. New York: Springer Verlag.

Weiner, B. (1992). *Human Motivation: Metaphors, theories and research*. Newbury Park, CA: Sage Publications.

Weiner, B. (1994). Integrating social and personal theories of achievement striving. *Review of Educational Research, 64*, 557–573.

Weiner, B. (1995). *Judgments of responsibility: A foundation for a theory of social conduct*. New York: Guilford Press.

Weiner, B. (2000). Intrapersonal and interpersonal theories of motivation from an attributional perspective. *Educational Psychology Review, 12*, 1–14.

Weiner, B., & Hareli, S. (2000). Social emotions and personality inferences: A scaffold for a new research direction in the study of achievement motivation. Unpublished manuscript.

Weiner, B., & Peter, N. (1973). A cognitive–developmental analysis of achievement and moral judgments. *Developmental Psychology, 9*, 290–309.

Weiner, B., Russell, D., & Lerman, D. (1978). Affective consequences of causal ascriptions. In J. Harvey, W. Ickes, & R. Kidd (Eds.), *New directions in attribution research, Vol. 2* (pp. 59–90). Hillsdale, NJ: Erlbaum.

Weiner, B., Russell, D., & Lerman, D. (1979). The cognition-motion process in achievement-related contexts. *Journal of Personality and Social Psychology, 37*, 1211–1220.

Weinstein, R. (1976). Reading group membership in first grade: Teacher behaviors and pupil experience over time. *Journal of Educational Psychology, 68*, 103–116.

Weinstein, R. (1985). Student mediation of classroom expectancy effects. In J. Dusek (Ed.), *Teacher Expectancies* (pp 329–350). Hillsdale NJ: Erlbaum.

Weinstein, R. (1989). Perceptions of classroom processes and student motivation: Children's views of self-fulfilling prophecies. In C. Ames & R. Ames (Eds.), *Research on motivation in education, Vol. 3: Goals and cognitions* (pp. 187–221). New York: Academic Press.

Weinstein, R. (1993). Children's knowledge of differential treatment in school: Implications for motivation. In T. Tomlinson (Ed.), *Motivating students to learn: Overcoming barriers to high achievement* (pp. 197–224). Berkeley: McCutchan.

Weinstein, R., Madison, S., & Kuklinski, M. (1995). Raising expectations in schooling: Obstacles and opportunities for change. *American Educational Research Journal, 32*, 121–159.

Weinstein, R., & Middlestadt, S. (1979). Student perceptions of teacher interactions with male high and low achievers. *Journal of Educational Psychology, 71*, 421–431.

Weinstein, R., Soule, C., Collins, F., Cone, J., Mehlorn, M., & Stimmonacchi, K. (1991). Expectations and high school change: Teacher-researcher collaboration to prevent school failure. *American Journal of Community Psychology, 19*, 333–363.

Weisz, J., & Stipek, D. (1982). Competence, contingency and the development of perceived control. *Human Development, 25*, 250–281.

Wentzel, K. (1989). Adolescent classroom goals, standards for performance, and academic achievement: An interactionist perspective. *Journal of Educational Psychology, 81*, 131–142.

Wentzel, K. (1991). Social and academic goals at school: Motivation and achievement in context. In M. Maehr & P. Pintrich (Eds.), *Advances in motivation and achievement, Vol. 7* (pp. 185–212). Greenwich, CT: JAI Press.

Wentzel, K. (1992). Motivation and achievement in adolescence: A multiple goals perspective. In D. Schunk & J. Meece (Eds.), *Student perceptions in the classroom* (pp. 287–306). Hillsdale, NJ: Erlbaum.

Wentzel, K. (1993a). Does being good make the grade? Social behavior and academic competence in middle school. *Journal of Educational Psychology, 85*, 357–364.

Wentzel, K. (1993b). Motivation and achievement in early adolescence: The role of multiple classroom goals. *Journal of Early Adolescence, 13*, 4–20.

Wentzel, K. (1994). Relations of social goals pursuit to social acceptance, and perceived social support. *Journal of Educational Psychology, 86*, 173–182.

Wentzel, K. (1996). Social goals and social relationships as motivators of school adjustment. In J. Juvonen & K. Wentzel (Eds.), *Social motivation: Understanding children's school adjustment.* New York: Cambridge University Press.

Wentzel, K. (1997). Student motivation in middle school: The role of perceived pedagogical caring. *Journal of Educational Psychology, 89*, 411–419.

Wharton-McDonald, R., Pressley, M., & Hampston, J. (1998). Literacy instruction in nine first-grade classrooms: Teacher characteristics and student achievement. *Elementary School Journal, 99*, 101–128.

White, R. (1959). Motivation reconsidered: The concept of competence. *Psychological Review, 66*, 297–333.

Wigfield, A., & Eccles, J. (1989). Test anxiety in elementary and secondary school students. *Educational Psychologist, 24*, 159–183.

Wigfield, A., & Eccles, J. (1990). Test anxiety in the school setting. In M. Lewis & S. M. Miller (Eds.), *Handbook of developmental psychopathology: Perspectives in developmental psychology* (pp. 237–250). New York: Plenum.

Wigfield, A., & Eccles, J. (1992). The development of achievement task values: A theoretical analysis. *Developmental Review, 12*, 265–310.

Wigfield, A., & Eccles, J. (1994). Children's competence beliefs, achievement values, and general self-esteem: Change across elementary and middle school. *Journal of Early Adolescence, 14*, 107–137.

Wigfield, A., Eccles, J., Blumenfeld, P., Harold, R., Arbreton, A., Freedman-Doan, C., & Yoon, K. (1997). Changes in children's competence beliefs and subjective task values across the elementary school years: A three-year study. *Journal of Educational Psychology, 89*, 451–469.

Wigfield, A., Eccles, J., Mac Iver, D., Reuman, D., & Midgley, C. (1991). Transitions during early adolescence: Changes in children's domain-specific self-perceptions and general self-esteem across the transition to junior high school. *Developmental Psychology, 27*, 552–565.

Wigfield, A., Eccles, J., & Pintrich, P. (1996). Development between the ages of 11 and 25. In D. Berliner & R. Calfee (Eds.), *Handbook of educational psychology* (pp. 148–185). New York: MacMillan.

Wigfield, A., & Guthrie, J. (1997). Relations of children's motivation for reading to the amount and breadth of their reading. *Journal of Educational Psychology, 89*, 420–432.

Wigfield, A., & Harold, R. (1992). Teacher beliefs and children's achievement self-perceptions: A developmental perspective. In D. Schunk & J. Meece (Eds.), *Student perceptions in the classroom* (pp. 95–121). Hillsdale, NJ: Erlbaum.

Wigfield, A., & Meece, J. (1988). Math anxiety in elementary and secondary school students. *Journal of Educational Psychology, 80*, 210–216.

Williams, J., & Montgomery, D. (1995). Using frame of reference theory to understand the self-concept of academically able students. *Journal for the Education of the Gifted, 18*, 400–409.

Williams, B., Williams, R., & McLaughlin, T. (1991). Classroom procedures for remediating behavior disorders. *Journal of Educational Psychology, 80*, 210–216.

Wine, J. (1980). Cognitive-attentional theory of test anxiety. In I. Sarason (Ed.), *Test anxiety: Theory, research, and applications* (pp. 349–384). Hillsdale, NJ: Erlbaum.

Winfield, L. (1986). Teacher beliefs toward academically at risk students in inner urban schools. *Urban Review, 18*, 253–268.

Winterbottom, M. (1958). The relation of need for achievement to learning experiences in independence and mastery. In J. Atkinson (Ed.), *Motives in fantasy, action, and society.* Princeton: Van Nostrand.

Wolters, C., & Pintrich, P. (1998). Contextual differences in student motivation and self-regulated learning in mathematics, English, and social studies classrooms. *Instructional Science, 26*, 27–47.

Wolters, C., Yu, S., & Pintrich, P. (1996). The relation between goal orientation and students' motivational beliefs and self-regulated learning. *Learning and Individual Differences, 8*, 211–238.

Wong, B. (1999). Metacognition in writing. In Ronald Gallimore and L. Bernheimer (Eds.), *Developmental perspectives on children with high-incidence disabilities* (pp. 183–198). Mahwah, NJ: Erlbaum.

Wood, D., Rosenberg, M., & Carran, D. (1993). The effects of tape-recorded self-instruction cues on the mathematics performance of students with learning disabilities. *Journal of Learning Disabilities, 26,* 250–258.

Wood, R., & Bandura, A. (1989a). Impact of conceptions of ability on self-regulatory mechanisms and complex decision making. *Journal of Personality and Social Psychology, 56,* 407–415.

Wood, R., & Bandura, A. (1989b). Social cognitive theory of organization management. *Academy of Management, 14,* 361–384.

Woolfolk, A., & Hoy, W. (1990). Prospective teachers' sense of efficacy and beliefs about control. *Journal of Educational Psychology, 82,* 81–91.

Yamauchi, H., & Tanaka, K. (1998). Relations of autonomy, self-referenced beliefs, and self-regulated learning among Japanese children. *Psychological Reports, 82,* 803–816.

Yasutake, D., Bryan, T., & Dohrn, E. (1996). The effects of combining peer tutoring and attribution training on students' perceived self-competence. *Remedial and Special Education, 17,* 83–91.

Young, A. (1997). I think, therefore I'm motivated: The relations among cognitive strategy use, motivational orientation and classroom perceptions over time. *Learning and Individual Differences, 9,* 249–283.

Zahorik, J. (1996). Elementary and secondary teachers' reports of how they make learning interesting. *The Elementary School Journal, 96,* 551–564.

Zatz, S., & Chassin, L. (1985). Cognitions of test-anxious children under naturalistic test-taking conditions. *Journal of Consulting and Clinical Psychology, 53,* 393–401.

Zeidner, M. (1994). Personal and contextual determinants of coping and anxiety in an evaluative situation: A prospective study. *Personality and Individual Differences, 16,* 899–918.

Zeidner, M. (1995). Adaptive coping with test situations: A review of the literature. *Educational Psychologist, 30,* 123–133.

Zeidner, M. (1998). *Text anxiety: The state of the art.* New York: Plenum.

Zeidner, M., Klingman, A., & Papko, O. (1988). Enhancing students' test coping skills: Report of a psychological health education program. *Journal of Educational Psychology, 80,* 95–101.

Zeidner, M., & Nevo, B. (1992). Test anxiety in examinees in a college admissions testing situation: Incidence, dimensionality, and cognitive correlates. In K. Hagtvet & T. Johnsen (Eds.), *Advances in test anxiety research, Vol. 7* (pp. 288–303). Amsterdam: Swets & Zeitlinger.

Zeldin, A., & Pajares, F. (2000). Against the odds: Self-efficacy beliefs of women in mathematical, scientific, and technological careers. *American Educational Research Journal, 37,* 215–246.

Zigler, E., & Harter, S. (1969). The socialization of the mentally retarded. In D. Goslin (Ed.), *Handbook of socialization theory and research* (pp. 1065–1102). Chicago: McNally.

Zimmerman, B. (1995). Self-efficacy and educational development. In A. Bandura (Ed.), *Self-efficacy in changing societies* (pp. 202–231). New York: Cambridge University Press.

Zimmerman, B. (1998). Academic studying and the development of personal skill: A self-regulatory perspective. *Educational Psychologist, 33,* 73–86.

Zimmerman, B., & Bandura, A. (1994). Impact of self-regulatory influences on writing course attainment. *American Educational Research Journal, 31,* 845–862.

Zimmerman, B., & Martinez-Pons, M. (1986). Development of a structured interview for assessing student use of self-regulated learning strategies. *American Educational Research Journal, 23,* 614–628.

Zimmerman, B., & Martinez-Pons, M. (1992). Perceptions of efficacy and strategy use in the self-regulation of learning. In D. Schunk & J. Meece (Eds.), *Student perceptions in the classroom* (pp. 185–207). Hillsdale, NJ: Erlbaum.

Zimmerman, J., & Silverman, R. (1982). The effects of selected variables on writing anxiety. *Diagnostique, 8,* 62–70.

Zuckerman, M., Porac, J., Lathin, D., Smith, R., & Deci, E. (1978). On the importance of self-determination for intrinsically motivated behavior. *Personality and Social Psychology Bulletin, 4,* 443–466.

AUTHOR INDEX

SUBJECT INDEX